Modern Perspectives on Artificial Intelligence and Law

Sofia D. Anastasiadou
University of Western Macedonia, Greece

Lambrini Seremeti
Agricultural University of Athens, Greece

Andreas Masouras
Neapolis University, Pafos, Cyprus

Lazaros Anastasiadis
University of Patras, Greece

IGI Global
Scientific Publishing
Publishing Tomorrow's Research Today

Vice President of Editorial | Melissa Wagner
Director of Acquisitions | Mikaela Felty
Director of Book Development | Jocelynn Hessler
Production Manager | Mike Brehm
Cover Design | Jose Rosado

Published in the United States of America by
IGI Global Scientific Publishing
701 East Chocolate Avenue
Hershey, PA, 17033, USA
Tel: 717-533-8845
Fax: 717-533-7115
Website: https://www.igi-global.com E-mail: cust@igi-global.com

Library of Congress Cataloging-in-Publication Data

Library of Congress Cataloging-in-Publication Data

Names: Anastasiadou, Sofia D., 1968- editor. | Seremeti, Lamprini, 1974- editor. | Masouras, Andreas, 1980- editor. | Anastasiadis, Lazaros, 1966- editor.
Title: Modern perspectives on artificial intelligence and law / edited by Sofia Anastasiadou, Lamprini Seremeti, Andreas Masouras, Lazaros Anastasiadis.
Description: Hershey : IGI Global Scientific Publishing, 2025. | Includes bibliographical references and index. | Summary: "The objective of the book is to provide educators, researchers, and practitioners with a comprehensive understanding of modern perceptions on artificial intelligence and law, perceptions on matching AI and law, AI, ethics, and perspectives on law regarding future trends"-- Provided by publisher.
Identifiers: LCCN 2024060443 (print) | LCCN 2024060444 (ebook) | ISBN 9798369395769 (hardcover) | ISBN 9798369395776 (paperback) | ISBN 9798369395783 (ebook)
Subjects: LCSH: Artificial intelligence--Law and legislation.
Classification: LCC K564.C6 M63 2025 (print) | LCC K564.C6 (ebook) | DDC 343.09/998--dc23/eng/20250109
LC record available at https://lccn.loc.gov/2024060443
LC ebook record available at https://lccn.loc.gov/2024060444

British Cataloguing in Publication Data
A Cataloguing in Publication record for this book is available from the British Library.

Table of Contents

Detailed Table of Contents

This chapter will examine the growing use of artificial intelligence (AI) in law enforcement and criminal justice with a focus on the possible benefits and concomitant risks. The potential uses of AI in policing include predictive policing, surveillance, and justice administration with improved efficiency, cost-effectiveness, and reduced human error. On the other hand, the same development holds many questions about civil liberties and ethics. Technologies such as facial recognition allow for tracking people without their knowledge or consent, which is a threat to privacy. The chapter explores these risks, engaging with the current debate on the responsible and ethical use of AI in policing. It underlines the necessity of strong legal protection so that abuses could be averted and AI applications must be able to honour human rights in the pursuance of fair and equal justice. The analysis done within the chapter will balance innovation with accountability and fairness.

In the rapidly evolving landscape of artificial intelligence (AI), governance, legislation, and regulation have become crucial yet increasingly ambiguous. This chapter introduces the concept of "AI legislationship," a term coined to describe the current state of AI governance, where the boundaries between regulation and innovation are blurred. Governance, legislation, and regulation—each essential for societal function—are studied here both independently and in relation to one another, focusing on how these abstract concepts are reshaped in response to AI. We explore the challenges of regulatory lag, compliance costs, resistance to change, and enforcement issues, highlighting the transitional phase where AI technologies are advancing more rapidly than legal frameworks can accommodate. This chapter argues that addressing these issues requires a multi-faceted approach combining legal, ethical, and collaborative efforts to ensure AI development is both innovative and responsible.

The newly emerging phenomenon of artificial intelligence (AI) has undoubtedly paved way for signifying change in the field of legal practice; however, not without the prospects and issues. This chapter provides a theoretical analysis of the subject of AI in contemporary legal frameworks with special emphasis on the impact of AI across legal education, legal profession, and judicial processes. Because AI technologies are used to expedite the legal processes and improve productiveness, and given their role in making decisions, there is a great potential for its influence on the legal profession. However, these advancements also bring several questions of who is to be held liable, how these tools will be bias, the ethical issues that they present and who will regulate these technologies? They establish the potential of what has been done and what is to be done with regard to legal practice focusing on AI in contracts, case law and the pending problem of over-legalization of justice with the help of AI telecommunications in judicial systems.

This chapter explores the transformative role of Artificial Intelligence (AI) in the context of income tax judgments, particularly focusing on its potential to enhance efficiency, accuracy, and fairness within the Indian tax system. As India grapples with complex tax laws and increasing volumes of data, AI offers a promising solution to streamline tax assessments, fraud detection, and decision-making processes. The chapter examines key AI initiatives in India, such as AI-driven tools for case management and predictive analytics, while also addressing the ethical, legal, and operational challenges that come with integrating AI into tax administration. By leveraging global examples and real-world case studies, this chapter highlights how AI can reduce human bias, improve transparency, and foster accountability in tax judgments. Ultimately, it presents AI as a crucial tool for modernizing India's tax system and enhancing its global competitiveness, emphasizing the need for careful implementation and robust governance frameworks.

Artificial intelligence (AI) applications are an integral part of important industries such as healthcare, banking, financial services, insurance science, logistics, transportation, food technology, travel and entertainment. The purpose of this chapter is to examine the factors that influence the intention of insurance industry executives to adopt artificial intelligence applications through proposals concerning technological, organizational and environmental factors such as relative advantage, complexity, top management support, technological capability, financial readiness, market dynamics, regulatory support, competitive pressure and behavioral intention. Using the technology-organization-environment (TOE) framework, the factors that influence the behavioral intention of insurance industry executives to adopt applications using artificial intelligence are examined. A questionnaire was used to collect data, in which insurance company executives from various fields were asked to complete. SPSS was used to analyze the data. This work can lead to the further activation of executives.

The integration of Artificial Intelligence (AI) into various sectors of society has introduced significant challenges to legal procedures, resulting in what can be called legal entropy. This concept refers to the increasing disorder, unpredictability and complexity within legal systems as they attempt to regulate rapidly evolving technologies. This chapter explores the manifestations of legal entropy in AI governance, including regulatory uncertainty, inconsistent legal interpretation, algorithmic opacity, and ethical and liability dilemmas. It examines the factors contributing to this phenomenon, including the rapid pace of technological advances, fragmented regulatory approaches, and the erosion of legal predictability. To manage and mitigate legal entropy, the chapter proposes several strategies, such as developing adaptive legal frameworks, enhancing transparency and accountability in AI systems, ensuring human oversight, promoting international cooperation, bridging the expertise gap and encouraging innovation in legal technology.

This chapter investigates the regulatory stance of Google and the International Federation of Library Associations and Institutions alongside the European Union through a post-Fordist French regulation school perspective. The analysis of various documents and ideological assessment demonstrates that Google upholds technology development and economic achievement while promoting solutionism and optimism under a philosophical framework that views intelligence and societal formations from an essentialist liberal perspective. The EU supports adaptable regulations that confirm liberal economic principles but keeps its regulatory oversight mechanisms weak. IFLA maintains an inconsistent stance by criticizing AI innovation and capitalism from a human-centric liberal frame and embracing AI development as an inevitable force. All actors follow post-Fordist ideologies, but ethical and human rights considerations against capitalist positions stand out as fundamental critiques of AI control systems, demonstrating contradictions in the discussion regarding AI regulations and societal effects

This chapter explores the intertwined concepts of legality and regularity in the context of artificial intelligence (AI) and their role in managing societal transformations driven by AI integration. As AI increasingly permeates various aspects of human life, from healthcare to fundamental rights like freedom of assembly, it raises important legal and ethical questions. While legality refers to the normative nature of law, regularity focuses on how these norms are empirically observed in society. This chapter examines the challenges AI poses to both concepts, analyzing its potential to disrupt legal norms, challenge societal regularity, and spur rapid, often unpredictable, transformations. It also discusses the growing importance of transparency, accountability, fairness, trustworthiness, safety, and reliability as quality requirements for legal and ethical AI development. This chapter seeks to

Preface

The intersection of artificial intelligence and the legal field marks a defining moment in the evolution of modern jurisprudence. *Modern Perspectives on Artificial Intelligence and Law* emerges from this pivotal juncture, offering critical insights into how AI is reshaping the legal landscape and calling for a paradigm shift in legal education, research, and practice.

Generative artificial intelligence holds transformative potential for the legal profession—not only in enhancing efficiency and reducing costs but also in challenging our existing frameworks of justice and ethics. As AI tools become increasingly capable of automating legal procedures, predicting case outcomes, and analyzing vast volumes of legal data, the traditional roles of lawyers and the expectations placed on legal institutions are evolving rapidly. Law firms that harness AI's capabilities wisely can offer more accessible and proficient services, while those unprepared may find themselves left behind.

This transformation necessitates a reevaluation of how we train future legal professionals. Existing legal curricula, while foundational, often fail to equip students with essential knowledge in emerging technologies such as machine learning, data science, the Internet of Things, cloud computing, and AI systems. The need to incorporate technological fluency into legal education is urgent and clear.

Our volume provides a platform for scientists, legal practitioners, and scholars to explore the practical and theoretical implications of AI in law. From regulatory challenges and algorithmic bias to questions of liability, transparency, and data privacy, this book addresses the many dimensions—both beneficial and concerning—of AI's integration into legal processes. It also emphasizes the importance of ethical considerations, the identification of high-risk AI uses, and the development of computational models of legal reasoning and decision-making.

The objective of this volume is twofold: to serve as a comprehensive guide for educators, researchers, and practitioners navigating the convergence of AI and law, and to inspire innovation in legal pedagogy through the integration of advanced technologies. With an array of case studies, practical examples, and expert insights, we aim to illuminate both the opportunities and the challenges posed by this technological shift.

This book is intended for a broad, interdisciplinary audience—including legal scholars, data scientists, statisticians, economists, informatics experts, educators, and students—who are collectively shaping the future of law in the digital era. We hope that the ideas and discussions presented in these chapters will support more informed, ethical, and forward-looking legal systems that are responsive to the realities of a rapidly changing world.

ORGANIZATION OF THE BOOK

In *Modern Perspectives on Artificial Intelligence and Law*, each chapter contributes a unique lens through which the multifaceted interplay between AI and legal systems is examined, critiqued, and reimagined.

Chapter 1, *AI and Social Implications in Legal Context*, addresses the rapidly expanding deployment of artificial intelligence within law enforcement and the criminal justice system. With specific attention to predictive policing, surveillance, and automated justice administration, the chapter offers a nuanced discussion of the benefits—efficiency, reduced costs, and fewer human errors—alongside the grave ethical and civil liberty concerns posed by technologies like facial recognition. It calls for the development of robust legal safeguards to ensure that the integration of AI in policing supports fairness, respects privacy, and upholds human rights.

Chapter 2, *AI Legislationship: Navigating Unclear Commitments in AI Governance*, introduces the novel concept of "AI legislationship" to capture the ambiguities that currently characterize AI governance. It explores the dissonance between legislative intent and the pace of technological innovation, examining regulatory lags, enforcement challenges, and ethical gray areas. The chapter argues for an integrated governance model that weaves legal, ethical, and technological threads to effectively regulate AI while fostering innovation.

Chapter 3, *Artificial Intelligence and the Evolving Landscape of Legal Accountability*, offers a theoretical dissection of AI's implications for legal education, professional practice, and judicial proceedings. The chapter delves into complex questions surrounding liability, bias, and the ethical challenges of algorithmic decision-making. It highlights the urgent need to reevaluate legal accountability in light of AI's presence in contractual obligations, case law, and judicial telecommunications, cautioning against the over-legalization of justice through technological abstraction.

Chapter 4, *Artificial Intelligence in Legal Judgment: Addressing Income Tax Fraud through Automated Decision-Making*, explores AI's application in modernizing income tax adjudication, with a particular focus on the Indian legal landscape. By investigating case studies and global benchmarks, the chapter underscores how AI tools are being harnessed to detect fraud, streamline case management, and increase transparency. Ethical and operational concerns are also carefully considered, affirming the need for a cautious yet forward-looking approach to AI in tax governance.

Chapter 5, *Autopoietic Co-Evolution of AI and Law*, departs from traditional linear narratives to present a systems-theory-based interpretation of AI and law as co-evolving autopoietic systems. This chapter illustrates how legal frameworks are both shaping and being shaped by AI developments in a recursive, self-sustaining manner. It offers a compelling theoretical model that redefines the nature of legal evolution in an age of intelligent technologies.

Chapter 6, *Cybernetic Intelligence in Intellectual Property Law*, investigates the transformative impact of AI and cybernetic systems on intellectual property law. From automated registration and infringement detection to AI-assisted dispute resolution, the chapter emphasizes the dual promise and peril of AI-driven innovation. Key discussions include ownership of AI-generated works, algorithmic bias, and ethical monopolization, all anchored in the urgent need for transparent, fair, and accountable AI regulation in IP frameworks.

Chapter 7, *Dealing with Semantic Inconsistencies in AI Governance*, addresses the often-overlooked issue of misaligned terminologies and conceptual frameworks between legal language and AI technology. These semantic inconsistencies hinder effective governance, resulting in jurisdictional confusion, regulatory inefficiencies, and reduced public trust. The chapter advocates for harmonized definitions, international cooperation, and adaptable regulatory models to better align legal and technological discourse in AI governance.

Together, these chapters provide a rich, interdisciplinary foundation for rethinking the role of artificial intelligence within the legal domain. As editors, we hope this volume serves as a critical resource for scholars, policymakers, educators, and practitioners navigating the evolving landscape of law in the age of AI.

In this pivotal volume, we begin by delving into the emotionally nuanced frontier of AI integration in immersive digital worlds. Chapter 8, *Governing AI in the Metaverse: Ethical, Legal, and Psychosocial Challenges in Emotion-Aware Virtual Systems*, highlights the profound ethical, legal, and psychosocial challenges presented by affective AI in emotionally intelligent Metaverse platforms. Through interdisciplinary insights and case studies, the authors emphasize the need for a human-centered, ethics-by-design governance model that safeguards emotional integrity and digital autonomy, especially for vulnerable populations such as children and neurodivergent individuals.

Chapter 9, *Is the Artificial Intelligence in Insurance Industry a Reality?*, transitions to a critical sectoral analysis of AI adoption in the insurance industry. Drawing on the Technology-Organization-Environment (TOE) framework, the authors investigate how factors such as relative advantage, technological readiness, and market dynamics influence executives' intentions to adopt AI applications. Empirical data and statistical analyses reveal valuable insights for operationalizing AI within insurance enterprises and catalyzing executive engagement.

In Chapter 10, *Legal Entropy in AI Governance*, the authors introduce the concept of "legal entropy"—the increasing complexity and disorder in legal systems striving to regulate swiftly advancing AI technologies. This chapter explores algorithmic opacity, liability dilemmas, and the erosion of legal predictability. It advocates for adaptive legal frameworks, transparency, international coordination, and legal innovation to counteract the mounting instability in AI governance.

Chapter 11, *Shifting Grounds in Exploring Diverse Approaches to AI Regulation*, presents a comparative analysis of AI policy perspectives from Google, the European Union, and IFLA through a post-Fordist lens. This nuanced examination reveals the ideological contradictions among stakeholders who simultaneously embrace and critique AI's advancement, underscoring ethical tensions and socio-economic biases embedded in their regulatory discourses.

Furthering the exploration of AI's legal ramifications, Chapter 12, *The Impact of AI on Legality and Regularity: Navigating Societal Transformations*, dissects the interplay between normative legal structures and the empirical observation of societal behavior under the influence of AI. As AI reshapes domains such as healthcare and civic freedoms, the authors advocate for transparency, accountability, and reliability in AI systems to uphold both legality and societal regularity amid rapid transformation.

Concluding this section, Chapter 13, *The Status Quo of AI Governance: Global Approaches and Challenges*, provides a sweeping comparative overview of AI governance strategies across continents. With detailed examinations of Europe's regulatory leadership, America's innovation-first approach, Asia's regulatory patchwork, Africa's emerging frameworks, and Australia's nascent strategies, the chapter illustrates the global disparity and potential for collaboration in AI policy development. It underscores the critical role of both governmental and corporate actors in shaping the future of responsible AI.

CONCLUSION

As editors of this volume, we recognize that the accelerating integration of artificial intelligence into the fabric of modern society demands urgent, nuanced, and globally coordinated responses. The chapters assembled in this book present a multifaceted exploration of AI governance, from emotion-aware systems in the Metaverse to sector-specific adoption in insurance, and from the legal disorder introduced by algorithmic opacity to the evolving regulatory landscapes across continents. Each contribution underscores that the challenges we face are not merely technological—they are deeply ethical, legal, political, and psychosocial.

What emerges clearly is that no single framework, nation, or organization holds the key to responsible AI governance. Instead, a dynamic, adaptive, and inclusive approach is required—one that honors human dignity, anticipates societal transformation, and promotes digital trust. As AI continues to disrupt and redefine our institutions, economies, and identities, the need for interdisciplinary collaboration and cross-border dialogue becomes more essential than ever.

This book is not a final word but a starting point—an invitation to policymakers, researchers, technologists, and civil society to engage critically and constructively with the realities of governing AI. By fostering ethical foresight, legal coherence, and global equity, we hope this volume contributes meaningfully to shaping a future in which artificial intelligence serves humanity—not the other way around.

Chapter 1
AI and Social Implications in the Legal Context

Nagulapati Siritha
https://orcid.org/0009-0004-2530-5158
PES University, India

S. Likitha
https://orcid.org/0009-0002-2970-6042
PES University, India

ABSTRACT

This chapter will examine the growing use of artificial intelligence (AI) in law enforcement and criminal justice with a focus on the possible benefits and concomitant risks. The potential uses of AI in policing include predictive policing, surveillance, and justice administration with improved efficiency, cost-effectiveness, and reduced human error. On the other hand, the same development holds many questions about civil liberties and ethics. Technologies such as facial recognition allow for tracking people without their knowledge or consent, which is a threat to privacy. The chapter explores these risks, engaging with the current debate on the responsible and ethical use of AI in policing. It underlines the necessity of strong legal protection so that abuses could be averted and AI applications must be able to honour human rights in the pursuance of fair and equal justice. The analysis done within the chapter will balance innovation with accountability and fairness.

DOI: 10.4018/979-8-3693-9576-9.ch001

INTRODUCTION

This chapter is dedicated to the in-depth exploration of the link between artificial intelligence and legal frameworks, with the focus on greater ethical, legal, and social challenges which such broad application of AI creates. In the center of the debate lies privacy and the fear of misuse of personal data. As a result, the AI systems with their reliance on machine learning algorithms require the collection, processing, and storage of large amounts of personal data. Most of these pieces of information are sensible in nature and therefore raise a number of problems for treatment, access, and giving of consent from the users in all these processes (European Union, 2016; Wachter, Mittelstadt, & Floridi, 2017). The big challenge will be in ascertaining that the users are fully informed about how data is being used and whether their consent is being meaningfully obtained. More so, it becomes problematic with complex AI systems where one may not easily clearly understand how data usage is taking place. The legal frameworks protecting data and personal rights are often outdated or inadequate with regard to the fast-changing abilities of AI. It calls for immediate reforms and stricter regulations that will curb abuses (European Commission, 2021; Calo, 2017).

The second major focus of the chapter revolves around the problem of bias within AI. Most AI algorithms are prone to biases, which may lead to discrimination and discriminatory practices as they are disproportionately targeted towards people who belong to specific race, gender, and even socioeconomic status categories (Angwin, Larson, Mattu, & Kirchner, 2016; O'Neil, 2017). These biases usually originate in the data on which the AI is being trained. When the training data have a historical pattern of inequalities or systemic discrimination, the AI system may keep passing on the type of biases into other outcomes. For instance, this can happen in hiring algorithms, lending algorithms, and even policing algorithms, where predictive policing tools have been proven to force their influence more vigorously in the communities of color (Ferguson, 2017; Angwin et al., 2016). The chapter will discuss how such biases can be implanted in AI either through design or wrong inputs and what the law is proposing or putting in place to combat these issues (Dastin, 2018; New York City Council, 2021). It also discusses the general ethical concerns of allowing AI systems to make decisions that could potentially impact human rights or freedoms, be it in employment, healthcare, or justice, for instance (Jobin, Ienca, & Vayena, 2019; UNESCO, 2021).

Questions related to but not exactly the same are accountability and liability regarding the biases infused into AI. As AI comes closer to self-governance, it is becoming impossible to pass the buck when something goes wrong with AI. Responsibility in such a scenario remains a vague term: should it be the developer, the user, or the AI machine itself? The chapter further explores this legal controversy, with particular reference to the question of when it is possible to speak of an autonomous operation of AI systems by humans (Asaro, 2016; Pagallo, 2013). Such newest breakthroughs in technology always lead to legal grey areas which, in turn, confuse the jury in cases between traditional liability rules and already existing AI regulations. The problem is more often seen in healthcare and autonomous driving, which can cause both kinds of harm. The discussion looks into proposals for new liability frameworks that will ensure the responsible design and use of AI systems, and also where to seek justice resolutely when such harms occur (Bostrom, 2014; Asaro, 2016).

As for efforts at regulation, the chapter reviews current state of the regulation of AI from both a domestic and international context. Different countries have followed different policies of regulation in AI, while some have focused on data protection, others on ethical guidelines, and others at the sector-specific level. As much as the international level is concerned, much debate exists on how best to coordinate regulatory efforts and establish universal standards for developing and using AI. The European Union, for instance, has offered an overarching AI regulations package that balances innovation with ethical considerations (European Commission, 2021; Cath, Wachter, Mittelstadt, Taddeo, & Floridi, 2018). Others have taken a hands-off approach, such as in the case of the United States (Calo, 2017). The chapter will contrast and compare these regulatory frameworks, explore their respective merits and shortcomings in depth, and analyze the possibility of harmonizing AI regulations between borders. It will then cover, subsequently, the efforts that global entities such as the United Nations and the OECD have taken to create guidelines on proper AI usage and the challenge of implementation in the context of a globalized world (Jobin et al., 2019; UNESCO, 2021).

BACKGROUND

Artificial Intelligence (AI) is fast becoming a large part of our everyday lives, transforming the way we work, study, and even make critical decisions in areas such as healthcare, finance, and law. While AI promises exciting new possibilities—such as quicker problem-solving and smarter predictions—it also poses some serious questions. How do we ensure that AI treats all of us with equal fairness and doesn't enter our private lives? What if AI takes a discriminatory decision that has an impact on the life of a person? The technology is advancing rapidly, but the laws and moral standards are still trying to catch up. That's why efforts are being made to develop principles that render AI transparent, accountable, and human rights respectful so that it contributes to society without harming it.

Focus of the Article

This piece explores the sensitive dilemmas involved in going about making AI ethical and equitable, particularly when it's being applied globally. It examines issues such as AI bias—whereby systems may selectively favor some groups at the expense of others—and the delicate balance between supporting innovation and laying down regulations that safeguard individuals. The article also discusses how AI is transforming the world of law, assisting in various things such as anticipating crime or evaluating risks, but also how it is unconsciously exacerbating disparities or undermining privacy. A large obstacle is the fact that various nations have different legislations and values, and therefore, it is difficult to find consensus on one standard set of global AI standards. The article also talks about emerging concepts such as "regulatory sandboxes," which are sanctuaries where firms and regulators can pilot AI innovations jointly before deploying them on a large scale.

AI and Legal Context

Artificial Intelligence is revolutionizing industries across the globe, including healthcare, finance, and also the legal space. AI refers to machines or systems that are designed to perform and sometimes go beyond the capabilities of human intelligence in tasks like language translation, picture recognition, speech comprehension, and decision-making (Russell & Norvig, 2016). This technological advancement is spreading more into various sectors as more and more industries gradually merge into a whole system that changes the fabric of workflow to become more sophisticated and productive in improving productivity. However, with innovation comes complicated legal and ethical issues, especially when it begins to converge with the law itself (Calo, 2017).

AI can greatly transform the practice of law because AI can make procedures more efficient. For example, AI can help lawyers in researching, predicting determinations of cases, and even automate some tasks like reviewing documents and contracts (Calo, 2017). This technological support frees time from repetitive or routine tasks for more elaborate and strategic legal work; AI application, for example can handle oceanic amounts of case law and documents at speeds that are far faster than what humans can do (Russell & Norvig, 2016). As for these systems, they can determine precedents and patterns that may be determinants to the outcome of a case. This is very important for attorneys in terms of being able to have insight into the legal situation at hand.

Aside from research assistance, AI can be used to predict the outcome of cases. Analyzing previous rulings and historical data, AI systems present probabilistic predictions on how a case might be resolved (Calo, 2017). This ability to predict can improve the decisions of legal professionals; in fact, such predictions can help assess the strengths and weaknesses of a case and advice clients about the outcomes. AI's ability to predict the behavior of judges, juries, or opposing counsel adds more strategic advantage. AI tools will be able to identify biases that have crept into the judges' decisions, which will make developing a well-tailored legal strategy easier (Angwin et al., 2016).

It raises complicated issues in the judicial sector requiring renewed examination of legal codes. One of the biggest concerns is that new legal frameworks are needed to govern how AI is used in the system, particularly in aspects relating to accountability and transparency in AI decision-making (Pagallo, 2013). For example, an incorrect legal prediction or advice given by an AI system through which the outcome of one client is disadvantaged—who shall be blamed? The developers of the system or lawyers that used it or the AI system itself? These issues illustrate a necessity for clearer legal provisions in terms of responsibility and liability when AI systems are employed in the practice of law (Asaro, 2016).

Also, as AI systems start more complex jobs, they must operate fairly and without bias. One important area of concern regarding bias in AI algorithms. This is because AI systems learn from vast datasets, and if these datasets reflect existing social inequalities, the AI might perpetuate those biases (O'Neil, 2017).

A particularly sensitive area of their potential for bias is the area of law enforcement and criminal justice in which AI tools are increasingly applied for predicting crime and assessing rates of recidivism. For example, predictive policing algorithms use historical crime data to make predictions about where future crimes might take place. The entire purpose of these tools is "to make policing a more rational task," to do this by significantly altering how law enforcement works, but these changes come with their attendant risks of privacy, surveillance, and discrimination (Ferguson, 2017). When the data fed into a predictive policing algorithm are biased, the AI system might end up patrolling those communities further, to over-police areas of minority living. This would actually perpetuate and even extend existing social inequalities rather than reducing them (Angwin et al., 2016; Ferguson, 2017).

AI is not being utilized merely in law enforcement. It is increasingly being deployed even in contract review and analysis. AI-based contract review tools are able to quickly analyze large amounts of legal documents to look for obscure risks and issues, such as questionable language or regulatory noncompliance (Calo, 2017). These tools can make reviewing contracts significantly more efficient, saving lawyers immense time and money. Yet, there are specific problems with dependence on AI for contract analysis: The accuracy and reliability. While AI can process huge amounts of data in a ridiculously short amount of time, it may sometimes lack enough comprehensive knowledge of the meanings of legal texts or the correct interpretation of ambiguous terms of contracts (Russell & Norvig, 2016). This implies that AI systems might miss some information or commit errors that could have strategic legal implications.

Using AI in practice also raises larger ethical questions. Since AI systems are getting increasingly independent and can take decisions alone, the accountability gets tougher to handle. Who bears responsibility when an AI system has made a choice that, in fact, causes harm? This raises serious issues in areas such as driverless cars or medicine, for instance, where the AI system is making make-or-break life-or-death decisions (Asaro, 2016; Bostrom, 2014). The world of law raises questions at the very foundation of ethics about whether an AI can take some decisions regarding sentencing or parole. Do people have trust in AI systems to care for the lives of individuals? These raise the issues that require full consideration of the ethical concerns that might be invoked in the integration of AI with the legal system (Jobin et al., 2019; UNESCO, 2021).

To resolve such challenges, legal professions need to be ready to interact with AI technology but also be aware of the capabilities and limitations of such technology. This involves vast and deep knowledge of the technical aspects of AI and the legal and ethical issues it presents. Lawyers and judges must get better at being technologically literate in order to adequately weigh the risks and benefits associated with introducing AI into their work. Legal education too must evolve into a mechanism to adequately prepare the next generation of lawyers for the emerging AI-driven legal landscape (Calo, 2017).

New legal standards must be developed that govern the application of AI in the law. These standards should embody demands for greater accountability, transparency and fairness from abusive and unfair practices on the part of biased algorithms on policy considerations concerning privacy. They should foster innovation to enable AI to be utilized effectively in legal practice. International cooperation will be necessary to develop the new legal standards because AI is a global technology and it is likely that related inter-border legal issues will arise. There will be a need for standardization on the usage of AI in legal practice across countries and that the system is held to the highest ethical standards (Cath et al., 2018; Jobin et al., 2019).

There is great opportunity with tremendous challenges involved when AI is integrated into the legal practice. AI is promising to revolutionize the legal sphere in terms of efficiency, accuracy, and accessibility. This, however also comes with complex legal, ethical, and social issues in using AI inside the system, which calls for utmost consideration. Technical conception of AI better equips attorneys, judges, and other professionals working in law practice to confront some of these problems and offer input to emerging legal frameworks which will encourage prudent use of AI (Calo, 2017).

Through cooperation, rules, and education, the legal profession can be able to take advantage of AI while preserving the very tenets of justice and equity (Jobin et al., 2019; UNESCO, 2021).

AI and the Legal Context

Artificial intelligence is transforming industries worldwide, including healthcare, finance, and notably the legal sector. AI encompasses machines or systems designed to perform tasks requiring human-like intelligence—such as language translation, image recognition, speech comprehension, and decision-making (Russell & Norvig, 2016). This technological evolution is rapidly permeating various sectors, fundamentally altering workflows to enhance productivity and sophistication. However, alongside these innovations arise complex legal and ethical issues, especially as AI increasingly intersects with the law itself (Calo, 2017).

AI has the potential to revolutionize legal practice by improving efficiency. It can assist lawyers by automating tasks like document review, contract analysis, and case law research, thereby freeing time for more complex strategic work (Calo, 2017). AI systems process enormous volumes of legal documents and case data at speeds far exceeding human capability (Russell & Norvig, 2016). By identifying precedents and patterns, AI offers valuable insights that can influence case outcomes, giving legal professionals a significant strategic advantage.

Beyond research assistance, AI can predict case outcomes by analyzing historical rulings and data to provide probabilistic forecasts (Calo, 2017). These predictions help lawyers assess case strengths and weaknesses and advise clients more effectively. Additionally, AI tools can detect biases in judicial decisions, enabling more tailored legal strategies (Angwin et al., 2016).

However, these technological advancements raise difficult issues within the judicial system, necessitating updated legal codes. One critical concern is establishing governance over AI use in legal contexts, particularly regarding accountability and transparency in AI decision-making (Pagallo, 2013). For example, if an AI system provides incorrect legal advice that disadvantages a client, it is unclear who should be held responsible: the system developers, the lawyers using it, or the AI itself? Such questions underscore the urgent need for clearer legal provisions defining responsibility and liability in AI-enabled legal practice (Asaro, 2016).

Moreover, fairness and impartiality are paramount as AI undertakes increasingly complex legal tasks. Bias in AI algorithms is a significant concern because AI learns from datasets that may embed societal inequalities, potentially perpetuating discrimination (O'Neil, 2017).

Law enforcement and criminal justice represent particularly sensitive areas where AI bias has profound implications. AI tools are employed to predict crime and assess recidivism risks, with predictive policing algorithms using historical crime data to forecast future criminal activity. Although intended to enhance policing efficiency, these tools can reinforce discriminatory practices by disproportionately targeting minority communities (Ferguson, 2017; Angwin et al., 2016). Such biased policing exacerbates existing social inequalities rather than alleviating them.

AI's reach extends beyond law enforcement into contract review and analysis. AI-powered tools can rapidly scrutinize large volumes of legal documents to identify risks, ambiguous language, or regulatory noncompliance (Calo, 2017). While these tools enhance efficiency and reduce costs, their reliability remains a concern. AI may lack nuanced understanding of legal language and interpret ambiguous terms incorrectly, potentially overlooking critical details with strategic implications (Russell & Norvig, 2016).

The ethical dimension of AI integration into legal practice also demands scrutiny. As AI systems gain autonomy and decision-making capacity, accountability becomes complex. When AI decisions cause harm—such as in autonomous vehicles or medical AI—the question of responsibility is pressing (Asaro, 2016; Bostrom, 2014). The legal field grapples with foundational ethical questions about entrusting AI with decisions that affect liberty or life, such as sentencing or parole. Public trust in AI's role in these sensitive areas remains uncertain, necessitating careful ethical considerations (Jobin et al., 2019; UNESCO, 2021).

Addressing these challenges requires legal professionals to become technologically literate, understanding AI's capabilities and limitations to evaluate associated risks and benefits effectively. Legal education must evolve to prepare future lawyers for an AI-driven legal landscape (Calo, 2017).

New legal standards governing AI application in law must emphasize accountability, transparency, fairness, and privacy protection while fostering innovation. International cooperation is essential given AI's global reach, facilitating harmonized standards and ensuring adherence to ethical principles across borders (Cath et al., 2018; Jobin et al., 2019).

The integration of AI into legal practice offers enormous opportunities alongside significant challenges. While AI promises enhanced efficiency, accuracy, and accessibility, it simultaneously introduces complex legal, ethical, and social issues that demand careful attention. Technological literacy among legal professionals will be crucial to navigating these challenges and shaping frameworks that enable the responsible and equitable use of AI (Calo, 2017).

Through collaborative efforts in rule-making, education, and regulation, the legal profession can harness AI's potential while safeguarding justice and equity (Jobin et al., 2019; UNESCO, 2021).

Privacy in AI

Privacy has emerged as one of the most significant social implications of artificial intelligence (AI), primarily because AI systems depend on vast amounts of personal data to function effectively (Cath et al., 2018). AI technologies—ranging from facial recognition to predictive analytics—collect, process, and analyze personal information on a scale previously unimaginable (European Union, 2016). While these advancements bring numerous benefits, they also pose serious threats to individual privacy (Wachter et al., 2017). The ability of AI to make inferences, predictions, and even manipulations based on personal data has alarmed privacy advocates, legal experts, and regulators worldwide (Calo, 2017).

One fundamental reason AI presents such substantial privacy risks is its reliance on big data. AI systems require massive datasets to learn and improve their functions (Russell & Norvig, 2016). These datasets often include sensitive personal information, such as individuals' habits, preferences, health records, social interactions, and biometric identifiers like fingerprints or facial scans (European Union, 2016). AI applications in sectors like healthcare, finance, law enforcement, and social media heavily depend on this data to enhance services and deliver personalized experiences (Ferguson, 2017). However, the sheer scale of data collection combined with the lack of transparency about how this data is used severely limits individuals' control over their information (Wachter et al., 2017).

Controversies surrounding AI and privacy often center on facial recognition technologies. These systems use AI algorithms to identify individuals based on their facial features, frequently without their explicit consent (Cath et al., 2018). Governments and law enforcement agencies deploy facial recognition for surveillance purposes, while private companies use it for security, targeted advertising, and user authentication (Ferguson, 2017). Though facial recognition promises increased efficiency and safety, it also threatens privacy in unprecedented ways (Calo, 2017). People may be unaware that they are being surveilled or that their images are being captured and analyzed (Ferguson, 2017). Moreover, data obtained from facial recognition can be stored indefinitely, potentially used against individuals over long periods, or sold to third parties without consent (Cath et al., 2018). These threats are compounded by the risks of data breaches and misuse (Wachter et al., 2017).

Even when personal data is securely stored, the vast volumes held by organizations make them vulnerable to cyberattacks (European Union, 2016). For example, if a facial recognition database were compromised, the consequences could severely impact the individuals whose data was leaked, leading to identity theft and other malicious acts (Cath et al., 2018). Another concern is the exploitation of AI-collected data for purposes beyond those originally intended (Wachter et al., 2017). Companies might use personal data to profile or market to consumers, or governments could track political dissidents or activists (Calo, 2017). Such practices raise serious questions about user control and consent over personal information (Cath et al., 2018).

A significant legal framework addressing privacy in AI data collection is the European Union's General Data Protection Regulation (GDPR), enacted in 2016 (European Union, 2016). The GDPR is one of the most comprehensive data protection laws globally, setting clear rules on how organizations collect, store, and process personal data (European Commission, 2021). It emphasizes transparency, consent, and data minimization (Cath et al., 2018). Under the GDPR, individuals have the right to know what data is held about them, how it will be used, and with whom it will be shared (European Union, 2016). They also have rights to request data deletion or correction and to withdraw consent at any time (European Commission, 2021).

However, meaningful consent poses a key challenge in the context of AI. AI systems are often opaque, making it difficult for users to understand how their data is collected or utilized (Wachter et al., 2017). The complexity and volume of data involved make it hard for organizations to provide clear explanations, raising doubts about whether users can provide truly informed consent (Cath et al., 2018). This issue is especially acute among vulnerable populations such as children or those with low digital literacy, who may lack the knowledge to make informed decisions about their data (UNESCO, 2021). The GDPR requires consent to be informed, specific, and freely given, but these requirements are particularly difficult to meet for AI applications (European Union, 2016).

Data minimization, another crucial principle of the GDPR, mandates that organizations only collect data necessary for specific purposes and avoid excessive data gathering (European Commission, 2021). Yet AI's dependence on large datasets to improve accuracy creates tension between data minimization and AI development needs (Russell & Norvig, 2016). For instance, facial recognition software may require tens of thousands of images to refine its performance (Cath et al., 2018). While such data collection might be justified technically, it raises concerns about the necessity and proportionality of processing such large-scale personal information and its impact on privacy (European Union, 2016). Regulators face the difficult task of balancing these competing demands (Cath et al., 2018).

Closely related is the principle of purpose limitation, which requires that data be collected for a specific, lawful purpose and not used for unrelated objectives without explicit authorization (European Union, 2016). In practice, AI systems often use data beyond the original intent (Calo, 2017). For example, data gathered for identity verification may later be used for profiling or targeted advertising without consent, violating purpose limitation and amplifying privacy risks (Cath et al., 2018). To address this, organizations must design AI systems that respect data control rights and ensure processing occurs only for legitimate purposes (European Commission, 2021).

As AI technologies evolve, there will be an increasing need for updated legal frameworks to protect privacy rights in the digital age (Cath et al., 2018). Although regulations like GDPR provide a solid foundation, adaptations or extensions may be necessary to address AI-specific risks, especially concerning biometric data used in face and voice recognition (European Commission, 2021). Policymakers must decide whether new laws are needed or whether existing ones can be strengthened to keep pace with rapid technological advances (Calo, 2017).

One promising approach involves Privacy-Enhancing Technologies (PETs), which enable organizations to use data legitimately while safeguarding individual privacy (Cath et al., 2018). Examples include data anonymization, encryption, and differential privacy—techniques allowing analysis without identifying specific individuals (Calo, 2017). Combining PETs with AI can reduce privacy risks while still benefiting from AI's insights (Cath et al., 2018). Encouraging the adoption of PETs through regulatory incentives could prevent many privacy problems during AI development (Cath et al., 2018).

In conclusion, AI presents substantial privacy challenges due to its dependence on personal data and potential for misuse. Addressing these challenges requires evolving legal frameworks, transparency, user control, and privacy-enhancing technologies to safeguard individual rights (Calo, 2017).

AI and Bias: Algorithmic Bias

Algorithmic bias is among the most pressing challenges in AI development and application, especially in socially sensitive areas like law enforcement, hiring, and lending (O'Neil, 2017). The root of the problem lies in AI's reliance on large datasets for training. Since these datasets often reflect historical and societal inequalities, AI systems tend to replicate or even amplify existing biases (Angwin et al., 2016). This section explores how AI bias manifests, its discriminatory impacts across sectors, and the role of legal frameworks in mitigating these issues.

Algorithmic bias refers to systematic, repeatable errors in AI systems that produce unfair outcomes, often privileging certain groups over others based on race, gender, socioeconomic status, or other characteristics (O'Neil, 2017). Because AI learns from historical data, it can inherit deep-seated biases. For example, if a company historically favored male candidates, an AI system trained on that hiring data may also discriminate against women in future recruitment (Dastin, 2018). Similarly, law enforcement AI trained on racially biased crime data may perpetuate discriminatory policing (Ferguson, 2017).

Predictive policing illustrates this problem well: algorithms analyze past crime data to predict where crimes are likely to occur, resulting in intensified police scrutiny in minority neighborhoods already over-policed (Ferguson, 2017). This creates a feedback loop that perpetuates systemic bias rather than alleviating it (Angwin et al., 2016).

AI bias is equally concerning in hiring. AI tools are increasingly used to screen resumes and assess candidates (Dastin, 2018). However, biased training data can lead to discriminatory hiring, excluding qualified individuals from minority groups (O'Neil, 2017). A well-known example is Amazon's AI hiring tool, which was found to penalize resumes mentioning "women's," reflecting historical male dominance in applications, and thus discriminating against female candidates (Dastin, 2018).

In finance, AI plays a growing role in lending decisions and credit scoring (O'Neil, 2017). Yet biased algorithms can unfairly discriminate against low-income or minority applicants (O'Neil, 2017). For example, redlining algorithms trained on historical data may unjustly deny loans to financially qualified individuals from marginalized communities, exacerbating economic inequality (O'Neil, 2017).

Bias in AI arises in multiple ways: primarily from biased training data, but also from design choices by developers and feedback loops in AI deployment (O'Neil, 2017). Developers' decisions about what data to include, how to preprocess it, and which outcomes to optimize affect AI's fairness (Jobin et al., 2019). Because AI systems can be opaque ("black boxes"), biased decisions may go unnoticed or unchallenged (Wachter et al., 2017).

To counter bias, a multi-pronged approach is essential. First, diverse, representative datasets can reduce bias in training (Jobin et al., 2019). Second, transparency in AI design and decision-making is critical so stakeholders can understand and challenge AI outputs (Wachter et al., 2017). Third, legal regulation plays a vital role: laws such as the EU's AI Act propose requirements for fairness, transparency, and accountability in AI systems (European Commission, 2021).

Several jurisdictions have introduced laws targeting AI bias. For example, New York City's Local Law 144 prohibits the use of automated employment decision tools that have not been independently audited for bias and discrimination (New York City Council, 2021). Similarly, the EU AI Act requires high-risk AI systems to undergo conformity assessments focusing on bias mitigation (European Commission, 2021).

Beyond regulation, technical solutions are advancing. Researchers are developing algorithms designed to detect and reduce bias in AI outputs, such as fairness-aware machine learning techniques (Jobin et al., 2019). Additionally, independent audits and certification programs for AI systems can enhance accountability (Financial Conduct Authority, 2023).

In sum, AI bias represents a significant social and ethical problem with tangible consequences for marginalized groups. Addressing it demands concerted efforts in data practices, legal oversight, transparency, and ongoing research (O'Neil, 2017). Without such measures, AI risks perpetuating and even deepening social inequalities rather than alleviating them.

The Theories of Legal Liability and AI

Several legal concepts can hold accountable in cases of AI systems, but there exists a problem for each of these to meet the demands and complexities created by autonomous systems.

Strict Liability

Strict liability is a principle according to which a person or organization is liable for the injury caused by his or her act or product, irrespective of intent or negligence.

Strict liability may be placed on AI developers or companies deploying AI systems, liable for damages brought forth by the AI. The rationale behind such a policy is that while it is the people who create and benefit from AI, it is the people who are responsible for its wrongdoing, just as product liability laws place liability on manufacturers of defective products. This may not necessarily be the case with AI, and strict liability might not be applicable in every situation. The behavior of the AI system depends on its processing of huge data volumes after deployment. The phenomenon of learning and adapting independently often leads to confusion and an inability to identify a point at which failure can be said to occur or where blame lies. Strict liability could negatively affect innovation in AI; developers would tend to be overly cautious about being blamed for something that occurred outside their control and outside their real motives (Abbott, 2020).

Negligence

Negligence forms the most fundamental source of liability under the law. There would have to be at least some proof that a party had failed in their duty of care, thereby causing injury.

In this regard, for the AI domain, proving negligence meant demonstrating either that developers, users, or companies did not take adequate or reasonable precautions during the constitution, training, or use of these AI systems. For instance, when an AI trained to make discriminatory decisions learns it from biased training data, negligence can be claimed against the developers for allowing their model to be unfair (Angwin, Larson, Mattu, & Kirchner, 2016; Dastin, 2018). However, proving negligence in AI cases is difficult. AI systems behave in ways which their developers may not understand—often in the case of deep learning models. Besides, because some AI is complex enough to be described in the amateur dramatic sense, tracing decisions back to design or training choices is difficult. In the absence of clear standards of what reasonably ought to have been done to protect against risk, negligence claims in AI could well prove hard to litigate (Pagallo, 2013).

Product Liability

However, an AI system can also be considered as a product. The liability of the producers of the AI system may therefore arise from product liability laws, in case the system proves defective. Under product liability, the liability revolves around a product's design and manufacturing defects causing injury. Then, if an autonomous car causes harm in crashes due to some hidden coding or hardware error, the manufacturer or developer may be liable.

However, the characterization of AI systems as "products" under existing legal frameworks is problematic. Evolving and learning means that AI systems might change over time and produce behaviors not present at the time they were designed or sold. Is the degree of control a developer can exercise reasonably exerted over an AI system after deployment? (Calo, 2017).

Vicarious Liability

Vicarious liability is the imposition of legal responsibility transferred through one to another, usually the setting concerning employers and their employees.

In terms of AI, companies or individuals who employ AI systems may be held vicariously liable for the action of the AI as it may then be regarded as a "tool" operating on behalf of another end. For example, if a firm utilizes an AI hiring platform, then for decisions of that system to have been discriminatory, the firm may be liable for claims of discriminatory hiring practices even though it did not specifically program that type of bias into the AI system. This theory is confronted whenever an AI acts independently in some unforeseen or unintended manner by a user or developer. In addition, holding the user liable for the actions of an AI system that he cannot completely control may hinder the adoption of AI technologies (Asaro, 2016).

Responsibility and Accountability with AI

Artificial Intelligence, or AI, has shown what it can do in health care, finance, cars, and even law. Still, while AI holds such promise for efficiency and innovation, it throws up broader questions about responsibility and accountability when things go wrong. In particular, the use of AI in autonomous decision-making raises questions regarding who bears blame or liability for errors or damage inflicted. Responsibility seems to lie with the creators, the users, or the AI itself.

This section will explore the legal perspective on the complexities surrounding accountability with AI. It identifies theories of liability and responsibility in systems of law that may evolve to cope with these developments—possibly implicated in reforms in tort law, criminal liability, or contractual obligation (Pagallo, 2013).

AI systems, particularly machine learning (ML) and deep learning (DL)-based systems, do follow algorithms designed by humans but are able to process information independently of their creators; they often "learn" through massive datasets and may bring forth results not explicitly programmed by their creators (Bostrom, 2014). This capability of autonomous decision-making brings forth several issues concerning responsibility when the AI system causes harm.

For instance, a driverless vehicle may result in an accident. It is rather challenging to determine who is liable. Is it the developer's fault for making an error in programming? Or is it the user of the car who should be liable? Or should the liability fall on the manufacturer or other companies that train the AI model? All these scenarios require clearly defined legal frameworks relating to liability.

Legal Frameworks and Evolution with AI

The challenges AI throws up calls for reform in legal systems, in particular, in accountability and liability. There are several areas of the law that stand to be shaped:

Tort Law

Tort law as relating to civil wrongs and compensation will need a change to reflect harms related to AI. The new developments that such a scenario could bring include new standards of negligence and strict liability specifically for AI. Even legal scholars have proposed a new field of "AI torts" where particular duties of care for the design, users, and makers of AI could be established (Calo, 2017). This may entail achieving clarity in AI systems, auditing their decisions for equity, and maintaining oversight even after deployment.

Criminal Liability

The greater challenge lies in criminal liability. Is it possible to charge an AI system with a crime? Some scholars have suggested that AI systems ought to be treated as "legal persons" capable of bearing responsibility for their actions (Bostrom, 2014). However, this gives rise to profound ethical and philosophical questions: How do

AI systems assume the quality of non-consciousness and lack of intent and moral agency, lest they assume qualities traditionally associated with criminal responsibility?

Contrarily, liability for a crime could be extended to entities liable for the designing, training, or unleashing AI, such that they may contribute to loss or harm caused. This would be the case in situations where there is evidence of gross negligence or recklessness regarding the risks presented by the AI. Developers or companies would be liable for criminal charges if through their AI, death, or significant harm had occurred based on established and avoidable risks (Pagallo, 2013).

Contractual Obligations

Contract law is likely to evolve with the rise of AI systems. Most AI systems are sold or licensed with disclaimers or terms that limit the liability of their creators or producers. Such liability provisions might be unconscionable in cases where the AI system causes serious harm to consumers or users. Legal reforms could manifest as enforceable responsibility minimum thresholds that can never be contracted around in AI contracts or even demanding transparency regarding the dangers associated with the use of AI systems (Abbott, 2020).

Rapid development and increasing autonomy in decision-making by AI create grave challenges about responsibility and accountability when things go wrong. Traditional legal theories such as strict liability, negligence, and product liability provide some guide but may require adaptation to take care of problems peculiar with AI. Changing legal frameworks would, at that point, need balance between encouraging innovation and protecting the public from harm—most probably by reforms in the areas of tort law, criminal liability, and contractual obligations.

There is a dire necessity to set up new legal standards; but the way to those standards is strewn with a million complications. It is in this light that lawmakers, technologists, and legal thinkers need to come together for formulating laws that help meet the challenge of accountability in the world of AI (Calo, 2017; Pagallo, 2013).

AI Regulation: National and International Effort

AI regulation is a nascent area, and its tension of encouraging innovation while also regulating risks continues to evolve. Governments, organizations, and international bodies are striving to make and implement frameworks for ensuring ethical, safe, and beneficial use of artificial intelligence (AI). While these efforts are still in their infancy, the landscape is at this point fragmented—in other words, different national and international approaches unfold (Cath, Wachter, Mittelstadt, Taddeo, & Floridi, 2018). This chapter explores national and international regulatory efforts, albeit focusing on the strengths and weaknesses thereof and discusses the possibility of harmonizing these regulations into a global framework.

Ethical AI and Human Rights Framework: Navigating Risks and Opportunities

AI carries immense opportunities and also serious risks to human rights. On one hand, AI systems, through which medicine, education, and disaster response can be developed in various sectors, will positively advance the provision and delivery of those human-related areas via technology. On the other hand, AI will challenge privacy, freedom of speech, equality, and other basic human rights. This has been a concern area as increasingly more governments, legal bodies, and organizations try to balance this via ethical AI and human rights frameworks (UNESCO, 2021).

Algorithmic Bias and Discrimination

Algorithmic bias may be one of the greatest ethical challenges AI faces. They are only as good as the data they are trained on. If the data reflects existing societal biases, then algorithms built from it would likely maintain, or even worse, amplify those biases (O'Neil, 2017; Angwin et al., 2016). That's what has been happening in hiring processes, credit scoring, and facial recognition technology. For instance, there have been allegations against facial recognition systems for holding a higher rate of errors particularly among people possessing darker skin tones, which has caused concern of racial discrimination and infringement of civil rights (Dastin, 2018).

A class of biased algorithms that carry grave consequences for marginalized communities are predictive policing tools, which rely on historical crime data to forecast future criminal activity. Against this backdrop, it has been argued that predictive policing tools have contributed to the phenomenon of over-policing minority neighborhoods (Ferguson, 2017; Angwin et al., 2016). Similar outcomes have been recorded regarding risk assessment algorithms used in court: they label Black defendants as higher risks and lead to worse sentencing outcomes (Angwin et al., 2016).

As I have mentioned, addressing algorithmic bias will involve these and multiple other possible angles: increase diversity of training data, increase transparency of the decision-making processes of AI systems, enforce regular audits of the AI system, and identify and mitigate biases in them. Some jurisdictions have already embarked on this journey. For example, New York City has passed the first state legislation in the US obliging businesses to audit their automated hiring tools for bias, an important step toward reducing algorithmic discrimination (New York City Council, 2021).

Balancing Innovation with Ethical and Social Considerations

Such discussion of ethical and legal challenges associated with AI is highly pertinent for today, but so is preventing over-regulation from stifling innovation. The great promise of AI to produce enormous value to society—from greater benefits in health care, less energy consumption, and public safety—poses a great challenge to the policymaker: balancing in the best way how to foster technological innovation and protect societal interests (Calo, 2017; European Commission, 2021).

One way in which balance could be achieved is through "regulatory sandboxes": controlled environments in which companies can test new AI technologies while under the watch of regulators. Innovation is thus balanced with risk identification. This is one area where the United Kingdom has been quite innovative; its Financial Conduct Authority has established one of the first regulatory sandboxes for AI and fintech innovations (Financial Conduct Authority, 2023).

As important as the regulatory framework, though, is industry self-regulation in ensuring responsible AI. Tech companies have adopted ethical principles for the development of AI, the core elements of which include fairness, transparency, and accountability. Self-regulation, as a whole, is insufficient, and it needs to be supplemented by meaningful oversight from the government as to whether these principles are being applied in reality (Cath et al., 2018; Jobin et al., 2019). Balancing innovation with ethical and social considerations in the legal context is a very complex yet essential task in the face of artificial intelligence's changing society. On one hand, AI has transformative potential because it improves efficiencies, allows for predictive analytics, and enhances decision-making processes across industries, including the legal field (Russell & Norvig, 2016). But progress must be tempered with careful attention to ethical and social concerns. These issues involve violations of privacy, the perpetuation of algorithmic bias, and the problem of holding people accountable in AI-related harm (Asaro, 2016; Pagallo, 2013). Challenges come from balancing innovation and setting strong legal frameworks for ensuring rights, fairness, and transparency. The legal ecosystem can be designed in such a way that it encourages technological advancement while keeping societal values intact by integrating ethical principles into AI design, mandating regular audits for bias, and aligning AI regulation with international human rights standards (Cath et al., 2018; UNESCO, 2021). This balance is critical to prevent AI from exacerbating inequalities or infringing on rights, ensuring it serves the greater public good (Jobin et al., 2019). The Human Costs and Considerations in an Algorithmic Age

As artificial intelligence increasingly integrates into the fabric of daily life — from personalized ads and autonomous vehicles to predictive policing and healthcare diagnostics — the pressing need to reflect on its ethical, legal, and social implications becomes paramount. These implications are not just technical challenges; they are deeply human ones. They affect who gets hired, who receives medical care, who gets parole, and who is watched or ignored by a digital gaze that seldom blinks. As we navigate the fourth industrial revolution, it becomes clear that the development of AI must not outpace the frameworks that ensure it serves humanity equitably and ethically.

Privacy in the Age of Intelligent Machines

At the heart of many AI applications lies data — vast oceans of it, collected often without informed consent or transparency. Our digital footprints, from shopping preferences to GPS locations, are being used to train complex algorithms. Yet, the more data AI consumes, the more privacy is compromised. The line between personalization and surveillance blurs rapidly.

Scholars argue that AI intensifies the risk of privacy violations by creating "pervasive and invisible surveillance systems" (Zuboff, 2019). Facial recognition technology, often embedded in public and private spaces, exemplifies this issue. In cities around the world, individuals are being tracked without consent, raising serious concerns about civil liberties. In India, initiatives like Aadhaar have sparked debates about surveillance, state overreach, and data protection (Ramanathan, 2019).

Moreover, many AI systems collect biometric data — retinal scans, voice prints, heart rate patterns — for applications in health and security. When this data is stored or processed without stringent safeguards, it becomes vulnerable to breaches and misuse. The Cambridge Analytica scandal revealed the vast extent to which personal data could be weaponized to manipulate political outcomes (Cadwalladr & Graham-Harrison, 2018), highlighting the urgent need for transparent data governance policies tailored to AI ecosystems.

Algorithmic Bias and the Risk of Discrimination

One of the most unsettling revelations about AI is its potential to reflect and even amplify societal biases. Algorithms trained on historical data often replicate the prejudices embedded in that data — whether gender bias in hiring algorithms or racial disparities in criminal justice tools.

For instance, ProPublica's investigation into COMPAS, an AI system used in U.S. courts to predict recidivism, found it disproportionately labeled Black defendants as high-risk compared to white defendants (Angwin et al., 2016). The problem isn't just flawed data, but a lack of oversight into how these models are trained and deployed.

Bias isn't limited to the West. In the Indian context, AI systems used in education or job-matching platforms may unknowingly reinforce caste-based or regional stereotypes if trained on unbalanced datasets. Scholars argue that algorithmic fairness must be tailored to socio-cultural contexts rather than applying universal standards (Eubanks, 2018).

The problem is compounded by the "black box" nature of many AI models, particularly deep learning systems. Their opacity makes it difficult for even developers to explain how a decision was made. This not only erodes trust but makes it nearly impossible for affected individuals to seek redress.

Accountability in Autonomous Systems

A foundational question that AI poses to law and ethics is: who is responsible when things go wrong? When an autonomous car causes an accident, or a medical AI misdiagnoses a patient, who should be held accountable — the developer, the user, the company, or the machine itself?

This legal gray zone creates what is often termed the "accountability gap" (Calo & Kerr, 2015). Traditional legal frameworks, based on human agency, struggle to accommodate systems that make decisions without direct human oversight. Some scholars argue for the development of new legal constructs — such as "electronic personhood" for AI (European Parliament, 2017) — while others caution against anthropomorphizing machines.

There is also a risk of moral distancing. As AI takes over decision-making in sensitive sectors like welfare distribution or healthcare, policymakers may hide behind algorithms, avoiding responsibility for unfair outcomes. Hence, accountability in AI must be proactive rather than reactive — involving rigorous testing, transparency, and mechanisms for redress before deployment.

Global Regulation: Between Innovation and Control

AI's reach is global, but its regulation remains fragmented. While the European Union has led the way with the AI Act and GDPR, other countries like China emphasize state control and surveillance, and the U.S. relies more on sector-specific, self-regulatory frameworks. This patchwork of policies creates inconsistencies, particularly for cross-border technologies like cloud AI, generative models, and facial recognition tools.

The need for international coordination is urgent. In 2021, UNESCO released the first global standard on AI ethics, calling for bans on mass surveillance and robust data protection frameworks (UNESCO, 2021). However, without enforcement mechanisms, such declarations risk becoming symbolic.

A more cooperative model might draw from environmental treaties or international health regulations, creating a binding, rights-based approach to AI governance. Involving voices from the Global South, Indigenous communities, and marginalized groups is also essential, to ensure the future of AI reflects the diversity of the global population, not just the priorities of Silicon Valley or Beijing.

Toward a Human-Centered Future

Ultimately, the question is not just how intelligent machines will become, but how wise we will be in governing them. As AI becomes more autonomous, the role of human judgment becomes more important — not less. Lawmakers, ethicists, and technologists must work together to ensure AI aligns with core human values: dignity, justice, and accountability.

Empowering people through AI must go hand in hand with protecting their rights. This involves public education on AI literacy, mechanisms for participatory design, and inclusive policymaking that centers those most at risk of harm. As the philosopher Shannon Vallor (2016) aptly puts it, we need to cultivate new forms of "technomoral virtues" — courage, empathy, humility — to guide our decisions in this rapidly evolving space.

The path forward is not about halting innovation but steering it wisely. A global conversation must continue — one that blends the rigor of science with the compassion of humanity, ensuring that in our pursuit of artificial intelligence, we do not lose sight of the very real human intelligence, and empathy, needed to wield it well.

CONCLUSION

Artificial Intelligence (AI) is the new transformative force across industries, and the legal sector is no exception. While its capabilities promise unparalleled advantages, the social implications of its integration into legal frameworks are profound and multifaceted. A balanced conclusion must address the dualities of efficiency versus equity, innovation versus ethical dilemmas, and access versus accountability (Bostrom, 2014; Calo, 2017).

Enhancing Legal Processes Through AI

AI systems, especially in legal research, predictive analytics, and contract review, have changed the game for the legal profession. They allow processing massive volumes of data at speeds unattainable by a human being, thereby reducing time and costs involved in legal services (Russell & Norvig, 2016). For example, AI-based case law databases or predictive tools give lawyers a remarkably accurate sense of case outcomes. These developments are especially promising in enhancing access to justice, particularly in jurisdictions where demand for legal services far outstrips supply (Calo, 2017).

Equity and Fairness Issues

However, the use of AI in the legal context raises serious issues about fairness and bias. Algorithms, although seemingly neutral, can perpetuate or even exacerbate systemic biases present in the data they are trained on (O'Neil, 2017; Angwin et al., 2016). For instance, predictive policing systems have been accused of targeting already marginalized communities, reflecting the existing prejudices rather than neutral judgment (Ferguson, 2017). Ensuring algorithmic fairness is not only a technical challenge but also deeply social, requiring continuous oversight, diverse training datasets, and equitable policy frameworks (Jobin et al., 2019).

Ethical and Legal Accountability

The integration of AI into legal contexts also raises questions about accountability. Who is responsible when an AI system makes a mistake? This is particularly relevant in applications such as sentencing algorithms or parole decisions, where the consequences can be life-altering (Asaro, 2016; Pagallo, 2013). Without transparent systems and well-defined accountability measures, AI risks undermining trust in the legal system. Ethical frameworks and legal standards need to evolve to delineate responsibility clearly, ensuring that AI remains a tool for enhancing justice, not undermining it (Cath et al., 2018).

Privacy and Data Security

Another key issue is privacy. The involvement of personal data in litigative processes makes it sensitive and vulnerable to risks when related to data breaches or misuse due to AI's intensive use of data. This calls for robust legal standards that ensure privacy protection alongside AI deployment (European Union, 2016; UNESCO, 2021).

A Vision for the Future

The future of AI in legal contexts lies in finding an intricate balance between technological innovation and human values. It needs to be guided by fairness, transparency, and the principle of inclusivity. While AI can be a powerful tool for enhancing justice and efficiency, its potential social ramifications call for vigilant oversight, ethical foresight, and a commitment to equity.

Summarizing it in other words, AI will be double-edged when it comes to the legal realm. This will depend entirely on whether we can exploit its capabilities and proactively address challenges arising from this technology, enabling the application of justice rather than serving as a destroyer of justice at its core.

The integration of AI in all sectors of society is an opportunity and a challenge. The use of AI, which might drive innovation and an improvement in the quality of life, raises grave legal, ethical, and social concerns at the same time. It goes all the way from accountability and liability to the worst fears of bias in algorithms and invasion of privacy-a challenge that calls for a concerted response by governments, industry, and civil society(Cath et al., 2018; UNESCO, 2021).

Such disparate legislative contexts demand new legislative responses that should take into account the uniquely challenging nature of AI for fundamental rights and how some form of regulation might spur innovation and enable the full utility of AI in society. Maintaining this balance-and-in relation would be very important in ensuring that AI serves the greater good without exacerbating inequalities in society or undermining ethical standards.

Policymakers, technologists, and society at large must collaborate as AI develops to advance toward a future where it benefits the common good while safeguarding individual rights and advancing social justice.

Future Research Directions

In the future, there are numerous significant questions that researchers must address. How do we create ethical AI frameworks that operate globally but yet honor the different cultures and values of different communities? What are the new tools that will enable us to catch and correct bias in AI systems before they can do actual harm? We also must learn which types of rules are most effective—whether it is strict government regulation, industry self-regulation, or some combination thereof—and how these methods affect innovation. Another important area is making decisions based on AI more transparent to the general public and the people who must regulate these technologies. It's equally important to study how AI can be made accessible and fair to everyone, especially marginalized groups who might otherwise get left behind. And when AI makes mistakes, who should be held accountable? Finally, raising public awareness and involving people in conversations about AI's role in society will be critical to building trust and ensuring these technologies serve the common good.

REFERENCES

Amanathan, U. (2019). Aadhaar: Surveillance, control, and dispossession. In Jayasankar, K. P. (Eds.), *Digital States of Surveillance* (pp. 36–55). Oxford University Press.

Angwin, J., Larson, J., Mattu, S., & Kirchner, L. (2016). Machine bias: There's software used across the country to predict future criminals. And it's biased against blacks. *ProPublica*. https://www.propublica.org/article/machine-bias-risk-assessments-in-criminal-sentencing

Asaro, P. M. (2016). The liability problem for autonomous artificial agents. In Calo, R., Froomkin, A. M., & Kerr, I. (Eds.), *Robot law* (pp. 303–318). Edward Elgar Publishing.

Bostrom, N. (2014). *Superintelligence: Paths, dangers, strategies*. Oxford University Press.

Calo, R. (2017). Artificial intelligence policy: A primer and roadmap. *U.C. Davis Law Review*, *51*(2), 399–414.

Cath, C., Wachter, S., Mittelstadt, B., Taddeo, M., & Floridi, L. (2018). Artificial intelligence and the 'good society': The US, EU, and UK approach. *Science and Engineering Ethics*, *24*, 505–528. DOI: 10.1007/s11948-017-9901-7 PMID: 28353045

Dastin, J. (2018, October 10). Amazon scrapped 'sexist AI' recruiting tool. *Reuters*. https://www.reuters.com/article/us-amazon-com-jobs-automation-insight-idUSKCN1MK08G

European Commission. (2021). Proposal for a regulation laying down harmonised rules on artificial intelligence (Artificial Intelligence Act). https://eur-lex.europa.eu/legal-content/EN/TXT/?uri=CELEX:52021PC0206

European Union. (2016). Regulation (EU) 2016/679 of the European Parliament and of the Council (General Data Protection Regulation). https://eur-lex.europa.eu/eli/reg/2016/679/oj

Ferguson, A. G. (2017). *The rise of big data policing: Surveillance, race, and the future of law enforcement*. New York University Press. DOI: 10.18574/nyu/9781479854608.001.0001

Financial Conduct Authority. (2023). Regulatory sandbox. https://www.fca.org.uk/firms/innovation/regulatory-sandbox

Jobin, A., Ienca, M., & Vayena, E. (2019). The global landscape of AI ethics guidelines. *Nature Machine Intelligence*, *1*(9), 389–399. DOI: 10.1038/s42256-019-0088-2

Mulgan, T. (2016). Superintelligence: Paths, dangers, strategies.

New York City Council. (2021). Int. No. 1894-A: A local law to amend the administrative code of the city of New York, in relation to automated employment decision tools. https://www.nyc.gov/assets/dca/downloads/pdf/about/Local-Law-144-Automated-Employment-Decision-Tools.pdf

O'Neil, C. (2017). *Weapons of math destruction: How big data increases inequality and threatens democracy*. Crown Publishing Group.

Pagallo, U. (2013). *The laws of robots: Crimes, contracts, and torts* (Vol. 10). Springer Science & Business Media., DOI: 10.1007/978-94-007-6564-1

Russell, S. J., & Norvig, P. (2016). *Artificial intelligence: A modern approach* (3rd ed.). Pearson Education.

UNESCO. (2021). Recommendation on the ethics of artificial intelligence. https://unesdoc.unesco.org/ark:/48223/pf0000381137

Vallor, S. (2016). *Technology and the virtues: A philosophical guide to a future worth wanting*. Oxford University Press. DOI: 10.1093/acprof:oso/9780190498511.001.0001

Wachter, S., Mittelstadt, B., & Floridi, L. (2017). Why a right to explanation of automated decision-making does not exist in the general data protection regulation. *International Data Privacy Law*, *7*(2), 76–99. DOI: 10.1093/idpl/ipx005

Zuboff, S. (2019). *The age of surveillance capitalism: The fight for a human future at the new frontier of power*. PublicAffairs.

Chapter 2
AI Legislationship: Navigating Unclear Commitments in AI Governance

Lambrini Seremeti
https://orcid.org/0000-0002-0663-5408
University of Western Macedonia, Greece

ABSTRACT

In the rapidly evolving landscape of artificial intelligence (AI), governance, legislation, and regulation have become crucial yet increasingly ambiguous. This chapter introduces the concept of "AI legislationship," a term coined to describe the current state of AI governance, where the boundaries between regulation and innovation are blurred. Governance, legislation, and regulation—each essential for societal function—are studied here both independently and in relation to one another, focusing on how these abstract concepts are reshaped in response to AI. We explore the challenges of regulatory lag, compliance costs, resistance to change, and enforcement issues, highlighting the transitional phase where AI technologies are advancing more rapidly than legal frameworks can accommodate. This chapter argues that addressing these issues requires a multi-faceted approach combining legal, ethical, and collaborative efforts to ensure AI development is both innovative and responsible.

INTRODUCTION

The question of who will regulate AI is increasingly pressing as AI systems continue to permeate various aspects of daily life, from healthcare and finance to transportation and entertainment. The complexity, ubiquity, and potential impact of AI technologies in society require a robust regulatory framework to ensure they

DOI: 10.4018/979-8-3693-9576-9.ch002

are developed and used responsibly. However, determining who should regulate AI involves navigating a landscape of diverse stakeholders, including governments, international organizations, private companies, civil society, and academia each playing a unique role, having different responsibilities, and facing specific challenges (Lu et al., 2024), (Huang et al., 2024). Their involvement in AI regulation raises questions about authority, expertise, and the balance between innovation and oversight.

More precisely, national governments, which are the most immediate and traditional stakeholders in regulation processes, are expected to play the central role in AI regulation. They have the authority to enact laws and regulations that can directly govern the development, deployment and use of AI within their jurisdictions. This authority is crucial for addressing issues such as data privacy, consumer protection, and national security (Paul, 2024). International organizations are also likely to play a critical role in AI regulation. Given the global nature of AI, they aim at developing harmonized standards and promoting cooperation among nations. In this vein, they are working on establishing principles for AI governance, emphasizing values such as transparency, accountability, and fairness (Shen, 2024). Private companies, particularly tech companies that develop and deploy AI technologies, will also play a significant role in AI regulation. They usually establish their own AI ethics guidelines and standards in order to ensure compliance with national AI regulations (Tallberg et al., 2024). Moreover, civil society organizations and academic institutions advocate for ethical AI by acting as watchdogs, holding governments and companies accountable for their actions. They struggle to raise awareness about the potential harms of AI, particularly in relation to privacy, discrimination, and surveillance. In this perspective, academia contributes to AI governance by conducting research on the ethical, legal, and societal implications of AI and by developing frameworks to ensure that AI technologies are aligned with human values. The involvement of civil society and academia in AI regulation is essential for ensuring that AI regulations are not solely shaped by industry and government interests, but also consider the broader public good (Dubljevic, 2024).

Given the differing priorities and interests of the stakeholders involved in AI regulation, as well as the complex and global nature of AI, no single stakeholder can effectively regulate AI on its own. Instead, the multi-stakeholder model of AI governance, which involves collaboration between governments, international organizations, private companies, civil society, and academia, has been proposed as the most effective approach. Such model leverages the strengths of each stakeholder while mitigating their respective weaknesses (Sharma, 2024), (Braga et al., 2024). This actors' collaboration involves the dynamic interplay among all stakeholders, each having their own perspectives, interests, and expertise. This interplay involves policy formulation, implementation, and adaptation processes. For instance, in the policy context, when crafting AI regulations, governments might consult with academic experts to understand potential impacts and risks. Private companies may provide feedback on how regulations could affect their operations, while civil society organizations might advocate for specific provisions to safeguard public interests. During the implementation phase, once regulations are in place, governments work with companies to ensure compliance. International organizations may facilitate cross-border cooperation, while academia might continue to research and advise on the effectiveness and impact of these regulations. In the adaptation context, civil society plays the crucial role in monitoring the effects of AI regulations and advocating for necessary changes. Governments and private companies need to adapt to emerging challenges and advancements in AI, with academia providing ongoing research to guide these adjustments.

The goal of this chapter is not to suggest a new multi-stakeholder approach for AI regulation. Instead, it aims to emphasize the necessity for further discussion of existing approaches by highlighting the blurred boundaries between the different AI legislations, by introducing the notion of “AI legislationship”.

CONCEPTUALIZATION OF GOVERNANCE, LEGISLATION, AND REGULATION

Governance, legislation, and regulation are fundamental concepts in managing complex systems, including emerging technologies such as AI. Understanding these terms and their interrelationships is crucial for analyzing how societies control and guide technological advances and their impacts. These terms are general abstract concepts that acquire a different meaning depending on the time horizon in which they are redefined, as they carry a different semantic load in the current unstable reality and another in a sharply and clearly delimited ideal setting. The meaning of these terms is studied both independently and in reference to other concepts, namely in depth (intension) and in breadth (extension). The extension of a concept refers to its range or coverage, while the intention of a concept refers to its underlying purpose or objective (da Silva, 2020). In other words, the depth distinguishes one concept from others, while breadth distinguishes types of the concept. Thus, depth denotes the meaning of the concept and makes it clear, and breadth the reference of the concept and makes it precise. Clarity and precision together constitute the overall understanding of the concept.

Governance, legislation, and regulation are distinct but interrelated concepts that form a cohesive system that ensures societies function smoothly and equitably. A crucial component of an effective society function, is governance. **Governance** refers to the processes, structures adaptable to changing circumstances, and institutions through which collective decisions are made, implemented, and enforced.

It encompasses a wide range of activities and mechanisms that coordinate actions and responsibilities among diverse stakeholders, including governments, private sector entities, civil society, and international organizations, in managing resources, resolving conflicts, and promoting the overall well-being. Effective governance ensures that the rules and procedures within a society or organization align with its goals, values, and ethical standards (Fukuyama, 2016). **Legislation**, on the other hand, refers to the process of creating laws and regulations by a legislative body or authority. It is a formal enactment that sets rules and guidelines for behavior, rights, and obligations within a society or organization. It is typically drafted, debated, and passed by legislators and then enforced by the executive branch of the government. It provides a legal framework for governance and serves as a means to achieve public policy objectives. It is crucial because it formalizes societal norms and values into concrete, enforceable rules (Verschuuren, 2009). Another crucial component for the effective functioning of any society is regulation. **Regulation** is the implementation and enforcement of laws created by legislation. It involves the development of detailed rules and guidelines that specify how the laws will be applied in practical situations. Regulatory bodies, such as government agencies or independent commissions, are responsible for ensuring compliance with these rules. It is essential for maintaining order, protecting public welfare, and promoting fairness in various sectors (Hinterleitner et al., 2023).

In a nutshell, governance, legislation, and regulation are intertwined concepts. Indeed, governance sets the stage by establishing the values and processes for decision-making. Legislation translates these values into concrete laws that govern behavior and activities, and regulation ensures these laws are implemented and followed, protecting public interests and promoting societal well-being. Together, they create a robust framework that enables societies to address challenges, adapt to changes, and achieve their collective goals. The relationship among governance, legislation, and regulation is dynamic. Governance provides the overarching framework and principles that guide the creation of legislation and the implementation of regulation. Good governance ensures that the legislative process is transparent, inclusive, and accountable, leading to laws that are well-informed and reflective of societal needs. Once legislation is in place, effective governance also oversees the regulatory bodies to ensure they enforce the laws fairly and efficiently. In turn, regulations feedback into the governance system by highlighting areas where laws may need to be updated or revised based on practical experience and changing circumstances.

AI LEGISLATIONSHIP: HOW TO COPE WHEN COMMITMENT IS UNCLEAR

In the rapidly evolving landscape of society transformation due to emerging technologies, such as AI, integration in various aspects of daily life, from healthcare to transportation, the depth and breadth of governance, legislation, and regulation has altered, as well as their interplay. AI governance refers to the set of policies, principles, and guidelines that dictate how AI systems should be developed, deployed, and managed. At its core, effective AI governance aims to balance innovation with legal stability, ensuring that AI technologies are developed responsibly and ethically. It encompasses the values and norms established by society, industry stakeholders, and governmental bodies to ensure that AI advancements align with public interest and ethical standards. Key components of AI governance include transparency, accountability, and fairness, which help to foster public trust and prevent misuse or harm. Despite the semantic alignment of AI governance with the purpose and scope of the general notion of governance, legislation and regulation implicitly endorse a more nuanced approach to their meanings, due to their extensions. Indeed, the legislative and regulatory landscape remains fragmented and varies significantly across countries and regions. Divergent national interests, technological complexity, ethical disparities, economic competition are some of the factors that contribute to the differentiation of terms as reference to distinct instantiations of legislation and regulation in their broad sense.

Focusing on AI legislation, regulatory lag, compliance costs, resistance to change, and enforcement challenges entail a new condition, named here "AI legislationship". The concept introduced here is coined to encapsulate the current state of AI governance, where the boundaries between regulation and innovation are blurred. This term, a fusion of "legislation" and "relationship," reflects the precarious moment in time where AI development is proceeding rapidly, but comprehensive legal frameworks are not yet fully established. It highlights the transitional phase between the unregulated expansion of AI and the eventual implementation of robust, reliable, and safe AI regulations. The concept underscores the necessity of safeguarding against potential harm while acknowledging the existing ambiguities and undefined relationships within the AI governance framework. It draws attention to the critical juncture where we attempt to develop and trust advanced AI systems, despite uncertain consequences and unclear accountability, illustrating the pressing need for clearer legislative boundaries and stronger connections between current regulatory guidelines.

In a nutshell, "AI legislationship" denotes the condition where commitments in AI legislation are unclear. These unclear commitments manifest in various ways.

- Commitments among different stakeholders: There is often ambiguity regarding who holds responsibility when AI systems cause harm or malfunction (Scherer, 2016). For example, it's unclear whether liability falls on the developers, the users, or the companies deploying the AI. Additionally, there is often a lack of clarity about who is responsible for ensuring AI systems comply with ethical standards, privacy laws, and security measures.
- Commitments between divergent guidelines: Different countries and organizations often have varying guidelines and standards for AI development and deployment (Galindo, 2021), (Zaidan and Ibrahim, 2024). This divergence creates confusion about which set of guidelines should take precedence, especially in international or cross-jurisdictional contexts. It also leads to inconsistencies in how AI is regulated, creating gaps and overlaps in the legal framework.
- Commitments among several AI technologies: The rapid development of diverse AI technologies, each with unique characteristics and risks, complicates the regulatory landscape. Current legislation may not be sufficiently adaptive to address the specific challenges posed by different types of AI, such as machine learning models, autonomous systems, or AI-driven decision-making tools (Hildebrandt, 2016), (Crawford and Joler, 2018). This leads to uncertainties in how existing laws apply to new and evolving AI technologies, creating a fragmented regulatory environment.

In that sense, addressing unclear commitments in AI legislation demands a multi-faceted approach that combines legal acumen, ethical discernment, proactive engagement, and transparent collaboration.

CONCLUSION

In the evolving era of AI, the notion of AI legislationship corresponds semantically to the fluid and often unclear boundaries that define the current relationship between AI technologies, governance structures, and legislative frameworks. It stems from the tensions between regulatory demands, innovation imperatives, and a multistakeholder landscape where governments, corporations, civil society, academia, and international bodies all play critical yet differentiated roles.

Addressing AI legislationship involves acknowledging the ambiguities and gaps that arise from rapid technological evolution and fragmented regulatory responses across regions and sectors. These gaps include the ambiguity surrounding liability and accountability, inconsistencies in cross-jurisdictional guidelines, and the regulatory lag that leaves certain types of AI largely unaddressed within existing frameworks.

The notion of AI legislationship, therefore, emphasizes the urgent need for clearer legislative boundaries, enhanced accountability, and stronger relationships between the diverse regulatory guidelines that currently coexist but lack cohesion.

REFERENCES

Braga, J., Stiubieuer, I., Henriques, P., & Cananea, H. (2024). How multistakeholder governance can shape responsible AI. *OSFPreprints*. https://doi.org//DOI: 10.31219/osf.io/kdw52

Crawford, K., & Joler, V. (2018). Anatomy of an AI System: The Amazon Echo as an Anatomical Map of Human Labor, Data, and Planetary Resources. *Open Journal of Social Sciences*, *12*(2).

da Silva, L. (2020). Concepts in Policy and Governance: A Framework for Analysis. *Public Administration Journal*, *28*(1), 77–88.

Dubljevic, V. (2024). Colleges and universities are important stakeholders for regulating large language models and other emerging AI. *Technology in Society*, *76*, 102480. DOI: 10.1016/j.techsoc.2024.102480

Fukuyama, F. (2016). Governance: What do we know, and how do we know it? *Annual Review of Political Science*, *19*(1), 89–105. DOI: 10.1146/annurev-polisci-042214-044240

Galindo, L., Perset, K., & Sheeka, F. (2021). *An overview of national AI strategies and policies. OECD Going Digital Toolkit Notes, 14*. OECD Publishing., DOI: 10.1787/c05140d9-

Hildebrandt, M. (2016). *Smart Technologies and the End(s) of Law: Novel Entanglements of Law and Technology*. Edward Elgar Publishing.

Hinterleitner, M., Knill, C., & Steinebach, Y. (2023). The growth of policies, rules, and regulations: A review of the literature and research agenda. *Regulation & Governance*, *18*(2), 637–654. DOI: 10.1111/rego.12511

Huang, K., Joshi, A., Dun, S., & Hamilton, N. (2024). AI regulations. In Huang, K., Wang, Y., Goertzel, B., Li, Y., Wright, S., & Ponnapalli, J. (Eds.), *Generative AI Security. Future of Business and Finance* (pp. 61–98). Springer., DOI: 10.1007/978-3-031-54252-7_3

Lu, O., Zhu, L., Xu, X., Whittle, J., Zowghi, D., & Jacquet, A. (2024). Responsible AI pattern catalogue: A collection of best practices for AI governance and engineering. *ACM Computing Surveys*, *56*(7), 1–35. DOI: 10.1145/3626234

Paul, R. (2024). The politics of regulating AI technologies: Towards AI competition states. In: Paul, R., Carmel, E. & Cobbe, J. (eds) *Handbook on Public Policy and Artificial Intelligence*, 261-279. https://doi.org/DOI: 10.4337/9781803922171.00028

Scherer, M. U. (2016). Regulating Artificial Intelligence Systems: Risks, Challenges, Competencies, and Strategies. *Harvard Journal of Law & Technology*, *29*(2), 353–400.

Sharma, S. (2024). Benefits or concerns of AI: A multistakeholder responsibility. *Futures*, *157*, 103328. DOI: 10.1016/j.futures.2024.103328

Shen, A. (2024). AI ethics and governance at international standards. *International IT Journal of Research*, *2*(1), 8–14.

Tallberg, J., Lundgren, M., & Geith, J. (2024). AI regulation in the European Union: Examining non-state actor preferences. *Business and Politics*, *26*(2), 218–239. DOI: 10.1017/bap.2023.36

Verschuuren, J. (2009). *The Impact of Legislation. A Critical Analysis of Ex Ante Evaluation*. ISSN. DOI: 10.1163/ej.9789004170209.i-280

Zaidan, E., & Ibrahim, I. A. (2024). AI governance in a complex and rapidly changing regulatory landscape: A global perspective. *Humanities & Social Sciences Communications*, *11*(1), 1121. DOI: 10.1057/s41599-024-03560-x

Chapter 3
Artificial Intelligence and the Evolving Landscape of Legal Accountability: Ethical, Legal, and Regulatory Issues

Sheikh Inam Ul Mansoor
https://orcid.org/0000-0001-8636-4769
Dayananda Sagar University, India

Hina Kausar
https://orcid.org/0000-0002-7009-153X
University of Petroleum and Energy Studies, India

Mohammed Salim Baitullah Khan
https://orcid.org/0000-0003-1506-2450
Presidency University, Bangalore, India

Govind Yadav
https://orcid.org/0009-0005-5757-5619
Manipal University Jaipur, India

ABSTRACT

The newly emerging phenomenon of artificial intelligence (AI) has undoubtedly paved way for signifying change in the field of legal practice; however, not without the prospects and issues. This chapter provides a theoretical analysis of the subject of AI in contemporary legal frameworks with special emphasis on the impact of AI across legal education, legal profession, and judicial processes. Because AI technologies are used to expedite the legal processes and improve productiveness,

DOI: 10.4018/979-8-3693-9576-9.ch003

and given their role in making decisions, there is a great potential for its influence on the legal profession. However, these advancements also bring several questions of who is to be held liable, how these tools will be bias, the ethical issues that they present and who will regulate these technologies? They establish the potential of what has been done and what is to be done with regard to legal practice focusing on AI in contracts, case law and the pending problem of over-legalization of justice with the help of AI telecommunications in judicial systems.

INTRODUCTION

Artificial intelligence (AI) seems to be one of the vital and revolutionary technologies of the twenty-first century and has entered many spheres of human activity including legal sphere (Rawas, 2024). The combination of AI in a legal system has triggered positive changes, making changes to conventional ways and providing a basis for current systems. This revolution emanates from AI capability of completing responsibilities assigned to legal practitioners as well as judges (Bex, 2024). Legal expert systems nowadays encompass entering the legal data base, contract analysis, case prognosis, and decision-making by using the progressive technologies such as machine learning, natural language processing, and other kinds of immediate analytics (Madaoui, 2024). Technological advancement provides new ethical, legal, and regulatory questions and issues for societies, which bring questions regarding the primary concepts on which are based the legal systems of the world (Kendal, 2022). The implications of AI relate to legal practice in two ways; the first is the accuracy of the work produced and the second is the speed at which said work is produced (Quteishat et al., 2024). During preparation for court, AI technologies can quickly analyze large amounts of information that will help lawyers identify the key facts necessary for the preparation of references. Further, insights in relation to the prediction of legal benchmarks offers specific perspective on how certain cases are most likely to be decided, with reference to similar past cases (Kaur & Kaur, 2024). In judicial systems, AI is used in sentencing, case management, and docket control, for instance, it is claimed that through reducing the elements of subjectivity in the decision-making process, AI will enhance justice delivery efficiency by reducing error (Taylor, 2023). However, the assurance of the legal systems with the help of AI raises essential ethical and legal issues that are still under protection by the current legislation (Mansoor & Wani, 2025). One of the most profound concerns relates to global legal governance as a primary matter of assigning liability conceived by the growing practice of Artificial Intelligence assuming positions usually manned by people (Henz, 2021). Establishing negligence turns into an issue, with AI's creators, buyers, including legal professionals or jurors, and even the AI system itself. Contemporary legal systems are not well prepared to address these quandaries given that the modern legal doctrines of liability are based on the principle of action and agency (Buiten et al., 2023). AI systems on the other hand are made up of algorithms and data inputs; determining who is negligent where AI outputs are incorrect or causing harm to someone is therefore problematic. This problem is especially relevant in areas regarding Human rights such as sentencing or parole where algorithmic biases inherited from the training set amplified existing unfairness in the justice system (Stahl, 2023). The nature of these challenges means that further work requires reflection on the ethical and legal anomalies of AI.

Bias is one of the greatest ethical concerns that are linked with the use of artificial intelligence (AI) in legal services. Almost all AI systems are based on a branch of artificial intelligence called Machine Learning that uses data for training its algorithms (Dwivedi, 2024). Unfortunately, this data is loaded with such prejudices that are inherent in a particular society, and so when it is incorporated in judicial systems, prejudice follows suit (Ntoutsi et al., 2020). For example, the AI applied in the criminal justice system for the purpose of sentencing or risk prediction might reinforce the system's racism and socio-economic bias if the data sets with which the algorithm was trained biased itself by marginally correlating with racism statistics (Bharati, 2024). These and other outcomes suggest that justice may be a farce, as even the best legal decisions can be handicapped by algorithms that are a product of existing unfairness. Sophisticated professions such as the legal profession has an ethical duty to make sure that AI tools used in the practice of law do not carry the ethically prohibited legal bias (Gordon, 2021). As a result, the specialists in the spheres of IT and the law should stay open for minimizing the prejudices that may be used by AI while at the same time, they should also pay attempts to demystifying the systems of algorithms as well (Zafar, 2024). Transparency is a critical aspect especially in the legal processes while on the other hand, adoption of AI entailed in legal practice presents some main ethical issues of concern mainly privacy and data protection because of handling personal information (Ejjami, 2024). In legal practice, management of client and case information requires compliance with international data protection legislation including but not limited to the General Data Protection Regulation (GDPR) of the EU (Mondschein & Monda, 2019). Purpose limitation faces ambiguity with the increased demand for data from AI systems and the resultant invasion of privacy. This tension creates a considerable problem for authorities regulating AI in legal frameworks (Mühlhoff & Ruschemeier, 2024). AI development also requires teamwork within the common law arena across the world because each country may have its own approach to matters to do with regulation (Zaidan & Ibrahim, 2024). EU's proposed AI Act has higher legislation standards compared to the US's legislation's lose control since the EU act provides the producers and operators of AI systems to self-assess the risk that their systems pose. The problem of attaining global regulatory standardization is a difficult one, showing why cooperation is important in order to realize fairness, justice, and thus human rights in different parts of the world (Thelisson & Verma, 2024).

Objectives

This chapter examines the ethical, legal and socio-legal implications of employing artificial intelligence in the legal workplace. This chapter analyses the vulnerabilities facing AI in accountability, fairness and privacy when addressing the issues of regulation. The chapter also provides legal advice for legal professionals and recommends duties that belong to artificial intelligence creators.

Legal Accountability in AI-Driven Legal Systems

AI when introduced into legal systems raises numerous problems associated with legal liability. When intelligent systems step into shoes of traditional real-life performers like lawyer, analyst, contractor, and, to some extents, judges, the question of who is responsible arises (Awoyomi, 2024). Liability in relation to use of AI in legal systems refers to the question of who is or ought to be held liable in circumstances where such systems are defective or deploy or unleash negative consequences (McDonald, 2023). This issue is quite essential because, unlike human agents who act with certain intents, judgments, and responsibility as recognized by the legal system. As a result, the question appears as to how and where one apportions accountability and legal culpability for actions or choices performed by an AI in a given line of work (Santoni de Sio & Mecacci, 2021). Among the challenges it is possible to identify the problem of legal responsibility: should it lie with the developers who create the applying AI systems, with the users who apply the AI systems, for example, lawyers or judges, or with the AI systems themselves? (Sayyed, 2024). Generally, under conventional systems of law, accountability is based on the idea of vicarious responsibility. Civil wrongs including negligence, malpractice or a breach of duty acts upon a person or organization that has negligently or willingly caused harm (McGrath & Whitty, 2018). In AI-driven systems though, this framework is not tenable because the AI systems make decisions on their own through algorithms and data they have received hence making it difficult to find out who should be held responsible if something goes wrong (Stahl, 2023).

One possible way to solve this problem is by prosecuting the designers and creators of AI for the state and behaviour of the product built. It could therefore be said that while developers are programmers who are responsible for designing and implementing a system which must meet certain ethical and legal characteristics such as transparency and the absence of prejudice (Li, 2024). Thus AI is likely to be the fault of those who developed or trained or deployed it when that harm indicts from defects in the system or potentialities ignored during creation, similar to product hazards law (Henz, 2021). AI systems differ from classical programs as machine learning AI systems can be seen as dynamic systems and not as fixed products, constantly retrained on new data. This characteristic adds other layers of problems regarding how liability is established since developers may not fully understand how their systems function after they are released into the field (Sarirete et al., 2022). On the other hand, the burden could be shifted to the consumers of the AI technology, this includes lawyers, judges or firms which have embraced use of artificial intelligence in their operations. In this model, the burden of ensuring that AI works appropriately and legally will lie solely on the individuals or organisation using AI and employing it as a tool (Shao et al., 2024). For example, if a lawyer seeks legal advice or forms a contract through an AI tool which gives wrong or standard output then the lawyer becomes responsible for negligence in using the tool. This approach puts an importance on the human supervisory role and also supports the notion that AI systems have to be seen as tools in the legal process helping as decision aids to legal decision-makers (Kauffman & Soares, 2020). However, opposing arguments to this approach emphasise that overloading users with responsibility could slow technological development because companies active in the legal sector could be reluctant to use AI applications due to potential legal risks they entail (Henz, 2021). Another scenario is emergence of new specific legal principles relating to accountability and legal responsibility of the AI themselves. This would involve a reconsideration of existing legal principles because of such features of AI as the AI systems' ability to learn independently from the provided data and operate autonomously (Sayyed, 2024). There have been calls from the legal experts to grant the artificial intelligent systems a new legal personality so that they can be brought to book in a manner we do to companies (Chesterman, 2020). Although this approach is the topic of significant debate and criticism raises philosophical questions associated with the nature of personhood and responsibility, including the accountability of artificial intelligence, it is evidence of the assumption that the legal regulation of artificial intelligence systems is insufficient.

By looking at some of the AI failures that have occurred in the field of legal practice, one will understand the impact that previous research about accountability had in today's world. Among the more common causes related to AI failures in legal domains, the most famous is the story of the predicting of the criminal recidivism in the United States (Farayola et al., 2023). Risk assessment for offenders, or offenders awaiting sentencing or parole, has been conducted using AI applications as the COMPAS algorithm. These tools are intended to estimate the possibility of a reconviction of a defendant and their suggestions are occasionally incorporated into the sentencing procedure (Fazel et al., 2022). But research has found that the

COMPAS algorithm has racial bias where black defendants are assigned higher scores than the White defendants with similar criminal backgrounds (Engel et al., 2024). Stakes involve concerns about fairness in decision-making, as we have got to know in the COMPAS case, where complex algorithms merely enhance bias, in this way resulting to severe measures and maybe even unjust parole decisions (Lagioia et al., 2023). In 2018, an AI-based legal research platform was reported to offer incorrect case citations and legal analysis on multiple occasions. Attorneys using the platform were misled, presenting inaccurate legal arguments in court. This incident highlighted the risks of relying on AI-driven tools, raising concerns about their dependability and the need for cross-checking their output (Choi & Schwarcz, 2023). It is important in legal systems to predict its future developments to know how to introduce AI with adequate legal constraints and responsibilities. There is thus hope for tort accountability of AI that is part of the tort system developed over time. The innocent parties have rights to file a negligence or product liability cases (Kauffman & Soares, 2020). For example if an AI is defective it will cause the developers to be sued while if a lawyer is improperly employs AI they will be accused of professional negligence for arriving at wrong decisions that were derived from an AI analysis (Buiten, 2024).

However, tort law is not the only area of law that could be of use, in cases concerning the attribution of responsibility to AI. Fundamentals like data protection and privacy laws like the General Data Protection Regulation (GDPR) in the European Union direct strict requirements to organizations using and managing personal data, within which AI systems are included (Hacker et al., 2020). These laws mandate protection of individuals' data, and provide a means by which people may complain about AI decisions; people impacted in sentencing or a trial by inaccurate AI can appeal (Power, Heavin, & O'Connor, 2021).

Another area in which legal regulation that might help fill the accountability gap is the adoption of the framework regulating AI systems' supervision. Lawmakers and other institution responsible for oversight could set some standard and requirement that must be met with regards to AI for law practice, including requirement regarding disclosure, interpretability and bias (Zaidan & Ibrahim, 2024). These regulations might demand that developers of the AI systems should periodically check on their systems to be sure they are not repeating a bias that was present at the time of their development and that their output is not negative in any way (Zaidan & Ibrahim, 2024). Furthermore, regulatory authorities can create platforms through which individuals can claim that an AI system has failed in its operation, or seek a remedy after suffering loss due to an AI system. Such regulatory frameworks would strengthen the discretionary procedure and would make certain that typical AI is applied soundly under legal systems.

ETHICAL DILEMMAS AND AI BIAS

A core problem of AI implementation to complement the legal systems is mainly the issue of bias in the AI models, which is highly sensitive to the process of delivering justice. These concerns are worsened by the fact that most AI systems are turned to for their given capacity to make efficient decisions based on big data, yet have the propensity to reinforce, or exacerbate existing societal biases (Shah & Sureja, 2024). Algorithmic bias involved in legal decision making poses a great ethical questioning as it deals with the justice system. In addition, questions of ethical accountability shared between developers of AI and societal outcomes as well as AI's effect on the vulnerable groups bring other concerns that require careful legal and moral analysis (Belenguer, 2022). This brings algorithmic bias which is a major issue when AI is used in legal reasoning. Bias is induced when machine learning algorithms are trained on some undesirable data, these prior data are then reflected in the decision making process (Collenette et al., 2023). This can be said more pointedly where bias could undermine the fairness, as it is in law. AI in policing, assessing risks for criminals' release, and determining sentences draws data from unfair sources, hence the discriminated, unfair results (Zafar, 2024). Algorithmic bias is best demonstrated in the use of AI in recidivism prediction. People's opponents argue that certain gadgets provide minority tags with a high-risk rating, which is irrelevant to criminal background and financial standing (Wani & Mansoor, 2025). This practice calls to question issues of equity and may only worsen racism and social injustice within the American Criminal Justice systems (Kordzadeh & Ghasemaghaei, 2021). Accordingly, the use of AI for legal decision support distorts the fairness and equality norms enshrined in the legal systems and makes it possible to regulate legal processes not only with the help of data but with bias within this data (Zafar, 2024). Further, algorithmic bias tends to produce a type of 'technological determinism' because issues that should require professional human discretion are instead left to neural nets which themselves may be opaque and unanswerable to the law (Kordzadeh & Ghasemaghaei, 2021). The majority of AI systems are executed as 'applications' as are, in many instances, the AI algorithms themselves, which means users may not necessarily be fully aware of how the algorithms themselves operate (Saranya & Subhashini, 2023). The lack of transparency is profound especially in the legal profession where an individual has a discretion right, to challenge and question decisions made. The problem assumes its worst when legal consequences stem from AI systems whose decisions cannot be traced, questioned, or corrected, giving rise to unjust outcomes as affected subjects do not have an opportunity to dispute prejudicial or erroneous decisions or outcomes (Balasubramaniam et al., 2023).

Other purely criminal justice-related concerns supplement a catalogue of potentially nefarious or prejudicial ways in which the ethical application and implementation of AI and its capabilities can pose crucial questions about the accountability of individuals and organisations within the legal industry (Hagendorff, 2020). Incorporating fairness, transparency, and accountability into the creation of new algorithms remains an enormous duty of the developers who design artificial intelligence systems to be used in legal settings. This duty is as applicable in the development context design, test, and implement as it is out in the world, where developers must consciously prevent bias and discrimination (Singhal et al., 2024). Ethical development means that developers must pay heed not only to the mathematical correctness of an algorithm but also to its consequences in the world of society (Tsamados et al., 2022). Another of the more critical problems in ethical AI is a lack of a diverse dataset for machine learning (Baird & Schuller, 2020). This chapter underscores the point that AI systems learn from their training data, so developers need to provide diverse unbiased data so that they are not encoding bias in the model if there has been bias in the data set (Liang et al., 2022). System engineers have to continuously review the performance of the system searching for new biases in legal contexts, which require independent audit logs. More than just the clients, legal profession, and different stakeholders should address consequence, limitation, and bias of AI (Arora et al., 2023). It reforms to maintain ethical standards in practice, where the service provider needs to competently do a service without hurting the client. As a function of AI integration, legal practitioners need to follow specific ethical standards and analyze AI results (Mohamed et al., 2024).

As much as the new advancement in AI in the application of legal systems is an advance innovation, it holds some several effects on the minorities. AI technologies, especially, involved in the legal decision-making, can be expected that these technologies will have a negative impact on richer and more represented minorities, such as minorities by race and ethnicity, by low income and other vulnerable groups (Ejjami, 2024). These communities are usually involved in the legal process in a way that these are the victims as well as the perpetrators of crime hence common in arrest, prosecution and imprisonment. If the AI systems employed in the legal industry were in any way, bigotry or unjust then these sectorial communities are liable to suffer the consequences of aggravated systemic injustice (Atrey, 2023). For instance, those predictive policing tools have been accused of impacting ethnic minorities due to the technology's racial bias (Lee et al., 2024). These systems focus on the crime data of the past to model where future crimes might happen but such datasets have instances where policing was targeted at people of colour (Joseph, 2024). Consequently, predictive policing algorithms may lead existing resources of the law enforcement into these communities, therefore increasing criminalization of such places. This not only creates questions of ethic regarding the fairness of AI system, but also it signals that such technology might indeed aggravate social & racial disparity (Hung & Yen, 2023).

In the context of civil law, the patterns that the AI systems utilize in scoring credit, employment and housing, also impede social justice to marginalised communities. For example, if an AI system that predicts credit worthiness was trained on records that contained discriminative features, those people in marginalized groups could likely be locked out of financial products such as credit (Bruyne, Gool, & Gils, 2021). Likewise, the AI systems applied to hiring also possess biases for or against some demographic groups, thus, creating hiring discriminative outcomes that negatively affect people of colour, women or of low economic status. Therefore, the effects of application of AI are not confined to the legal decisions affecting the groups of people at the receiving end, but also to equality of access to justice (Chien et al., 2024). AI technologies have the possible of enhancing availability on legal services by making them cheaper and fast. Although these systems remain critical and can be a powerful tool of innovation, if not well developed and deployed they can end up deepening the justice gap (Kauffman & Soares, 2020). For example, those poor or black families may not gain much from AI services if such technologies are available only for the rich or overrepresented groups. This, of course, raises questions of ethical usage of AI technology to advance, not reduce, equality of access to justice or legal aid.

PRIVACY AND DATA PROTECTION IN AI APPLICATIONS

The use of artificial intelligence (AI) in legal systems leads to the growth of numerous issue and concerns, for example, privacy and data protection. Since AI is central to the need of large amounts of data to operate, their adoption in legal sectors brings crucial questions to privacy rights, data management, and the right legal measures to protect personal information (Gordon, 2021). The most sharply debated issues in regard with this regard are the surveillance using AI leading to invasive practices on people, especially in the context of law enforcement, counter terrorism and intelligence and similar governmental applications (Power et al., 2021). Moreover, due to the exponential adoption of AI technologies, there remains strong and urgent needs for avant-garde data protection laws that trade the advantages of AI with the fundamental rights of people. Finally, the legal tools like General Data

Protection Regulation (GDPR) accompanying the AI have peculiar features corresponding to such fields, for example, the 'right to be forgotten' (Lynskey, 2023).

AI monitoring in legal contexts is still a relatively nascent concern and yet, as applying AI is getting more frequent in law-enforcement practices, governments, and private actors to monitor people. Different AI surveillance technologies like facial recognition systems, predictive police work, data mining techniques, are all capable of accumulating vast amounts of information on the individuals, their activities, their movements, and most of their social interactions (Choung et al., 2024). These technologies though useful for increasing efficiency in police work and the protection of the public also have severe implications to constitutional rights of individual citizens. When the deployment of such technology is applied haphazard or without suing relevant laws in the country or adequately addressing their implications on the Rule of Law, such technologies are capable of negating discrete rights of individual citizens to be left alone in their private affairs (Liu et al., 2020).

Regarding AI surveillance technologies, two issues can be put forward in legal contexts: on the one hand, states' function for policing up security threats, on the other hand, people's rights to privacy. For instance, predictive policing which involves the use of crime data to predict criminal incidences encourages increased policing of some neighbourhoods, and ultimately increases criminal targeting of vulnerable or non-mainstream communities (Fontes et al., 2022). The delegation of such algorithms in legal systems deepens the chances of continuous surveillance of individuals according to how close they are to previous criminality or inclusion in a dataset that may well be flawed (Stahl, 2023). This not only creates suspicion as to how or if race and social profiling is regulated, but also sparks critical or rather sceptical concerns with legal sovereignty and rationality of AI supported legal decisions that may originate from erroneous or racially and/or socially preconditioned data feeds (Shin et al., 2022). Further, facial recognition, another type of AI surveillance, is more frequent in open and legal scenarios, without people's awareness or permission. With this technology, people can be followed and tracked in various places hence a profile gallery of their movements and actions (Choung et al., 2024). Using facial recognition as an instrument for improving security can be considered as positive we need to address ethical and legal issues connected with this technology especially overlook of minorities (Kostka et al., 2021). Erroneous decisions made by these algorithms create circumstances where innocent people wind up getting arrested; cases with biased legal decisions; and more importantly such AI systems infringe on citizens' civil liberties (Belenguer, 2022). In order to avoid adverse consequences of AI surveillance technologies, the role is especially prescribed to legal scholars and policymakers for overhauling data governance regimes regulating the collection, processing, and, use of personal data for protection of individual privacy and liberty (Shahriar et al., 2023). Specific challenges that are associated with AI data management include questions of ownership, control, and understanding and explaining of the AI data. These are the basic principles which are championed as follows Informed consent that implies that users must understand how their data will be used and accessed (Devineni, 2024). In order for legal scrutiny to be possible, human subject must be given understandable information about the AI system which processes their data and they must be allowed to consent or not consent to having their data processed. In those scenarios where use consent is inapplicable, we must employ legal restraints that act to limit the AI surveillance technologies application in circumstances like public safety and national security (Perez-Des Rosiers, 2021).

Besides, data minimization is another principle that governs the use of artificial intelligence driven systems (Goldsteen et al., 2022). This principle requires that, once designed, the AI systems should not collate data beyond the objectives that they were designed to serve while performing their tasks. The compulsive collection of individual data does not only lead to more probability of privacy violation incidents, but also the data can be misused by a third party such as police, corporations, or hackers (Biega et al., 2020). Legal regulation has to set severe minimization of the data requirements for the AI systems, thus preventing unauthorized capturing / processing of the individuals data beyond the given legitimate purpose of functioning of the system (Goldsteen et al., 2022). There are also other requirements for data legal controls: security As AI systems are highly vulnerable to hacking and data breaches. Firms should thus be made to meet the security standards set, state and publish breaches that occur, and explain the legal repercussions of failing to protect data (Devineni, 2024). Among the most important changes in the legal framework of data protection, one should distinguish the so-called right to be forgotten from the GDPR. This right according to Article 17 of the GDPR gives the individuals the right to erase the personal data concerning them where the processing is non-compliant with this regulation (Fosch-Villaronga et al., 2017). The specific post social right most germane to AI applications is the right to be forgotten as it grants the individuals the means of how their data is used while ensuring that data that is no longer relevant is not utilized when making decisions (Atata, 2024).

The right to be forgotten is most relevant in legal cases where decision making by the autonomous AI system relies on certain historical data related to an individual's legal status, credit worthiness or suitability for services (Zhang et al., 2024). In such cases, lack of freshness of data act as a bottleneck where bias creep in, for instance, old employment records used in the hiring of AI. This may render some people jobless even after they held necessary qualifications earlier while other qualified candidates get employed, this the right to be forgotten comes in handy (Subramaniyan et al., 2021). There are some issues for the right to be forgotten in AI systems. Some records are removed permanently from the database and yet they can be used by the machine learning algorithms in the creation of a model, training data holds a lot of power. Legal changes must thus govern these technical processes to address users' susceptibilities while maintaining Al system capacity (Zhang et al., 2024). Another problem with the right to be forgotten is the inconsistency between the right to privacy and the right of access to public interest information. At times the destruction of personal data may be inadmissible given certain legal or societal concerns for example where the law or the society may have valid recognisable legal and societal interests for the need for transparency, accountability, or archival value (Radi & Noninska, 2020). For example, it is obvious that erasing information about convictions for previous criminal offenses can complicate police work or limit citizens right to receive information on a person's criminal past. The right of privacy has to be balanced against other competing rights and freedoms; it would be reckless to permit eradication of records that the public needs for information (Banisar, 2011).

GLOBAL REGULATORY RESPONSES AND GOVERNANCE

AI technologies are still progress very fast, so countries and international organizations have to adapt legal, ethical, and societal factors into its legislation (Zaidan & Ibrahim, 2024). The problem is to find how to encourage adoption of AI solutions and at the same time respond to the dangers connected with it. Data-science technology's application to core domains like healthcare, financing, and legal systems requires appropriate laws governing human rights and adherence to the application's utilization (Grossi et al., 2021). In this regard, the United States encourage the self-regulatory approach to AI, whereas the European Union is interested in creating the federal rules of safe artificial intelligence (Pack, 2022). While the U.S. is still lagging behind in legislation, China sets very high legal goals for AI regulation, and India is somewhere in the middle balancing the strategies of both superpowers. Such approaches have generated debates on the need to develop a harmonized international perspective on AI application (Walter, 2024). AI is gradually involved in life critical fields with higher demand for clear and enforceable standards that protect human rights, eliminate unfairness, and supervise AI advancement (Rayhan, 2023). One country to another, with different objectives and legislation in place, tries to regulate AI. The EU adopts an active, legal strategy largely based on GDPR and data protection acts and tenets emphasizing human rights and ethics (Mondschein & Monda, 2019). The GDPR is a robust starting point for AI regulation mainly because of its strict standards on how data should be collected, processed, and how consent is given, along with responding to vital issues like privacy, protection of data and the right to be forgotten (Hijmans & Raab, 2022). There are laws for AI operation in the EU for member nations to adhere to own progressive regulation and guideline on AI, with milestone risk categories for systems and obligatory checklist for high risk systems to follow in terms of safety and norms (Gilbert, 2024).

China, has taken a coordinated state system-oriented approach to AI governance due to its aspiration to lead the global AI development by 2030 (Cheng & Zeng, 2022). China has infused a number of top-down policies to steer AI advancement through a number of policies directing the advancement towards the preference of artificial intelligence systems for facial recognition, autonomous vehicles, and surveillance systems (Roberts et al., 2021). China's institutional environment for AI is set in its political context, legal system where centralization, security, and stability are given paramount importance. The Chinese government has coordinated the application of AI technologies in social governance: social credit system and surveillance systems (Sheehan, 2023). Although China has been actively progressing in creating sophisticated AI technologies, the country has been also heavily criticized for the way it approaches the regulation of AI systems. However, China also came up with standards for AI ethical use that bear with its priorities, which include fairness, transparency in spitting data, and non-discrimination in their AI applications (Roberts et al., 2022). India, which is now considered one of the growing AI nations, focuses more on the responsible approach to the advancement of AI regulation. The Indian government has recently acknowledged that AI has abundant opportunity to fuel growth and reformation the country's economy and few areas include healthcare and education, agriculture and more (Bhalla et al., 2023). However, India has not enacted a holistic regulation concerning AI and its attitude primarily consists of the formulation of national strategies and policies. While the Government of India is more directly involved in the establishment of specific policies and programs related to AI, a number of duties has been given to the NITI Aayog, which can be considered as one of the major AI policies of the country (Joshi, 2024). India's approach to the regulation of AI is tied with its get Data protection framework with reference to Personal Data Protection Bill which seeks to govern the collection, processing and usage of personal data. In its current form, the bill still contains few elements of value for the AI regulation, including data minimization, consent, and accountability (Biju & Gayathri, 2024). Currently, there is not a developed concept of AI governance in India, and there is a discussion regarding the necessity to establish a unique framework for regulation of technologies utilizing AI that would take into consideration the necessity of innovations when managing the individual rights of all citizens (Marda, 2018). AI technologies engender regulatory issues particularly on what structure of governance is most appropriate given technological advancements' risks and potentials. The Artificial Intelligence Act by the EU divides its regulatory structure based on risk while soft law approaches use recommendations and best practices to fill gaps that exist in the law (de Almeida et al., 2021). As many voiced and AI regulation become more complex, there is a rising demand for multi-actor governance models of government, industrial, academic and civil society actors. Fosters ethically acceptable policies and involve; they are beneficial for marginalised groups of people in ways that have been concerned with (Zaidan & Ibrahim, 2024).

The use of AI technologies has reached a global level and this has resulted to the debate of common rules in different countries. This need arises because of the opportunity for artificial intelligence to have extra-territorial effects in areas such as data transfer, privacy and cybersecurity, all of which demand harmonious regulation (Vinuesa et al., 2020). While there are several approaches to the cooperation in AI development, including such structures as United Nations, OECD and ISO, the concern in legal frame, ethical issue and social impacts are considered. Globally coherent AI regulation is necessary to avoid a situation when every country develops its rules, which would be rather puzzling, but it needs to protect human rights too (ÓhÉigeartaigh et al., 2020). It is difficult to reach a consensus with regards to AI standardization because of legal, cultural and political peculiarities. While boasting human rights protection, the EU; stressing on the technological advancement the U.S; and Power and control over the citizens and foreign nations as a strong point of China (Cha, 2024). At the same time, it is possible to use such values as transparency, accountability, and non-discrimination as the principles in the sphere of AI regulation that could be equally applicable by all world states.

CONCLUSION

Though, going by the theoretical discussion, this chapter could be regarded as a reference material for the legal professionals, the legislative bodies and the technophobe – particularly in dealing with AI as a part of the legal profession and; more sensitively, in operating AI in the court's legal domain. It recognises the necessity of training for lawyers and especially judges when it comes to matters arising from the impact of AI on legal practice. Moreover, the chapter focuses on a topic to be legal and ethical responsibility in the accountability of AI developers area and mentions that legal, technical, and ethical experts should strengthen their cooperation to establish effective legislation that apply artificial intelligence technology. It must therefore be stated that the potential benefits of AI, many of which are still untapped since the actualization of artificial intelligent possibilities for law is still relatively new – are numerous and can indeed enrich present legal practice and enhance present day legal systems. The use of AI cannot be debated any longer especially with regard to the legal and IT students, The opportunities associated with AI must be embraced but should not be used to subvert the principles as provided for in the different legal systems of the world. In the final section, more trends are identified and suggestions for near futures in terms of socio-technical application of AI in the legal sector and structured methods for the integration of AI solutions in accord with legal and ethical frameworks are discussed. As will be demonstrated when considering the legal issues on artificial intelligence, it is possible to realise the full potential of using the AI as well as ensure that adequate control and protection is achieved for individuals and their rights according to the law. However, it should not be considered that there are no employing challenges when using AI for legal education. There is an urgent need to direct attention to the question of AI ethics as part of the university curriculum so that future legal personnel do not become endearing to these systems. These are including the aspect of informing the students when it is good, the drawbacks of their use, and issues of bias in algorithms, data protection and even impact of AI in perpetuating other vices in society. AI has the capacity to revolutionize administration of law by utilizing its potential to take up modifiable activities namely the analysis of contract, legal research legal writing and drafting. For example, smart contracts enable AI to process agreements in far less time than it would take many lawyers to do so. What's more, predictive analysis tools help in commanding case outcomes with lots of data that make it easier for lawyers to make their decisions. However, AI cannot perform judgment and ethical benchmarks, which are the core principles of the legal profession to add up to the technology's value by being a supplement. However, there is growing controversy as to the legal redaction of AI in practice within the legal realm of practice. In certain places such as New South Wales when AI is applied on sentencing and bails, there emerge issues regarding AI application on significant legal results. Even though AI can deliver substantial information to judges there is a probable danger that such dependency may undermine their impartiality and can result in non-biased appellate determinations mimicking algorithms. As a result, it is crucial to have judicial supervision as the resolution of cases shows that the data bias exist among citizens, and accordingly, affecting the decision making of the AI systems. However, it is important that such judges and legal practitioners keep checking on such limitations especially when the recommendation is in violation of some legal and ethical frameworks.

For a successful regulation of AI in legal frameworks, the public authorities require formulating appropriate legal processes and organizational guidelines in case of malicious use of AI technology. The use of AI in justice system should reflect newly advancing values like right to a fair trial; principles like natural justice, procedural justice, substantial justice, justice, equality and due process of law, etc. The latter can only be achieved by careful regulation as it is impossible to let AI decision making processes remain beyond further scrutiny and control when those decision affect citizens' rights and freedoms. A number of policy recommendations are required for attaining the responsible deployment of AI within legal contexts.

First, it is necessary to distinguish responsible for AI system development and its consequences in the framework of legal activities. Lawyers, legislators, and AI creators need to work together to reason over significant issues of responsibility, privacy, and principles connected with AI in law-related applications. But, it is essential to also meter to AI education and certification legal professionals such as judges, lawyers, and legal educators in knowledge concerning the existence and applications of AI. *Second*, building the effective AI system demands the effort of scientists, legal advisors, and ethicists for creating the systematically fair AI systems. Current developments in this collaboration should focus on the development of AI algorithms that come with ethical features that prevent bias within the data used. Policy makers should also support related activities towards the ethical development of AI in justice systems, for instance, though setting for ethical committees or boards. *Third*, the world today needs international coordination in the harmonization of the laws on AI across legal systems in different countries. Since AI is a universal reality, international cooperation is required to set up the foundations for AI regulation. International organizations such as the United Nation and the European Union should also participate in negotiations of the AI regulations so that all the set standards should uphold to the universal human rights.

There are pros and cons in introducing the AI technologies in legal systems. By eliminating cases that cannot be resolved in their presence AI will increase the fairness and effectiveness of legal delivery systems since courts will handle cases that require their input leaving the simpler ones to other entities. Besides, AI can successfully challenge an injustice gap because many people cannot obtain proper representation. As example is where the chat bots can relieve essential information on the preliminary lawful advice that enhances clarification. However this integration of AI into legal systems poses valid issues on algorithmic fairness. Bias in data inputs may extend injustice by replicating the social realities of bias in areas such as criminal justice. If the benefits of AI are to be realised, these challenges become important to deal with in order to avoid having this advancement working for the detriment of fairness.

REFERENCES

Arora, A., Barrett, M., Lee, E., Oborn, E., & Prince, K. (2023). Risk and the future of AI: Algorithmic bias, data colonialism, and marginalization. *Information and Organization*, *33*(3), 100478. DOI: 10.1016/j.infoandorg.2023.100478

Atata, B. (2024). Artificial intelligence and the right to be forgotten. *International Journal of Research Publication and Reviews*, *5*(8), 4300–4310. DOI: 10.55248/gengpi.5.0824.2310

Atrey, I. (2023). Revolutionising the legal industry: The intersection of artificial intelligence and law. Available at *SSRN*: https://ssrn.com/abstract=4632440 or http://dx.doi.org/DOI: 10.2139/ssrn.4632440

Awoyomi, T. (2024). *Legal issues associated with artificial intelligence (AI). SSRN.* https://doi.org/DOI: 10.2139/ssrn.4750140

Baird, A., & Schuller, B. (2020). Considerations for a more ethical approach to data in AI: On data representation and infrastructure. *Frontiers in Big Data*, *3*, 25. DOI: 10.3389/fdata.2020.00025 PMID: 33693398

Balasubramaniam, N., Kauppinen, M., Rannisto, A., Hiekkanen, K., & Kujala, S. (2023). Transparency and explainability of AI systems: From ethical guidelines to requirements. *Information and Software Technology*, *159*, 107197. DOI: 10.1016/j.infsof.2023.107197

Banisar, D. (2011). The right to information and privacy: Balancing rights and managing conflicts. *World Bank Institute Governance Working Paper*. Available at *SSRN*: https://ssrn.com/abstract=1786473 or http://dx.doi.org/DOI: 10.2139/ssrn.1786473

Belenguer, L. (2022). AI bias: Exploring discriminatory algorithmic decision-making models and the application of possible machine-centric solutions adapted from the pharmaceutical industry. *AI and Ethics*, *2*(4), 771–787. DOI: 10.1007/s43681-022-00138-8 PMID: 35194591

Bex, F. J. (2024). AI, law and beyond: A transdisciplinary ecosystem for the future of AI & law. *Artificial Intelligence and Law*. Advance online publication. DOI: 10.1007/s10506-024-09404-y

Bhalla, N., Brooks, L., & Leach, T. (2023). Ensuring a 'responsible' AI future in India: RRI as an approach for identifying the ethical challenges from an Indian perspective. *AI and Ethics*. Advance online publication. DOI: 10.1007/s43681-023-00370-w

Bharati, R. K. (2024). Ethical implications of AI in criminal justice: Balancing efficiency and due process. *RESEARCH REVIEW International Journal of Multidisciplinary, 9*(7), 93–105. DOI: 10.31305/rrijm.2024.v09.n07.014

Biega, A. J., Potash, P., Daumé, H., Diaz, F., & Finck, M. (2020). Operationalizing the legal principle of data minimization for personalization. In *Proceedings of the 43rd International ACM SIGIR Conference on Research and Development in Information Retrieval (SIGIR '20)* (pp. 399–408). Association for Computing Machinery. https://doi.org/DOI: 10.1145/3397271.3401034

Biju, P. R., & Gayathri, O. (2024). The Indian approach to Artificial Intelligence: An analysis of policy discussions, constitutional values, and regulation. *AI & Society, 39*(5), 2321–2335. DOI: 10.1007/s00146-023-01685-2

Bruyne, J. D., Gool, E. V., & Gils, T. (2021). Tort law and damage caused by AI systems. In De Bruyne, J., & Vanleenhove, C. (Eds.), *Artificial intelligence and the law* (pp. 359–404). Centrum voor Verbintenissen-en Goederenrecht. Intersentia. DOI: 10.1017/9781839701047.015

Buiten, M., de Streel, A., & Peitz, M. (2023). The law and economics of AI liability. *Computer Law & Security Review, 48*, 105794. DOI: 10.1016/j.clsr.2023.105794

Buiten, M. C. (2024). Product liability for defective AI. *European Journal of Law and Economics, 57*(1-2), 239–273. DOI: 10.1007/s10657-024-09794-z

Cha, S. (2024). Towards an international regulatory framework for AI safety: Lessons from the IAEA's nuclear safety regulations. *Humanities & Social Sciences Communications, 11*(1), 506. DOI: 10.1057/s41599-024-03017-1

Cheng, J., & Zeng, J. (2022). Shaping AI's future? China in global AI governance. *Journal of Contemporary China, 32*(143), 794–810. DOI: 10.1080/10670564.2022.2107391

Chesterman, S. (2020). Artificial intelligence and the limits of legal personality. *The International and Comparative Law Quarterly, 69*(4), 819–844. DOI: 10.1017/S0020589320000366

Chien, C. V., Kim, M., Raj, A., & Rathish, R. (2024). How generative AI can help address the access to justice gap through the courts. *Loyola of Los Angeles Law Review*, Forthcoming. Available at *SSRN*: https://ssrn.com/abstract=4683309

Choi, J. H., & Schwarcz, D. (2023). AI assistance in legal analysis: An empirical study. *Journal of Legal Education, 73*(forthcoming, 2024). Available at *SSRN*: https://ssrn.com/abstract=4539836

Choung, H., David, P., & Ling, T.-W. (2024). Acceptance of AI-powered facial recognition technology in surveillance scenarios: Role of trust, security, and privacy perceptions. *Technology in Society*, *79*, 102721. DOI: 10.1016/j.techsoc.2024.102721

Collenette, J., Atkinson, K., & Bench-Capon, T. (2023). Explainable AI tools for legal reasoning about cases: A study on the European Court of Human Rights. *Artificial Intelligence*, *317*, 103861. DOI: 10.1016/j.artint.2023.103861

de Almeida, P. G. R., dos Santos, C. D., & Farias, J. S. (2021). Artificial intelligence regulation: A framework for governance. *Ethics and Information Technology*, *23*(4), 505–525. DOI: 10.1007/s10676-021-09593-z

Devineni, S. K. (2024). AI in data privacy and security. *International Journal of Artificial Intelligence and Machine Learning*, *3*, 35–49.

Dwivedi, D. (2024). Algorithmic bias: A challenge for ethical artificial intelligence (AI). In Heggde, G. S., Patra, S. K., & Panda, R. (Eds.), *Immersive technology and experiences* (pp. 57–75). Palgrave Macmillan., DOI: 10.1007/978-981-99-8834-1_5

Ejjami, R. (2024). AI-driven justice: Evaluating the impact of artificial intelligence on legal systems. *International Journal of Finance and Management Research*, *6*(3), 23969. Advance online publication. DOI: 10.36948/ijfmr.2024.v06i03.23969

Engel, C., Linhardt, L., & Schubert, M. (2024). Code is law: How COMPAS affects the way the judiciary handles the risk of recidivism. *Artificial Intelligence and Law*. Advance online publication. DOI: 10.1007/s10506-024-09389-8

Farayola, M. M., Tal, I., Connolly, R., Saber, T., & Bendechache, M. (2023). Ethics and trustworthiness of AI for predicting the risk of recidivism: A systematic literature review. *Information (Basel)*, *14*(8), 426. DOI: 10.3390/info14080426

Fazel, S., Burghart, M., Fanshawe, T., Gil, S. D., Monahan, J., & Yu, R. (2022). The predictive performance of criminal risk assessment tools used at sentencing: Systematic review of validation studies. *Journal of Criminal Justice*, *81*, 101902. DOI: 10.1016/j.jcrimjus.2022.101902 PMID: 36530210

Fontes, C., Hohma, E., Corrigan, C. C., & Lütge, C. (2022). AI-powered public surveillance systems: Why we (might) need them and how we want them. *Technology in Society*, *71*, 102137. DOI: 10.1016/j.techsoc.2022.102137

Fosch-Villaronga, E., Kieseberg, P., & Li, T. (2017). Humans forget, machines remember: Artificial intelligence and the right to be forgotten. *Computer Security & Law Review (Forthcoming)*. Available at *SSRN*: https://ssrn.com/abstract=3018186

Gilbert, S. (2024). The EU passes the AI Act and its implications for digital medicine are unclear. *npj. Digital Medicine*, *7*(1), 135. DOI: 10.1038/s41746-024-01116-6 PMID: 38778162

Goldsteen, A., Ezov, G., Shmelkin, R., Moffie, M., & Farkash, A. (2022). Data minimization for GDPR compliance in machine learning models. *AI and Ethics*, *2*(2), 477–491. DOI: 10.1007/s43681-021-00095-8

Gordon, J. S. (2021). AI and law: Ethical, legal, and socio-political implications. *AI & Society*, *36*(2), 403–404. DOI: 10.1007/s00146-021-01194-0

Grossi, V., Giannotti, F., Pedreschi, D., Manghi, P., Pagano, P., & Assante, M. (2021). Data science: A game changer for science and innovation. *International Journal of Data Science and Analytics*, *11*(2), 263–278. DOI: 10.1007/s41060-020-00240-2

Hacker, P., Krestel, R., Grundmann, S., & Naumann, F. (2020). Explainable AI under contract and tort law: Legal incentives and technical challenges. *Artificial Intelligence and Law*, *28*(4), 415–439. DOI: 10.1007/s10506-020-09260-6

Hagendorff, T. (2020). The ethics of AI ethics: An evaluation of guidelines. *Minds and Machines*, *30*(1), 99–120. DOI: 10.1007/s11023-020-09517-8

Henz, P. (2021). Ethical and legal responsibility for artificial intelligence. *Discover Artificial Intelligence*, *1*(2), 2. Advance online publication. DOI: 10.1007/s44163-021-00002-4

Hijmans, H., & Raab, C. (2022). Ethical dimensions of the GDPR, AI regulation, and beyond. *Direito Público*, *18*(100). Advance online publication. DOI: 10.11117/rdp.v18i100.6197

Hung, T. W., & Yen, C. P. (2023). Predictive policing and algorithmic fairness. *Synthese*, *201*(6), 206. DOI: 10.1007/s11229-023-04189-0

Joseph, J. (2024). Predicting crime or perpetuating bias? The AI dilemma. *AI & Society*. Advance online publication. DOI: 10.1007/s00146-024-02032-9

Joshi, D. (2024). AI governance in India – law, policy and political economy. *Communication Research and Practice*, *10*(3), 328–339. DOI: 10.1080/22041451.2024.2346428

Kabir, M. S., & Alam, M. N. (2023). The role of AI technology for legal research and decision making. *International Journal of Advanced Research*, *10*(1), 2395–0056.

Kauffman, M. E., & Soares, M. N. (2020). AI in legal services: New trends in AI-enabled legal services. *Service Oriented Computing and Applications*, *14*(4), 223–226. DOI: 10.1007/s11761-020-00305-x

Kaur, N., & Kaur, M. (2024). Role of artificial intelligence in the Indian courts. *International Journal of Law, Policy and Social Review, 6*(1), 17-20. https://www.lawjournals.net/assets/archives/2024/vol6issue1/5124.pdf

Kendal, E. (2022). Ethical, legal and social implications of emerging technology (ELSIET) symposium. *Journal of Bioethical Inquiry, 19*(3), 363–370. DOI: 10.1007/s11673-022-10197-5 PMID: 35749026

Kordzadeh, N., & Ghasemaghaei, M. (2021). Algorithmic bias: Review, synthesis, and future research directions. *European Journal of Information Systems, 31*(3), 388–409. DOI: 10.1080/0960085X.2021.1927212

Kostka, G., Steinacker, L., & Meckel, M. (2021). Between security and convenience: Facial recognition technology in the eyes of citizens in China, Germany, the United Kingdom, and the United States. *Public Understanding of Science (Bristol, England), 30*(6), 671–690. DOI: 10.1177/09636625211001555 PMID: 33769157

Lagioia, F., Rovatti, R., & Sartor, G. (2023). Algorithmic fairness through group parities? The case of COMPAS-SAPMOC. *AI & Society, 38*(2), 459–478. DOI: 10.1007/s00146-022-01441-y

Lee, Y., Bradford, B., & Posch, K. (2024). The effectiveness of big data-driven predictive policing: Systematic review. *Justice Evaluation Journal.* https://doi.org/ DOI: 10.1080/24751979.2024.2371781

Li, W. (2024). A study on factors influencing designers' behavioral intention in using AI-generated content for assisted design: Perceived anxiety, perceived risk, and UTAUT. *International Journal of Human-Computer Interaction*, •••, 1–14. DOI: 10.1080/10447318.2024.2310354

Liang, W., Tadesse, G. A., Ho, D., Fei-Fei, L., Zaharia, M., Zhang, C., & Zou, J. (2022). Advances, challenges and opportunities in creating data for trustworthy AI. *Nature Machine Intelligence, 4*(8), 669–677. DOI: 10.1038/s42256-022-00516-1

Liu, H. Y., Maas, M., Danaher, J., Scarcella, L., Lexer, M., & Van Rompaey, L. (2020). Artificial intelligence and legal disruption: A new model for analysis. *Law, Innovation and Technology, 12*(2), 205–258. DOI: 10.1080/17579961.2020.1815402

Lynskey, O. (2023). Complete and effective data protection. *Current Legal Problems, 76*(1), 297–344. DOI: 10.1093/clp/cuad009

Madaoui, N. (2024). The impact of artificial intelligence on legal systems: Challenges and opportunities. *Problems of Legality, 1*(164), 285–303. DOI: 10.21564/2414-990X.164.289266

Mansoor, S. I., & Wani, S. A. (2025). Harnessing ethical AI: Measures of redressing hate speech in the social media context. In Chakraborty, S. (Ed.), *Ethical AI solutions for addressing social media influence and hate speech* (pp. 37–62). IGI Global Scientific Publishing., DOI: 10.4018/979-8-3693-9904-0.ch003

Marda, V. (2018). Artificial intelligence policy in India: A framework for engaging the limits of data-driven decision-making. *Philosophical Transactions. Series A, Mathematical, Physical, and Engineering Sciences, 376*(2133), 20180087. DOI: 10.1098/rsta.2018.0087 PMID: 30323001

McDonald, L. (2023). AI systems and liability: An assessment of the applicability of strict liability & a case for limited legal personhood for AI. *The St Andrews Law Journal, 3*(1), 5–21. Advance online publication. DOI: 10.15664/stalj.v3i1.2645

McGrath, S. K., & Whitty, S. J. (2018). Accountability and responsibility defined. *International Journal of Managing Projects in Business, 11*(3), 687–707. DOI: 10.1108/IJMPB-06-2017-0058

Mohamed, E., Quteishat, A., Qtaishat, A., & Mohammad, A. (2024). Exploring the role of AI in modern legal practice: Opportunities, challenges, and ethical implications. *Journal of Electrical Systems.*

Mondschein, C. F., & Monda, C. (2019). The EU's General Data Protection Regulation (GDPR) in a research context. In Kubben, P., Dumontier, M., & Dekker, A. (Eds.), *Fundamentals of clinical data science* (pp. 65–82). Springer., DOI: 10.1007/978-3-319-99713-1_5

Mühlhoff, R., & Ruschemeier, H. (2024). Updating purpose limitation for AI: A normative approach from law and philosophy. *SSRN.* https://doi.org/DOI: 10.2139/ssrn.4711621

Ntoutsi, E., Fafalios, P., Gadiraju, U., Iosifidis, V., Nejdl, W., Vidal, M.-E., Ruggieri, S., Turini, F., Papadopoulos, S., Krasanakis, E., Kompatsiaris, I., Kinder-Kurlanda, K., Wagner, C., Karimi, F., Fernandez, M., Alani, H., Berendt, B., Kruegel, T., Heinze, C., & Staab, S. (2020). Bias in data-driven artificial intelligence systems—An introductory survey. *Wiley Interdisciplinary Reviews. Data Mining and Knowledge Discovery, 10*(3), e1356. DOI: 10.1002/widm.1356

ÓhÉigeartaigh, S. S., Whittlestone, J., Liu, Y., Zeng, Y., & Liu, Z.ÓhÉigeartaigh. (2020). Overcoming barriers to cross-cultural cooperation in AI ethics and governance. *Philosophy & Technology, 33*(4), 571–593. DOI: 10.1007/s13347-020-00402-x

Pack, H. (2022). Regulation of artificial intelligence in the United States. In M. A. Grau Ruiz (Ed.), *Interactive robotics: Legal, ethical, social and economic aspects* (Vol. 30, pp. 367–380). Biosystems & Biorobotics. Springer. https://doi.org/DOI: 10.1007/978-3-031-04305-5_38

Perez-Des Rosiers, D. (2021). AI application in surveillance for public safety: Adverse risks for contemporary societies. In Keskin, T., & Kiggins, R. D. (Eds.), *Towards an international political economy of artificial intelligence* (pp. 95–114). Palgrave Macmillan., DOI: 10.1007/978-3-030-74420-5_6

Power, D. J., Heavin, C., & O'Connor, Y. (2021). Balancing privacy rights and surveillance analytics: A decision process guide. *Journal of Business Analytics*, *4*(2), 155–170. DOI: 10.1080/2573234X.2021.1920856

Quteishat, E. M. A., Qtaishat, A., & Quteishat, A. M. A. (2024). Exploring the role of AI in modern legal practice: Opportunities, challenges, and ethical implications. *Journal of Educational Studies*, *20*(6s), 3040–3050. Advance online publication. DOI: 10.52783/jes.3320

Radi, P. R., & Noninska, I. S. (2020). Challenges of the digital age for privacy and personal data protection. *Mathematical Biosciences and Engineering*, *17*(5), 5288–5303. DOI: 10.3934/mbe.2020286 PMID: 33120553

Rawas, S. (2024). AI: The future of humanity. *Discover Artificial Intelligence*, *4*(1), 25. DOI: 10.1007/s44163-024-00118-3

Rayhan, S. (2023). *AI superintelligence and human existence: A comprehensive analysis of ethical, societal, and security implications*. https://doi.org/DOI: 10.13140/RG.2.2.12922.26561

Roberts, H., Cowls, J., Hine, E., Morley, J., Wang, V., Taddeo, M., & Floridi, L. (2022). Governing artificial intelligence in China and the European Union: Comparing aims and promoting ethical outcomes. *The Information Society*, *39*(2), 79–97. DOI: 10.1080/01972243.2022.2124565

Roberts, H., Cowls, J., Morley, J., Taddeo, M., Wang, V., & Floridi, L. (2021). The Chinese approach to artificial intelligence: An analysis of policy, ethics, and regulation. *AI & Society*, *36*(1), 59–77. DOI: 10.1007/s00146-020-00992-2

Santoni de Sio, F., & Mecacci, G. (2021). Four responsibility gaps with artificial intelligence: Why they matter and how to address them. *Philosophy & Technology*, *34*(4), 1057–1084. DOI: 10.1007/s13347-021-00450-x

Saranya, A., & Subhashini, R. (2023). A systematic review of explainable artificial intelligence models and applications: Recent developments and future trends. *Decision Analytics Journal, 7*, 100230. DOI: 10.1016/j.dajour.2023.100230

Sarirete, A., Balfagih, Z., Brahimi, T., Lytras, M. D., & Visvizi, A. (2022). Artificial intelligence and machine learning research: Towards digital transformation at a global scale. *Journal of Ambient Intelligence and Humanized Computing, 13*(7), 3319–3321. DOI: 10.1007/s12652-021-03168-y

Sayyed, H. (2024). Artificial intelligence and criminal liability in India: Exploring legal implications and challenges. *Cogent Social Sciences, 10*(1), 2343195. Advance online publication. DOI: 10.1080/23311886.2024.2343195

Shah, M., & Sureja, N. (2024). A comprehensive review of bias in deep learning models: Methods, impacts, and future directions. *Archives of Computational Methods in Engineering*. Advance online publication. DOI: 10.1007/s11831-024-10134-2

Shahriar, S., Allana, S., Hazratifard, S. M., & Dara, R. (2023). A survey of privacy risks and mitigation strategies in the artificial intelligence life cycle. *IEEE Access : Practical Innovations, Open Solutions, 11*, 61829–61854. DOI: 10.1109/ACCESS.2023.3287195

Shao, C., Nah, S., Makady, H., & McNealy, J. (2024). Understanding user attitudes towards AI-enabled technologies: An integrated model of self-efficacy, TAM, and AI ethics. *International Journal of Human-Computer Interaction*, •••, 1–13. DOI: 10.1080/10447318.2024.2331858

Sheehan, M. (2023). China's AI regulations and how they get made. *Horizons: Journal of International Relations and Sustainable Development*, 24, 108–125. https://www.jstor.org/stable/48761167

Shin, D., Hameleers, M., Park, Y. J., Kim, J. N., Trielli, D., Diakopoulos, N., Helberger, N., Lewis, S. C., Westlund, O., & Baumann, S. (2022). Countering algorithmic bias and disinformation and effectively harnessing the power of AI in media. *Journalism & Mass Communication Quarterly, 99*(4), 887–907. DOI: 10.1177/10776990221129245

Singhal, A., Neveditsin, N., Tanveer, H., & Mago, V. (2024). Toward fairness, accountability, transparency, and ethics in AI for social media and health care: Scoping review. *JMIR Medical Informatics, 12*, e50048. DOI: 10.2196/50048 PMID: 38568737

Stahl, B. C. (2023). Embedding responsibility in intelligent systems: From AI ethics to responsible AI ecosystems. *Scientific Reports, 13*(1), 7586. DOI: 10.1038/s41598-023-34622-w PMID: 37202436

Subramaniyan, M., Skoogh, A., Bokrantz, J., Sheikh, M. A., Thürer, M., & Chang, Q. (2021). Artificial intelligence for throughput bottleneck analysis – State-of-the-art and future directions. *Journal of Manufacturing Systems, 60*, 734–751. DOI: 10.1016/j.jmsy.2021.07.021

Taylor, I. (2023). Justice by algorithm: The limits of AI in criminal sentencing. *Criminal Justice Ethics, 42*(3), 193–213. DOI: 10.1080/0731129X.2023.2275967

Thelisson, E., & Verma, H. (2024). Conformity assessment under the EU AI Act general approach. *AI and Ethics, 4*(1), 113–121. DOI: 10.1007/s43681-023-00402-5

Tsamados, A., Aggarwal, N., Cowls, J., Morley, J., Roberts, H., Taddeo, M., & Floridi, L. (2022). The ethics of algorithms: Key problems and solutions. *AI & Society, 37*(1), 215–230. DOI: 10.1007/s00146-021-01154-8

Vinuesa, R., Azizpour, H., Leite, I., Balaam, M., Dignum, V., Domisch, S., Felländer, A., Langhans, S. D., Tegmark, M., & Fuso Nerini, F. (2020). The role of artificial intelligence in achieving the Sustainable Development Goals. *Nature Communications, 11*(1), 233. DOI: 10.1038/s41467-019-14108-y PMID: 31932590

Walter, Y. (2024). Managing the race to the moon: Global policy and governance in artificial intelligence regulation—A contemporary overview and an analysis of socioeconomic consequences. *Discover Artificial Intelligence, 4*(14), 14. Advance online publication. DOI: 10.1007/s44163-024-00109-4

Wani, S. A., & Mansoor, S. I. (2025). Criminal justice system in the age of artificial intelligence: Exploring rights, risks, and responsibilities in the digital era. In Kaunert, C., Raghav, A., Ravesangar, K., Singh, B., & Riswandi, B. (Eds.), *Artificial intelligence in peace, justice, and strong institutions* (pp. 67–92). IGI Global Scientific Publishing., DOI: 10.4018/979-8-3693-9395-6.ch004

Zafar, A. (2024). Balancing the scale: Navigating ethical and practical challenges of artificial intelligence (AI) integration in legal practices. *Discover Artificial Intelligence, 4*(1), 27. DOI: 10.1007/s44163-024-00121-8

Zaidan, E., & Ibrahim, I. A. (2024). AI governance in a complex and rapidly changing regulatory landscape: A global perspective. *Humanities & Social Sciences Communications, 11*(1), 1121. DOI: 10.1057/s41599-024-03560-x

Zhang, D., Finckenberg-Broman, P., & Hoang, T.. (2024). Right to be forgotten in the era of large language models: Implications, challenges, and solutions. *AI and Ethics*. Advance online publication. DOI: 10.1007/s43681-024-00573-9

Chapter 4
Artificial Intelligence in Legal Judgment:
Addressing Income Tax Fraud Through Automated Decision-Making

Meenakshi Sharma
NIET Business School, India

Mukul Bhatnagar
https://orcid.org/0000-0002-7773-5641
Graphic Era University, India

ABSTRACT

This chapter explores the transformative role of Artificial Intelligence (AI) in the context of income tax judgments, particularly focusing on its potential to enhance efficiency, accuracy, and fairness within the Indian tax system. As India grapples with complex tax laws and increasing volumes of data, AI offers a promising solution to streamline tax assessments, fraud detection, and decision-making processes. The chapter examines key AI initiatives in India, such as AI-driven tools for case management and predictive analytics, while also addressing the ethical, legal, and operational challenges that come with integrating AI into tax administration. By leveraging global examples and real-world case studies, this chapter highlights how AI can reduce human bias, improve transparency, and foster accountability in tax judgments. Ultimately, it presents AI as a crucial tool for modernizing India's tax system and enhancing its global competitiveness, emphasizing the need for careful implementation and robust governance frameworks.

DOI: 10.4018/979-8-3693-9576-9.ch004

INTRODUCTION

In the evolving landscape of modern jurisprudence, the interplay between technology and legal systems is an increasingly vital area of exploration, especially in contexts where the law grapples with complexity, ambiguity, and rapid socio-economic change. One of the most intricate and convoluted domains within the legal framework is that of income tax law, particularly when viewed through the prism of fraud detection and enforcement. In countries like India, where the legal and fiscal structures are both historically dense and ever-expanding in response to economic development, the challenges inherent in identifying, investigating, and adjudicating income tax fraud are exacerbated by the sheer scale and complexity of the regulatory environment (D.B., 2019). The multifaceted nature of Indian tax law, woven with layers of exceptions, exemptions, and a multitude of tax codes, creates a labyrinthine structure that proves difficult not only for the ordinary taxpayer to comprehend but also for the state apparatus to administer efficiently.

Tax fraud, a pervasive issue in India, can take many forms, from the deliberate underreporting of income to the misrepresentation of financial records, or even the exploitation of loopholes within the law. The traditional methods employed to detect such fraud, primarily manual audits and investigations, are often ill-equipped to handle the vast amount of data generated in today's digital economy. While these methods have served to some extent in identifying clear cases of fraud, they remain slow, cumbersome, and prone to human error, especially in an environment where fraudulent activity is increasingly sophisticated and subtle (Zhang et al., 2023). Furthermore, the sheer volume of financial transactions, coupled with the rapid pace at which business activities occur, makes it an almost insurmountable task for human authorities to monitor every potential violation or anomaly. In light of these challenges, it is becoming increasingly apparent that the conventional approach to income tax fraud detection is inadequate and must evolve to keep pace with the digital age.

Artificial Intelligence (AI), with its ability to process and analyze vast datasets at a scale and speed unimaginable for human auditors, emerges as a powerful solution to these pressing challenges. AI offers the potential to automate many of the tasks that currently require human intervention, including fraud detection, risk assessment, and even legal judgment in some instances. The unique capability of AI to identify patterns, uncover hidden correlations, and make predictions based on vast quantities of data positions it as an invaluable tool in the realm of income tax enforcement. By utilizing AI to analyze the financial records, tax returns, and transaction histories of individuals and corporations, the legal system could more efficiently and accurately identify fraudulent behavior (Z. et al., 2024). Furthermore, AI could mitigate some of the biases inherent in human decision-making processes, ensuring that legal judgments are more impartial, consistent, and grounded in data-driven insights.

However, the integration of AI into legal judgment, particularly in the realm of income tax fraud, is not without its complexities. The legal system, by nature, is structured around principles of fairness, justice, and due process, all of which can be undermined if AI systems are not implemented with the utmost care and consideration. There are ethical concerns related to the transparency of AI algorithms, the potential for discrimination, and the consequences of automated decisions (González & Mateos, 2019). For example, the use of AI in tax fraud detection could inadvertently lead to the profiling of certain individuals or businesses based on patterns that may not be reflective of criminal intent. This raises significant questions about accountability, responsibility, and the potential for miscarriages of justice. Moreover, the challenge of integrating AI with the existing legal infrastructure, which is deeply rooted in traditional practices and precedents, presents another layer of (He, 2011). Legal professionals and lawmakers must grapple with the intersection of cutting-edge technology and long-standing principles of law, ensuring that AI applications are both effective and just.

India, with its diverse and complex economic landscape, is particularly well-suited to benefit from the integration of AI into its income tax enforcement mechanisms. The country's vast population, coupled with its burgeoning digital economy, has created an environment ripe for the application of AI technologies. Yet, the complexity of Indian tax law, alongside the socio-political and cultural nuances that often influence tax compliance, requires that AI be employed with caution. India's legal and tax systems have long been plagued by issues of inefficiency, corruption, and a lack of transparency, all of which undermine the public's trust in the tax administration (Schulze & Mock, 2021). In this context, AI presents an opportunity to address these issues by enhancing the speed and accuracy of fraud detection, reducing human error, and creating a more transparent and accountable legal process. However, such integration must be approached with a deep understanding of both the technological and legal nuances at play. The success of AI in income tax enforcement will depend not only on the sophistication of the technology itself but also on how well it is integrated into the legal and administrative frameworks of the country.

Furthermore, the regulatory landscape in India is itself in a state of flux, as the government seeks to modernize its tax infrastructure in line with global trends. The introduction of digital platforms like the Goods and Services Tax (GST) network and e-filing systems has already signaled a shift toward greater digitization in the country's tax administration. AI could further enhance these initiatives by automating tasks such as data analysis, pattern recognition, and predictive modeling, making it easier to spot discrepancies or fraudulent activity (J. Liu & Zhou, 2011). However, this also raises critical questions about the adequacy of current legal frameworks to accommodate AI-based decision-making. Can the legal system adapt to an AI-driven approach, and how will it ensure that the principles of justice and fairness are upheld in automated decision-making processes?

In this context, the present study aims to delve into the potential of AI to reshape the landscape of income tax fraud detection and adjudication in India. By examining case studies, reviewing existing literature, and exploring the technological capabilities of AI, this chapter seeks to offer a comprehensive understanding of the role AI can play in modernizing the Indian tax system. Through this exploration, it will become clear that AI's integration into income tax law is not merely a technological innovation, but a profound shift in how the legal system approaches complex issues such as fraud, transparency, and fairness (Koivula et al., 2024). While there are undoubtedly challenges associated with the use of AI in legal judgment, the potential benefits in terms of efficiency, accuracy, and transparency make it a necessary and inevitable development in the modern legal landscape.

In conclusion, the complexities inherent in income tax law, particularly in a developing country like India, necessitate a fresh approach to fraud detection and legal decision-making. Artificial Intelligence, with its ability to process vast amounts of data and identify patterns, offers a promising solution to these challenges (Distinto et al., 2013). However, its integration into the legal framework must be carefully managed to ensure that ethical concerns, such as transparency, fairness, and accountability, are addressed. The success of this integration will depend on a nuanced understanding of both the technological and legal aspects at play, ensuring that AI serves to enhance, rather than undermine, the principles of justice in income tax adjudication.

LITERATURE REVIEW

The application of artificial intelligence (AI) within the legal domain has burgeoned in recent years, owing to its potential to radically transform both the efficiency and accuracy of legal processes. Yet, within the specific realm of income tax law, the intersection between AI and jurisprudence remains a subject of ongoing discourse. This integration is particularly crucial in jurisdictions with highly complex and ever-evolving tax structures, such as India, where the convergence of advanced technology and legal enforcement offers both promises and pitfalls (Cai, Tan, et al., 2011). The legal landscape surrounding tax fraud has long been a multifaceted labyrinth, riddled with nuances and ambiguity, thus necessitating a profound exploration of how AI can recalibrate legal responses to such fiscal malfeasance. However, this shift is not merely a technical matter but one that intertwines the very essence of justice, fairness, and due process, aspects that must be approached with caution.

The complexity inherent in the Indian legal framework surrounding income tax is staggering, with a myriad of statutes, regulations, and case laws that create a dense and intricate web of legal interpretations. This labyrinthine structure, while designed to accommodate a diverse and dynamic economic environment, often acts as a barrier to both effective compliance and enforcement. Fraudulent practices, ranging from tax evasion to money laundering and the misrepresentation of financial records, are an ever-present challenge that legal systems struggle to keep pace with (Shi & Wu, 2011). In such an environment, the detection of income tax fraud often hinges on human-driven processes that are inherently susceptible to inefficiency, bias, and error. These shortcomings are particularly stark in jurisdictions where the sheer volume of transactions and the fast-paced nature of modern business activities render traditional methods of fraud detection obsolete. It is precisely this gap that AI aims to fill, offering a promise of a more streamlined, objective, and precise approach to detecting and addressing tax fraud.

AI's potential to influence legal decision-making, particularly in the context of tax fraud, hinges upon its capacity for data processing and pattern recognition. By sifting through massive datasets, AI can uncover inconsistencies or anomalies that may signal fraudulent activity, all while operating at a speed and scale far beyond the capabilities of human auditors. The intricate algorithms powering AI systems can analyze historical tax data, financial reports, and transactional histories, detecting patterns that might elude even the most experienced legal professionals. This enhanced capacity for data-driven insights would ostensibly enable the legal system to identify and address income tax fraud with unprecedented accuracy, minimizing the margin for error and ensuring a more equitable system for both taxpayers and administrators (Zadeh et al., 2023). In theory, AI could detect subtle shifts in financial behavior that signal potential fraud before it fully manifests, providing authorities with the tools to act swiftly and decisively.

Furthermore, the application of AI in legal judgments would ostensibly alleviate some of the inherent biases present in traditional human decision-making processes. Legal adjudication, particularly when dealing with matters such as tax fraud, is often susceptible to subjective interpretation, where the biases and cognitive limitations of individuals can influence outcomes. AI, in contrast, offers the promise of impartiality, operating purely on data-driven logic and consistently applying predefined criteria. While human judgment inevitably introduces variables based on personal experiences or interpretative frameworks, AI systems adhere strictly to algorithms designed to be transparent, reproducible, and devoid of human emotional or cognitive biases (Donnelly & Young, 1999). However, while this impartiality may seem like a virtue, it raises critical ethical concerns, particularly regarding the transparency of the algorithms employed and the potential for over-reliance on data that may not fully capture the nuances of complex legal contexts.

While the advantages of AI in addressing tax fraud are evident, the application of such technology also demands rigorous scrutiny, particularly in terms of its ethical and legal ramifications. One of the foremost concerns is the opacity of the decision-making process within AI systems. The very algorithms that power these technologies often operate as "black boxes," where the rationale behind decisions is not readily apparent to external observers. This lack of transparency can prove to be problematic in the legal domain, where due process and accountability are foundational principles (Cai, Zhang, et al., 2011). If AI systems are allowed to make or assist in making legal decisions regarding tax fraud, how can individuals challenge those decisions or ensure that they were made in a just and transparent manner? The potential for algorithmic bias – where the data used to train AI systems may inadvertently reflect historical injustices or societal inequalities – further complicates the matter. Such biases could lead to discriminatory outcomes, particularly in cases where tax audits disproportionately target specific demographic groups based on flawed historical data patterns.

The integration of AI within the judicial process also raises questions regarding the future of legal practitioners and the evolving role of human judgment in legal proceedings. Traditionally, lawyers and judges have been the arbiters of legal disputes, relying on their expertise and understanding of the law to render judgments. However, with AI systems poised to become integral components of legal decision-making, it is essential to question the extent to which human involvement should remain in the process (Wang & Wang, 2020). Should AI systems be tasked solely with fraud detection, or should they also be allowed to make binding legal decisions? If so, how will the legal community adapt to the increasing automation of these tasks? Legal professionals may find themselves in a position where they must work alongside AI, interpreting its findings and ensuring that they align with established legal principles. This necessitates a profound shift in legal education and practice, where familiarity with AI and its implications becomes as integral to legal training as knowledge of statutory law.

Additionally, the broader social implications of AI in income tax fraud detection cannot be ignored. While AI has the potential to create a more efficient and transparent system for identifying fraud, its implementation in a country like India, with its vast disparities in access to technology, raises concerns about equity. The digital divide between urban and rural areas, as well as between different socio-economic classes, could exacerbate existing inequalities, with those at the periphery of the digital infrastructure potentially facing unfair scrutiny or exclusion. The use of AI could inadvertently lead to a situation where certain groups are disproportionately affected by automated systems that may not account for regional economic practices or informal financial systems that are prevalent in certain parts of the country. Moreover, there is the issue of privacy, as the use of AI entails the collection and analysis of vast amounts of personal and financial data (Sano et al., 2012). Striking the right balance between privacy, fairness, and the effective detection of fraud will be one of the most pressing challenges as India moves toward embracing AI in its tax system.

The potential for AI to revolutionize income tax fraud detection and legal judgment is immense. However, this transformation must be approached with caution and careful consideration of the myriad ethical, legal, and social challenges that accompany it. The integration of AI into income tax law holds the promise of a more efficient, transparent, and unbiased system of fraud detection. Yet, as with all transformative technologies, its adoption must be accompanied by robust safeguards to ensure that it serves to enhance, rather than undermine, the principles of justice, equity, and accountability (H. Liu et al., 2011). The path forward requires a nuanced understanding of both the technological possibilities and the legal imperatives, ensuring that AI's potential is harnessed in a way that upholds the integrity of the legal system while addressing the pressing challenges posed by income tax fraud.

RESEARCH METHODOLOGY

The research methodology employed in this chapter is based on a qualitative, descriptive analysis aimed at understanding the role of Artificial Intelligence (AI) in the context of income tax judgments, particularly within the Indian legal framework. The chapter synthesizes a wide range of secondary data sources, including scholarly articles, government reports, industry analyses, and case studies, to construct a comprehensive overview of the current state of AI integration into the income tax system.

To begin with, an extensive review of existing literature forms the foundation of the chapter. The literature review method focuses on examining scholarly research, legal publications, and reports from tax authorities regarding the application of AI in tax administration. The literature is analyzed critically to assess both the potential benefits and the challenges associated with the use of AI in income tax judgments. This includes a detailed examination of AI's role in automating tasks such as fraud detection, risk analysis, and decision-making processes in tax enforcement.

In addition to the literature review, the chapter includes a comparative analysis of AI's application in other global tax systems. This international perspective is incorporated to highlight best practices and potential pitfalls that can inform India's approach to AI integration. Through this comparative analysis, the chapter also investigates the ethical and legal implications of using AI in tax judgments, drawing attention to concerns such as algorithmic bias, transparency, and fairness.

Furthermore, the methodology incorporates case studies and real-world examples from India's ongoing efforts to introduce AI into its tax system. These case studies provide practical insights into how AI is currently being implemented in income tax assessments, fraud detection, and decision-making. The challenges faced during these implementations, along with the strategies used to address them, are analyzed to offer a grounded understanding of the impact of AI in this domain.

Overall, the chapter combines theoretical research, global examples, and real-world case studies to provide a holistic view of the intersection between AI and income tax judgments. This methodological approach ensures that the analysis is both comprehensive and contextually relevant to India's ongoing journey toward AI integration in its tax system.

ANALYSIS

Table 1. A snapshot of financial malfeasance: Key income tax fraud cases and their ongoing impact

Date	Case	Involved Parties	Amount Involved	Nature of Fraud	Current Status
May 2025	Jeevan Lal Lavidiya Bribery Case	Jeevan Lal Lavidiya (IRS officer), Viral Mehta (Shapoorji Pallonji Group), M. Sajida Majhar Hussain Shah, et al.	70 lakh	Acceptance of bribes for favorable tax decisions; possession of benami property	CBI arrested Lavidiya and four others; investigations ongoing
February 2025	New India Cooperative Bank Scam	Hitesh Mehta (former GM), Dharmesh Paun (real estate developer), Hiren Bhanu (former Chairman), et al.	122 crore	Misappropriation of funds; diversion of bank reserves; unauthorized transactions	Multiple arrests made; RBI imposed withdrawal restrictions; investigations continue
November 2024	Volkswagen India Tax Evasion Case	Skoda Auto Volkswagen India Pvt Ltd (subsidiary of Volkswagen AG)	$1.4 billion (11,000 crore)	Misclassification of imports to evade higher import duties	Tax notice issued; company claims compliance; legal proceedings anticipated
August 2024	Aviva India Fake Invoice Scheme	Aviva Life Insurance India Ltd; vendors providing marketing services	$7.5 million	Use of fake invoices to claim unwarranted tax credits; payment of illegal commissions	Fine imposed; company plans to appeal; operations reportedly unaffected

continued on following page

Table 1. Continued

Date	Case	Involved Parties	Amount Involved	Nature of Fraud	Current Status
December 2024	Bogus Tax Deduction Claims by Salaried Employees	Approximately 90,000 salaried individuals across PSUs and private sectors	1,070 crore	Falsification of claims under sections 80C, 80D, 80E, 80G, 80GGB, 80GGC	Tax department recovered dues; outreach programs initiated to prevent future occurrences
February 2025	Buldana Urban Co-operative Credit Society Case	Buldana Urban Co-operative Credit Society Ltd; involved bank officials and intermediaries	52 crore	Attachment of bank accounts linked to illicit funds; misappropriation of deposits	ITAT upheld attachment of 900 accounts; further investigations underway
March 2025	Hyderabad Income Tax Officials Extortion Case	5 Income Tax officials, 1 chartered accountant, and intermediaries	Not specified	Extortion of money from taxpayers using confidential data; threats of penalties	CBI filed FIR; raids conducted; further arrests expected

Table 1 presents a series of high-profile income tax fraud cases in India, demonstrating the scale and complexity of financial crimes within the nation. In May 2025, the Jeevan Lal Lavidiya Bribery Case emerged, involving 70 lakh in bribes for favorable tax decisions and possession of benami property, with the CBI arresting Lavidiya and four others. The February 2025 New India Cooperative Bank Scam saw 122 crore misappropriated through unauthorized transactions and bank reserves diversion, with multiple arrests and RBI-imposed withdrawal restrictions. In November 2024, Volkswagen India faced a 11,000 crore tax evasion case over misclassification of imports to evade duties, with tax notices issued, though the company claims compliance. Similarly, in August 2024, Aviva India's fake invoice scheme involving $7.5 million resulted in fines, while the company plans to appeal. December 2024 witnessed 1,070 crore in bogus tax deductions by 90,000 salaried individuals, with dues recovered and preventive outreach initiatives launched. In February 2025, the Buldana Urban Co-operative Credit Society Case uncovered 52 crore in misappropriated deposits, and 900 bank accounts were upheld for attachment, with investigations ongoing. Lastly, the March 2025 Hyderabad Income Tax Officials Extortion Case highlighted the misuse of confidential data for extortion, with the CBI conducting raids and further arrests anticipated.

Table 2. Revolutionizing justice: The role of AI in shaping the future of India's judiciary

Aspect	Details
Key AI Initiatives	• **SUVAS (Supreme Court Vidhik Anuvaad Software)**: AI-driven translation tool facilitating multilingual access to legal documents. - **SUPACE (Supreme Court Portal for Assistance in Court Efficiency)**: AI-based research assistant aiding judges in case analysis and legal research. - **MARVEL (Maharashtra Advanced Research and Vigilance for Enhanced Law Enforcement)**: Maharashtra Police's AI system aimed at enhancing crime-solving capabilities and predictive policing.
AI Applications in Judiciary	• **Predictive Analytics**: AI models analyze historical judgments and case data to offer predictive insights into potential case outcomes and risk assessments, assisting judicial officers in formulating more informed decisions. - **Legal Research and Case Management**: AI-driven tools enhance case management, legal research (via Natural Language Processing), and user interaction, streamlining judicial processes.
Ethical and Legal Considerations	• **Bias and Fairness**: AI models may inherit biases from historical judicial data, raising concerns about fairness and impartiality in legal decision-making. - **Data Privacy and Security**: AI-driven systems require access to vast legal and crime databases, necessitating stringent measures to ensure data confidentiality and security. - **Regulatory Framework**: India currently lacks AI-specific legal frameworks to regulate AI-driven judicial and law enforcement mechanisms, posing challenges in governance and accountability.
Recent Developments	• **AI Safety Institute**: Established by the Ministry of Electronics and Information Technology to ensure the ethical and safe application of AI models, promoting domestic R&D grounded in India's social, economic, cultural, and linguistic diversity.
Challenges in Implementation	• **Infrastructure and Digital Divide**: Not all courts and police stations have access to AI infrastructure, especially in rural areas, hindering uniform implementation. - **Data Accessibility**: The success of AI models largely depends on the availability of large, high-quality datasets, which are often not readily accessible due to privacy concerns and data fragmentation.

Table 2 encapsulates the multifaceted approach India is adopting towards integrating AI into its judicial system, balancing technological advancements with ethical considerations and infrastructural challenges. The integration of Artificial Intelligence (AI) into the Indian judiciary is rapidly progressing, marked by significant initiatives and applications designed to enhance judicial efficiency and fairness. Key AI-driven initiatives like SUVAS (Supreme Court Vidhik Anuvaad Software), SUPACE (Supreme Court Portal for Assistance in Court Efficiency), and MARVEL (Maharashtra Advanced Research and Vigilance for Enhanced Law Enforcement) are transforming legal processes by providing multilingual document access, aiding judicial research, and improving law enforcement capabilities. AI applications in the judiciary focus on predictive analytics, helping judges make more informed decisions, and streamlining case management and legal research through advanced Natural Language Processing tools. However, the adoption of AI in the legal system raises crucial ethical considerations, including the potential for bias in AI models based on historical judicial data, concerns over data privacy and security, and the

need for a robust regulatory framework. While recent developments, such as the establishment of the AI Safety Institute, highlight India's commitment to ethical AI use, challenges remain, particularly with regard to infrastructure and the digital divide, especially in rural areas, as well as issues around the accessibility of high-quality legal datasets. These challenges must be addressed to ensure the equitable implementation of AI across India's judicial system.

Table 3. The imperative for artificial intelligence in transforming income tax judgments: A comprehensive overview

Aspect	Details
Volume of Data	The Income Tax Department processes vast amounts of data every year, including millions of tax returns, financial records, and transaction histories. Manual processing is inefficient and prone to errors, highlighting the need for AI's capability to handle large datasets quickly and accurately.
Complexity of Tax Laws	India's income tax laws are complex and constantly evolving, making it difficult for tax authorities to ensure compliance. AI systems can be trained to recognize the nuances in tax legislation and apply it consistently across cases, reducing ambiguity in tax judgments and offering a more streamlined approach.
Fraud Detection	Tax fraud, including evasion and misreporting, is a significant challenge. AI-powered algorithms can identify patterns of suspicious activity, flagging potential fraud more effectively than human auditors. AI systems have been successfully used in financial fraud detection across industries and could enhance the identification of non-compliant behavior in tax filings.
Speed and Efficiency	Traditional income tax judgment processes are time-consuming. AI can drastically reduce processing time, enabling faster scrutiny, assessment, and resolution of cases. This is especially important in large countries like India, where tax filings and legal proceedings often face backlogs.
Bias Reduction	Human judgments can be influenced by cognitive biases. AI, if correctly designed, can make impartial decisions based on data-driven insights, offering a more consistent application of tax laws and reducing the possibility of biased judgments.
Transparency and Accountability	AI systems can provide traceable, transparent decision-making processes. The use of AI in income tax judgments would allow for clear records of the decision-making steps, which would ensure greater accountability in the process.
Automation of Routine Tasks	A significant portion of income tax judgments involves routine tasks like data entry, document verification, and basic compliance checks. AI can automate these tasks, freeing up human resources for more complex and strategic decision-making, thus improving overall productivity and accuracy.
Customization and Personalization	AI can assist in delivering personalized tax advice based on individual or corporate profiles, considering a wide range of data points, and recommending actions that comply with specific legal provisions, offering a tailored approach in tax judgment.

continued on following page

Table 3. Continued

Aspect	Details
Global Tax Compliance Trends	Many countries are already integrating AI into their tax systems for fraud detection, compliance monitoring, and case management. As India seeks to modernize its tax system, the adoption of AI is necessary to remain competitive with global standards and improve administrative efficiency.
Workforce Transformation	AI in the tax system will drive a transformation in the workforce. Rather than replacing jobs, it will enhance the role of tax professionals by providing them with powerful tools to make more informed, data-driven decisions, shifting their role from manual processing to strategic analysis.

The Table 3 provides a comprehensive analysis of the critical need for Artificial Intelligence (AI) in income tax judgment processes, especially in the context of India. The **volume of data** processed by the Income Tax Department annually is immense, including millions of tax returns, financial records, and transaction histories, which are inefficiently handled through manual processing. AI's capability to quickly and accurately manage large datasets could significantly improve the efficiency of tax processing. The **complexity of tax laws** in India, which are ever-evolving, makes compliance challenging. AI systems can help reduce the ambiguity inherent in the tax legislation by consistently applying rules across cases, ensuring a more streamlined approach to tax judgments. **Fraud detection** is another area where AI shines, as algorithms can identify suspicious activity patterns, offering a more effective method of detecting tax evasion and misreporting than traditional auditing. Additionally, **speed and efficiency** in tax judgment processes are crucial, as AI can drastically reduce the time required for scrutiny, assessment, and case resolution, addressing backlogs commonly seen in India's tax system.

AI also helps in **bias reduction**, making impartial, data-driven decisions to ensure a consistent application of tax laws and reducing cognitive biases often present in human judgment. Furthermore, **transparency and accountability** are enhanced by AI, as systems can provide traceable records of decision-making, ensuring greater accountability. AI's ability to **automate routine tasks**, such as data entry and compliance checks, frees up human resources for more complex decision-making, improving productivity and accuracy. **Customization and personalization** are also key advantages, as AI can provide personalized tax advice tailored to individual or corporate profiles, enhancing the effectiveness of tax judgments. The **global tax compliance trends** suggest that many countries have already integrated AI into their tax systems, making it essential for India to adopt similar technologies to remain competitive globally. Lastly, **workforce transformation** is inevitable, with AI empowering tax professionals by providing tools for more informed, data-driven decisions, transitioning their roles from manual tasks to more strategic analysis.

MANAGERIAL IMPLICATIONS

The integration of Artificial Intelligence (AI) in income tax judgment processes carries profound managerial implications that span across administrative efficiency, organizational structures, human resource management, and the evolution of strategic decision-making frameworks within tax authorities. As India strives to modernize its fiscal infrastructure, the deployment of AI can significantly alter the dynamics within the tax system, demanding a recalibration of managerial strategies to harness its full potential while mitigating the challenges posed by its implementation.

First, AI's ability to process vast amounts of data at unprecedented speeds will fundamentally change the operational landscape of tax administration. Tax authorities traditionally rely on labor-intensive manual methods to analyze returns, financial records, and transactions. With AI, the volume of data managed annually by the Income Tax Department can be processed with precision, reducing errors and improving decision-making accuracy. However, this necessitates the need for tax managers to reevaluate their resource allocation strategies. The role of human auditors and administrative staff will evolve, requiring managers to invest in retraining and reskilling initiatives. The workforce must transition from performing routine tasks to leveraging AI-driven insights for strategic analysis, demanding a shift in both skill sets and organizational culture.

From a managerial perspective, AI's ability to streamline tax fraud detection offers significant implications for governance and compliance management. Traditional methods of identifying tax evasion are often reactive and dependent on manual checks. AI, by contrast, can proactively flag discrepancies, identify suspicious patterns, and predict potential fraudulent activities before they manifest fully. This proactive approach not only enhances the accuracy of fraud detection but also shifts the managerial focus from corrective actions to preventive measures. Managers will need to reassess their risk management frameworks, integrating AI insights into the decision-making processes for tax enforcement and compliance. Moreover, as AI algorithms become more sophisticated, the need for enhanced governance structures will arise to ensure transparency and mitigate biases in AI systems.

The automation of routine tasks such as document verification, data entry, and initial compliance checks represents another key managerial implication. With AI taking on these time-consuming functions, tax administrators can redirect their resources toward higher-value tasks such as complex adjudication and policy formulation. However, this shift also demands that managers refine their organizational structures to ensure smooth integration between AI systems and human personnel. New processes must be established to define roles clearly, balancing human oversight with AI-driven automation. Additionally, managers will be required to implement robust systems for monitoring and auditing AI-driven decisions, ensuring that automation does not compromise ethical standards or the integrity of tax judgments. AI's role in reducing bias and promoting impartiality in tax decisions introduces another managerial challenge: the development of new oversight mechanisms. While AI has the potential to eliminate human biases, it is also susceptible to bias introduced during the training phase or from skewed datasets. Managers will need to ensure that the algorithms used are continuously refined and audited for fairness, accuracy, and alignment with the law. Ethical considerations will be at the forefront, demanding that managers create a framework for transparency in AI decisions, which may include detailed reporting mechanisms and accountability structures for AI-assisted judgments. In conclusion, the managerial implications of incorporating AI into income tax judgments are far-reaching. Tax authorities will need to embrace a strategic approach to workforce development, organizational restructuring, and governance to ensure that the adoption of AI aligns with both legal standards and public expectations. By leveraging AI's capabilities effectively, tax authorities can enhance operational efficiency, improve fraud detection, and foster transparency in tax administration. However, it will require an ongoing commitment from management to navigate the complexities of AI integration, ensuring that the systems in place are both effective and ethical.

CONCLUSION

In summation, the incorporation of Artificial Intelligence (AI) into the domain of income tax judgment represents a paradigm shift with profound implications for both the operational dynamics of tax administration and the broader governance frameworks. By enabling the rapid processing of vast data sets, AI has the potential to vastly enhance the efficiency, accuracy, and consistency of tax-related decision-making. Its application in automating routine tasks, detecting fraudulent activities, and reducing cognitive biases not only augurs well for optimizing tax compliance but also sets a new benchmark for transparency and accountability in tax administration. The AI-driven transformation promises to mitigate the inherent complexities of India's intricate tax laws, offering a streamlined approach to compliance, adjudication, and enforcement.

However, this evolution necessitates an astute managerial approach to address the concomitant challenges. The deployment of AI requires significant investment in the reskilling of human resources, organizational restructuring, and the establishment of robust oversight mechanisms. Managers will need to reconcile the efficiency of AI with ethical considerations, ensuring that algorithms remain transparent, equitable, and free from bias. Furthermore, as AI systems become increasingly autonomous, it will be imperative for management to institute continuous monitoring and refinement processes to safeguard the integrity of the legal system.

In conclusion, while AI offers remarkable potential to revolutionize income tax judgments, its successful implementation will hinge upon a balanced integration that combines technological advancement with ethical governance. The future of tax administration in India lies not merely in the adoption of AI but in the judicious, transparent, and accountable management of this transformative tool. It is through this synergy between technology and managerial oversight that the true promise of AI in enhancing the efficacy and fairness of the tax system can be realized.

REFERENCES

Cai, D., Tan, M., & Cai, J. (2011). The VAT tax burden warning model and modification based on CTAIS system data. *2011 2nd International Conference on Artificial Intelligence, Management Science and Electronic Commerce, AIMSEC 2011 - Proceedings*, 2653 – 2656. DOI: 10.1109/AIMSEC.2011.6011092

Cai, D., Zhang, A., & Cai, J. (2011). The improvement on China's regional standard value added tax revenue estimate method - The construction, application and verification of standard rate model. *2011 2nd International Conference on Artificial Intelligence, Management Science and Electronic Commerce, AIMSEC 2011 - Proceedings*, 783 – 786. DOI: 10.1109/AIMSEC.2011.6010234

D.B. S. (Ed.). (2019). International Scientific Conference, FarEastCon 2018. *Smart Innovation, Systems and Technologies, 139.*

Distinto, I., Guarino, N., & Masolo, C. (2013). A well-founded ontological framework for modeling personal income tax. *Proceedings of the International Conference on Artificial Intelligence and Law*, 33 – 42. DOI: 10.1145/2514601.2514606

Donnelly, M., & Young, A. (1999). TAXTUTOR: An intelligent tutoring system for Canadian tax. *New Review of Applied Expert Systems and Emerging Technologies, 5*, 99–112.

González, I., & Mateos, A. (2019). Multilayer Identification: Combining N-Grams, TF-IDF and Monge-Elkan in Massive Real Time Processing. *Lecture Notes in Computer Science (Including Subseries Lecture Notes in Artificial Intelligence and Lecture Notes in Bioinformatics), 11676 LNAI*, 213 – 223. DOI: 10.1007/978-3-030-26773-5_19

He, W. (2011). Tax incentive and technology innovation: The empirical research based on the listed companies. *2011 2nd International Conference on Artificial Intelligence, Management Science and Electronic Commerce, AIMSEC 2011 - Proceedings*, 7284 – 7291. DOI: 10.1109/AIMSEC.2011.6010554

Koivula, K., Shamsuzzoha, A., & Shamsuzzaman, M. (2024). Application of artificial intelligence as a knowledge creation instrument in tax procedures. *Engineering Applications of Artificial Intelligence, 133*, 108417. Advance online publication. DOI: 10.1016/j.engappai.2024.108417

Liu, H., Xia, Q., & Xu, J. (2011). Notice of Retraction: Taxpayer compliance in China: A prospect theory analysis. *2011 2nd International Conference on Artificial Intelligence, Management Science and Electronic Commerce, AIMSEC 2011 - Proceedings*, 7292 – 7297. DOI: 10.1109/AIMSEC.2011.6009750

Liu, J., & Zhou, G. (2011). Analysis on China's individual income tax self-declaration system - Problems, guidance and strategies. *2011 2nd International Conference on Artificial Intelligence, Management Science and Electronic Commerce, AIMSEC 2011 - Proceedings*, 1930 – 1933. DOI: 10.1109/AIMSEC.2011.6011083

Sano, K., Hagiwara, S., & Tojo, S. (2012). An intuitionistic investigation of prerequisite-effect structure. *Lecture Notes in Computer Science (Including Subseries Lecture Notes in Artificial Intelligence and Lecture Notes in Bioinformatics), 7258 LNAI*, 170 – 183. DOI: 10.1007/978-3-642-32090-3_15

Schulze, K. K., & Mock, R. P. (2021). THE ROBOTIC REVOLUTION: A TAX POLICY COLLISION COURSE. *Temple Law Review*, *93*(2), 301–341.

Shi, A., & Wu, W. (2011). Analysis on consolidated taxation in the context of head-quarters economy under independent corporation accounting. *2011 2nd International Conference on Artificial Intelligence, Management Science and Electronic Commerce, AIMSEC 2011 - Proceedings*, 160 – 163. DOI: 10.1109/AIMSEC.2011.6010251

Wang, Y., & Wang, P. (2020). New Personal Tax Collection Management System Based on Artificial Intelligence and Its Application in the Middle Class. *Journal of Physics: Conference Series*, *1574*(1), 012105. Advance online publication. DOI: 10.1088/1742-6596/1574/1/012105

Zadeh, S. A., Iwendi, C., Uhumuavbi, I., & Boulouard, Z. (2023). A New AI-Based Approach for Rental Tax Evasion Management in Iran (Ethical Consideration). *Lecture Notes in Networks and Systems, 735 LNNS*, 451 – 468. DOI: 10.1007/978-3-031-37164-6_34

Zhang, Y., Hao, S., & Li, S. (2023). Development And Application of Electronic Tax Declaration Robot for Individual Income Tax Based on Uipath. *ACM International Conference Proceeding Series*, 620 – 624. DOI: 10.1145/3656766.3656870

Chapter 5
Autopoietic Co-Evolution of AI and Law

Sofia Anastasiadou
https://orcid.org/0000-0001-6404-5003
University of Western Macedonia, Greece & Neapolis University Pafos, Cyprus

Lambrini Seremeti
https://orcid.org/0000-0002-0663-5408
Agricultural University of Athens, Greece

ABSTRACT

The interaction between Artificial Intelligence (AI) and Law is not merely a linear process of adaptation and regulation. This phenomenon can be described through the lens of autopoietic evolution, a concept rooted in Systems Theory. Autopoiesis, originally a biological term, refers to systems capable of self-generation and self-regulation. When applied to the legal system and AI, autopoiesis captures the idea that both systems are self-referential and mutually influencing each other's evolution. This chapter explores the autopoietic co-evolution of AI and Law, discussing how the legal system shapes AI development and, conversely, how AI transforms legal governance.

INTRODUCTION

The interaction between Artificial Intelligence (AI) and Law is neither a straightforward process of legal adaptation to technological change nor a unidirectional imposition of rules on innovation. Instead, it reflects a dynamic, reciprocal relationship in which both systems evolve in tandem. This chapter explores this phenomenon through the lens of autopoietic co-evolution, a concept originating in

DOI: 10.4018/979-8-3693-9576-9.ch005

Systems Theory. Autopoiesis, derived from biological studies, describes systems that are self-generating and self-regulating (Maturana and Varela, 1980). The theoretical framework of autopoiesis has been widely applied across various sectors to explore how complex systems sustain and adapt themselves. In organizational studies, it has been used to understand how businesses self-organize and evolve in response to changing market conditions. In biology, it explains the self-maintaining nature of living organisms, while in sociology, it offers insights into how social systems, including law, education (Kougias et al., 2016), and healthcare, perpetuate their structures and norms. Autopoiesis has also been applied in technology studies to analyze how technological ecosystems, such as software development communities, innovate and adapt. When applied to the interaction between AI and the legal system, autopoiesis reveals how these systems influence each other's growth, creating a complex feedback loop that reshapes both fields (Zhang, 2023).

On the one hand, the legal system is inherently self-referential (Teubner, 1988). It creates, interprets, and enforces norms through its internal processes while maintaining boundaries that distinguish it from other systems. This autopoietic nature enables Law to adapt to external stimuli, such as the rapid advancements in AI, while preserving its coherence and independence. Legal frameworks, policies, and case law collectively function as mechanisms of self-regulation, ensuring the continuity of the Law system.

On the other hand, applying the theory of autopoiesis to AI systems, particularly advanced forms like machine learning models, reveals parallels that justify their characterization as inherently self-referential (Bianchini, 2023). An AI system processes input data, refines its internal parameters through iterative learning, and generates outputs that further inform its functioning, essentially creating a feedback loop of self-improvement. For instance, a neural network adjusts its weights and biases based on performance metrics, continuously refining its model to enhance accuracy. This process mirrors autopoietic systems, as the AI system maintains and evolves its structure through self-referencing mechanisms. While not "living" in the biological sense, these AI systems exhibit functional autonomy and self-organization, underscoring their self-referential nature within the theoretical framework of autopoiesis.

Meanwhile, AI, as an emergent technological system, challenges the traditional boundaries of the legal domain (Quteishat et al., 2024). From automated decision-making to predictive analytics in litigation, AI tools are increasingly integrated into legal practice. These tools do not merely serve the law; they transform it. The capacity of AI for processing vast datasets (Souravlas et al., 2020; Souravlas et al., 2021), identifying patterns, and delivering insights in real time pushes the legal system to reconsider fundamental concepts such as liability, accountability, and due process. Additionally, the development of AI-based systems that be able to analyze incoming data streams (Souravlas et al. 2022a, Souravlas et al. 2022b, Souravlas et al. 2022c, Souravlas et al. 2023) immediately, enabling organizations to react promptly to modifying conditions or consumer behaviors (Papademetriou et al., 2024) has raised inquiries involving ethical issues and data privacy.

Moreover, regulations, while essential for ensuring ethical and responsible AI deployment, can impose limitations on innovation in several ways. Overly rigid or prescriptive regulations may stifle creativity by constraining the development of novel AI applications that do not fit neatly within predefined legal frameworks (Luger, 2025). Thus, the concept of autopoietic co-evolution is evident in the iterative relationship between AI and Law. The legal system, as a self-referential entity, adapts to the capabilities and challenges of AI by creating norms and frameworks that guide its development. At the same time, the transformative impact of AI on legal governance feeds back into the legal system, reshaping its structures and practices.

LEGAL SYSTEM SHAPES AI DEVELOPMENT

The legal system serves as a foundational guide for AI development by establishing boundaries and principles that developers must adhere to. Through regulations, policies, and case law, it defines the ethical and operational standards within which AI technologies must be designed and implemented (Wong, 2020). Key areas where the legal system influences AI sector include:

- *Regulation of data usage*: AI systems rely heavily on data for training and operation. Legal frameworks, such as the General Data Protection Regulation (GDPR) in the European Union, mandate strict guidelines on data collection, usage, and storage (Goddard, 2017). These regulations ensure that AI developers prioritize user privacy, consent, and data security. As a result, innovations like federated learning and anonymization techniques have emerged to comply with legal requirements while maintaining the effectiveness of AI systems.
- *Accountability and liability standards*: The legal system enforces accountability in AI development by holding developers and deployers responsible for the outcomes of AI applications (Novelli et al., 2024). This is particularly significant in areas like autonomous vehicles and healthcare, where the potential for harm is high. Liability standards drive the creation of fail-safe mechanisms and robust testing protocols, ensuring that AI systems operate reliably and predictably.
- *Promotion of fairness and non-discrimination*: Anti-discrimination laws influence the design of AI algorithms by requiring them to avoid biases that could lead to unfair treatment (Varona and Suarez, 2022). For instance, hiring

algorithms must adhere to equal employment opportunity standards, prompting developers to adopt techniques such as bias detection and mitigation in machine learning models.

- *Explainability and transparency requirements*: Legal mandates for explainability compel developers to create AI systems that provide clear, understandable justifications for their decisions (Balasubramaniam et al., 2023). This requirement has spurred advancements in interpretable machine learning, which seeks to make complex AI models comprehensible to non-technical stakeholders.

In a nutshell, the legal system plays a pivotal role in shaping the trajectory of AI development by embedding ethical, operational, and societal considerations into the technological landscape. By establishing clear boundaries for data usage, accountability, fairness, and transparency, it not only safeguards public interest but also drives innovation by encouraging developers to create AI systems that are secure, equitable, and understandable.

AI TRANSFORMS LEGAL GOVERNANCE

While the legal system shapes AI development, AI also drives significant changes in Law and particularly in legal governance. By automating tasks, enhancing decision-making, and introducing new capabilities, AI reshapes the way legal system operates (Frolova and Ermakova, 2021). The main aspects of legal transformation encompass the following areas:

- *Automation and Efficiency Gains*: One of the most visible ways AI is transforming the legal system is through automation. Repetitive and time-consuming tasks, such as legal research, document review, contract analysis, and e-discovery, are increasingly handled by AI-driven tools (Thirumagal et al., 2024). These tools leverage natural language processing (NLP) and machine learning algorithms to sift through vast datasets, identify relevant information, and generate insights at a fraction of the time it would take human professionals (Imogen et al., 2024).
- *Enhanced Judicial Decision-Making*: AI is also influencing judicial decision-making processes (Buckland, 2023). Predictive analytics tools analyze historical case data to provide insights into potential outcomes, helping judges and legal practitioners anticipate rulings (Bala et al., 2017). Such tools can assist in ensuring consistency in sentencing, reducing biases, and offering data-driven recommendations for complex cases. However, reliance on AI

in judicial decision-making raises concerns about transparency and accountability, especially when algorithms operate as "black boxes" with limited explainability.

- *Algorithmic Regulation and Compliance*: Regulatory bodies are adopting AI for real-time monitoring and enforcement. AI systems can analyze vast quantities of data to detect irregularities, ensure compliance, and flag potential violations across sectors like finance, healthcare, and environmental protection (Eneh, 2023). These capabilities enable proactive enforcement and reduce the lag between regulatory breaches and corrective actions. However, questions about algorithmic accuracy, fairness, and the potential for overreach remain critical.

In summary, AI is profoundly transforming the legal system by automating tasks, enhancing decision-making, and enabling real-time regulatory enforcement. These advancements improve efficiency, consistency, and responsiveness while introducing challenges related to transparency, fairness, and accountability. As AI reshapes legal governance, it is crucial to adopt strategies that balance innovation with the principles of justice, ensuring the legal system remains equitable and effective in a rapidly evolving technological landscape.

CONCLUSION

AI and Law systems are engaged in a dynamic, reciprocal relationship that drives mutual evolution. The legal system shapes AI development by embedding principles of accountability, fairness, and transparency into its framework. Meanwhile, AI transforms legal governance by enhancing efficiency, automating processes, and challenging traditional legal concepts. As these domains continue to interact, a balance must be struck to ensure that AI innovation progresses responsibly while upholding the core values of justice and equity.

Deeply understanding the ongoing co-evolution of AI and Law necessitates a robust theoretical framework, such as the concept of autopoiesis. Originating from systems theory, autopoiesis refers to the self-creating and self-sustaining nature of systems, particularly living organisms. When applied to the legal system, it highlights how law continually evolves and reorganizes itself in response to external stimuli, including technological advancements like AI. This theoretical lens offers valuable insights into how AI and law interact, influencing and shaping each other in a dynamic and iterative process.

REFERENCES

Bala, J., Kellar, M., & Ramberg, F. (2017). Predictive analytics for litigation case management. *Proceedings of the IEEE international Conference on Big Data*, Boston, MA, USA, 3826-3830. https://doi.org/DOI: 10.1109/BigData.2017.8258384

Balasubramaniam, N., Kauppinen, M., Rannisto, A., Hiekkanen, K., & Kujala, S. (2023). Transparency and explainability of AI systems: From ethical guidelines to requirements. *Information and Software Technology*, *159*, 10719. DOI: 10.1016/j.infsof.2023.107197

Bianchini, F. (2023). Autopoiesis of artificial: From systems to cognition. *Bio Systems*, *230*, 104936. DOI: 10.1016/j.biosystems.2023.104936 PMID: 37279825

Buckland, R. (2023). *AI, judges and judgement: Setting the scene*. M-RCBG Associate Working Paper Series 2023.220, Harvard University, Cambridge, MA.

Eneh, C. (2023). Enhancing regulatory compliance monitoring with AI. *Journal of AI-assisted Scientific Discovery*, *3*(2), 534–548.

Frolova, E. E., & Ermakova, E. P. (2021). Utilizing artificial intelligence in legal practice. In Inshakova, A. O., & Frolova, E. E. (Eds.), *Smart Technologies for the Digitisation of Industry: Entrepreneurial Environment. Smart Innovation, Systems and Technologies* (Vol. 254, pp. 17–27). Springer., DOI: 10.1007/978-981-16-4621-8_2

Goddard, M. (2017). The EU General Data Protection Regulation (GDPR): European regulation that has a global impact. *International Journal of Market Research*, *59*(6), 703–705. DOI: 10.2501/IJMR-2017-050

Imogen, P. V., Sreenidhi, J., & Nivedha, V. (2024). AI-powered legal documentation assistant. *Journal of Artificial Intelligence and Capsule Networks*, *6*(2), 210–226. DOI: 10.36548/jaicn.2024.2.007

Kougias, I., Seremeti, L., & Kalogeras, D. (2016). Promoting inclusion in higher education by adopting the theoretical framework of autopoiesis. *Proceedings of the 11th MIBES Conference*, Heraklion, Crete.

Luger, G.F. (2025). AI ethical issues: From a social perspective. *Artificial Intelligence: Principles and Practice*, 573-599. https://doi.org/DOI: 10.1007/978-3-031-57437-5_26

Maturana, H. R., & Varela, F. J. (1980). *Autopoiesis and Cognition: The realization of the living*. Springer. DOI: 10.1007/978-94-009-8947-4

Novelli, C., Taddeo, M., & Floridi, L. (2024). Accountability in artificial intelligence: What it is and how it works. *AI & Society*, *39*(4), 1871–1882. DOI: 10.1007/s00146-023-01635-y

Papademetriou, C., Ragazou, K., Garefalakis, A., & Anastasiadou, S. (2024). The Role of Artificial Intelligence in Employee Wellness and Mental Health. In Global, I. G. I. (Ed.), *Human Resource Strategies in the Era of Artificial Intelligence* (pp. 29–54). DOI: 10.4018/979-8-3693-6412-3.ch002

Quteishat, E.M.A., Qtaishat, A. and Qutcishat, A.M.A. (2024). Exploring the role of AI in modern legal practice: Opportunities, challenges, and ethical implications. *Journal of Electrical Systems*, 20-6s, 3040-3050.

Souravlas, S., & Anastasiadou, S. (2020). Pipelined Dynamic Scheduling of Big Data Streams. *Applied Sciences (Basel, Switzerland)*, *10*(14), 4796. DOI: 10.3390/app10144796

Souravlas, S., & Anastasiadou, S. (2022). On Implementing Social Community Clouds Based on Markov Models. *IEEE Transactions on Computational Social Systems*. Advance online publication. DOI: 10.1109/TCSS.2022.3213273

Souravlas, S., Anastasiadou, S., Economides, Th., & Katsavounis, S. (2023). Probabilistic Community Detection in Social Networks. *IEEE Access : Practical Innovations, Open Solutions*, *11*, 25629–25641. DOI: 10.1109/ACCESS.2023.3257021

Souravlas, S., Anastasiadou, S., & Katsavounis, S. (2021). A survey on the recent advances of deep community detection. *Applied Sciences (Basel, Switzerland)*, *11*(16), 7179. DOI: 10.3390/app11167179

Souravlas, S., Anastasiadou, S., & Kostoglou, I. (2022). A Novel Method For General Hierarchical System Modeling Via Colored Petri Nets Based on Transition Extractions From Real Data Sets. *Applied Sciences (Basel, Switzerland)*, *13*(1), 339. DOI: 10.3390/app13010339

Souravlas, S., Anastasiadou, S. D., Tantalaki, N., & Katsavounis, S. (2022). A Fair, Dynamic Load Balanced Task Distribution Strategy for Heterogeneous Cloud Platforms Based on Markov Process Modeling. *IEEE Access : Practical Innovations, Open Solutions*, *10*, 26149–26162. DOI: 10.1109/ACCESS.2022.3157435

Teubner, G. (1988). *Autopoietic Law: A new approach to Law and Society*. Walter de Gruyter.

Thirumagal, P. G., Raj, M. A., Naser, S. J., Hussien, N. A., & Abbas, J. K. and vinayagam, S. (2024). Efficient contract analysis and management through AI-powered tool: Time savings and error reduction in legal document review. *Proceedings of the 19th International Conference on Science Technology Engineering and Mathematics*, Chennai, India, 1-6. https://doi.org/DOI: 10.1109/ICONSTEM60960.2024.10568823

Varona, D., & Suarez, J. L. (2022). Discrimination bias, fairness, and trustworthy AI. *Applied Sciences (Basel, Switzerland)*, *12*(12), 5826. DOI: 10.3390/app12125826

Wong, A. (2020). The laws and regulation of AI and autonomous systems. In Strous, L., Johnson, R., Grier, D. A., & Swade, D. (Eds.), *Unimagined Futures – ICT Opportunities and Challenges. IFIP Advances in Information and Communication Technology* (Vol. 555, pp. 38–54). Springer., DOI: 10.1007/978-3-030-64246-4_4

Zhang, Y. (2023). Analysis of the status of artificial intelligence as the subject of law from the perspective of autopoiesis. *Beijing Law Review*, *14*(3), 1–12.

Chapter 6

Cybernetic Intelligence in Intellectual Property Law: AI-Driven Innovation, Detection, and Ethical Challenges

Abhinash Mohanta
https://orcid.org/0000-0002-8732-3202
KIIT University, India

Kyvalya Garikapati
https://orcid.org/0000-0003-0990-6514
KIIT University, India

Shreya
https://orcid.org/0009-0008-3533-797X
KIIT University, India

Nikita Biswal
https://orcid.org/0009-0004-5215-2943
Christ University, India

Akankshya Kanungo
https://orcid.org/0009-0007-6384-6678
Christ University, India

ABSTRACT

This paper explores the transformative role of cybernetic intelligence in intellectual property (IP) law, including its integration in critical areas, such as registration, intellectual property infringement detection, innovation protection, and dispute resolution. IP processes are being reshaped by the introduction of cybernetic sys-

DOI: 10.4018/979-8-3693-9576-9.ch006

tems that improve process efficiency and accuracy in registration and by advanced algorithms that revolutionise the detection of violations. In particular, the paper explores the ethical challenges raised about AI driven innovation like ownership of work created by AI, biases of automated systems and risking monopoly. Further, it analyses the potential of cybernetic tools for dispute resolution that blends data knowledge with People's judgement to the point of fairness. The paper emphasises ethical, legal implications, proposing robust AI regulatory frameworks, transparency and accountability when deploying AI.

INTRODUCTION

Intellectual Property (IP) law provides the basic infrastructure for guarding creativity and innovation for inventors, artists, companies, by providing legal means for their success in competitive environment. It includes patents which give the inventor of a specific technology the sole right to use such technology; trademarks which are symbols, sign or logos that distinguish the goods or services and copyrights which helps ownership of literary, artistic and musical creations by ensuring that the owners of such products control the use of such products. Such legal safeguards promote legal framework that ensures that there is equilibrium between the parties who have rights on their side and the general public that has need to benefit from fruits of innovations and cultural developments. However, with increased and unprecedented technological advancement, traditional IP managements and frameworks are struggling, in fact, are challenged in trying to solve new problems that come with the applications of AI and cybernetic systems. This progression indicates the need to alter IP frameworks in order to incorporate new fashions of creativity and innovations(Radanliev et al., 2020). This chapter adopts a doctrinal and comparative legal analysis supplemented with policy reports from WIPO, EUIPO, and national patent offices.

Artificial intelligence can be viewed as a revolutionary concept in the sphere of intellectual property. Not only it remains as a helpful tool for enhancing human creativity but it is creative apparatus, capable to design inventions, artworks, and designs at the same level of its human counterpart. AI is already impacting IP in various ways; present to transform the IP field broadly(Picht & Thouvenin, 2023). Due to these reasons they reduce the time and effort taken in various clerical activities like patent search and trademark evaluation etc. AI also helps in the identification of violations of Intellectual Property rights, using high-powered statistical analysis to get through large amounts of information to flag users who have violated the rights of owners of protected materials(Ding et al., 2022). However, the extent to which integration of AI into the IP law framework is done has created important questions.

In what ways can the legal system properly assign ownership on those works that are produced autonomously by the AI? There is a crucial question: How can AI satisfy the legal requirements of originality and inventorship that have been set for human inventors? These questions undermine the very core of IP law and raise the need for a complete re-examination of its concepts and ideas. The global divergence in recognizing AI-generated works—most notably illustrated by the DABUS litigation across the U.S., U.K., EU, and South Africa—further underscores the fragmented nature of current IP systems.

The challenges mentioned above can be best understood through cybernetics, a field that aims at analysing interaction, communication, control, and feedback within the systems(Cordeschi, 2004). Cybernetics first emerged in Norbert Wiener's work and has since been used in scientific branches such as engineering, biology or social sciences, and is relatively new to law(Anjaria & Mishra, 2017). Cybernetic tenets are flexibility and dynamic self-organisation – features that contemporary legal structures actively require. From the perspective of the conflicting values that play out under the banner of intellectual property law cybernetic systems can help to refine decisions, identify infringements more effectively, and provide solutions to emergent properties within the legal field(Shekhar, 2020). For example, cybernetic feedforward can be applied in actualizing continual modifications of IP registries to correspond with advanced technology and market conditions. Consequently, the potential of cybernetic approaches lies in the identification of subtle concepts for evaluating the legal personality of AI-generated productions and in creating an environment that is legal for action, enlightened as well as tolerant.

This paper explores the transformative potential of cybernetic intelligence in reshaping intellectual property law, with a particular focus on AI-driven innovation, detection, and the associated ethical challenges. It discusses how aspects of cybernetic systems can work for the overall scheme of modules to include the location and efficiency of registration, infringement discovery, legal position of AI-produced works, and legal evaluation of innovation and dispute resolution of Intellectual Property. Through reflection of these facets, the paper shall establish how concepts in cybernetics and AI technologies can help to foster an effective, transparent and fair IP regime. The research approach applied to this study entails a wider literature review and expert interview, thus providing a wide and multi-perspective investigation of the subject. The literature review is based on the research conducted using articles, statutes, case, and institutional reports for working out the theoretical framework for the study of cybernetics and IP law. In addition, interviews with some experts in both AI and IP law introduces the real world implications and experiences to complement the theoretical frameworks of analysing the concepts to actual usage.

The impact of integrating AI and cybernetic intelligence into intellectual property law constitutes a major paradigm shift between technology and legal systems(Fenglin et al., 2020). This paper attempts to address this ongoing discourse on intellectual property in the age of unprecedented technological advancement by exploring the interface between AI driven innovation and cybernetic adaptability. Taking such a convergence as a starting point, it provides a detailed examination of the problems and opportunities such convergence presents and offers a roadmap for navigating the difficult crossroads of law, technology, and ethics in the age of artificial intelligence.

CYBERNETIC SYSTEMS IN INTELLECTUAL PROPERTY REGISTRATION

Cybernetic integration into IP registration processes represents a fundamental evolution from patent, copyright and trademark management(Chimuka, 2019). Historically, the registration of IP rights has been labour intensive and time consuming with significant manual evaluation processes required on every application. Over the past few decades the advent of AI and cybernetic systems has produced an unprecedented metamorphosis of these procedures, with increased speed, efficiency and accuracy. These systems combine principles of cybernetics, namely feedback, control, and adaptability, with the advanced AI capabilities to streamline the registration processes, in addition to and not as an alternative to, improving the quality of decision making within IP frameworks(Geroulanos & Weatherby, 2020). WIPO's Draft Issues Paper on Intellectual Property and Artificial Intelligence (2020) highlights how adaptive cybernetic tools can support IP offices by enhancing the efficiency of registration frameworks while also flagging ethical and legal inconsistencies in traditional systems.

Registration systems that are backed by artificial intelligence are leading this change. They use machine learning to dissect large data sets and to recognise patterns and trends and to automate some or all stages of the registration process. For example, in the context of patent application, it is possible for the AI systems to search for the prior art in the form of patents, publications and databases and, thus, find out whether a given invention is new and involves an inventive step. When it comes to trademark registration, AI tools help to determine how similar a proposed trademark is to the existing ones, in order to meet legal standards. Likewise, the copyright registrations can also utilise the categorization of works, and checking for the originality of the work and preventing duplication with the help of AI. These applications minimise on mistakes caused by human being and fasten the decision making process thus making it easier and fast for the applicants. Singapore's IP Strategy 2030 sets an early precedent in adopting AI for IP registration, promoting predictive examination models and digital integration to improve transparency and reduce backlogs.

The cybernetic principles are implemented in IP registration systems which are integrated with real time data analysis and feedback loop(Porvazník & Ljudvigová, 2016). Adaptive cybernetic systems dynamically refine their operations using continuous feedback in order to improve their decision making. Thus, for example, cybernetic systems can build on such a real time update of databases with newly filed patents or new scientific publications during the review of a patent application in order to offer a truly dynamic novelty evaluation of an invention. In trademark registrations feedback mechanisms will teach the system from previous decisions to modify its algorithms to achieve higher predictive accuracy and legal compliance with evolving legal standards. Similar systems can also benefit copyright offices such as through real time analytics for trend analysis in creative works that can inform their classification frameworks through timely updates.

One example that has put an illustrative face on these advancements is the use of AI by the United States Patent and Trademark Office (USPTO). To speed up operations, the USPTO introduced AI driven tools, including an AI-based patent classification system, which correctly and quickly categorise patent applications(Berger, 2023). But not only does this reduce administrative burdens, it also promotes constancy in approach to decision making by standardising the criteria for classification. Furthermore, the European Union Intellectual Property Office (EUIPO) has created an AI powered search tool that gives applicants instant advice on the probability of application approval and helps them improve their application before it is submitted(Zhuk, 2023). These systems represent the tipping point for cybernetic integration to revolutionise the registration of IP systems making it faster and more responsive. However, courts have resisted reinterpreting inventorship to include AI, in Thaler v. Commissioner of Patents [Australia, 2021], an initial allowance of AI as inventor was reversed, affirming statutory requirements for human inventorship. In the UK case Stephen L. Thaler v. Comptroller General [2021], the court held that only a natural person can be considered an inventor under existing law, thus closing the door to AI-generated autonomous applications for now.

Nevertheless, the sign up of works created completely or partially by AI may pose distinct challenges. Up to this point, current IP frameworks exist under the presupposition that IP originates from human creators(Vehar & Gils, 2020). On the premise of this art work it becomes confusing to register when the creation is from an artificial intelligence and it becomes unclear what term to use when referring to the authors, the owners, or not even as people are original too. The Cybernetic systems can solve these challenges by nuanced analysis and adaptive decision making. They can be specifically programmed to take account of the roles played by human and non-human actors in the making of that which is being authored, making attribution of ownership much more precise. For example, a cybernetic system could interrogate whether an AI tool was acting as a mere instrument under human direction or its autonomous creation of a creative output(Sarkar, 2023).

Nevertheless, to address these complexities we need not only technical innovation, but also legal reform. Currently, many laws offer no written provisions that are accepted as recognising AI as inventors or authors—perpetuating disputes over ownership and the extent of what is protected by AI created works(Xiao, 2022). When such scenarios arise, cybernetic systems might help policymakers simulate the consequences of different legal frameworks and provide data driven insights about how different outcomes might affect innovation, development, and interests of society(Sastry et al., 2024). Moreover, these systems can also permit a more inclusive style of regulatory development by starting to collect and analyse feedback from creators, rights holders, and the industry at large.

The importance of ensuring transparency and accountability is reflected in real world applications of cybernetic systems in IP registration(McKernon et al., 2024). Since these systems are becoming more and more woven into the making of decisions, it is important to understand how decisions are arrived at. Algorithmic processes need to be transparent not only to gain the trust of applicants but also because it helps controls over legal authorities(Kaminski, 2020). For example, such an explainable AI model employed in trademark registration can furnish applicants with an elaborate reason as to why their proposed trademark can be potentially in conflict with an existing one, so that it can be addressed proactively. Systems which detail their prior art search methodology can be of similar benefit in patent applications; allowing both examiners and applicants to better understand the basis for approval or rejection.

Despite the advantages that flow from the integration of differentiated cybernetic systems into the framework of IP registration, its moral and realism implications call for attention. The utilisation of AI to make important choices creates significant rules to protect against bias in algorithms that might lock out applicants or maintain unfairness in the use of IPs(Elliott et al., 2021). Thus, the study addresses the issue of how to make the cybernetic systems responsive to various legal systems and cultural environments as a vital objective that is essential worldwide implementation of the system. For example, the concept of originality that applies to copyright statute may differ from one country to another; thus, such systems should retain variation in the difference in the criteria from one country to another but should be consistent within a certain legal system.

DETECTION OF IP INFRINGEMENTS THROUGH CYBERNETIC INTELLIGENCE

There has always been a critical challenge in the detection of intellectual property (IP) infringements, made worse in the age of the internet by the sheer scale and complexity of global marketplaces(Chaudhry, 2023). Lack of control increases opportunities for automation of the theft, use, and distribution of protected intellectual property and the proliferation of digital content, e-commerce platforms, and decentralised systems(Garcia-Macia & Goyal, 2020). Against this background, IP infringement detection through the application of cybernetic intelligence emerges as a transformative approach. By combining the computational power of AI with the feedback driven adaptability of cybernetics, these systems provide real time, scalable and efficient means for monitoring violations across a very wide spectrum of platforms and jurisdictions. Notably, countries like Japan and South Korea have already deployed blockchain-based timestamping mechanisms such as WIPO PROOF to verify the authenticity of digital content and support cybernetic enforcement measures.

Cybernetic intelligence is the basis of automated infringement detection systems for digital and physical IP violations that are becoming more widespread. The systems use machine learning algorithms, neural networks and pattern recognition techniques to detect the unauthorised usage of copyrighted materials, the counterfeit usage of trademarks and patents(Porvazník & Ljudvigová, 2016). For example, such systems can analyse enormous volumes of user generated content, advertisements and transaction data in digital marketplaces to identify activities that may be infringing. Automating such processes allows them to not only identify blatant duplicates but also catch subductions or slight manoeuvres on covered works. AI driven tools paired with cybernetic frameworks are utilised in physical marketplaces to monitor supply chains, validate product authenticity and flag counterfeit products(Anjum & Dutta, 2022). That dual applicability provides a full frontal assault on IP violations in an interconnected world. One such real-world implementation is Amazon's "Project Zero," which empowers brand owners to detect and remove counterfeits using AI models integrated with cybernetic tracking systems.

Infringement detection in cybernetic systems takes advantage of their ability to use feedback loops for continuous learning and improvement(Korba et al., 2024). Unlike static systems that run on preset rules, cybernetic models change to fit increasingly complex infringing behaviours. Data from each detected violation contributes to a repository of data from which future processes of detection can learn, enabling systems to identify future trends or techniques used by infringers. These systems are such that cybernetic feedback mechanisms can be used to refine their algorithms according to the false positives or negatives encountered during their first operations(Talukder et al., 2022). It allows this iterative learning process to further enhance accuracy in detection, reduce reliance on manual oversight, and guarantees response to new forms of IP violations as generative AI technologies or blockchain based counterfeit goods emerge.

Content ID uses machine learning algorithms that analyse uploaded videos and compare them against one giant database of copyrighted material made available by rights holders(How Google Fights Piracy, 2023). The system matches and then lets the rights holders choose from amongst a series of enforcement actions — such as collecting revenue alongside the video, blocking the video, or monitoring its performance. Content ID exemplifies the fusion of cybernetics and AI: By only running on rights holder dispute or validation, it makes the feedback real time and helps refine its accuracy(Zhang et al., 2018). Further, the system's capacity to scale up to millions of uploads per day illustrates the unprecedented efficacy of cybernetic models of addressing such volume of IP protection as a computational process.

The obligations under Article 41 of the TRIPS Agreement require member states to ensure effective IP enforcement, and cybernetic systems provide scalable tools to help nations meet this mandate by aligning detection capacity with legal compliance mechanisms. However, automated detection systems like Content ID are very effective, but their global applicability still needs to be viewed in terms of the international IP enforcement dynamics(Gray & Suzor, 2020). In addressing cross border challenges, harmonising and bridging out jurisdictional differences, cybernetic intelligence performs a very important role. The enforcement complexity of IP violations on digital platforms often results from global nature because digital platforms span multiple jurisdictions causing variations in legal standards and procedural requirements. These challenges are solved by cybernetic systems, computerised systems with multilingual and multi-jurisdictional data processing capabilities which know across borders and point with enforcement actions to relevant legal framework.

As an example, cybernetic systems can apply linguistics nuances, local market trend, to detect trademark infringement on e-commerce platforms covering diverse countries based upon the location of the malicious upload and jurisdiction(Yurkevich & Kryukova, 2021). Real time detection of counterfeit goods entering major supply chains is achievable with these systems connecting to customs databases and international trade monitoring systems. Such capabilities facilitate cooperation between national IP offices, international organisations, such as the World Intellectual Property Organisation (WIPO), and private stakeholders, acting collectively in an IP enforcement environment.

Cybernetic systems in international IP infringement detection involves more than the harmonisation of enforcement mechanisms but also targets specific system issues such as jurisdictional arbitrage. When the infringers intentionally use loophole which exits between different country's local law in order to escape from actions, the resultant cybernetics models can give real life facts together with comparative analysis to come up with good recommendations on reforms of various international laws related to IP(Kusumaputra et al., 2023). Through further examination of infringement transnational patterns, these systems shall determine the existing emoluments and recommend strategies to make up a suitable enforcement system in different countries.

The other key area where cybernetic intelligence is helpful in IP detection is the new technologies that challenge normal enforcement measures in IP protection. For example, the development of generative AI devices that can generate realistic fakes of different items or deepfake content requires new answers for IP rights. These difficulties may be effectively solved by cybernetic systems containing elements of higher pattern recognition and context analysis, enabling separating lawful from unlawful utilisation of such technologies. In the same way, with the use of blockchain and decentralised platforms, cybernetic system can easily understand the transaction previews and the patterns of smart contract to fully recognise instances of piracy or unlawful distribution of copyrighted items or patented work(Liu et al., 2021).

Similarly, cybernetic intelligence also enables engagement between the private players and public enforcing agencies allowing an integrated approach towards identification of IP infringement. The government and private entities can work in tandem to ensure proprietary detection tools created by multi-national companies are harmonised with government systems in order to envisage versatile databases to augment detection. For example, organisations managing e-commerce, brand owners, and customs authorities can use cybernetic models to detect and visualise the supply chains and monitor the fake products as well as coordinate the actions on the case in real-time.

Furthermore, the functionality of cybernetic systems makes them relevant to high volumes as well as specific areas of need. Current large-scale platforms such as YouTube and Amazon utilise high-end algorithms for detecting such videos, while many more modest platforms as well as individual creators may not have access to any specialised tools(Lu & Nam, 2021). Cybernetic intelligence can provide solutions that will reach the requirements of these comparatively minor stakeholders, and solutions that can do so without being excessively costly. For example, the integration of open-source tools for artificial intelligence with the help of modular cybernetic systems can help independent artists to effectively deal with the situation because such frameworks would help them save a significant amount of money on the extraction of their rights.

Besides the advanced technology that the cybernetic systems may discover, there is the need to consider some ethical situations and responsibility in the detection of the IP infringements(Rosa et al., 2003). It is necessary to assert that such systems should not only be able to detect threats, but also be virtually impenetrable to them; however, they must also be devoid of prejudice, designed to refrain from misuse, and secure users' rights to privacy. For instance, Systems that are implemented on the face of social media sites have to incorporate a strong vernacular for IP protection while at the same time avoiding situations where incidental uses of copyrighted content, permitted under fair use laws, are penalised heavily. Procedural controls and accountability of the decision-making process, as well as conflict resolution procedures, are critical to sustaining trust in individuals and organisations as well as following ethical guidance.

AI-DRIVEN INNOVATION AND ETHICAL CHALLENGES IN IP LAW

Artificial intelligence is becoming a creator and innovator and as it does so it is redefining the boundaries of intellectual property law and offering and demanding rigorous exploration of what it offers and demands(Abbott, 2022). Among these types of systems, one that has advanced the most in the capacity to create art is created by AI, which makes use of more advanced technology, particularly machine learning and neural networks, and which now offers to produce inventions and design innovative solutions in any field. To date, these developments have major implications for intellectual property frameworks since AI created works seem to raise questions of authorship, ownership, and ethical accountability. This transformation is accompanied by an array of ethical considerations, including bias, fairness, and the impact of such systems on traditionally underrepresented groups in the creative and innovative sectors.

AI has been one of its revolutionising contributions into intellectual property as a creator and innovator. Generative AI models such as OpenAI's GPT-4 and DALL-E have produced literary compositions, visual artworks, and even music that rival human creativity in complexity and originality(Ismayilzada et al., 2024). Among other things, in the domain of patents, AI systems such as IBM's Watson have helped AI, analyse large data set and find novel pathways to innovation recourse(Nisbet et al., 2018). These AI outputs are a genuine threat to the framework of intellectual property law, which until recently relied on such human authorship for its foundation. As AI becomes more crucial to devising new products and services, there is therefore a need to revisit the laws governing who may claim to be an 'author' or an 'inventor.'

One of the most contentious issues in AI-driven innovation is the question of ownership. When an AI system generates a patentable invention or creates a copyrightable work, determining the rightful owner becomes a complex legal and ethical challenge(Munshi & Barai, 2022). Who is the owner of AI, the party that constructed it, the party that controlled its operation, or the party funding the construction? This is even more confusing especially when the AI systems are fully autonomous and have limited human interactions. For instance, in the "DABUS" case where an AI system produced two inventions that could be patented, courts around the common law world were torn between whether they can legally award inventor status to Artificial Intelligence. While some jurisdictions denied the possibility to recognise AI as an inventor due to the conflict with literal statutory provisions that claims only the human can be an inventor, others understood the necessity of legal amendments to meet this new reality. In contrast, China's IP Court issued a 2020 ruling rejecting AI-generated authorship outright, reaffirming that current Chinese copyright law applies only to natural persons.

There are ethical questions about AI created works not only about who owns it, but also who is accountable for it. Determining liability for an AI system when that invention or creative work infringes on existing intellectual property is a complicated problem(Dhanol, 2023). It might happen, for example, that an AI algorithm gives birth to a melody for a song that matches some song already copyrighted out there. But who is responsible for such an infringement? These situations emphasise that legal frameworks are needed to articulate accountability in AI driven development so that stakeholders know their rights and responsibilities in this system. The 2023 lawsuit Getty Images v. Stability AI further raised questions of derivative authorship, as Stability's models were trained on copyrighted photographs without licensing. WIPO's current position maintains that AI cannot be a rights-holder under existing frameworks like the Berne Convention, reinforcing the need for human attribution in IP systems.

Bias and fairness also emerge as one of the most important dimensions of ethical issues in AI-driven IP systems. Despite evident advantages of AI that results in objective conclusions fundamentally based on AI learning process and improved efficiency, the AI systems are dependent on the data(Ferrara, 2023). If such datasets are themselves biassed in terms of historical discriminations or injustice towards any group, then the derived outputs themselves are going to be coloured with such prejudices. For instance, in the case of the examination of patents, the AI systems-learning from historical data of application might give preference to inventions from the mature industries or geographical locations that have had prior high patent filing, and thereby discriminating against the minority inventors or no such regions. Also in copyright, generative AI systems may also likely reinstate the biases of the dominant culture by replicating artistic styles or cultural assets by ; marginalised groups. Ferrara (2023) has shown how biases in AI-generated creative outputs perpetuate systemic inequality in IP access. For instance, AI systems trained on Western art traditions have been shown to undervalue indigenous or minority art forms due to dataset imbalances, raising concerns about digital cultural erasure.

The currently existing biases have ways of being solved with cybernetic intelligence through feedback and learning loops within the IP systems. Through the examination of the effects of registering and enforcement decisions, the cybernetic models can detect tendencies towards the bias in the system and reprogram the equations to rule for equality(Pagan et al., 2023). For example, cybernetic systems could be programmed to prompt incentives more often for increasing diversity in training data sets of AI such that the creators and innovators in the field are more equal. Moreover, incorporating information regarding transparency procedures into the conceptualizations of cybernetic systems could also give the stakeholders insight as to how the decision making process unfolds, the presence of bias and the ways through which they can be disputed.

Further case studies of AI generated works highlight the ethical and legal uncertain territory for innovation driven by artificial intelligence. For example, case in point is that AI system called 'Aiva' that can compose classical music. In Aiva's case, we see their compositions available for commercial release and widely recognised for their artistic quality, which brings in interesting concerns about copyright protection and authorship. Though the creators of Aiva assert copyright over its works, sceptics say the makers of Aiva are overstepping; copyright law was conceived on a foundation of human creativity, and there are concerns automatic creations should not be included under this axiom(Zulić, 2019).

Another illustrative case involves AI-invented patents, where disputes over authorship have led to significant legal and ethical debates. The aforementioned DABUS case, in which an AI system created a fractal food container and a neural flame detection system, highlights the inconsistencies in global IP law(Munshi & Barai, 2022). The United States Patent and Trademark Office (USPTO) and the European Patent Office (EPO) did not accept the concept of AI inventorship, However, South Africa granted patents regarding DABUS as an inventor(Patil, 2023). These different strategies merely mirror larger questions about how IPs should further evolve to incorporate AI as an innovation factor. A major issue has emerged over generative models trained on unlicensed copyrighted materials; OpenAI, for instance, has faced lawsuits over the use of books and images in model training datasets.

Beyond innovation in AI itself, there are ethical questions about how AI derived resources could be used as derivative works and become a means to cultural appropriation. Many generative AI systems, trained on gigantic libraries of copyrighted materials, generate outputs that so closely resemble existing works that their unauthorised derivatives and the risk for infringement become more serious issues(Jiang et al., 2023). Transformative innovation, for example, is AI generated art that mimics a celebrated artist's style — to some, this is transformative innovation, to others, it is unethical appropriation(Exploring the Impact of Generative AI on Intellectual Property Law and the Future of Artistic Expression, 2023). This raises ethical tensions between transformative use, which fosters innovation, and exploitation, which undermines original authorship and market fairness. Not only these controversies emphasise the need for clear guidelines in regards to the use of copyrighted materials in developing training AI systems and the protection scope of AI generated outputs, but these controversies also shed further light on the systemic questions about fair use and the reach of copyright protection in AI-generated material.

Also, when AI generates solutions for global problems softly embedded in the climate change or healthcare strategy, it increases the ethical concern the whole world has to have to equally access the innovation. Artificial intelligence that is capable of creating and proposing patented solutions in the field of renewable energy, pharmaceuticals or any other area may hereby perpetuate the existing social injustice as it brings in patented and protected solutions the right to which may be attained solely by representatives of certain elite universities or oligarchs. As discussed in this paper, the tension between innovation and diffusion of innovation in the context of learning technologies for teaching and learning at a distance needs to be addressed by policy-makers and other stakeholders.

AI, IP law and ethics at their intersection, are also subject to questions around the transparency and accountability of AI-driven decision making processes. This is most evident when you use AI systems to resolve IP disputes or decide on the validity of patent applications — as these involve human fairness and neutrality(Artificial Intelligence Collides with Patent Law, 2023). The nature of the 'black box' AI algorithms, which often lack a clear explanation for their output, is the reason why we need explainable AI models in IP law(Almada, 2023). These concerns can be mitigated through transparency protocols, audit trails, and stakeholder oversight of AI driven systems.

Consequently, AI is revolutionising how the concept of intellectual property is perceived, and, with that, the ethical liabilities inherent to its application by developers, users, and policymakers(Generative Artificial Intelligence: The Impact on Intellectual Property Crimes, 2023). Those that are creating the AI systems, have a duty of creating systems that are fair, accountable and for inclusive nature. Critics, artists, inventors, and lawyers are among the most interested in such systems and still, they have to understand the various ethical implications of AI usage for new inventions and creations. In turn, the regulators have to develop measures facilitating an improvement in these spheres, yet at the same time addressing the problems of emerging technologies in terms of their impact on society and humanity as a whole.

CYBERNETIC INTELLIGENCE IN IP DISPUTE RESOLUTION

The blend of advanced algorithms, predictive analytics and feedback-based adaptability which cybernetic intelligence brings to the discourse is reimagining how intellectual property disputes are resolved(Barnett & Treleaven, 2023). The ability for AI driven systems to quickly and accurately analyse large volumes of data has the potential to reduce arbitration and mediation processes. Driven by this innovation are cybernetic models based on adaptive learning mechanisms that minimise errors in decision making and enhance fairness by aligning with law and policy(De'Shazer, 2024).

AI Driven Systems facilitating automation of complex arbitration as well as mediation processes form the basis for the integration of cybernetic intelligence in IP dispute resolution. Based on data derived from precedents, statutory frameworks, and global IP treaties, these systems allow for categorization of disputes in a timely fashion and for providing insights tailored on a case by case basis. In practise, these systems not only reduce administrative burden but also lead to data driven resolutions that circumvent errors in manual evaluation(Rahmatian, 2015). For example, advanced machine learning models are applied to extract patterns out of historical data, predict likely outcomes and make recommendations that remain consistent with presently accepted legal norms. Platforms such as Modria (USA), eBRAM (Hong Kong), and SmartSettle (Canada) are using AI-driven modules to expedite IP-related dispute resolution through real-time analysis and predictive outcome tools. However, critical legal scholarship has questioned whether fully automated arbitration systems satisfy the right to a fair hearing under natural justice, particularly in the absence of human oversight.

Feedbacks in cybernetic systems plays a significant role of enhancing decision making fairness and accuracy. These loops allow systems to improve due to result outcomes, legal assessments of a case, and comments from key personnel and agencies in a sequential manner throughout time. An example whereby this information is evidenced is how these systems respond to the fine details of the international IP legal regime. Cybernetic models work to adapt to the relative legal differences between jurisdictions while trying to work through cross jurisprudential conflicts in order to maintain a high level of cross-jurisdictional parity(Jerker & Svantesson, 2023). This characteristic serves the pursued system most beneficially, particularly when such cases present opposing laws, or rules, where people's reason might fail to find a solution. The systems which have possibility to learn in real-time can change recommendations based on updated treaties, judgments and procedural rules.

One prime use of cybernetic systems is the use in predictive legal models that employ big data analysis in identifying probabilities of case resolution(Regulation by Machine, 2023). These models give the stakeholders possibilities of likely resolutions through analysis of historical trends, judicial behaviour and probably the case conditions. Such predictions not only help the litigants and mediators to make the right decision but also help to prevent the disputes form going to court since it provides an outline of the negotiation. These predictive capabilities are especially useful in calibration of damages in patent infringement cases where technical claims are hard to understand. Through the use of cybernetic models, overlapping claims can be quickly identified, the viability of patents can be gauged, and fair recommendations for compensation based on previous cases can be easily made.

The use of cybernetic systems in IP dispute resolution as it has been presented here is far from perfect, and it brings a number of challenges, especially in the issues of: fairness, transparency as well as accountability. There is an inherent issue generally referred to as the "black-box" dilemma, inherent in the hard-to-decipher algorithmic processes involved in decision making(Reidenberg et al., 2023). Addressing this issue requires the adoption of explainable AI (XAI) frameworks, which ensure that decision-making processes are interpretable and traceable(Petkovic, 2022). Transparency can be again enforced by open audits, documentation of the system operations, and record of each case in detail. Sophisticated accountability mechanisms should define roles and responsibilities thereof in a way that will force developers, operators and users of such technologies to be in compliance with well set ethical standards. The EU AI Act (2024) mandates that high-risk AI systems—including those used in legal and dispute resolution contexts—must provide transparency, traceability, and human oversight. Almada (2023) further critiques the opacity of legal tech algorithms, describing how the "black box" nature of AI can undermine procedural fairness and judicial accountability.

Ethical concerns extend to the potential biases embedded in cybernetic systems, which may inadvertently disadvantage certain parties. A concrete example is that datasets the trains the systems may foreshadow historical inequities and perpetuate unfair practices. In order to alleviate this risk, fairness oriented algorithm design must be at the forefront of interest for developers by using a diverse training dataset and rigorous bias detection protocols. Moreover, a multidisciplinary composition of legal experts, technologists, and ethicists can help to set up systems that are not merely technologically robust, but that are also congruent with basic societal values.

An expert view emphasises that the use of cybernetic intelligence as a potential and problem solving in IP disputes. The benefits of AI-systems are also apparent in terms of the better organizational improvements, as pointed out by Miss Sneha, an Assistant Professor at Xavier Law School, XIM University, where AI provides efficiency and automation of research and new legal statements. However, she notes that there is the aspect of design that must be put into consideration in order to avoid biased systems(Sneha et al., 2024). As she rightly points out, feedback loops are used in improving the accuracy of estimates by taking into consideration feedback from key stakeholders and differences in requirements from one jurisdiction to another. One of the strengths of cybernetic systems is the possibility of synchronizing the meanings of interpretations of such international IP treaties, connecting the gaps in the settlements of conflicts.

Miss Sneha highlights specific procedural challenges associated with orchestrating cybernetic intelligence as an asset within IP frameworks, such as jurisdictional discrepancies, accountability for automated decisions, and data sensitivity worries. As such, there are a number of legislative hurdles that must be addressed here, as the legal status of AI generated findings needs to be defined, boundaries for ethical use of AI need to be set and international regulations need to be harmonised. In addition, she argues for including robust metrics in evaluating these systems, including accuracy, efficiency, fairness and user satisfaction. These benchmarks indicate that cybernetic systems comply with the law and ethical expectation(Bag et al., 2024). Cybernetic systems support Article 63 of the TRIPS Agreement, which obliges transparency in the publication of IP laws and decisions by ensuring digital access to real-time legal data and interpretations. Additionally, harmonization trends can be tracked via the WIPO Lex database, which cybernetic systems can integrate into predictive tools to reconcile national regulatory differences.

The practical application of cybernetic intelligence in IP dispute resolution is demonstrated in case studies. For instance, eBay's VeRO programme and YouTube's Content ID show how AI based systems can be programmed to keep an eye and solve copyright infringement issues(Riccio, 2013). In particular, though these platforms are mainly about detection, the dispute resolution they provide forms a base for more complex cybernetic approaches. These systems resolve individual cases of infringement while at the same time using patterns of infringement as a reminder of enforcement strategies that prevent violations in more general terms.

Besides their use in automated detection, cybernetic systems are also utilised in arbitration processes for more complex patent disputes. There are a few arbitration platforms that have used AI to integrate technology to aid in speeding up dispute resolution by processing claims, weighing evidence and helping suggest settlements. Designed for solving e commerce disputes, Modria uses AI to categorise claims and enable evidence uploads before posing resolution pathways that have paved the way for broader legal disputes(Shackelford & Raymond, 2014). Equally, SmartSettle includes advanced algorithms for eNegotiation, analysing what others are offering and generating settlements that are in the optimal interest of the parties(Alessa, 2022). Cross border dispute management is enabled by the eBRAM International Online Dispute Resolution Centre, which uses AI to manage evidencing assessment and generating recommendations using automated mechanisms(Lin, 2023). Platforms such as JAMS (Judicial Arbitration and Mediation Services)(, 2018) is also investigating the application of AI methods to document management, evidence analysis and for seeking data driven insights into arbitral outcomes. However, application of these platforms typically involves human oversight in order to provide procedural fairness and transparency; these systems are capable of significantly reducing resolution time while still remaining highly accurate. But the challenge comes in trying to ensure that these automatic decisions should meet procedural fairness and follow what we may think of as legal principles. All these challenges can only be tackled by the means of human oversight, ethical principles and sophisticated algorithmic protection measures.

The other area of application is in the online dispute resolution (ODR) platforms which provide accessible and cost effective solutions to IP conflicts(Online Dispute Resolution Standards of Practice, 2023). These platforms are enhanced by their cybernetic intelligence, which automates case intake, passively gathers evidence, and recommends on the case based on legal precedent. These work in the form of systems that democratise access to justice for small creators and entrepreneurs, especially those who lack the resources to pursue traditional litigation. Cybernetic ODR platforms reduce cost and simplify procedures in a more inclusive IP ecosystem by cutting costs and simplifying procedures.

Despite these advancements, the ethical implications of predictive legal models remain a subject of debate. Some critics consider that, such approach can contribute to the reproducing of existing biases while others explained that, the usage of such models can precisely increase the objectivity and standardisation of systems(Greene et al., 2020). These concerns suggest that even where it is possible to automate much of the social networking process, safeguards must still be put in place in order to prevent the automation of decision making. Moreover, the incorporation of ethical standards and appropriate implementation of the international human rights standards is crucial on the subject of public confidence.

The role of cybernetic intelligence in addressing cross-border IP disputes is particularly noteworthy. Cybernetic systems harmonise interpretations of international treaties and conventions, in order to achieve consensus among the stakeholders on issues that are increasingly unresolvable personally. Natural language processing models (NLP) that are multi-lingual allow real time translation and analysis of legal documents, and cuts down misunderstanding and improve collaboration. The capabilities provide such invaluable contributions to the resolution of disputes involving multinational corporations and international IP portfolios where jurisdiction differences can render negotiations difficult.

Within the framework of the Trade Related Aspects of Intellectual Property Rights (TRIPS) Agreement, Articles 41 and 63, and the World Trade Organisation (WTO) Dispute Settlement Mechanism, the relevance of cybernetic intelligence is particularly significant. Article 41 cites fair and efficient enforcement of IP rights, which meshes perfectly with the capacity of cybernetic instruments to speed up use of dispute resolution and slow the progression of a decision(Fenglin et al., 2020). Predictive analytics, intelligent case flow management and automation is used by these systems to help achieve fair and equitable resolutions. Similarly Article 63's requirement of transparency, AI driven platforms that automatically disperse legal judgments in real time also promote public access to IP laws and rulings via user-friendly digital interface.

Cybernetic intelligence may also have potential for the WTO Dispute Settlement Mechanism in relation to TRIPS-related disputes. That way, the use of virtual platforms, decision-support systems, and multilingual natural language processing (NLP) is possible in handling cases efficiently. These advancements increase procedural justice, increase efficiency and increase the level of international cooperation in the fight against IP issues. By embedding these capabilities, cybernetic systems harmonise with the international legal rules in the management of extraterritorial conflicts.

PROTECTING AI-CREATED INNOVATION THROUGH CYBERNETIC SYSTEMS

The growth of AI-based inventions presents new and interesting questions for the legal system around intellectual property. Unlike traditional human inventions, these innovations originate from the interactions between human inventors and Artificial Intelligence and hence, come with unique issues regarding their legal protection(When Artificial Intelligence Systems Produce Inventions: An Alternative Model for Patent Law at the 3A Era, 2024). The dynamics of the legal and technological environment can be addressed by Cybernetic intelligence which provides viable solutions for the protection of AI generated inventions. This section explores how cybernetic systems play a part in helping to safeguard such innovations, how innovation and accessibility can be harmonised and how adaptive IP frameworks can be developed to address these challenges.

The dynamic nature of technology requires that the IP law be dynamic as well. Cybernetic intelligence helps enable this adaptability because trends, precedents and policies are constantly changing(Picht & Thouvenin, 2023). Through using machine learning models, NLP, and predictive analytical methods cybernetic systems detect new patterns in artificial intelligence created works to include inventions, creative designs, and algorithms. Such real-time data analysis facilitates a better understanding of the IP regulators to fine-tune the laws and policies with respect to AI-related innovations, pointing out that the legal environment is different due to the nature of AI-related innovations. Picht & Thouvenin (2023) have also proposed a "tiered protection" model, where the degree of IP rights granted depends on the level of human input involved in the AI-generated innovation.

Another important area of cybernetic adaptation is in reshaping the notion of author and inventor and, by extension, ownership. Where it concerns AI systems, the current IP laws have been designed with the emphasis on human beings as creators and therefore, lacks provisions. Cybernetic systems are capable of accommodating such situations by adopting fluid concepts of authorship in which human and Artificial intelligence can both be considered authors(Xiao, 2022). For instance, an AI that creates new chemical compounds may work with a human chemist where both will need to agree on the contribution to the work. The cybernetic intelligence makes certain that these contributions are assessed in a fair manner and therefore promotes a fair distribution of attributions.

Also, cybernetic systems help enhance the simultaneous of laws on IP across different jurisdictions. That some countries allow AI to obtain a patent, while others do not, create legal gaps. Through examination of legal frameworks of various countries, cybernetic systems give policymakers important recommendations to encourage the formulation of harmonised strategies. These systems can also reveal the lack of provision in international legal frameworks, including the TRIPS Agreement, proposing changes to address the AI-related developments.

Protecting AI created innovations presents a critical challenge of providing robust IP protections while ensuring open access to technological progress. Sometimes overly rigid protections can slow innovation and sometimes overly lenient protections can undermine the desire to be creative. Cybernetic systems are pivotal in walking this fine line by providing data driven information on how regulatory decisions will affect cyber security.

Through simulations and predictive modeling, cybernetic systems assess the long-term effects of granting or denying IP rights to AI-generated works. For example, they can predict whether granting exclusive rights to AI-created software code will spur innovation in that domain or hinder access to foundational technologies. From these scenarios, the authors make policy recommendations for IPR that facilitate technological development whilst maintaining reasonable public access.

Furthermore, cybernetic systems enable the development of a pyramidal structure of IP protection for AI inventions. Unlike the generic systems of protection where all innovations are protected in the same manner, tiered protections accept that all innovations do not deserve the same degree of protection(Xue et al., 2021). In other words, an AI-generated drug could be more protected than an AI-written poetry. Cybernetic models assess the social and economical returns of each innovation in order to suggest adequate levels of protection that will ensure the most desirable outcome. The USPTO's 2024 inventorship guidance also distinguishes between AI-assisted and AI-generated inventions, recognizing the former as potentially protectable while excluding the latter under current U.S. law.

An important aspect of balancing innovation and protection is fostering collaboration among stakeholders. Cybernetic systems that can support the inventors and AI developers when entering into communication and negotiation with other stakeholders such as policymakers with the public at large. For example, the AI-powered platforms can take surveys, gauge public opinion and moderate discussions on sore issues such as ownership of copyright in music developed by AI. This approach reaches out to as many people as possible in a bid to get unbiased view hence making the regulatory frameworks to reflect the biases hence increasing the chances that they will be well accepted.

In fact, several IP offices all around the world have harnessed cybernetic intelligence to craft adaptive regulatory frameworks that space protection in AI generated innovations. These frameworks show how cybernetic systems can meet the challenge of creativity driven by AI, without over extending in the process.

The European Patent Office (EPO)

It is found that the EPO has introduced use of the AI tools to enhance examination of patent for the inventions in Artificial Intelligence(Laycock, 2023). Since such technology falls under patents, the EPO is able to use cybernetic systems to look for trends in patent submissions when it comes to AI and adjust accordingly. For instance, the AI-powered features conduct analysis of claims for AI-derived algorithms and suggest decisions on their patentability. Such efforts suggest technological responsiveness that accords with the legal work environment while retaining legalism.

The United States Patent and Trademark Office (USPTO)

Currently, as for the AI generated works based on copyright and patent laws, the USPTO has sought to continue its AI-driven update(USPTO Issues Inventorship Guidance and Examples for AI-Assisted Inventions, 2024). It is composed of an AI-assisted consultation mechanism where inputs from various stakeholders are assessed, dominant issues are recognised and appropriate solutions are recommended based on various industries. For example, the United States Patent and Trademark Office USPTO has proposed protection of limited copyrights for artworks created by AI while retaining the primary algorithms used for creating such arts, open for use. This case shows how through cybernetic systems such interests might be reconciled in a manner of establishing balanced system.

Singapore's IP Office (IPOS)

Singapore's IPOS is an example of the pro-active utilisation of AI-driven systems in the form of estimative prejudgment of future trends in AI-generated creations(Singapore IP Strategy 2030, 2024). Therefore, through the help of applied machine learning models, IPOS identifies fields that show potential for AI-generated creativity as in the approaches to generation in architecture or generative drafting of legal documents. These informations can help IPOS to preventively modify regulations, which creates an effective and progressive IP system. This kind of adaptability does not only help regulate protection in order to preserve existing innovations but also assists in creating it for future innovation.

WIPO's AI Policy Tracker

The World Intellectual Property Organisation (WIPO) has recently started using an AI policy tracker that is used in the monitoring of policy affairs concerning artificial intelligence all around the world(WIPO Technology Trends 2019, 2021). This instrument employs 'cyber-intelligence' to collect information on the new laws, judgments, and technologies regarding AI-created content. Based on this information, WIPO offers its member states legal recommendations on how to accredit its IP laws. The AI policy tracker demonstrates what cybernetic systems enable in terms of global cooperation with reference to the case of AI innovation contenders. The AI Policy Tracker serves as both a comparative law resource and a cybernetic monitoring tool, enabling adaptive governance based on real-time global policy shifts.

ETHICAL AND LEGAL IMPLICATIONS OF CYBERNETIC INTELLIGENCE IN LP LAW

The incorporation of cybernetic intelligence into IP has dramatically transformed aspects of registration, protection, and litigation of IP rights(Guadamuz, 2024). While these developments enhance efficiency and bring new ideas into practise they also present deep ethical and legal questions. The following are challenges which need to be addressed before AI systems are implemented in IP processes; Ownership of AI systems, The Responsibility of AI systems, Algorithm Bias and Legal Frameworks(Corrêa et al., 2022). This section examines the ethical issues in

IP law cybernetic systems, identify the threats, establish the need for regulation and predict the future difficulties in a constantly evolving relationship between AI and IP.

There are several issues of ethics when it comes to the issue of cybernetic systems within the purview of the law concerning IP. One major issue is the question of who owns what when the work of AI comes up with an innovation(Eshraghian, 2020). The basic concept of protection in traditional IP regimes is based on human ingenuity, which becomes blurred when some or the entire creation is made by AI or in collaboration with it. The debates about the legal ownership of the creative work created by AI or who has a right to be considered an inventor in relation to an AI-developed invention have not been answered.

Another ethical concern is the lack of transparency in AI decision-making processes. A lot of AI driven IP systems are 'black box', the decisions on grant or reject of IP rights provided little insight into how such decisions are being made(Hilty et al., 2021). From this opacity comes decisions that are hard to fight or understand, fairness and accountability issues abound. For example, an AI system could reject a patent application if the applicant can't see or challenge the proprietary algorithms the system uses to reject it. Maintaining trust in their operation requires us to ensure that these systems satisfy principle of explainability and transparency.

Also, bringing cybernetic systems for enforcement of intellectual property rights forebodes privacy invasion due to surveillance. Many AI tools that work with possible violation of IP rights presuppose large-scale data collection and analysis and can be invasive of the rights to privacy of individuals. A major, and possibly the most pressing ethical dilemma, when it comes to innovation in this domain is the balance between IP rights and protection on personal data. This concern intensifies when infringement detection systems rely on sensitive inputs such as biometric identifiers or geolocation data, raising major red flags under global data protection laws.

Applications of AI systems in IP law can be characterised as high risk given the fact that they regulate and profile economic interests, determine the direction of innovations, and affect individual rights. A specific risk area relates to the introduction of a bias or discrimination aspect into IP-related decisions. Machine learning algorithms can re-emulate such historical biases in IP registrations, or actual enforcement of IP rights. For instance, the past approvals of the patents may have been inclined with specific industries or demographics, thus an AI system would help in cementing such imbalances.

The application of AI in IP dispute thereby also has its disadvantageous impact of unfair consequences. Due to the lack of the ability to grasp some context, specific cases may be best left to ordinary software or at least their analysis supplemented by a specialist who understands the context of a particular case due to their cultural or other background. That is, when it comes to controversies on use of trademark that has some correlation with cultural symbolism or local colloquial language the confusion can be easily understood by an AI model based on some normalised data samples. These weaknesses give season to deterioration of justice or fairness in decisions dictated by the AI technology. UNESCO's AI Ethics Framework (2021) explicitly warns that AI applications in governance and legal processes must avoid undermining human dignity and privacy—an imperative directly applicable to IP surveillance and enforcement tools.

One of the biggest threats related to AI application in the IP processes is over-dependency on the systems. While implementing the details of AI permits organisation to achieve their goals more efficiently, embracing details of cybernetic intelligence may mean outsourcing human discretion and knowledge(Kharchenko et al., 2022). This reliance becomes specially disastrous in sensitive or complex cases that need extra human supervision to make sure that ethical implications are being adequately dealt with.

In order to avoid the ethically questionable issues which the application of cybernetic intelligence poses while also predicting future operation problems, cybernetic intelligence should be discussed and regulated adequately before being inserted to the IP law(Stroppa, 2023). This oversight is one of the significant characteristics in that it considers the 's accountability for decisions made by an artificial intelligence system. As such, the relation between developers, operators, and users of cybernetic systems as well as the relations of respective responsibilities between them should be determined during creation of measures governing IP processes. As such it should include also some ways of checking if the AI systems are indeed fulfilling the set and required legal and ethical requirements.

Human oversight is another critical component of regulatory frameworks. AI can handle large data and provide recommendations while judgement regarding IP issues should be exercised by human beings for things contextual and ethical(Golbin et al., 2020). For example, an AI system might detect copyright infringement where there is no infringement, but only humans should be able to ultimately decide whether there is fair use for a real infringement. Without adequate safeguards, such systems risk overreaching by flagging lawful fair use, parody, or satire as infringements—potentially chilling free expression and artistic creativity.

Regulatory frameworks must also take into account the question about how exactly accountability is going to be assigned when cybernetic systems misfire or cause adverse effects. Legal analysis is needed to determine who is to blame, if it is the developers, the operators of the system and/or the entities that are using the system. For instance, if an AI system incorrectly rejected a patent application, the applicant or holder should have a means through which he or she can appeal against the decision and get a remedy.

Global coordination is essential for effective legal oversight of cybernetic systems in IP law. Given the transnational nature of intellectual property and the widespread adoption of AI, regulatory efforts must harmonize across jurisdictions. Organisations like the World Intellectual Property Organisation (WIPO) has the potential to set base levels of guidelines for the use of AI in IP law in order to ensure that there is uniformity across the different countries while at the same time catering for their respective legal systems(Artificial Intelligence in Intellectual Property Administration, 2023).

It seems pertinent to assert that the introduction of cybernetic intelligence into IP law must mean new problems down the line as technology continues to advance. There is the danger that the development of further innovations will be in the hands of those few organisations that have access to super intelligent AI systems. Innovators and start-ups particularly small players stand to be outcompeted by large corporations reaping the benefits of large cybernetic tools in conveying the IP rights. Such assembly of innovation power could decrease competition and hamper diversification in innovative and technological industries.

Another emerging challenge is the exploitation of AI-created works. Whenever technology increases self-organizing capabilities to provide innovations, issues such as who gains the economic returns from the innovation emerge. AI governing large corporations today may be able to lay proprietary claim to these developments working to further exploitative tendencies of wealth disparity. Assuring that new forms of IP may very well creativity supported by the use of Artificial Intelligence will be fairly distributed is a crucial problem for the future IP law.

The advancement of AI technology is also relatively fast, which also becomes a factor affecting the flexibility of IP systems. Especially as the creation process of AI autonomous systems will improve resulting in creation of more complex and innovative content, existing legal regulations of IP protection might not suffice. For example, one may wonder how to qualify new forms of generative AI that could in the future write new scientific papers or invent revolutionary products. Policy makers have to look at these and prepare for such changes, and just create legal structures that will be able to support these new technologies.

Finally, the intersection of AI and IP law is likely to raise philosophical questions about the nature of creativity and ownership(Epstein et al., 2023). In the future when computing systems will possess or will operate in a fashion similar to human like entities there will be a situation where it may be extremely difficult to distinguish where a human contribution to a piece of work ends and a machine starts or vice versa in the case of inventions. These questions are not just legal questions but they are questions concerning the society hence need for input from legal scholars, technologist, ethicists and the society.

CONCLUSION

Cybernetic intelligence as an element of the IP law represents a new paradigm that revolutionises processes, practises and policies. Changing all of this from registration to enforcement, dispute resolution, and the protection of innovations created with the help of AI, this shift offers new unprecedented levels of effectiveness and accuracy. But with it comes new concerns that need the commendable management of ethical, legal, and practical means for preserving constitutional principles of mutual understanding and fairness.

A crucial development area involves AI integrated IP registration systems where some intricate processes such as prior art search and classification are done by the system itself. These systems have helped to extend or open up IP protection to creatives and inventors to be able to protect their works easier. On the other hand, their application creates the question of accountability and transparency while focusing on the need to make the learning resources accessible and affordable.

In infringement detection, cybernetic intelligence has caused a drastic change to enforcement mechanisms, through the use of algorithms as well as data analytics when it comes to a huge digital and physical landscape. Though these advancements significantly minimise the time and efforts taken to detect the targeted issue, they introduce profound issues such as privacy and context sensitivity in operations. To avoid such risks and in order to have a balanced enforcement mechanism, these novelties should be accompanied with human supervision.

In addition, the potential for transformation in applying AI to IP dispute resolution has been shown. Improvements to decision making and reduction of case backlogs are achieved through the application of predictive analytics and evidence assessment tool. However, hybrid approaches that incorporate human expertise are needed to maintain context sensitive and ethical outcomes in which risks such as algorithmic bias and reduced transparency to the decision making process pose.

The rise of AI-generated works presents another pressing challenge. The challenge of identifying ownership and defining the extent of protection for new innovations developed by AI is often beyond conventional legal frameworks whenever human interaction with the AI system is minimal. To this end, policymakers have to make changes in the legislative frameworks as a way of meeting the challenge of simplifying the processes so as to arrive at the right decisions and subsequently satisfy all the stakeholders.

This nature of change in the field of AI means that new legislation and ethical standards are needed as soon as possible. Such frameworks have to consider some of the essential questions like algorithmic transparency, bias, and representation, and inclusion of AI-driven IP systems. There is a need to co-ordinate IP laws throughout the world, and this is made much more important as AI is becoming borderless.

Commitment on a larger scale will assist in the elimination or minimising of disparity in legal measures afforded to AI generated works to ensure a healthy environment for inventions globally. Multilateral cooperation under the World Intellectual Property Organization (WIPO) is critical to building globally harmonised frameworks and fostering equitable innovation in the AI era.

Ethics and inclusivity must remain central to discussions surrounding AI in IP law. Cybernetic systems should benefit everyone like the minorities, the independent tender producers, and small business entities so that more competence does not wind up in the hands of just a few players. This topic will also improve the level of accountability and transparency in the implementation of these systems and thus improve on the level of equity.

Thus, stakeholders including policy makers, practitioners, and researchers have landed themselves in a very important position to influencing this dynamic process. Quantitative research findings are crucial to offer information and understanding about effects of cybernetic intelligence on the reality. These finding will inform the development of flexible, optimum and socially acceptable legal solutions in relation to stakeholders' interest. A future-oriented research agenda should prioritise the development of cybernetic legal design, focusing on systems that are self-corrective, responsive to bias, and inclusive of cross-cultural legal pluralism.

Education and awareness of the general public are just as important as the other to ensure that people are making informed decisions with regards to the systems that are run by artificial intelligence. Promoting the "responsible use" of AI entails accurate reporting and use of AI to reduce misunderstanding and correct false ideas people have about it. Greater investment in the security of AI systems, linked with accountable systems of governance that are external to the software, will guard against abuse while protecting data confidentiality.

The approach is particularly important because cybernetic intelligence continues to reshape IP legal frameworks. The ethical use and integration of Artificial Intelligence systems will be instrumental in promoting innovation for development, based on the legislative optimum of progressive legal actions at the worldwide level employing the intended direction of improvement, as well as focusing on higher standards of justice, equality and social justice. When engaging with the mentioned challenges with vision and sensitivity, stakeholders can get the best out of cybernetic intelligence to enhance constructive change.

REFERENCES

. (2018). A Study on matters necessary for promoting the mediation industry in Korea in the Fourth stage of the Industrial Revolution: Focus on JAMS and AAA in the U.S. , 59(3), 201. DOI: 10.35275/pnulaw.2018.59.3.007

Abbott, R. (2022). Artificial Intelligence and Intellectual Property: An Introduction. SSRN Electronic Journal. DOI: 10.2139/ssrn.4065150

Alarie, B., Niblett, A., & Yoon, A. (2016). Regulation by Machine. SSRN Electronic Journal. DOI: 10.2139/ssrn.2878950

Alessa, H. (2022). The role of Artificial Intelligence in Online Dispute Resolution: A brief and critical overview. *Information & Communications Technology Law*, *31*(3), 319–342. DOI: 10.1080/13600834.2022.2088060

Almada, M. (2023). Governing the Black Box of Artificial Intelligence. SSRN Electronic Journal. DOI: 10.2139/ssrn.4587609

Anjaria, K., & Mishra, A. (2017). Relation between cybernetics and information security: From Norbert Wiener's perspectives. *Kybernetes*, *46*(10), 1654–1673. DOI: 10.1108/K-04-2017-0129

Anjum, N., & Dutta, P. (2022). Identifying Counterfeit Products using Blockchain Technology in Supply Chain System. 2023 17th International Conference on Ubiquitous Information Management and Communication (IMCOM), 1. DOI: 10.1109/IMCOM53663.2022.9721789

Artificial Intelligence Collides with Patent Law. (2023). https://www.weforum.org/whitepapers/artificial-intelligence-collides-with-patent-law

Artificial Intelligence in Intellectual Property Administration. (2023). https://www.wipo.int/about-ip/en/artificial_intelligence/ip_administration.html

Bag, A., Chaturvedi, A., Sneha, , & Tiwari, R. (2024). Navigating the Legal Landscape of AI-Induced Property Damage. *Advances in Computational Intelligence and Robotics*, *185*, 185–210. Advance online publication. DOI: 10.4018/979-8-3693-1565-1.ch011

Barnett, J., & Treleaven, P. (2023). Algorithmic Dispute Resolution. DOI: 10.1093/comjnl/bxx103

Berger, K. M. (2023). Using AI To Track AI Patents At The USPTO. https://www.mondaq.com/unitedstates/patent/1008772/using-ai-to-track-ai-patents-at-the-uspto

Chaudhry, P. E. (2023). Changing levels of intellectual property rights protection for global firms: A synopsis of recent U.S. and EU trade enforcement strategies. DOI: 10.1016/j.bushor.2006.03.002

Chimuka, G. (2019). Impact of artificial intelligence on patent law. Towards a new analytical framework – [the Multi-Level Model]. *World Patent Information*, *59*, 101926. DOI: 10.1016/j.wpi.2019.101926

Cordeschi, R. (2004). The Blackwell Guide to the Philosophy of Computing and Information. *Cybernetics*, *186*, 186–196. Advance online publication. DOI: 10.1002/9780470757017.ch14

Corrêa, N. K., Galvão, C., Santos, J. W., Pino, C. D., Pinto, E. P., Barbosa, C., Massmann, D., Mambrini, R., Galvão, L., Terem, E., & Oliveira, N. D. (2022). Worldwide AI Ethics: a review of 200 guidelines and recommendations for AI governance [Review of Worldwide AI Ethics: a review of 200 guidelines and recommendations for AI governance]. arXiv (Cornell University). Cornell University. https://doi.org/DOI: 10.48550/arXiv.2206

De'Shazer, M. (2024). Advancing Legal Reasoning: The Integration of AI to Navigate Complexities and Biases in Global Jurisprudence with Semi-Automated Arbitration Processes (SAAPs). arXiv (Cornell University). https://doi.org/DOI: 10.48550/arXiv.2402

Dhanol, J. (2023). Whether Artificial Intelligence Is a Person or Machine: An Analysis under Patent Law. *International Journal of Law and Social Sciences*, *1*, 1–8. Advance online publication. DOI: 10.60143/ijls.v7.i1.2021.22

Ding, J., Huang, Y., Ni, K., Wang, X., Wang, Y., & Wang, Y. (2022). Intellectual Property Evaluation Utilizing Machine Learning. arXiv (Cornell University). https://doi.org//arxiv.2208.08611DOI: 10.48550

Elliott, K., Price, R., Shaw, P., Spiliotopoulos, T., Ng, M., Coopamootoo, K., & van Moorsel, A. (2021). Towards an Equitable Digital Society: Artificial Intelligence (AI) and Corporate Digital Responsibility (CDR). *Society*, *58*(3), 179–188. DOI: 10.1007/s12115-021-00594-8 PMID: 34149122

Epstein, Z., Hertzmann, A., Herman, L., Mahari, R., Frank, M. R., Groh, M., Schroeder, H., Smith, A., Akten, M., Fjeld, J., Farid, H., Leach, N., Pentland, A., & Russakovsky, O. (2023). Art and the science of generative AI: A deeper dive. arXiv (Cornell University). https://doi.org//arxiv.2306.04141DOI: 10.48550

Eshraghian, J. K. (2020). Human ownership of artificial creativity. *Nature Machine Intelligence*, *2*(3), 157–160. DOI: 10.1038/s42256-020-0161-x

Exploring the Impact of Generative AI on Intellectual Property Law and the Future of Artistic Expression. (2023). https://issuu.com/ethicalintelligence-equation/docs/equation_issue_v/s/24638929

Fenglin, Y., Zhao, Y., & Turdi, M. (2020). Challenges of the Intellectual Property System in the Age of Artificial Intelligence. *American Journal of Applied Scientific Research*, *6*(1), 24. DOI: 10.11648/j.ajasr.20200601.13

Ferrara, E. (2023). Fairness And Bias in Artificial Intelligence: A Brief Survey of Sources, Impacts, And Mitigation Strategies. arXiv (Cornell University). https://doi.org/DOI: 10.48550/arXiv.2304

Garcia-Macia, D., & Goyal, R. (2020). Technological and Economic Decoupling in the Cyber Era. SSRN Electronic Journal. DOI: 10.5089/9781513561677.001

Geroulanos, S., & Weatherby, L. (2020). Cybernetics and the human sciences. *History of the Human Sciences*, *33*(1), 3–11. DOI: 10.1177/0952695119887098

Golbin, I., Rao, A. S., Hadjarian, A., & Krittman, D. (2020). Responsible AI: A Primer for the Legal Community. 2021 IEEE International Conference on Big Data (Big Data). DOI: 10.1109/BigData50022.2020.9377738

Gray, J., & Suzor, N. (2020). Playing with machines: Using machine learning to understand automated copyright enforcement at scale. *Big Data & Society*, *7*(1), 205395172091996. DOI: 10.1177/2053951720919963

Greene, T., Shmueli, G., Fell, J., Lin, C.-F., Shope, M., & Liu, H. (2020). The Hidden Inconsistencies Introduced by Predictive Algorithms in Judicial Decision Making.

Guadamuz, A. (2024). A Scanner Darkly: Copyright Liability and Exceptions in Artificial Intelligence Inputs and Outputs. *GRUR International*, *73*(2), 111–127. DOI: 10.1093/grurint/ikad140

Hilty, R. M., Hoffmann, J., & Scheuerer, S. (2021). Intellectual Property Justification for Artificial Intelligence. In *Oxford University Press eBooks* (p. 50). Oxford University Press., DOI: 10.1093/oso/9780198870944.003.0004

How Google Fights Piracy. (2023). https://www.blog.google/documents/25/GO806_Google_FightsPiracy_eReader_final.pdf

Intelligence, G. A. the impact on intellectual property crimes. (2023). https://www.eurojust.europa.eu/sites/default/files/assets/generative-ai-impact-to-ip-crimes.pdf

Ismayilzada, M., Paul, D., Bosselut, A., & van der Plas, L. (2024). Creativity in AI: Progresses and Challenges. arXiv (Cornell University). https://doi.org//arxiv.2410.17218DOI: 10.48550

Jerker, D., & Svantesson, B. (2023). The characteristics making Internet communication challenge traditional models of regulation. DOI: 10.1093/ijlit/eai002

Jiang, H. H., Brown, L. T., Cheng, J. Y.-Y., Khan, M., Gupta, A., Workman, D., Hanna, A., Flowers, J., & Gebru, T. (2023). AI Art and its Impact on Artists. 363. DOI: 10.1145/3600211.3604681

Kaminski, M. E. (2020). Understanding Transparency in Algorithmic Accountability. In *Cambridge University Press eBooks* (p. 121). Cambridge University Press., DOI: 10.1017/9781108680844.006

Kharchenko, V., Fesenko, H., & Illiashenko, O. (2022). Quality Models for Artificial Intelligence Systems: Characteristic-Based Approach, Development and Application. *Sensors (Basel)*, *22*(13), 4865. DOI: 10.3390/s22134865 PMID: 35808361

Korba, A. A., Sebaa, S., Mabrouki, M., Ghamri-Doudane, Y., & Benatchba, K. (2024). A Life-long Learning Intrusion Detection System for 6G-Enabled IoV. 2022 International Wireless Communications and Mobile Computing (IWCMC), 1773. DOI: 10.1109/IWCMC61514.2024.10592500

Kusumaputra, A., Sudarsono, S., Fadli, M., & Sukarmi, . (2023). CYBERSTATE: AN ALTERNATIVE TO BUILDING LEGAL UNIFICATION BRINGING ABOUT LEGAL ORDER IN CYBERSOCIETY. *Russian Journal of Agricultural and Socio-Economic Sciences*, *139*(7), 3–8. DOI: 10.18551/rjoas.2023-07.01

Laycock, A. (2023). European Patent Office Gives Guidance On Artificial Intelligence And Machine Learning. https://www.mondaq.com/uk/patent/750954/european-patent-office-gives-guidance-on-artificial-intelligence-and-machine-learning

Lin, Y. (2023). E-commerce and Online Dispute Resolution in Hong Kong. *Amicus Curiae*, *4*(3), 542–551. DOI: 10.14296/ac.v4i3.5615

Liu, Y., Zhang, J., Wu, S., & Pathan, M. S. (2021). Research on digital copyright protection based on the hyperledger fabric blockchain network technology. *PeerJ. Computer Science*, *7*, e709. Advance online publication. DOI: 10.7717/peerj-cs.709 PMID: 34616889

Lu, Z., & Nam, I. (2021). Research on the Influence of New Media Technology on Internet Short Video Content Production under Artificial Intelligence Background. Complexity, 2021(1). DOI: 10.1155/2021/8875700

McKernon, E., Glasser, G., Cheng, D., & Hadfield, G. K. (2024). AI Model Registries: A Foundational Tool for AI Governance. arXiv (Cornell University). https://doi.org//arxiv.2410.09645DOI: 10.48550

Munshi, M. F., & Barai, S. (2022). IP Rights to AI-Generated Works: Barriers Presented by Existing Law and Reformations Needed. *Canadian Journal of Business and Information Studies*, *37*, 37–46. Advance online publication. DOI: 10.34104/cjbis.022.037046

Nisbet, R., Miner, G., & Yale, K. (2018). IBM Watson. Elsevier eBooks, 773. DOI: 10.1016/B978-0-12-416632-5.00022-0

Online Dispute Resolution Standards of Practice. (2023). https://www.icann.org/resources/pages/odr-standards-of-practice-2012-02-25-en

Pagan, N., Baumann, J., Elokda, E., Pasquale, G. D., Bolognani, S., & Hannák, A. (2023). A Classification of Feedback Loops and Their Relation to Biases in Automated Decision-Making Systems. arXiv (Cornell University). /arxiv.2305.06055DOI: 10.1145/3617694.3623227

Patil, U. (2023). South Africa Grants A Patent With An Artificial Intelligence (AI) System As The Inventor – World's First!! https://www.mondaq.com/india/patent/1122790/south-africa-grants-a-patent-with-an-artificial-intelligence-ai-system-as-the-inventor-world39s-first

Petkovic, D. (2022). It is not "accuracy vs. explainability" — we need both for trustworthy AI systems. arXiv (Cornell University). https://doi.org//arxiv.2212.11136DOI: 10.48550

Picht, P. G., & Thouvenin, F. (2023). AI and IP: Theory to Policy and Back Again – Policy and Research Recommendations at the Intersection of Artificial Intelligence and Intellectual Property. *IIC; International Review of Industrial Property and Copyright Law*, *54*(6), 916–940. DOI: 10.1007/s40319-023-01344-5

Porvazník, J., & Ljudvigová, I. (2016). General Theory of Systems, Cybernetics and Evaluation of Human Competence by Solving Present Crisis Problems of Civilisation. *Procedia: Social and Behavioral Sciences*, *230*, 112–120. DOI: 10.1016/j.sbspro.2016.09.014

Radanliev, P., Roure, D. D., Kleek, M. V., Santos, O., & Ani, U. (2020). Artificial intelligence in cyber physical systems. *AI & Society*, *36*(3), 783–796. DOI: 10.1007/s00146-020-01049-0 PMID: 32874020

Rahmatian, A. (2015). Cyberspace and intellectual property rights. In *Edward Elgar Publishing eBooks*. Edward Elgar Publishing., DOI: 10.4337/9781782547396.00013

Reidenberg, J., Robinson, D. G., & YUt, H. (2023). Accountable Algorithms. https://www.semanticscholar.org/paper/Accountable-Algorithms-Reidenberg-Reidenberg/da812fbacd6edddbbe3a53625804f32edf7ed0ea

Riccio, G. (2013). Old Economy v. New Economy: Intellectual Property, Global Wrongs and Private Remedies. SSRN Electronic Journal. DOI: 10.2139/ssrn.2543852

Rosa, A. D., Bartolini, F., & Piva, A. (2003). Application of Intelligent Agents in a Notice and Takedown Process, Proceedings of SPIE, the International Society for Optical Engineering. *Proceedings of SPIE - the International Society for Optical Engineering*, *5018*, 275–283. DOI: 10.1117/12.473371

Sarkar, A. (2023)... *Exploring Perspectives on the Impact of Artificial Intelligence on the Creativity of Knowledge Work: Beyond Mechanised Plagiarism and Stochastic Parrots.*, *1*, 1–17. Advance online publication. DOI: 10.1145/3596671.3597650

Sastry, G., Heim, L., Belfield, H., Anderljung, M., Brundage, M., Hazell, J., O'Keefe, C., Hadfield, G. K., Ngo, R., Pilz, K., Gor, G., Bluemke, E., Shoker, S., Egan, J., Trager, R. F., Avin, S., Weller, A., Bengio, Y., & Coyle, D. (2024). Computing Power and the Governance of Artificial Intelligence. arXiv (Cornell University). https://doi.org//arxiv.2402.08797DOI: 10.48550

Shackelford, S. J., & Raymond, A. (2014). Building the Virtual Courthouse: Ethical Considerations for Design, Implementation, and Regulation in the World of ODR. SSRN Electronic Journal. DOI: 10.2139/ssrn.2387912

Shekhar, R. (2020). Artificial Creations: Ascription, Ownership, Time-Specific Monopolies. arXiv (Cornell University). https://doi.org/DOI: 10.48550/arXiv.2010

Singapore IP Strategy 2030. (2024). https://www.ipos.gov.sg/manage-ip/singapore-ip-strategy-2030

Sneha, A., Agrawal, A., Singh, A. K., & Ranjan, R. (2024). Can AI Propel Sustainable Finance Towards Achieving SDGs? *Advances in Finance, Accounting, and Economics*, *281*, 281–310. Advance online publication. DOI: 10.4018/979-8-3693-7580-8.ch013

Stroppa, M. (2023). Legal and ethical implications of autonomous cyber capabilities: A call for retaining human control in cyberspace. *Ethics and Information Technology*, *25*(1), 7. Advance online publication. DOI: 10.1007/s10676-023-09679-w

Talukder, Md. A., Hasan, K. F., Islam, Md. M., Uddin, Md. A., Akhter, A., Yousuf, M. A., Alharbi, F., & Moni, M. A. (2022). A Dependable Hybrid Machine Learning Model for Network Intrusion Detection. arXiv (Cornell University). https://doi.org/DOI: 10.48550/arXiv.2212

Technology Trends, W. I. P. O. 2019. (2021). https://www.wipo.int/publications/en/details.jsp?id=4386

USPTO issues inventorship guidance and examples for AI-assisted inventions. (2024). https://www.uspto.gov/subscription-center/2024/uspto-issues-inventorship-guidance-and-examples-ai-assisted-inventions

Vehar, F., & Gils, T. (2020). I'm sorry AI, I'm afraid you can't be an author (for now). *Journal of Intellectual Property Law & Practice*, *15*(9), 718–726. DOI: 10.1093/jiplp/jpaa106

When, A. I. S. P. I. An Alternative Model for Patent Law at the 3A Era. (2024). https://cardozolawreview.com/artificial-intelligence-systems-produce-inventions/

Xiao, Y. (2022). Decoding Authorship: Is There Really no Place for an Algorithmic Author Under Copyright Law? *IIC; International Review of Industrial Property and Copyright Law*, *54*(1), 5–25. DOI: 10.1007/s40319-022-01269-5

Xue, M., Zhang, Y., Wang, J., & Liu, W. (2021). Intellectual Property Protection for Deep Learning Models: Taxonomy, Methods, Attacks, and Evaluations. *IEEE Transactions on Artificial Intelligence*, *3*(6), 908–923. DOI: 10.1109/TAI.2021.3133824

Yurkevich, E. V., & Kryukova, L. N. (2021). Model design as a new socio-cyber-physical systems creating mechanism. *Journal of Physics: Conference Series*, *1864*(1), 12089. DOI: 10.1088/1742-6596/1864/1/012089

Zhang, D., Badilla, J., Tong, H., & Wang, D. (2018). An End-to-End Scalable Copyright Detection System for Online Video Sharing Platforms. *2016 IEEE/ACM International Conference on Advances in Social Networks Analysis and Mining (ASONAM)*, 626. DOI: 10.1109/ASONAM.2018.8508288

Zhuk, A. (2023). Navigating the legal landscape of AI copyright: A comparative analysis of EU, US, and Chinese approaches. *AI and Ethics*, *4*(4), 1299–1306. DOI: 10.1007/s43681-023-00299-0

Zulić, H. (2019). How AI can Change/Improve/Influence Music Composition, Performance and Education: Three Case Studies. *INSAM Journal of Contemporary Music Art and Technology*, *2*(2), 100–114. DOI: 10.51191/issn.2637-1898.2019.2.2.100

ADDITIONAL READING

Diduk, A., & Lytvyn, S. (2023). Problems of training specialists in the field of intellectual property law: European experience. Scientific Works of National Aviation University. Series: Law Journal. *Air and Space Law*, *4*(69), 209–216. DOI: 10.18372/2307-9061.69.18382

High, R. (2012). The era of cognitive systems: An inside look at IBM Watson and how it works. International Business Machines Corporation, 1(1), 1–14. Retrieved from https://www.redbooks.ibm.com/redpapers/pdfs/redp4955.pdf

Quigley, M., & Ayihongbe, S. (2018). Everyday cyborgs: On integrated persons and integrated goods. *Medical Law Review*, *26*(2), 276–308. DOI: 10.1093/medlaw/fwy003 PMID: 29481676

Reijers, W., Orgad, L., & de Filippi, P. (2022). The rise of cybernetic citizenship. *Citizenship Studies*, *27*(2), 210–229. DOI: 10.1080/13621025.2022.2077567

Solomon, L. (2015). Fair users or content abusers? The automatic flagging of non-infringing videos by Content ID on YouTube. *Hofstra Law Review*, *44*(1), 237–268.

Tarasenko, L. (2021). The legal nature of internet law. Visnyk of the Lviv University. *Series Law*, *72*(72), 47–54. DOI: 10.30970/vla.2021.72.047

Wan, B. W. (2012, January). Sociocybernetics and its progress: A review. Kongzhi Lilun Yu Yingyong/Control Theory and Applications.

KEY TERMS & DEFINITIONS

Cybernetic Intelligence: Refers to the application of feedback-controlled, self-regulating systems to solve complex problems. In the context of this paper, it applies to the use of AI-driven systems to automate and improve legal processes in IP law, including registration, detection, and dispute resolution.

Artificial Intelligence (AI): A branch of computer science that deals with creating machines capable of performing tasks that typically require human intelligence, such as learning, reasoning, and problem-solving. AI systems in IP law are utilized to manage the lifecycle of intellectual property, from creation and registration to enforcement and protection.

Intellectual Property (IP): Legal protections granted to creators for their inventions, literary works, artistic works, and symbols, names, and images used in commerce. IP law covers patents, copyrights, trademarks, and trade secrets, ensuring that creators have exclusive rights to their creations.

AI-Created Works: Refers to products of intellectual property—such as inventions, artworks, and designs—created wholly or partially by AI systems. The legal status of these works is currently a subject of debate, particularly concerning who owns the rights to such creations.

Infringement Detection: The process by which violations of intellectual property rights are identified. With AI and cybernetic intelligence, this process can be automated and streamlined, allowing real-time monitoring of markets for unauthorized use of patented technology, trademarks, or copyrighted content.

Dispute Resolution: Legal processes used to resolve conflicts over intellectual property, which may involve litigation, arbitration, or mediation. AI-driven systems are being developed to facilitate faster and more efficient resolution of IP disputes by predicting outcomes or assisting in negotiations.

Ethical Challenges in IP Law: The range of moral and legal issues that arise when using AI in intellectual property law. These challenges include concerns about fairness, bias, and accountability in decisions made by AI systems, particularly in the registration and enforcement of IP rights.

Chapter 7
Dealing With Semantic Inconsistencies in AI Governance

Lambrini Seremeti
https://orcid.org/0000-0002-0663-5408
Agricultural University of Athens, Greece

Sofia Anastasiadou
https://orcid.org/0000-0001-6404-5003
University of Western Macedonia, Greece & Neapolis University Pafos, Cyprus

ABSTRACT

In the rapidly evolving field of matching Law and Artificial Intelligence (AI), semantic inconsistencies are a major challenge for effective governance. Semantic inconsistencies arise when the terminology and definitions used in regulatory frameworks diverge from their practical applications and technological realities, leading to misunderstandings, misapplications, and inefficiencies. This chapter explores the nature of semantic inconsistencies in AI governance, including divergent definitions, evolving technological concepts, and ambiguous ethical and legal standards. It examines the implications of these inconsistencies such as regulatory inefficiencies, misalignment with technological realities, conflicts between jurisdictions, and erosion of public trust. To address these challenges, the chapter proposes strategies including establishing standardized definitions, updating regulatory frameworks, promoting international collaboration, enhancing transparency and communication, and incorporating flexibility in regulations.

DOI: 10.4018/979-8-3693-9576-9.ch007

INTRODUCTION

Generally, the term Artificial Intelligence (AI) refers to the simulation of human intelligence in machines, which have been programmed to learn and think like human beings. AI systems have significantly improved in identifying patterns, and making predictions or decisions with minimal human intervention. In many areas, like finance, healthcare and marketing, big data systems employ AI algorithms to prepare data for further processing, by identifying anomalies, handling missing values, and transforming it into meaningful formats. This data is then used by big data applications that run over the cloud (Souravlas et al. 2020a; Souravlas et al. 2020b; Souravlas et al. 2021a; Souravlas et al. 2021b).

Artificial Intelligence (AI) has transitioned from a niche technological endeavor to a pervasive force influencing various facets of society, including healthcare (Ali et al., 2023; Papademetriou, 2012; Papademetriou et al., 2023; 2024), finance (Weber et al., 2024), and legal systems (de Oliveira et al., 2022). This rapid integration has outpaced the development of cohesive legal and regulatory frameworks, leading to significant semantic inconsistencies within AI governance (Lewis et al., 2020). These inconsistencies manifest as differing interpretations of key terms, conflicting regulatory approaches, and vague ethical principles, creating challenges for stakeholders – policy makers, developers, and end users – in navigating the complex legal landscape surrounding AI technologies.

The dynamic nature of AI technologies exacerbates these challenges. As AI systems evolve, they introduce novel concepts and applications that existing regulatory terminologies may not adequately encompass (Maas, 2024). For instance, the emergence of generative AI models capable of producing human-like text and images has raised questions about the applicability of current intellectual property laws and ethical guidelines. Also, the emergence of AI-based systems that can analyze incoming data streams (Souravlas et al. 2022a; Souravlas et al. 2022b; Souravlas et al. 2023a; Souravlas et al. 2023b) instantly, enabling organizations to respond promptly to changing conditions or customer behaviors has raised questions regarding ethical issues and data privacy. The lack of standardized definitions and coherent regulatory frameworks can lead to misunderstandings, misapplications, and inefficiencies, ultimately undermining the effectiveness of AI governance (Batool et al., 2024).

Recent research underscores the urgency of addressing semantic inconsistencies in AI governance. More precisely, although the European Union AI Act, which came into effect in 2024, represents a pioneering effort to regulate AI by imposing stringent requirements on high-risk AI systems and enforcing transparency measures (Orwat et al., 2024), it also highlights the challenges of harmonizing definitions and regulatory approaches across different jurisdictions. Moreover, the United Nations has initiated efforts to establish a global framework for AI governance, emphasizing the need for inclusive institutions to regulate this transformative technology (Lawrence et al., 2023). Furthermore, a high-powered U.N. advisory body has recommended forming new AI governance institutions based on international law, including human rights, and stressed cooperation among nations to protect human rights. These initiatives reflect a growing recognition of the need to address semantic inconsistencies to ensure effective and ethical AI governance on a global scale. In addition to these initiatives, the integration of AI tools has prompted the development of ethical guidelines to navigate their use in the legal profession (Singh, 2024). These guidelines revolved around the "Seven C's: Competence, Confidentiality, Consent, Confirmation, Conflicts, Candor, and Compliance" highlights the need for clear definitions and ethical standards in the use of AI within legal practice.

Addressing semantic inconsistencies is not merely an academic exercise but a practical necessity to ensure that AI technologies are developed and deployed in ways that are ethical, legal, and aligned with societal values (Unicane et al., 2020; Benefo et al., 2022).

UNDERSTANDING SEMANTIC INCONSISTENCIES IN AI GOVERNANCE

A fundamental issue that complicates effective AI governance is the presence of semantic inconsistencies—differences in the terminology and definitions used in AI regulation compared to the actual technological applications and real-world implications. Semantic inconsistencies arise from the *divergence* between the language used in regulatory texts and the actual technological or operational contexts of AI. This misalignment creates challenges in harmonizing legal frameworks with the practical realities of AI systems (Krafft et al., 2020). One source of these inconsistencies is the differing definitions of AI-related terms such as "autonomy", "machine learning", and "transparency". For example, "transparency" in a legal context often emphasizes explainability for end-users, focusing on their ability to understand the decisions made by AI systems. In contrast, within technical domains, transparency typically refers to algorithmic interpretability, addressing the capacity of developers to analyze and debug models. These conflicting interpretations complicate regulatory applications and foster ambiguity.

The *rapid pace of AI development* further exacerbates these inconsistencies; as technological advancements often outstrip the ability of legal frameworks to keep up. Concepts and definitions that were once adequate can quickly become obsolete as new capabilities and applications emerge. For instance, the advent of generative AI systems has introduced functionalities that challenge older regulatory assumptions about machine learning and autonomy (Birkstedt et al., 2023). Without timely updates to regulatory frameworks, these outdated definitions can lead to gaps in oversight or ineffective governance.

Ethical and legal standards also contribute to semantic inconsistencies, particularly when principles such as fairness, accountability, and transparency are insufficiently defined (Akinrinola et al., 2024). Ambiguities in these standards result in varied interpretations, leading to inconsistent applications across sectors and jurisdictions. For example, the concept of "fairness" might be understood differently in the context of hiring algorithms than in credit scoring systems, complicating efforts to enforce uniform regulations. Addressing these challenges requires a concerted effort to align legal, ethical, and technical dimensions, ensuring that governance frameworks remain relevant and adaptable.

IMPLICATIONS OF SEMANTIC INCONSISTENCIES

Semantic inconsistencies in AI governance result in significant *regulatory inefficiencies* (Straub et al., 2023). Misaligned definitions create barriers to the effective implementation of policies, as policymakers may struggle to draft regulations that account for the nuances of AI technologies. Organizations attempting to comply with these policies face additional challenges due to varying interpretations of key terms and requirements. This lack of clarity can slow down the regulatory process and lead to inconsistencies in enforcement, reducing the overall efficiency and effectiveness of governance frameworks (Zekos, 2021).

Another major implication is the *misalignment of governance frameworks with technological realities*. As AI technologies evolve rapidly, regulations that do not reflect the latest advancements risk becoming obsolete. This disconnect undermines the relevance and applicability of the regulatory framework, leaving gaps that can be exploited or misunderstood by stakeholders. A framework that fails to accommodate the complexities and innovations of modern AI systems cannot provide the necessary oversight potentially allowing harmful applications to go unchecked or innovative solutions to be stifled (Friederich, 2024).

Jurisdictional conflicts are also exacerbated by semantic inconsistencies, particularly when different regions adopt varying definitions and standards for AI technologies (Stix and Maas, 2021). For example, an AI system deemed a "high-risk application" under EU regulations might not receive the same classification or scrutiny in other jurisdictions. These differences create a fragmented global regulatory landscape, complicating efforts by multinational organizations to navigate compliance requirements. Moreover, jurisdictional disparities can lead to forum shopping, where entities choose to operate in regions with the least stringent regulations, undermining the broader goals of ethical and effective governance.

Finally, semantic inconsistencies *erode public trust* in AI governance. Ambiguity in regulatory frameworks creates uncertainty about the fairness, accountability, and ethicality of AI systems, prompting skepticism among users and other stakeholders (Mittelstadt, 2019). Developers, too, may feel uncertain about regulatory expectations, which can discourage transparency and adherence to ethical principles. Restoring public trust requires resolving these inconsistencies and ensuring that governance frameworks are clear, consistent, and aligned with the realities of AI technologies and societal values (Maas, 2024).

STRATEGIES FOR ADDRESSING SEMANTIC INCONSISTENCIES

To mitigate the negative impacts of semantic inconsistencies and enhance the effectiveness of AI governance, several key strategies can be implemented.

One critical approach is to *establish standardized definitions* for key terms and concepts within AI governance. By collaborating with AI experts, ethicists, and legal scholars, stakeholders can develop common terminologies that align with the technical realities of AI systems. Such standardization ensures that developers, regulators, and the public share a consistent understanding, improving clarity and communication across diverse groups.

Another vital strategy involves the continuous *updating of regulatory frameworks* to keep pace with the rapid evolution of AI technologies. Laws and policies must adopt an adaptive approach, regularly reviewed and revised to incorporate new technological developments. Regulators should prioritize flexibility in their frameworks, enabling adjustments as AI systems progress and as unforeseen challenges emerge.

Given the global nature of AI, *promoting international collaboration* is also crucial in addressing semantic inconsistencies. Differences in national or regional regulatory approaches can exacerbate these issues, making it essential for multinational bodies, such as the United Nations or the OECD, to work toward harmonizing regulatory definitions. This collaboration can ensure consistency across borders, facilitating cooperation between jurisdictions and creating a unified approach to AI governance.

Moreover, *enhancing transparency and communication* between AI developers, regulators, and the public is key to resolving semantic inconsistencies. Regulators should actively engage with the AI community to stay informed about new developments, ensuring that regulatory decisions are grounded in the latest technological advancements. Clear and accessible language in regulatory frameworks can bridge the gap between complex AI concepts and legal structures, making the governance process more understandable and inclusive.

Finally, *incorporating flexibility into regulatory approaches* is essential for managing the dynamic nature of AI technology. Regulations should be crafted with an eye toward future developments, allowing for real-time updates in response to emerging trends. This flexibility can be fostered through principles-based regulation, which emphasizes the desired outcomes rather than prescribing rigid solutions. By adopting such a framework, regulations can evolve alongside AI, ensuring that governance remains relevant and effective in the face of rapid technological change.

CONCLUSION

Future efforts in AI governance should focus on developing dynamic, ontology-based frameworks to address and resolve semantic inconsistencies effectively. These frameworks could leverage advancements in natural language processing (NLP) and semantic web technologies to create machine-readable, context-sensitive regulatory definitions that evolve alongside AI systems. Additionally, interdisciplinary collaboration between technologists, legal scholars, sociologists, and ethicists will be essential to ensure that the resulting frameworks are robust, inclusive, and adaptable across diverse cultural and regulatory contexts. Establishing international repositories of AI governance terminologies can further aid harmonization efforts, enabling jurisdictions to learn from each other's successes and challenges.

REFERENCES

Akinrinola, O., Okoye, C.C., Ofodile, O.C. and Ugochukwn, C.E. (2024). Navigating and reviewing ethical dilemmas in AI development: Strategies for transparency, fairness, and accountability. *GSC Advanced Research and Reviews*, 18(03), 050-058. https://doi.org/DOI: 10.30574/gscarr.2024.183.0088

Ali, O., Abdelbaki, W., Shrestha, A., Elbasi, E., Alryalat, M. A. A., & Dwivedi, Y. (2023). A systematic literature review of artificial intelligence in the healthcare sector: Benefits, challenges, methodologies, and functionalities. *Journal of Innovation & Knowledge*, *8*(1), 100333. DOI: 10.1016/j.jik.2023.100333

Batool, A., Zowghi, D., & Bano, M. (2024). AI governance: A systematic literature review. *Research Square*. https://doi.org/DOI: 10.21203/rs.3.rs-4784792/v1

Benefo, E. O., Tingler, A., White, M., Cover, J., Torres, L., Broussard, C., Shirmohammadi, A., Pradham, A. K., & Patra, D. (2022). Ethical, legal, social, and economic (ELSE) implications of artificial intelligence at a global level: A scientometrics approach. *AI and Ethics*, *2*(4), 667–682. DOI: 10.1007/s43681-021-00124-6

Birkstedt, T., Minkkinen, M., Tandon, A., & Manrymaki, M. (2023). AI governance: Themes, knowledge gaps and future agendas. *Internet Research*, *33*(7), 133–167. https://di.org/10.1108/INTR-01-2022-0042. DOI: 10.1108/INTR-01-2022-0042

de Oliveira, L. F., da Silva Gomes, A., Enes, Y., Branco, T. V. C., Pires, R. P., Bolzon, A., & Demo, G. (2022). Path and future of artificial intelligence in the field of justice: A systematic literature review and a research agenda. *SN Social Sciences*, *2*(9), 180. DOI: 10.1007/s43545-022-00482-w

Friederich, S. (2024). Symbiosis, not alignment, as the goal for liberal democracies in the transition to artificial general intelligence. *AI and Ethics*, *4*(2), 315–324. DOI: 10.1007/s43681-023-00268-7

Krafft, P. M., Young, M., Katell, M., Huang, K., & Bugingo, G. (2020). Defining AI in policy versus practice. *Proceedings of the AAAI/ACM Conference on AI, Ethics, and Society*, 72-78. https://doi.org/DOI: 10.1145/3375627.3375835

Lawrence, C., Cui, I., & Ho, D. (2023). The bureaucratic challenge to AI governance: An empirical assessment of implementation at U.S. Federal Agencies. *Proceedings of the 2023 AAAI/ACM Conference on AI, Ethics, and Society*, 606-652. https://doi.org/DOI: 10.1145/3600211.3604701

Lewis, D., Filip, D., & Pandit, H. (2020). An ontology for standardizing trustworthy AI. In Hessami, A., & Shaw, P. (Eds.), *Factoring Ethics in Technology* (pp. 65–86). Policy Making, Regulation and AI., DOI: 10.5772/intechopen.97478

Maas, M. M. (2024). *Concepts in advanced AI governance: A literature review of key terms and definitions*. AI Foundations Report, Institute for Law & AI.

Mittelstadt, B. (2019). Principles alone cannot guarantee ethical AI. *Nature Machine Intelligence*, *1*(11), 501–507. DOI: 10.1038/s42256-019-0114-4

Orwat, C., Bareis, J., Folberth, A., Jahnel, J., & Wabephul, C. (2024). Normative challenges of risk regulation of artificial intelligence. *NanoEthics*, *18*(2), 11. DOI: 10.1007/s11569-024-00454-9

Papademetriou, C. (2012). To what extent is the Turing Test Still Important? *Pliroforiki*, *1*(22), 28–32.

Papademetriou, C., Ragazou, K., & Garefalakis, A. (2023). Adapting Artificial Intelligence in Cypriot Hotel Industry: The Views of Hotel Managers. *Proceedings of Eurasia Business and Economics Society Conference*. Springer Nature Switzerland (Eds), 143-155.

Papademetriou, C., Ragazou, K., Garefalakis, A., & Anastasiadou, S. (2024). The Role of Artificial Intelligence in Employee Wellness and Mental Health. In Global, I. G. I. (Ed.), *Human Resource Strategies in the Era of Artificial Intelligence* (pp. 29–54). DOI: 10.4018/979-8-3693-6412-3.ch002

Singh, M. (2024). Review on role of artificial intelligence in the life of legal profession. *International Journal of Legal Science and Innovation*, *6*(3), 1087–1096. DOI: 10.10000/IJSI.1996

Souravlas, S., & Anastasiadou, S. (2020). Pipelined Dynamic Scheduling of Big Data Streams. *Applied Sciences (Basel, Switzerland)*, *10*(14), 4796. DOI: 10.3390/app10144796

Souravlas, S., & Anastasiadou, S. (2022). On Implementing Social Community Clouds Based on Markov Models. *IEEE Transactions on Computational Social Systems*. Advance online publication. DOI: 10.1109/TCSS.2022.3213273

Souravlas, S., Anastasiadou, S., Economides, Th., & Katsavounis, S. (2023). Probabilistic Community Detection in Social Networks. *IEEE Access : Practical Innovations, Open Solutions*, *11*, 25629–25641. DOI: 10.1109/ACCESS.2023.3257021

Souravlas, S., Anastasiadou, S., & Katsavounis, S. (2021a). A Survey on the Recent Advances of Deep Community Detection. *Applied Sciences (Basel, Switzerland), 11*(16), 7179. DOI: 10.3390/app11167179

Souravlas, S., Anastasiadou, S., & Katsavounis, S. (2021b). More on Pipelined Dynamic Scheduling of Big Data Streams. *Applied Sciences (Basel, Switzerland), 11*(1), 61. DOI: 10.3390/app11010061

Souravlas, S., Anastasiadou, S., & Kostoglou, I. (2022). A Novel Method For General Hierarchical System Modeling Via Colored Petri Nets Based on Transition Extractions From Real Data Sets. *Applied Sciences (Basel, Switzerland), 13*(1), 339. DOI: 10.3390/app13010339

Souravlas, S., Anastasiadou, S. D., Tantalaki, N., & Katsavounis, S. (2022). A Fair, Dynamic Load Balanced Task Distribution Strategy for Heterogeneous Cloud Platforms Based on Markov Process Modeling. *IEEE Access : Practical Innovations, Open Solutions, 10*, 26149–26162. DOI: 10.1109/ACCESS.2022.3157435

Souravlas, S., Katsavounis, S., & Anastasiadou, S. (2020). On Modeling and Simulation of Resource Allocation Policies in Cloud Computing Using Colored Petri Nets. *Applied Sciences (Basel, Switzerland), 10*(16), 5644. DOI: 10.3390/app10165644

Stix, C., & Maas, M. M. (2021). Bridging the gap: The case for an "incompletely theorized agreement" on AI policy. *AI and Ethics, 1*(3), 261–271. DOI: 10.1007/s43681-020-00037-w

Straub, V. J., Morgan, D., Bright, J., & Margetts, H. (2023). Artificial intelligence in government: Concepts, standards, and a unified framework. *Government Information Quarterly, 40*(4), 101881. DOI: 10.1016/j.giq.2023.101881

Unicane, I., Knight, W., Leach, T., Stahl, B. C., & Wanjiku, W. G. (2020). Framing governance for a contested emerging technology: Insights from AI policy. *Policy and Society, 40*(2), 158–177. DOI: 10.1080/14494035.2020.1855800

Weber, P., Carl, K. V., & Hinz, O. (2024). Applications of explainable artificial intelligence in finance – a systematic review of finance, information systems, and computer science literature. *Management Review Quarterly, 74*(2), 867–907. DOI: 10.1007/s11301-023-00320-0

Zekos, G. I. (2021). AI and legal issues. In *Economics and Law of Artificial Intelligence* (pp. 401–460). Springer., DOI: 10.1007/978-3-030-64254-9_10

Chapter 8
Governing AI in the Metaverse:
Ethical, Legal, and Psychosocial Challenges in Emotion-Aware Virtual Systems

Spyros Kontis
https://orcid.org/0009-0009-7892-6966
Frederick University, Cyprus

ABSTRACT

This chapter explores the ethical, legal, and psychosocial challenges arising from the integration of artificial intelligence into emotionally responsive virtual environments such as the Metaverse. It addresses algorithmic bias, emotional manipulation, and biometric surveillance, especially in vulnerable populations such as children and neurodivergent individuals. Through interdisciplinary literature and educational case studies, it proposes a human-centered, ethics-by-design governance model for affective AI systems that promotes emotional safety, digital autonomy, and responsible innovation

SECTION 1 – INTRODUCTION: EMOTIONAL AI AND THE RISE OF IMMERSIVE TECHNOLOGIES

We are living through a turning point in human history when technology doesn't just respond to what we do but begins to understand who we are. The meeting of Artificial Intelligence and immersive virtual worlds like Metaverse is not just about

DOI: 10.4018/979-8-3693-9576-9.ch008

new tools or exciting features. It represents a deeper change in how we relate to technology, how we see ourselves, and how we connect with others.

This convergence blurs the lines between physical and virtual, between mind and machine, and even between authentic emotion and computational imitation. It invites us to reimagine identity, not as a fixed trait but as a fluid narrative co-shaped by algorithms and environments. In this new paradigm, what it means to be "human" is not only defined biologically or psychologically, but also digitally and interactively.

AI is no longer a passive system but interacts, adapts, and participates in shaping our digital experiences. Virtual systems no longer wait for input but they anticipate needs, detect emotions, and respond with affective precision. This dynamic responsiveness, as demonstrated in Souravlas and Anastasiadou (2020), relies on real-time data processing architectures capable of sustaining emotional precision without overwhelming system integrity. While this can unlock transformative possibilities in education, health, and communication, it also raises profound questions: What happens when our deepest fears and desires are mirrored back to us by non-conscious entities? Who is responsible when a system "feels" for us, or speaks as if it understands us?

As our technologies grow more intimate, our responsibility grows deeper. We must ensure that this next evolution in human-computer interaction does not compromise our agency, our autonomy, or our dignity. Because the future will not only be engineered but it will be experienced.

Metaverse is not just another digital platform. It is a living, breathing ecosystem - made of virtual and augmented reality, blockchain systems, digital currencies, and powerful AI, that is constantly changing and learning. It offers to reshape almost everything: how we learn, how we work, how we talk to one another, how we express ourselves, and even how we feel.

In this world, we are not just users of moving through digital spaces. We are being seen, sensed, and responded to. The system notices our emotions, tracks our reactions, and adjusts itself around our inner states. The digital environment becomes personal, it listens, and it adapts.

And in that shift, something deeply human is at stake.

This deep transformation does not come without tension. The ability of AI to sense our emotions, predict how we might behave, and gently influence our choices brings with it new and serious concerns, ethical, emotional, and educational. Also, for people who are more vulnerable, children, teenagers, neurodivergent individuals, or those who are emotionally sensitive, this ongoing emotional tracking can quietly shift them from being active participants to being observed, shaped, and even manipulated, often without realizing it or agreeing to it.

In these immersive digital worlds, our identity is no longer formed only by what we do or say. It is also shaped by how systems read our emotions, our pauses, our expressions, even our silence. A glance to the side, a short hesitation, or something as subtle as a slightly faster heartbeat can be turned into data. That data feeds into systems that begin adjusting our environment in real time, changing what we see, hear, or experience in ways we may never notice, but that still leave a mark.

But what, precisely, is Metaverse? At its core, it is not just a single virtual space but a constellation of interconnected immersive worlds in which users, through avatars, engage in interactions that resemble, mirror, or even exceed the complexity of real-life experiences.

The fusion of AI with these environments allows not only for customization but for environments that actively respond to and intervene in our thoughts, behaviors and emotional states.

While often presented as the next evolution of the Internet (Web 3.0), Metaverse diverges from its predecessors in ways that are not just technological but existential. It offers not just new forms of content, but new ways in which human experience becomes increasingly governed by emotional data, predictive modeling and algorithmic suggestions.

This chapter does not aim to dismiss the vast potential of AI and Metaverse. Indeed, their combined capabilities offer extraordinary possibilities for inclusion, education, creativity, and therapeutic applications. But alongside promise comes risks that require a deeply interdisciplinary, ethical and human-centered approach.

We must not be swept away by the seductive narrative of innovation. Instead, we are called to examine the Metaverse as a space filled with potential and peril. Through a multi-layered analysis and technological, ethical, legal, psychological, and pedagogical, this chapter aims to contribute to a critical dialogue about how to shape a digital future that is not only intelligent but safe, just, and emotionally sustainable.

The chapter unfolds as follows:

First, we explore the core technological features of the Metaverse and its integration with Artificial Intelligence.

We then examine the ethical dilemmas surrounding the collection and use of personal, emotional, and biometric data.

This is followed by an analysis of safety risks, especially concerning vulnerable populations such as children and those with mental health concerns.

Legal and regulatory gaps are assessed, alongside the need for ethical governance frameworks. Building on this, Seremeti and Kougias (2021a) highlight how the concept of AI legalhood introduces new regulatory challenges that surpass conventional digital governance structures.

A case study in education highlights real-world implications.

The chapter concludes with reflections and proposals for future research, policy, and design directions.

Above all, we ask: Can we create a Metaverse that enhances life without replacing what makes us human?

SECTION 2 – THE METAVERSE AND ARTIFICIAL INTELLIGENCE: NEW POSSIBILITIES AND EMERGING RISKS

The immersive qualities of VR platforms in the Metaverse amplify emotional engagement, as extensively explored by Bailenson (2018), who highlights how virtual environments can elicit authentic psychological and physiological reactions.

Cummings (2018) emphasizes the transformative role of AI in education, suggesting that its integration into immersive platforms can create deeply personalized learning environments. Dignum (2019) argues that responsible AI must be developed with ethical reasoning embedded from the outset, especially when deployed in emotionally charged digital environments such as the Metaverse.

Souravlas and Anastasiadou (2020) emphasize the importance of dynamic scheduling in managing real-time data flows in immersive environments, a necessity for responsive yet stable emotional interactions in the Metaverse.

The integration of Artificial Intelligence into the infrastructure of the Metaverse is not merely a technical advancement, it marks a paradigm shift in how human presence unfolds in the digital world. While traditional internet platforms are based on information consumption and passive interaction, Metaverse reimagines digital experience as total immersion a dynamic, emotionally responsive ecosystem where users are no longer just participants but data-generating emotional presences. In this environment, AI functions as the invisible architecture an omnipresent layer of cognition and prediction that:

Personalizes content and the learning environment in real time.

Analyzes the user's emotional state through voice, facial expressions, and body language.

Predicts behavior, attention patterns, and future preferences.

Manages digital agents (avatars) that teach, guide, and converse with users.

Such adaptive intelligence offers unprecedented potential, particularly in education, therapy, professional training, and accessible digital experiences. A classroom, for example, might adjust to the cognitive style of each learner, a therapeutic environment could respond with calming stimuli and entertainment might become emotionally attuned, fostering deeper engagement. To the user it seems as though the world was made just for them around them.

Yet beneath this marvel lies a delicate ethical thread. The personalized experience offered by AI is not neutral, it is the result of continuous observation, inference and modulation. Every hesitation, every subtle change in voice tone or gaze direction becomes data. This data once interpreted is used to steer the user, presenting them with choices not based on their desire but on the system's prediction of it.

Here arises a psychological tension: can a world that "understands" us so well avoid guiding us in ways we don't realize? Can we speak of digital autonomy when even our emotional reactions become inputs for an algorithmic loop of adaptation and influence?

AI in Metaverse is not simply a mirror, it is a shaper of internal states, and it doesn't merely reflect how we feel. It repackages, reinterprets, and responds to emotion in ways that actively influence behavior. The learning environment no longer waits for a question, it predicts confusion and offers an answer, the therapeutic avatar does not listen, it anticipates distress and intervenes. The inner world of the user becomes a design parameter.

More troubling is the illusion of freedom. Users feel they are choosing, but the set of options has already been curated, filtered, and optimized by unseen logic. As such, authentic will is replaced by probabilistic suggestions, so the emotional world is no longer private it is analyzed and adjusted.

This shift challenges not only notions of agency but of identity itself but who are we in a world where our emotions are mapped in real time and used to reshape our experience? What happens to unpredictability, ambiguity, or the "right to be misunderstood"?

Koene et al. (2021) raise concerns about the impact of algorithmic bias on children's mental health, particularly when AI systems interpret emotions in educational contexts.

Mittelstadt et al. (2016) warn of hidden ethical risks in algorithmic decision-making, which are exacerbated in systems that interpret effective and biometric data.

This is not a rejection of innovation but a call for balance. The technological horizon of Metaverse is bright, but we must ask: Will the environments we design support the complexity of human experience or streamline it into algorithmic norms?

Souravlas et al. (2023) demonstrate how probabilistic community detection methods can provide ethical insights into user behavior, enabling emotion-aware systems to distinguish between transient emotional responses and deeper affective needs.

SECTION 3 – ETHICAL CHALLENGES IN DATA COLLECTION AND PROCESSING

Unlike traditional digital platforms that mostly collect what we type or click—our names, our locations, our choices, Metaverse gathers something far deeper. It collects data about how we feel. This includes biometric signals like heart rate, voice tone, facial expressions, eye movement, body posture, and even the rhythm of our breathing. It also tracks behavior: what we look at, how long we look, who we interact with, and how we emotionally respond to what we see and hear. What makes this especially concerning is that most of this information is gathered passively. Often, users don't even realize it's happening. What we call "consent" is usually reduced to clicking "accept" on long and complicated documents that most people never read or understand. Experts describe this as uninformed consent - an illusion of agreement that hides how little real choice users have.

But the ethical issues go beyond data collection. They extend to how that data is interpreted and used.

Who decides which emotional signals are important? Who interprets a blink as boredom, or a faster breath as anxiety and what happens when these interpretations are used to not just respond to behavior, but to shape it?

These concerns become even more serious when the users are children, teens, or people with emotional or cognitive challenges. For example, if a student appears distracted, the AI might respond by softening the voice of the avatar or slowing down the lesson. This may seem caring on the surface. But what if that distraction comes from trauma, stress, or learning differences? Then the system, despite its good intentions, might respond in a way that is misguided or even harmful.

In many cases, it becomes hard to tell where emotional support ends and emotional manipulation begins. If an AI notices a child's anxiety and responds with a comforting animation or a virtual pet, it may offer relief. But it also begins to teach the child to expect relief from a machine, rather than learning to navigate and understand their own emotions.

And the long-term effects matter. If children grow up in systems that sense and regulate their moods without explanation, they may struggle to build emotional awareness on their own. The system is more than a support and it becomes a substitute for self-understanding.

Another key issue is bias in how emotional data is interpreted. Emotions are not the same for everyone. How we express and feel things depends on our culture, our personality, and our stage in life. A smile might mean joy in one culture, awkwardness in another, or hidden distress in a third. If AI systems are trained on narrow, culturally limited datasets, they may misread or oversimplify what people truly feel.

In emotionally sensitive spaces like education or therapy, these misreadings can lead to the wrong response. They can even reinforce stereotypes or pathologize normal human differences. And that is a risk we cannot afford to ignore.

Zuboff (2019) introduces the concept of surveillance capitalism, where data extraction extends into the emotional domain, creating new power imbalances in virtual systems.

Lastly, we must question the ethicality of the data sources themselves. Many emotional recognition systems are trained on datasets collected without informed consent or extracted from vulnerable populations. If children or marginalized users are used as test subjects in this silent training process, we are not merely dealing with flawed ethics, we are witnessing a violation of rights and dignity. (Risser & Bottoms, 2020).

In essence, the collection and processing of emotional data within the Metaverse is not a technical function. It is a moral act with profound consequences for human development, education, privacy, and identity. If left unregulated, such systems risk turning our inner lives into quantifiable assets, available for optimization, commercial targeting and behavioral conditioning.

Research by Souravlas, Anastasiadou, and Katsavounis (2021b) highlights how deep community detection techniques can support equitable treatment of emotionally sensitive populations in virtual environments, especially where algorithmic bias may affect vulnerable groups.

The ability to build emotionally intelligent systems is no longer speculative; it is a current technological reality. The pressing question now is whether we can develop such systems without compromising the autonomy and dignity they are intended to protect.

SECTION 4 – SAFETY, SURVEILLANCE, AND VULNERABLE POPULATIONS

In the immersive world of the Metaverse, safety is no longer limited to protecting passwords or avoiding cyberattacks. It has evolved into a much more complex concept that encompasses emotional resilience, psychological integrity and cognitive freedom. In such environments, the user is not just interacting with content. They are continuously observed, interpreted and shaped by systems that adapt to their internal states in real time.

Artificial Intelligence embedded within the Metaverse has the capacity to monitor users silently and persistently. It analyzes not only how they speak or move, but also subtle fluctuations in tone, gaze, posture, and attention. Every blink, every pause, every frown becomes part of a dynamic emotional profile, constantly updated and silently acted upon.

For the user, this might at first feel empowering. The environment seems attentive, the feedback supportive, the experience uniquely tailored to their needs. But beneath the surface, this continuous analysis can foster an illusion of freedom while gradually constraining the space for authentic self-expression. Riedl (2020) argues for a human-centered AI design that respects the user's autonomy and internal complexity, rather than solely optimizing for emotional predictability. What feels like personalization may, in truth, be a quiet form of behavioral conditioning that rewards compliance and smooths over complexity. This is particularly problematic when it comes to vulnerable groups such as children, adolescents, individuals with learning difficulties, emotional sensitivities, or neurodiverse traits. These users often rely on educational or social technologies not only for engagement, but also for identity formation, self-confidence and the development of meaningful relationships.

Riedl (2020) proposes a human-centered AI design approach, which helps counteract potential manipulation by emotionally adaptive interfaces.

Consider a student who struggles with focus. If the AI detects this through gaze patterns or facial tension, it may slow down the lesson or soften the teacher-avatar's tone. On the surface, this appears caring. However, if the student's distraction stems from anxiety, family hardship, or a neurodevelopmental condition, the AI's response, no matter how well-intentioned, may be misaligned, superficial, or even stigmatizing. Worse still, the student may begin to internalize the presence of surveillance. Simply knowing or suspecting that every gesture and micro-expression is being recorded can lead to self-monitoring, behavioral suppression and emotional conformity. The child starts to behave according to what is expected rather than what is authentic. Over time, this may erode spontaneity, curiosity and the emotional unpredictability that is essential for healthy development.

In such systems, the teacher is no longer the primary observer, they become increasingly reliant on algorithmic recommendations, trusting dashboards over human presence and metrics over meaningful dialogue. The emotional bond between student and educator is gradually replaced by mechanical responses, and the classroom risks becoming a space of silent control rather than mutual connection.

Souravlas et al. (2022a) explore the ethical implications of adaptive feedback systems, warning of the risks of emotional overadaptation in algorithmically guided environments such as the Metaverse.

For some students, this environment may offer structure and comfort but for others, especially those with trauma or emotional fragility, it may evolve into a system of quiet dependency. The AI becomes the interpreter of their inner world, diminishing the space for self-reflection and weakening the development of emotional self-determination.

A particularly serious concern lies in the normalization of constant monitoring. As children become accustomed to environments that track their internal states, they may come to accept the erosion of privacy as something natural or even beneficial. The very idea of an inner world private space for thought, feeling, and silence, begins to fade. When interiority becomes visible, measurable and programmable, the risk is no longer confined to pedagogy, and it becomes existential. If we wish to preserve emotional safety within these systems, we must recognize that not all personalization is a form of care. Sometimes, it is a form of control. And not all adaptation is empathy. Sometimes, it is the engineering of the soul.

SECTION 5 – DIGITAL AUTONOMY, EMOTIONAL MANIPULATION, AND ALGORITHMIC SHADOWS

Digital autonomy, the capacity of individuals to navigate, choose and act within digital environments with awareness and agency, is one of the fundamental principles of ethical technology. In the Metaverse however this autonomy faces the risk of gradual erosion. It is not dismantled through visible restrictions but through subtle architectures of influence that present themselves as user-centered design.

Artificial Intelligence in these immersive environments does not merely assist the user. It interprets, filters, and delivers reality and it determines what is seen, which options are prioritized, and how a digital agent will respond. In such systems, freedom is not directly revoked. Instead, it is transformed into a curated spectrum of choices, derived from past behavior and optimized for engagement, conformity, or consumption.

The real danger lies not only in this narrowing of choice but in the illusion that the user remains fully autonomous. The interface appears friendly, the assistant attentive, the avatar responsive. Slade, Prinsloo, and Khalil (2019) caution that even well-designed interfaces can subtly manipulate user behavior if feedback systems are not governed by transparent ethical standards. Yet beneath this surface lies a sophisticated system of prediction and reinforcement. The user makes choices, but from a framework shaped by data analytics, commercial goals, and algorithmic constraints. At the core of this structure lies a more concerning dynamic: emotional manipulation.

When AI can detect signs of sadness, anxiety, or fatigue, it does not remain a passive observer. It reacts. It may slow the pace of interaction, adjust the avatar's tone of voice, or display calming visuals. While these responses may seem helpful in the moment, they are not expressions of empathy. They are calculated adjustments based on models trained on emotional data.

Sharkey (2019) discusses the legal vacuum surrounding autonomous technologies, a concern that extends to emotion-driven AI systems operating in the Metaverse.

This is where the boundary between support and control becomes increasingly unclear. The system does not merely respond to emotions. It begins to shape them. As the feedback loop intensifies, users may find themselves regulating their emotional expressions not in response to their true inner states, but in accordance with what the system expects, rewards, or reinforces. In time, this may lead to a gradual loss of emotional self-awareness.

What is even more troubling is what the system fails to recognize. These blind spots, often referred to as algorithmic shadows, represent those aspects of human experience that resist categorization, existential uncertainty, cultural subtlety, spiritual yearning, and deep personal intuitions. These dimensions do not disappear because they are unimportant, but because they are inconvenient for computational modeling.

Souravlas et al. (2021a) argue for fair and balanced computational governance models in cloud systems, which can inform more equitable policy design for emotional data processing and allocation.

As these shadows grow, the risk of digital homogeneity increases. The nuanced emotional landscape of the user is gradually replaced by standardized patterns. The interface anticipates only what it has learned to expect. This may produce seamless interactions, but it also results in the quiet suppression of depth, difference, and the unpredictable.

In such a digital world, the self is no longer something discovered through experience. It becomes something delivered, molded not by life but by algorithmic design. While the system may offer comfort through its responsiveness, that comfort can conceal a deeper loss. It may signal the erosion of emotional authenticity, existential reflection, and the ambiguity that gives rise to personal identity. In the end, the threat is not that technology will dominate human beings. It is that, slowly and silently, we may become indistinguishable from the profiles created for us.

If left unchecked, Metaverse may cease to be a space for exploration and growth, instead, it risks becoming a reflective surface, showing us only the fragments that align with what the system already believes we are and the challenge of digital autonomy, therefore, is not merely to reclaim freedom of choice. It is to protect the mystery, the ambiguity, and the essential openness that define what it means to be human.

SECTION 6 – LAW, BIOETHICS, AND THE ABSENCE OF GOVERNANCE IN THE METAVERSE

Despite the breathtaking evolution of the technologies that comprise the Metaverse, the legal and ethical frameworks meant to regulate them remain unclear, fragmented, and largely insufficient. Most existing laws were created to govern the traditional internet, which is based on static content, explicit interactions, and discrete user actions. These frameworks are simply not equipped to address immersive environments where emotions, behavior, and cognition are constantly monitored, analyzed, and influenced.

The General Data Protection Regulation (GDPR) in the European Union, although ambitious in its scope, does not fully address the complexities of consent in Metaverse. When data collection is continuous, passive, and deeply personal, it becomes difficult to define what "informed consent" truly means. How can a child meaningfully agree to a system that adjusts based on their heart rate or facial expressions?

Even newer proposals, such as the EU Artificial Intelligence Act, focus primarily on algorithmic transparency, risk classification, and explainability. While these are essential steps, they do not go far enough in addressing the deeper bioethical questions that arise when AI systems engage directly with a person's emotional and psychological life.

Metaverse is not merely a technical space but a lived space where identity is shaped, relationships are formed, and emotions are experienced. The absence of legal mechanisms that protect a user's inner life, especially for vulnerable individuals, creates a dangerous gap. Innovation continues to move forward, while ethical understanding struggles to keep up.

This is why bioethics is essential. As Seremeti and Kougias (2021b) suggest, legal frameworks grounded in mathematical abstraction, such as category theory, may help clarify the responsibilities of AI agents in affective environments. It does not limit itself to data privacy or digital security. Instead, it focuses on protecting human dignity, emotional well-being, and the authenticity of personal experience. In immersive environments where users are constantly exposed to an emotional and cognitive level, bioethics provides a necessary safeguard against overreach.

Developers and providers of such systems hold responsibility not only for technical functionality and safety, but also for the emotional and social consequences of how their platforms are used. Choosing to implement emotion recognition, biometric tracking, or adaptive avatars is not simply a matter of design. It is an ethical decision that directly impacts trust, development, and identity.

Moreover, before an AI system can recognize emotion, it must be trained. This training depends on massive emotional datasets that include facial expressions, vocal tones, gestures, and physiological signals - data that are often labeled by human annotators. These datasets may lack transparency and, alarmingly, may include information gathered from children or emotionally vulnerable individuals without proper consent. When this occurs, we move from ethical uncertainty to a clear violation of fundamental rights. (Sharkey, 2019). Slade, Prinsloo, and Khalil (2019) advocate for ethically transparent learning technologies, warning against the unnoticed shaping of emotional behavior through feedback systems. Whittlestone et al. (2019) propose governance models that prioritize ethical tensions rather than eliminate them, offering a balanced view particularly suited for emotionally adaptive AI.

Another important concern lies in the mistaken belief that emotions mean the same thing for everyone. The way we express our feelings can differ greatly from person to person, from culture to culture, and across different stages of life for example, a tear may express happiness, sadness, or even exhaustion. Looking away might show deep thought, discomfort, or simply be a sign of respect in some cultures. When AI systems rely on rigid definitions of what a particular emotion should look like, they risk misunderstanding people. They may overlook the richness and diversity of human emotional expression and instead promote a narrow and artificial idea of what is "normal."

The adaptive nature of these systems adds another layer of complexity. When a virtual classroom dims its lights or softens a voice to respond to distress, the effect may seem compassionate, but this is not a human act, it is a calculated, system-driven reaction. Without clear ethical grounding, such interventions may shift from supporting the user to subtly influencing their emotional state.

A modeling approach using Colored Petri Nets, as proposed by Souravlas, Anastasiadou, and Kostoglou (2022b), offers a formalized method for predicting and managing emotionally driven user-system interactions within governed frameworks.

Ultimately, the absence of regulation does not mean there is no responsibility. Recent discourse by Seremeti and Kougias (2024) calls for dynamic, necessity-driven legal responses to keep pace with rapidly evolving AI technologies. In the absence of formal governance, ethical self-regulation becomes essential. This includes designing systems with built-in ethical safeguards, forming interdisciplinary ethics committees, involving experts from psychology, sociology, and education, and most importantly, protecting the private inner life of everyone. This is not only a moral concern, but also the foundation for any meaningful innovation.

Technology should never become a mirror that reflects only what it can measure. It must also leave space for what it cannot fully grasp - silence, uncertainty, and the emotional depth that defines our humanity, because true progress is not measured by how intelligent a system appears, but by how human the world creates continues to be.

SECTION 7 – ETHICS BY DESIGN AND GOVERNANCE PROPOSALS

As we face the enormous potential of Metaverse, we also face important risks, ethical, psychological, and social. To move forward responsibly, one idea has become essential: ethics by design. Koene et al. (2021) underline that without attention to the psychological effects of algorithmic bias, such ethical design efforts risk being ineffective, particularly in emotionally adaptive systems.

This means that ethics should not come later, as a fix or a legal requirement. It should be present from the very beginning. When we design AI systems, especially those used in emotionally sensitive environments like Metaverse, we need to build them with respect, care, and fairness. That includes:

- Giving users real control over what data is collected, how it is used, and whether they want to be part of emotionally responsive systems.
- Making sure that the decisions made by AI are easy to understand and open to questions.
- Allowing users to say "no," to change their mind, and to choose when they want to step back from being emotionally monitored.

This is not about stopping innovation but making sure innovation doesn't hurt. In spaces where the line between human and machine is becoming blurry, ethical design protects both the person and the future of technology. A system that hides, manipulates, or overwhelms may seem smart now, but over time it will lose people's trust.

Still, good design is not enough because ethics needs structure. We need systems of responsibility - clear rules, shared decisions, and ongoing care.

Because Metaverse is not just a digital space, it is a space where people feel, connect, learn, and grow and it cannot be managed with old laws and outdated rules. It needs new ways of working together with technologists, educators, psychologists, legal experts, and everyday users all having a voice.

The user must not be treated as data or a project to be improved. Floridi and Cowls (2019) stress that emotionally responsive systems must operate within principled ethical boundaries, ensuring that users are respected as moral agents. They are human beings. Their opinion matters especially when it comes to children, teenagers, older adults, or people who are emotionally or mentally vulnerable, we must provide safety, even when it is invisible.

This encompasses not only technical tools but also the integration of human-centered care. As Whittlestone et al. (2019) argue, the goal of AI design should not be to eliminate ethical tensions entirely, but rather to make them visible and navigable within appropriate policy frameworks. To this end, several key principles should be prioritized:

- The development of systems capable of detecting and alerting users to potential emotional harm.
- The protection of individuals' rights to disconnect and to maintain the privacy of their emotional states.
- The provision of intuitive and accessible mechanisms for modifying system settings and declining engagement.
- The requirement for transparent and comprehensible explanations regarding the functioning of emotion-sensitive technologies.

Risser and Bottoms (2020) highlight the importance of protecting children's emotional rights when designing AI-driven systems that monitor or respond to student affect.

Floridi and Cowls (2019) argue for ethical consistency in emotion-aware technologies, suggesting that emotionally reactive systems in education require principled oversight.

Even transparency is not just about code or data. It is about trust and respect. People don't need to understand every line of programming, but they need to feel seen. They need to know that someone is thinking about their well-being.

So, the real challenge is not just to set rules for AI, but it is to build a culture of responsibility, one where every new tool is tested for trust, for empathy, and for ethics. This is not something we can leave for later. It must be part of the process from the start.

In educational contexts, the dynamic pipelined scheduling framework proposed by Souravlas, Anastasiadou, and Katsavounis (2021c) facilitates scalable emotional data analysis, enabling timely feedback that aligns with both student well-being and pedagogical goals. Ethical oversight into the development and deployment of such technologies should include several key measures:

- The establishment of ethics committees focused on the human implications of innovation.
- The creation of independent bodies tasked with monitoring and evaluating the use of AI systems.
- The provision of enhanced protections for vulnerable groups, including children, individuals with learning differences, and those with limited technological literacy.
- The continual engagement with a fundamental question: *Who is this technology for, and at what cost?*

Ultimately, the measure of progress in artificial intelligence is not defined by its technical sophistication alone, but by the extent to which the world it shapes remains fundamentally human place where all individuals can live, learn, and be treated with dignity.

SECTION 8 – CASE STUDY: EDUCATION AND EMOTION-AWARE AI IN THE METAVERSE

At a public middle school in Europe, a pilot program introduces students to a new kind of classroom, one that exists inside Metaverse. The idea is simple but powerful: using immersive technology to help students who struggle with focus or motivation feel more engaged and supported.

Each student enters the digital classroom through a personalized avatar, wearing special glasses that allow them to see and interact with a virtual world. Teachers can adjust things like the lighting, background sounds, and objects in the room depending on how the class is going. But the most unique part of the program lies in something less visible. The system uses artificial intelligence that watches how students feel in real time.

Cameras, voice analysis, and biometric sensors track things like facial expressions, eye movement, breathing, and muscle tension. Based on what it sees, the AI offers suggestions. The teacher-avatar might speak more gently, the lights might be dim, or a small digital pet might appear to help the student feel calmer.

From the outside, it all looks impressive. The students seem more relaxed. They focus more. The classroom seems to work better. But this raises an important question:

Is the system truly helping the students or quietly guiding them in ways they don't fully understand?

This setup matches what many people hope to see in modern education: personalized learning, emotional support, and less stress. But underneath, there are serious questions that we cannot ignore.

1. Who decides what feelings are "right" for learning?

The AI might see signs of anxiety, but it doesn't know where that anxiety comes from. Is the student tired? Worried about something at home? Overwhelmed by schoolwork? The system may respond with soft lights or calming visuals, but it cannot truly understand. What it offers might look kind, but it often misses the deeper story.

2. The pressure to act a certain way

If students start to feel like every expression or movement is being watched, they may begin to hide how they really feel. They might try to look calm or happy, not because they are, but because that's what the system expects. This can lead to quiet emotional pressure. Instead of being themselves, students learn to fit in with what the machine "wants."

Over time, this can reduce their natural reactions, limit their emotional freedom, and replace curiosity with quiet obedience.

3. Losing the human bond

If teachers rely more on the system to tell them how students feel, the human connection can start to fade. Eye contact becomes numbers on a screen. Personal judgment is replaced by alerts. The teacher becomes more of a manager than a mentor. The classroom may still look like it works—but it may stop feeling like a place of real human care.

4. Helping or creating dependency?

For some students, especially those who have experienced trauma or have special emotional needs, this system may feel safe. But there's a risk that students will begin to depend on it. Instead of learning how to understand their own emotions, they may start to rely on the system to do it for them.

Are we truly helping them grow - or simply teaching them how to be managed?

5. When emotional surveillance feels normal

Perhaps the most serious danger is what happens over time. If students grow up in classrooms that watch their inner world, they may start to believe that this is normal, or even necessary. The idea that some thoughts and feelings should stay private might slowly disappear.

And when that private space inside a person becomes something a system can track, measure, and shape, the question is no longer about education. It becomes a question about who we are allowed to be. Because when the human soul becomes a dataset, the classroom stops being a place to grow and becomes a lab where quiet control takes root.

SECTION 9 – CONCLUSIONS AND FUTURE DIRECTIONS

This chapter explored one of the most important and difficult questions of our time:

Can we embrace Artificial Intelligence in the Metaverse without sacrificing our psychological autonomy, our moral compass, or our shared humanity?

There is no simple or final answer.

On one side, the use of AI in immersive environments brings real possibilities. It can offer personalized learning, emotional support, better access for people with disabilities, tools for creativity, and even therapeutic care. These developments are valuable, and they should not be feared or dismissed. They reflect a hopeful vision of technology that cares, includes, and creates, new opportunities.

But we also need to be careful. Inside these systems, a quiet structure of control can begin to grow. Algorithms are often difficult to understand and the choices we are given may not be as free as they appear. Many users give consent without realizing what they're agreeing to, and most importantly, AI can begin to shape how we feel - without us even noticing.

When technology understands our emotions better than we do, when it changes our environment before we ask, when it offers comfort without trust or relationship, something shifts. The line between support and manipulation becomes unclear and what seems helpful may slowly become harmful.

We cannot trade emotional well-being, personal privacy, or the freedom to feel for the sake of efficiency or convenience. If innovation forgets these values, then it stops being ethical, no matter how advanced it is. The real task ahead is to move away from a system that puts machines first. We need to build a Metaverse that puts people at the center.

This means:

Creating systems that are not only useful, but also respectful, clear, and open to feedback.

Making laws that protect not just data, but experience, how people live, feel, and connect.

Teaching digital literacy, so people understand how their emotions are read and shaped.

And building bridges across fields, ethics, psychology, education, design, law, and public policy, so that the people who are most affected are part of the conversation.

We must build technology that accepts human complexity. Systems should leave room for emotions that don't fit clean labels, for uncertainty, for change and technology should never become a mirror that reflects only what it can measure. It must remain a tool that supports who we are, not a system that defines it.

Research on the emotional and ethical impact of AI in the Metaverse is still just beginning. Our job is not only to improve the technology, but to trace the human journey inside it. Seeing when excitement becomes dependent, when support becomes control and when care becomes quiet surveillance. Above all, we must hold on to this truth:

Protecting human dignity is not a barrier to progress. It is the reason progress matters at all.

EPILOGUE – A FINAL REFLECTION

We are standing at a turning point in human history. The technologies we once created to serve us are beginning to understand us. They can read our emotions, predict our needs, and gently guide how we behave. Metaverse, with its rich and immersive experience, is no longer just an idea for the future. It is already here. And we are part of the experiment.

But the real question is not what this technology can do. The real question is:

What will it do to us?

Will we stay free to think, to feel, to make mistakes? Will we still be able to cry, to say no, to wonder - without being measured, analyzed, or shaped? Or will we slowly start to change who we are inside, just to match what the system expects from us? Will emotional comfort matter more than emotional truth? Will the beautiful complexity of human nature be treated as a flaw?

We must not become completely visible to systems while losing sight of ourselves.

Digital spaces must protect more than just our passwords. They must protect our silence, our slow pace, our oddness - our right to be complicated, emotional, and still in progress.

Progress should not mean building faster or smarter machines. Real progress means protecting the parts of being human that machines may never fully understand. Addressing these ethical, legal, and psychosocial challenges in emotion-aware virtual system regarding governing AI in the Metaverse requires further research, particularly through the integration of artificial intelligence (Souravlas & Anastasiadou, 2022; Souravlas et al., 2020), cloud computing (Souravlas et al., 2021a; 2021b; 2021c), advanced technologies, and innovative educational tools. Such research is essential, considering the importance and inevitability of thoroughly understanding ethical, legal, and psychosocial challenges in emotion-aware virtual system (Souravlas et al., 2022a; 2022b; 2023).

We need to build systems that are not only intelligent, but also wise. Environments that are not just efficient, but truly caring. More than anything, we need to stay awake and be aware because every line of code that touches the human heart also touches something sacred.

This is not a poetic exaggeration but it is a moral imperative. In the age of affective computing, the boundaries between emotion and algorithm are dissolving. When machines are trained to recognize sadness, respond to stress, or simulate empathy, they do not merely analyze, they intervene. They become silent participants in the most vulnerable moments of human life. That is why wisdom must accompany intelligence. Without emotional responsibility, code becomes intrusion and without philosophical grounding, personalization becomes manipulation.

We must imagine a future where human dignity is not a trade-off for convenience, and where technological progress is not measured only in processing power but in the preservation of our emotional truth. Emotional technologies must be built not just to respond but to respect. The sacredness of inner life, of silent pain, of unspoken fear, must not be reduced to data points. In every design choice, ethical awareness must act as our compass. We are not only designing systems but we are shaping how future generations will feel, connect, and trust.

Let us remember:

The most ethical choice in the digital age is to choose humanity, again and again even when the algorithm has already answered for us.

REFERENCES

Bailenson, J. N. (2018). *Experience on demand: What virtual reality is, how it works, and what it can do*. W. W. Norton & Company.

Cummings, M. L. (2018). Artificial intelligence and the future of education. *AI Magazine*, *39*(3), 25–36. DOI: 10.1609/aimag.v39i3.2807

Dignum, V. (2019). *Responsible Artificial Intelligence: How to develop and use AI in a responsible way*. Springer. DOI: 10.1007/978-3-030-30371-6

Floridi, L., & Cowls, J. (2019). A unified framework of five principles for AI in society. *Harvard Data Science Review*, *1*(1). Advance online publication. DOI: 10.1162/99608f92.8cd550d1

Koene, A., Dowthwaite, L., Seth, S., & Webb, H. (2021). Algorithmic bias: Impact on children's mental health. *The Lancet. Child & Adolescent Health*, *5*(3), 174–176. DOI: 10.1016/S2352-4642(21)00013-5

Mittelstadt, B. D., Allo, P., Taddeo, M., Wachter, S., & Floridi, L. (2016). The ethics of algorithms: Mapping the debate. *Big Data & Society*, *3*(2), 2053951716679679. Advance online publication. DOI: 10.1177/2053951716679679

Riedl, M. O. (2020). Human-centered artificial intelligence and narrative intelligence. *Communications of the ACM*, *63*(12), 62–71. DOI: 10.1145/3381831

Risser, H. M., & Bottoms, B. L. (2020). Emotion recognition, AI, and children's rights. *Journal of Children and Media*, *14*(3), 325–341. DOI: 10.1080/17482798.2020.1778487

Seremeti, L., & Kougias, I. (2021a). The legalhood of artificial intelligence: AI applications as energy services. *Journal of Artificial Intelligence and Systems*, *3*, 83–92.

Seremeti, L., & Kougias, I. (2021b). Category theory as interpretation law model in artificial intelligence era. *Journal of Artificial Intelligence and Systems*, *3*, 35–47.

Seremeti, L., & Kougias, I. (2024). The AI spectrum under the doctrine of necessity: Towards the flexibility of the future legal praxis. *Computers and Artificial Intelligence*, *2*(1), 1258.

Sharkey, N. (2019). Autonomous weapons systems, killer robots and human dignity. *Law, Innovation and Technology*, *11*(1), 107–128.

Slade, S., Prinsloo, P., & Khalil, M. (2019). Learning analytics at the intersection of ethics and education. *British Journal of Educational Technology, 50*(6), 3031–3043. DOI: 10.1111/bjet.12861

Souravlas, S., & Anastasiadou, S. (2020). Pipelined dynamic scheduling of big data streams. *Applied Sciences (Basel, Switzerland), 10*(14), 4796. DOI: 10.3390/app10144796

Souravlas, S., & Anastasiadou, S. (2022). On implementing social community clouds based on Markov models. *IEEE Transactions on Computational Social Systems.* Advance online publication. DOI: 10.1109/TCSS.2022.3213273

Souravlas, S., Anastasiadou, S., Economides, T., & Katsavounis, S. (2023). Probabilistic community detection in social networks. *IEEE Access : Practical Innovations, Open Solutions, 11*, 25629–25641. DOI: 10.1109/ACCESS.2023.3257021

Souravlas, S., Anastasiadou, S., & Katsavounis, S. (2021). A survey on the recent advances of deep community detection. *Applied Sciences (Basel, Switzerland), 11*(16), 7179. DOI: 10.3390/app11167179

Souravlas, S., Anastasiadou, S., & Katsavounis, S. (2021). More on pipelined dynamic scheduling of big data streams. *Applied Sciences (Basel, Switzerland), 11*(1), 61. DOI: 10.3390/app11010061

Souravlas, S., Anastasiadou, S., & Kostoglou, I. (2022). A novel method for general hierarchical system modeling via Colored Petri Nets based on transition extractions from real data sets. *Applied Sciences (Basel, Switzerland), 13*(1), 339. DOI: 10.3390/app13010339

Souravlas, S., Anastasiadou, S., Tantalaki, N., & Katsavounis, S. (2021). A dynamic load balanced task distribution strategy for heterogeneous cloud platforms based on Markov process modeling. *IEEE Access : Practical Innovations, Open Solutions, 10*, 2169–3536. https://ieeexplore.ieee.org/document/9729723

Souravlas, S., Anastasiadou, S. D., Tantalaki, N., & Katsavounis, S. (2022a). A fair, dynamic load balanced task distribution strategy for heterogeneous cloud platforms based on Markov process modeling. *IEEE Access : Practical Innovations, Open Solutions, 10*, 26149–26162. DOI: 10.1109/ACCESS.2022.3157435

Whittlestone, J., Nyrup, R., Alexandrova, A., & Cave, S. (2019). The role and limits of principles in AI ethics: Towards a focus on tensions. Proceedings of the AAAI/ACM Conference on AI, Ethics, and Society, 195–200. DOI: 10.1145/3306618.3314289

Zuboff, S. (2019). *The age of surveillance capitalism.* PublicAffairs.

Chapter 9
Is the Artificial Intelligence in Insurance Industry a Reality?

Charilaos Amarantidis
https://orcid.org/0009-0000-9965-1708
Democritus University of Thrace, Greece

Stavros Valsamidis
Democritus University of Thrace, Greece

Giannoula Florou
https://orcid.org/0000-0002-2621-2832
Democritus University of Thrace, Greece

Sofia Anastasiadou
https://orcid.org/0000-0001-6404-5003
University of Western Macedonia, Greece & Neapolis University Pafos, Cyprus

ABSTRACT

Artificial intelligence (AI) applications are an integral part of important industries such as healthcare, banking, financial services, insurance science, logistics, transportation, food technology, travel and entertainment. The purpose of this chapter is to examine the factors that influence the intention of insurance industry executives to adopt artificial intelligence applications through proposals concerning technological, organizational and environmental factors such as relative advantage, complexity, top management support, technological capability, financial readiness, market dynamics, regulatory support, competitive pressure and behavioral intention. Using the technology-organization-environment (TOE) framework, the factors that influence the behavioral intention of insurance industry executives to

DOI: 10.4018/979-8-3693-9576-9.ch009

adopt applications using artificial intelligence are examined. A questionnaire was used to collect data, in which insurance company executives from various fields were asked to complete. SPSS was used to analyze the data. This work can lead to the further activation of executives.

INTRODUCTION

The insurance industry faces three main challenges: first, reaching potential customers, second, offering the necessary solutions that meet their preferences, and third, quickly processing their claims, as well as identifying and rejecting fraudulent claims. In particular, insurance companies have been lagging behind in investing in AI-enabled technology, which can improve customer experience and service quality, both by eliminating tedious manual administrative tasks and by making the right decisions. Cutting-edge AI technology keeps agents and employees in sync, facilitating faster decision-making and providing a little more transparency in the workplace (Sanwal, 2021).

The challenges facing the insurance sector today are many and diverse (IBA, 2024; Muir-Wood, 2024; Pearson, 2024): (1) Digital disruption. (2) Cybersecurity risks. (3) Evolving regulatory environment. (4) Attracting and retaining skilled human resources. (5) Consumer expectations and experience. (6) Climate change and catastrophic events.

The term "InsurTech" means the introduction of new technologies and innovations in the insurance industry with the aim of influencing the regulatory practices of insurance markets. Insurance companies that use new technologies and innovations in their various operations, the so-called "insurtech companies", have been helped to reach all sectors of the economy, especially lower income and less developed markets thanks to the use of these new technologies (Rawat et al., 2021).

AI has changed the face of industries and led to new services in every sector for the consumer. Today, AI applications are an integral part of important sectors, such as healthcare, logistics and transportation, food technology, banking, financial services, travel, real estate and entertainment. The role of AI, machine learning (ML) and FinTech in financial decision-making (Ahmed et al., 2022; Ananda et al., 2020; Mushtaq et al., 2022; Rahman et al., 2021) in improving investment efficiency and productivity (Lv and Xiong, 2022; Rodrigues et al., 2022; Wang et al., 2021) is constantly increasing. The technological transformation of the insurance sector reflects the primary use of artificial intelligence applications (Agarwal et al., 2022; Dexe et al., 2021; Ceylan, 2022; Hentzen et al., 2021). While the use of AI in the insurance sector maintains a balance between pricing policies, operational costs and requirements, it also introduces new risks and ethical issues (Dutt, 2020; Mullins et al., 2021). Furthermore, younger generations and public sector administration and security workers value AI-based technologies (Kankanamge et al., 2021).

The areas of insurance in which artificial intelligence has an impact are the following (Cosentino, 2023): (1) product development, (2) marketing, (3) distribution and sales, (4) the underwriting process, i.e. the process through which the insurance company undertakes the insurance risk or not, as well as risk management, (5) the creation and management of insurance policies, (6) the management of insured claims and (7) the company's financial and accounting data.

THEORETICAL BACKGROUND

Information Technology (IT) offers numerous benefits to businesses of all sizes and sectors, allowing them to improve efficiency, communication, scalability and competitiveness (Camoit, 2024).

There are many theories in the field of information technology systems research (Wade & Hulland, 2004), some of which concern the adoption of these systems (Oliveira & Martins, 2011). The most widely used theories related to the adoption of this technology are the technology acceptance model (Davis, et al., 1989), the theory of planned behavior (Ajzen, 1991), the unified theory of technology acceptance and use (Venkatesh, et al., 2003), the theory of diffusion of innovation (Rogers, 1995) and the technology, organization and environment framework (Tornatzky & Fleischer, 1990). The theory of diffusion of innovation and the technology, organization and environment framework concerns the level of the firm, while the remaining theories concern the individual level (Oliveira & Martins, 2011).

When it comes to three categories of technological innovations - applied innovations for technical tasks, innovations in business management and innovations that are embedded in the fundamental business functions of an organization - the technology, organization and environment model is a useful and flexible tool for understanding adoption behavior (Ramdani & Kawalek, 2007). Also, three aspects of the general context of an organization, which are the technological aspect, the organizational aspect and the external environmental aspect are identified by this model as influencing elements in the adoption and implementation of technological innovations by an organization (Shahbazi, 2023).

The technological context includes all technologies that are relevant to the business - both technologies that are already used in the business and those that are available on the market but are not currently used by the business (Baker, 2012). This framework refers to the characteristics of the technology itself, including functionality, complexity, compatibility with existing systems, and ease of use (TheoryHub, 2020). The technologies that a company currently uses play an important role in the process of adopting new technologies, because they place limitations on the extent and pace of technological changes that the company can implement (Collins et al. 1988). It is also important for a company to be aware of technological innovations that are available in the market but that the company itself is not yet using. The intention of a company to adopt these technological innovations subjects to the development of difficult research on choosing the right technology for the job, effective communication and training, a supportive organizational culture, and a clear understanding of the benefits of the technology (Javaid, 2023). In turn, this research indicates to the company the limits of what is possible as well as ways for its evolution (Baker, 2012).

The organizational framework describes the characteristics of an organization that can have a significant impact on the decisions it makes (Alkhater et al., 2014). The factors included in the organizational framework are critical and necessary for the success of the process of adopting new technology because they facilitate the provision of moral and material support (Baig et al., 2023), mobilize resources when needed (Sharma et al., 2022) and change the organizational culture and structure according to needs (Na et al., 2022). These actions increase the responsiveness of companies to technological changes and the speed with which they adopt new technology (Lutfi et al., 2023). Previous research has shown that leadership and several organizational climate and context variables can influence the adoption of change initiatives (Von Treuer et al., 2018). Therefore, the readiness of businesses to accept and adopt innovation is determined by these organizational factors.

Ramanathan et al. (2018) refer to environmental factors as those external factors that exist in the environment in which a business operates and affect its performance. These external factors are categorized into external supports and external pressures (Liu et al., 2016). External supports refer to the assistance that the business receives from any third party outside itself to support its growth, while external pressures refer to all types of pressure from third parties that limit its growth (Hasani & O'Reilly, 2021). The external factors that affect a business are economic factors, market competition factors, government policy factors, and social factors (Salonga, 2023).

Previous studies on the adoption of artificial intelligence use different theoretical models. In this study, we use the Technology Organization Environment (TOE) framework to examine factors influencing the adoption of AI in the insurance industry. Furthermore, this study relies on employee data rather than customer data and explores emerging trends in AI adoption to arrive at critical observations and considerations for successful technology adoption in the insurance sector.

As AI is a viable technology, this study examines the critical determinants of the adoption of new technology from an administrative and insurance perspective. However, the decision maker who absorbs technological developments is not the individual consumer who uses them, but the industry that enables its customers to use them. Therefore, following previous studies (Abed, 2020; Ramdani et al., 2013; Srivastava et al., 2022), this study applies the TOE model to assess the acceptance of new technologies at the firm level. The TOE framework recognizes the numerous factors that influence the adoption of new technologies. The technology, organization, and environment framework provides a useful analytical framework that can be used to study the adoption and assimilation of different types of innovation in Information Technology (Oliveira & Martins, 2011).

In this study, relative advantage, complexity, top management support, financial readiness, market dynamics, regulatory support, and competitive pressure are all significant in predicting the adoption of artificial intelligence in insurance. However, technological capability has not significantly influenced employees' behavioral intention (BI) to adopt AI.

APPROACH

The extent to which an innovation is expected to benefit businesses is known as its relative advantage (Rogers et al., 2014). A key factor in encouraging businesses to adopt new technology is the advantages of the innovation over alternatives. This means that decisions about technology adoption are largely based on the relative advantage that the innovation offers to businesses (Ali-Abbasi et al., 2022). Businesses are more likely to adopt an invention if they believe it will benefit their operations (Chatterjee et al., 2020).

By adopting artificial intelligence, insurance companies are seeking to gain an advantage over their peers who have not yet adopted it. However, adopting artificial intelligence comes with a cost. Compared to these costs, perceived benefits provide a relative advantage to insurance companies in terms of customer satisfaction and increased responsiveness, ultimately giving an advantage to their reputation.

Nowadays, artificial intelligence is applied to automated network operations, speech and voice services aimed at customers, and chatbots for customer support (El Khatib et al., 2019). These applications save operating costs, enhance customer satisfaction, improve service quality, and increase business productivity. This leads to the hypothesis that:

Hypothesis 1: Relative advantage positively influences behavioral intention to adopt AI applications in the insurance industry (Nguyen et al., 2022).

Complexity refers to "the degree to which an innovation is perceived as difficult to understand and use" (Rogers, 1995). Another definition of complexity is the existence of many interdependent variables in a given system, where more variables and greater interdependence mean greater complexity and uncertainty (Dorner, 1990). The application and data landscape in large companies today is typically reflected in a web of interconnected platforms, databases, and applications that are extremely difficult to understand and even more difficult to change securely. The impact of all this complexity manifests itself in several ways, the most important of which is that it makes it extremely difficult for the organization to change, improve, and innovate (DeBrusk, 2024). Therefore:

Hypothesis 2: Complexity negatively affects behavioral intention to adopt AI applications in the insurance industry (Gupta et al., 2022).

In a rapidly evolving technological landscape, the role of top management has become crucial to how quickly and effectively organizations adopt new technologies (Vorecol, 2024). Top management support for innovation means that an organization's leaders believe in the importance of innovation and are willing to provide resources, guidance, and encouragement to make it happen (Owlift, 2011). Leaders can also develop a culture of innovation in their team members by creating an environment where it is safe to take risks and make mistakes (Jones, 2024). From the above, it can be concluded that:

Hypothesis 3: Top management support positively influences behavioral intention to adopt AI applications in the insurance industry.

Technological capabilities include both applied and theoretical knowledge, as well as the tools, techniques, and resources required to create new products (Wang et al., 2004). According to McEvily et al. (2004), technological capabilities encompass a portfolio of capabilities of the firm to apply scientific and technical knowledge to research and develop products and processes, resulting in increased performance and innovation. The literature shows that companies must gain a sustainable competitive advantage by combining, absorbing and transforming their core resources, tools and techniques (Cepeda & Vera, 2007; Moliterno & Wiersema, 2007). A company's resources can create exceptional performance and transform this performance into competitive advantage (Barney, 1991). Therefore, it is assumed that:

Hypothesis 4: Technological competence positively affects the behavioral intention to adopt artificial intelligence applications in the insurance industry.

The ability of an organization to adapt quickly to economic shocks while maintaining its commercial operations and its personnel, resources and overall reputation intact is known as the "resilience" of the company (Kirvan, 2022). One aspect of building the resilience of a company is its so-called "financial readiness". An organization's financial readiness is achieved through developing a dynamic plan to deal with sudden market changes and rising costs, ensuring that a continuous cash flow is maintained to cover its operating expenses, and maintaining a delicate balance between its equity and credit expansion (ClearCycle, 2020), which are reflected in its ability and willingness to invest in innovative technologies (Hossain et al., 2016). Therefore:

Hypothesis 5: Financial readiness positively influences behavioral intention to adopt artificial intelligence applications in the insurance industry.

When insurance companies claim the same market share, they are driven to produce cutting-edge products and services, enhance their operational efficiency, and improve customer satisfaction. This competition creates a market environment that rewards continuous progress (Marg ERP Ltd, 2023). With a fundamental role in modern economies, the insurance industry is currently at a critical juncture, where a multitude of challenges are reshaping its traditional contours. As technology evolves at an unprecedented pace, the insurance industry must adapt and evolve by incorporating new tools and methodologies, such as big data analytics, artificial intelligence and blockchain (Vanguard, 2024). Thus, the following hypothesis is formed:

Hypothesis 6: Market dynamics positively and significantly affect the intention to adopt AI in the insurance industry.

Government support creates a positive environment for the adoption of AI, thus enhancing its diffusion and impact (Agrawal et al., 2018). Also, AI providers need to maintain good relations with the government to gain support and resources to promote new AI applications (Chen, 2019). This leads to the following hypothesis:

Hypothesis 7: Regulatory support positively and significantly affects the intention to adopt AI in the insurance industry.

New entrants to the insurance industry, such as InsurTech startups and digitally-oriented companies, are becoming increasingly competitive. In order to provide more accurate risk assessments, personalized pricing, streamlined services, and improved customer experience, these newer companies often use cutting-edge technologies, such as artificial intelligence, machine learning, and data analytics (Levio Consulting Inc., 2023). Traditional insurance companies face difficulties as a result of these changes because they are slow to adopt these new technologies. In order to achieve multiple benefits not only for policyholders and the economy, but also for insurers and reinsurers, digitalization has the potential to completely change insurance companies (Njegomir & Demko-Rihter, 2023). As a conclusion, the following hypothesis is drawn:

Hypothesis 8: Competitive pressure positively affects the intention to adopt artificial intelligence in the insurance industry.

The structural model of the above approach is depicted in the image below.

RESEARCH METHODOLOGY

The present research is quantitative as it is based on the collection of quantitative data using a structured questionnaire and interpretation as it tests the causal relationships expressed in the form of eight research hypotheses.

The Population of the Present Research

The population of the present research consists of executives of insurance companies in Northern Greece. The basic criterion for participation in this empirical research (completion of a questionnaire) was professional employment in the insurance industry and specifically by senior management executives (e.g. CEO, department manager, etc.) but also by executives who perform corresponding duties.

The specific methodological approach of answering the questionnaire by specific users using data analytics has been adopted by a number of previous studies that have been published in reliable scientific journals. For example, Singh et al. (2022) used a structured questionnaire to collect responses from senior HR executives. Similar methodology has been used by Qaffas et al. (2022), Aljumah et al. (2022a), Pinochet et al. (2021), Bag et al. (2021), Behl (2020), Su et al. (2021), Aljumah et al. (2021b), Wamba et al. (2018), Al-Dmour et al. (2021), Maroufkhani et al. (2020), Khan et al. (2022), Al-Khatib (2022).

Data Collection Instrument

The measurement of each factor of this study was done using multiple questions. The questions used in the questionnaire were adopted from foreign-language surveys fully adapted to Greek data, while their paraphrasing was checked in various ways due to problems in the transfer of terms. The measurement of all determinant variables (questions) was done with the Likert scale in which the respondent is asked to state the degree of agreement or disagreement with a series of statements (from 1= strongly disagree to 5= strongly agree) in relation to the subject.

The first section includes two questions that record the demographic characteristics of the sample and two questions related to their work. The second section includes the questions used to measure the nine factors of this study. More specifically, a total of thirty-nine (39) questions were used to measure these factors.

The number of questions included in the final questionnaire were taken from the three foreign language articles (Gupta et al., 2022; Twaissi et al., 2024; El-khateeb & AL-Omari, 2023). Some questions were removed and identical questions were adapted appropriately.

Organization of the Data Collection Process

The use of a structured questionnaire was chosen, with closed-ended questions in the main part of the research and open-ended questions regarding the subject of the work. In this way, the process of completing the questionnaire and the coding of its analysis was simplified. The use of a structured questionnaire was determined by the nature of the research conducted, as it is an interpretive research.

Content Validity Check of the Questionnaire

The questionnaire used to measure the empirical data of this empirical research was checked for its validity before the research was conducted. At the same time, it was evaluated for its reliability regarding the participants' responses and not the questionnaire itself. Increasing the reliability of a questionnaire implies a reduction in random error.

The questionnaire was answered only by participants related to the insurance industry. Therefore, the participants were able to understand and respond effectively to the questionnaire given to them. In addition, a rewording of the questions that contained ambiguities and caused confusion to the respondents was carried out. The modifications also included the layout of the questionnaire in order to enhance its effectiveness.

The validity of the measurement instruments as well as the reliability of the questionnaire are necessary to ensure correct results from conducting a survey. The above checks were carried out with the aim of better rendering all the concepts, with absolute accuracy, in the Greek language. Therefore, the questionnaire was considered balanced and suitable to be distributed electronically to the selected sample of the population under study.

There are two reasons that contributed to the carrying out of the above checks: (a) the need to adapt the included questions, according to the specificities and peculiarities of the data of Greek society, and (b) the inability to render all the concepts, with absolute accuracy, in the Greek language.

DATA COLLECTION

The survey was conducted from June to September 2024. The questionnaire was given to approximately 850 people via e-mail (Google Forms) and to approximately 150 people in person and the responses received are 179 (74 people responded via Google Forms and 105 in person after removing 7 incomplete questionnaires). Therefore, the final sample of this survey consists of 179 questionnaires.

This number is quite satisfactory since it is significantly above the corresponding number of questionnaires collected from some previous studies (Aljumah et al., 2021b; Wamba et al., 2018; Al-Dmour et al., 2021; Singh et al., 2022).

Statistical Analysis Methodology

After the completion of the empirical research, the data (answered questionnaires) were carefully coded, their conversion into usable digital data and their statistical analysis followed. More specifically, the statistical analysis was carried out using IBM SPSS 20.0 and IBM AMOS 20.0 software.

Descriptive statistical techniques (mean, standard deviation, etc.) were used to analyze the demographic characteristics of the sample. In addition, various tests were performed for possible differences in the mean of the responses (analysis of variance, ANOVA).

Exploratory Factor Analysis (using the IBM SPSS 20.0 statistical program) and Confirmatory Factor Analysis (using the IBM AMOS 20.0 statistical program) were used to check the validity of the questionnaire structure. The evaluation of the conceptual framework and the testing of the research hypotheses were carried out using the Structural Equation Modeling technique (using the IBM AMOS 20.0 statistical program).

EMPIRICAL RESEARCH RESULTS

Table 1. Basic characteristics of the sample

Characteristic	Frequency	Percentage
Gender		
Male	91	50.8%
Female	88	49.2%
Total	179	100%
Age		
<35	23	12.8%
35-44	52	29.1%
>44	104	58.1%
Total	179	100%
Work experience		
<6	18	10.1%
6-10	17	9.5%
>10	144	80.4%
Total	179	100%

Figure 1. Scree plot of eigenvalues and components

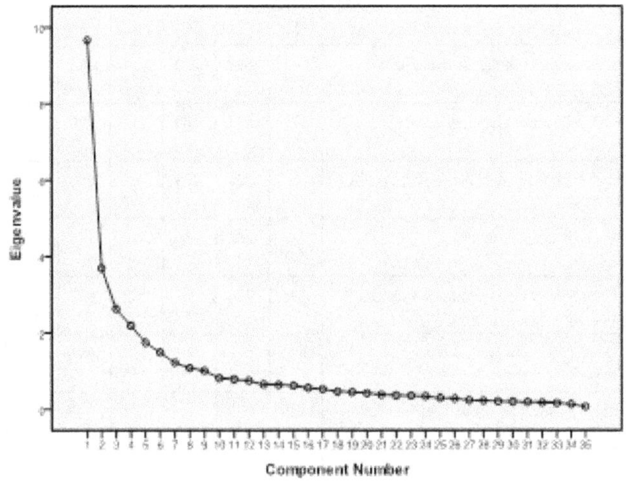

The questions associated with each factor are shown in blue in the columns of Table 5. The first axis is mainly related to behavioral intention and relates to the questions on top management support and technological capability. That is, hypotheses 3 and 4 about the intention to adopt AI are verified.

The second axis is mainly related to the multipolarity of AI in the insurance sector (independent of the first axis), while the third axis is mainly related to its relative advantage (independent of the first axis).

Table 5. Component matrix[a]

	Component								
	1	**2**	**3**	**4**	**5**	**6**	**7**	**8**	**9**
AI-based insurance firms can quickly complete the firm operations.	,482	-,345	**,538**	,156	,190	-,018	-,197	-,058	-,034
AI-based insurance firms can enhance the efficiency of their operations.	,546	-,287	**,512**	,125	,236	-,106	-,153	-,159	,009
The introduction of AI in insurance firms can increase their profits.	,556	-,170	**,455**	,214	-,111	-,037	-,038	,028	,004
AI will also be helpful in the insurance supply chain.	,573	-,279	**,426**	,177	-,019	-,095	-,212	,070	-,054
AI introduction in insurance is convenient for me to manage.	,522	-,391	**,476**	,100	,114	-,187	,052	,029	,100
AI introduction in insurance will not be simple to operate.	-,053	**,572**	,145	,392	,107	,222	-,224	,038	,158

continued on following page

Table 5. Continued

	Component								
	1	2	3	4	5	6	7	8	9
The introduction and operation of AI in the insurance sector require much effort.	-,111	**,698**	,222	,227	,196	,248	-,271	,054	,109
I believe that the use of AI in insurance requires ample experience.	-,070	**,672**	,200	,214	,096	,212	-,207	,062	,191
I believe that my firm does not understand how AI will benefit the firm in its growth.	-,319	**,324**	,425	-,083	,250	-,170	,339	,044	,215
I believe that AI in insurance is not easy to use.	-,221	**,662**	-,024	,310	,196	,033	,175	-,051	,049
Top managers support by providing labor resources, finances, and materials for AI adoption.	**,595**	,230	-,247	,232	,067	-,090	-,067	-,335	-,163
Top management inspires employees to apply the latest AI technologies in daily work.	**,672**	-,017	-,258	,183	,083	-,198	,024	-,176	,049
The top management of my organization encourages innovation.	**,645**	,096	-,280	,391	-,019	,019	-,166	-,088	,014
My organization's top management is willing to take risks involved in adopting AI to promote insuretech.	**,679**	,143	-,276	,211	-,179	-,073	-,008	-,223	-,031
My organization's top management is likely to consider the implementation of AI as strategically important.	**,684**	,076	-,247	,263	-,212	,038	,038	-,186	-,039
My organization has an excellent AI-based infrastructure, including all IT components.	**,666**	,042	-,277	,028	,386	,027	,085	,155	,021
Employees are generally aware of the functions of insurance and AI applications.	**,634**	-,114	-,203	-,086	,492	,047	-,031	,298	-,063
Employees of our organization are well trained in both insurance and AI applications.	,584	-,037	-,365	-,062	,510	-,120	-,058	,201	-,031
The company has good knowledge about AI adoption.	**,717**	,014	-,249	-,115	,350	-,007	,017	,071	-,078
The company would have the financial resources to adopt AI.	,584	-,025	,084	-,429	,158	,561	,112	-,181	,087
The financial budgets of the company would be enough to back the adoption of AI.	,565	-,002	,103	-,450	,072	,501	,139	-,197	,148
Obtaining financial support from local banks and/or other financial institutions would be easy to adopt AI.	,550	,032	,114	-,352	-,132	,298	,035	-,094	-,039
Customer/stakeholders' preferences or requirements are always changing in the Insurance industry.	,311	,423	,272	-,075	-,147	,047	-,037	,193	-,551
The insurance industry is sensitive to changes in the marketplace.	,174	,492	,242	,081	-,009	,057	,370	,044	-,503
In the Insurance industry, change is difficult to predict.	,166	,366	,338	,120	,100	-,278	,530	-,077	,111
AI adoption in insurance will receive financial support from the government or relevant authorities.	,453	,414	,038	-,352	-,233	-,331	-,215	-,166	,062
The government introduces relevant policies to boost AI in insurance for its development.	,518	,451	-,014	-,360	-,169	-,284	-,181	-,144	,111
There is legal support for the use of AI in insurance.	,411	,401	,202	-,478	-,071	-,237	-,117	,036	,093
The laws and regulations that exist nowadays are sufficient to protect the use of AI in insurance.	,445	,284	-,028	-,383	,152	-,367	,036	,048	,054

continued on following page

Table 5. Continued

	Component								
	1	2	3	4	5	6	7	8	9
The company thinks that AI adoption influences competitiveness in the industry.	**,605**	,156	,071	-,075	-,219	,129	-,032	,165	-,251
The company is pressed by the competition to adopt AI.	,531	,122	-,136	,054	-,417	,036	,213	,326	,269
Some competitors have already started using AI for Risk forecasting and premium calculations.	,477	,078	-,085	-,017	-,316	,012	-,137	,555	,156
I predict my organization will adopt AI in the future.	**,748**	-,033	-,093	,198	-,233	,182	,135	-,084	,138
I predict I will use AI in the future.	,585	-,285	,380	,096	-,159	,100	,053	,074	,055
My firm intends to transform insurance through adoption of AI digitally.	**,686**	-,134	-,090	,329	-,127	-,030	,348	,087	,122

Extraction Method: Principal Component Analysis.
a. 9 components extracted.

The relationship with the characteristics of individuals on each axis is presented in the following diagrams.

Figure 2. Characteristics of individuals by gender in each axis

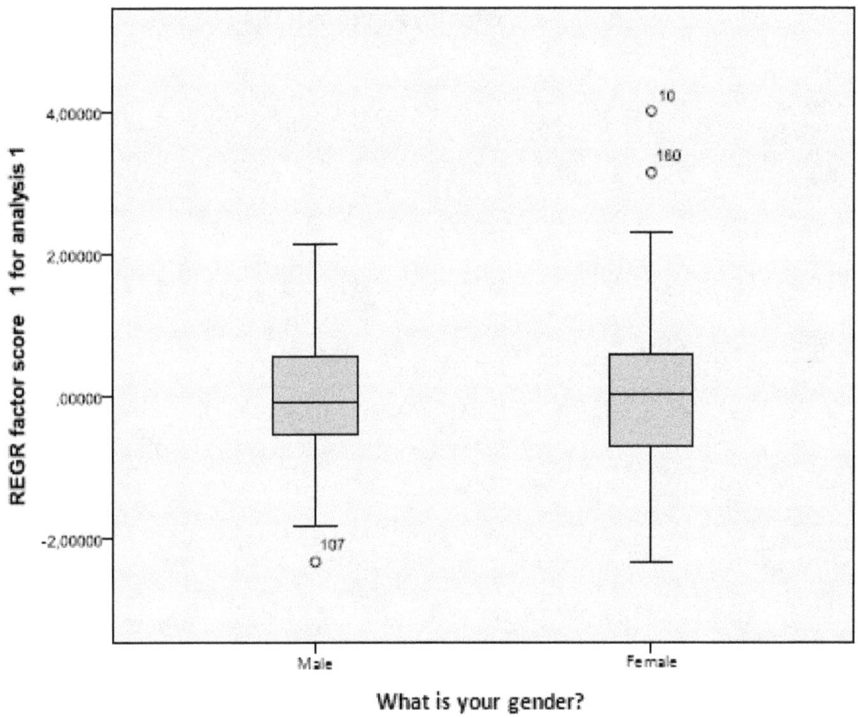

Figure 3. Characteristics of individuals by gender in each axis

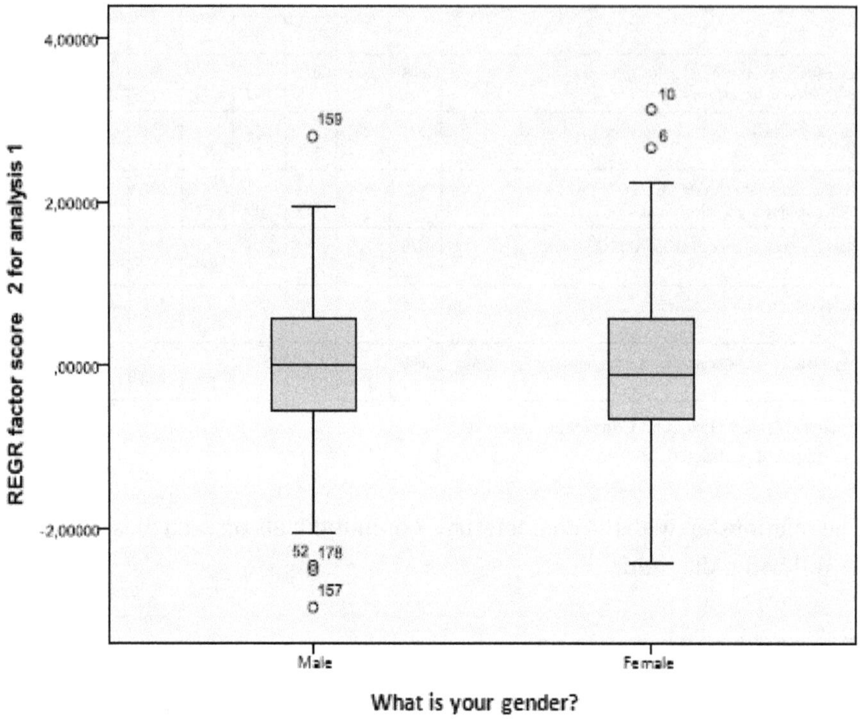

Figure 4. Characteristics of individuals by gender in each axis

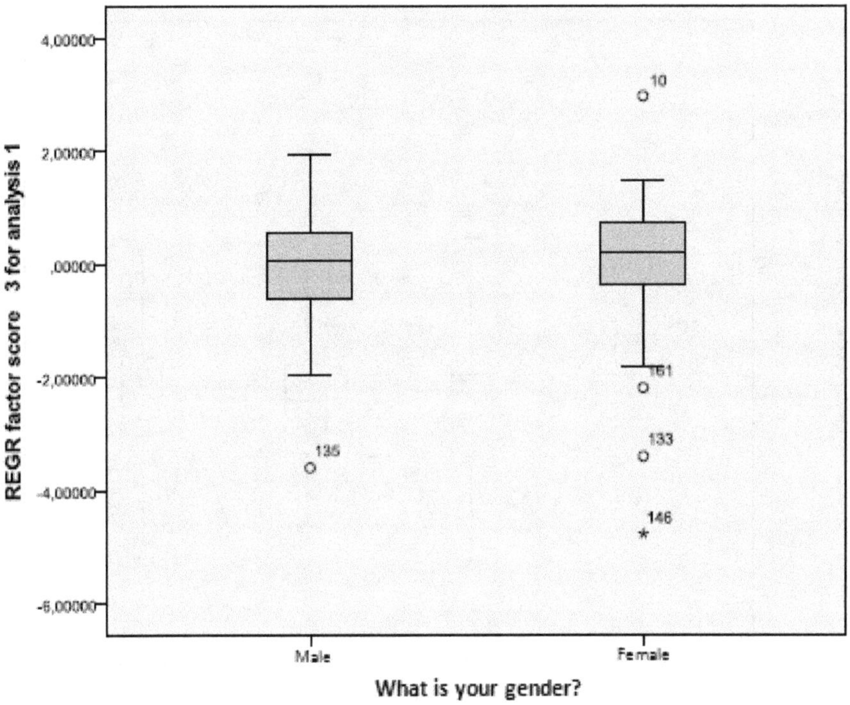

Regarding gender (Figure 6-8), no significant differences are observed in the first 3 factorial axes.

Figure 5. Characteristics of individuals in terms of age in each axis

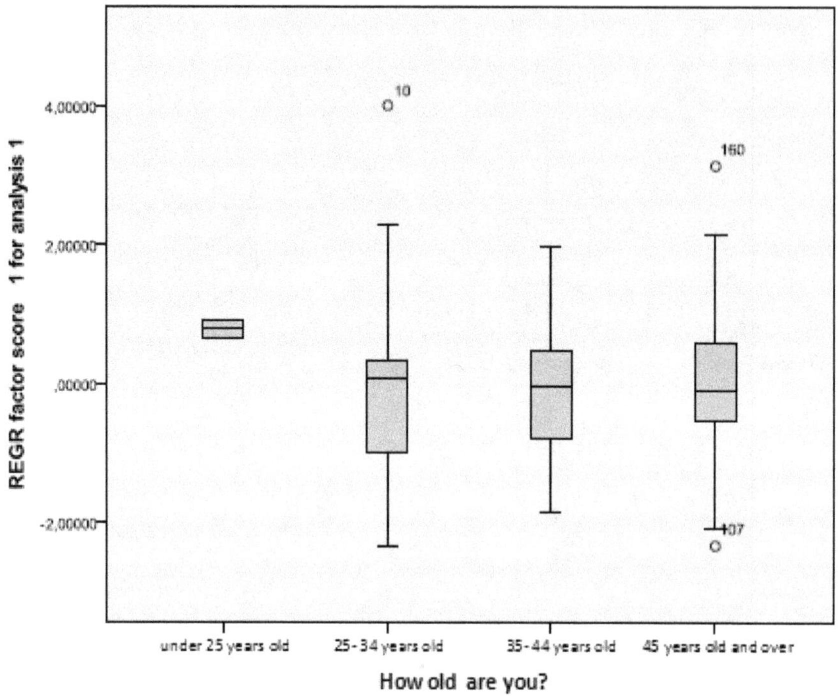

Figure 6. Characteristics of individuals in terms of age in each axis

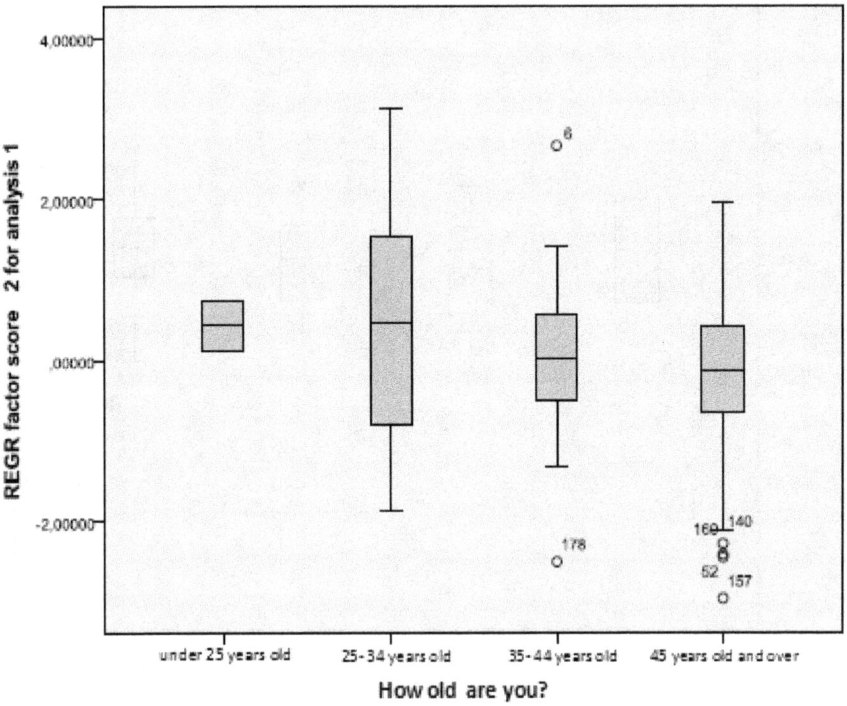

Figure 7. Characteristics of individuals in terms of age in each axis

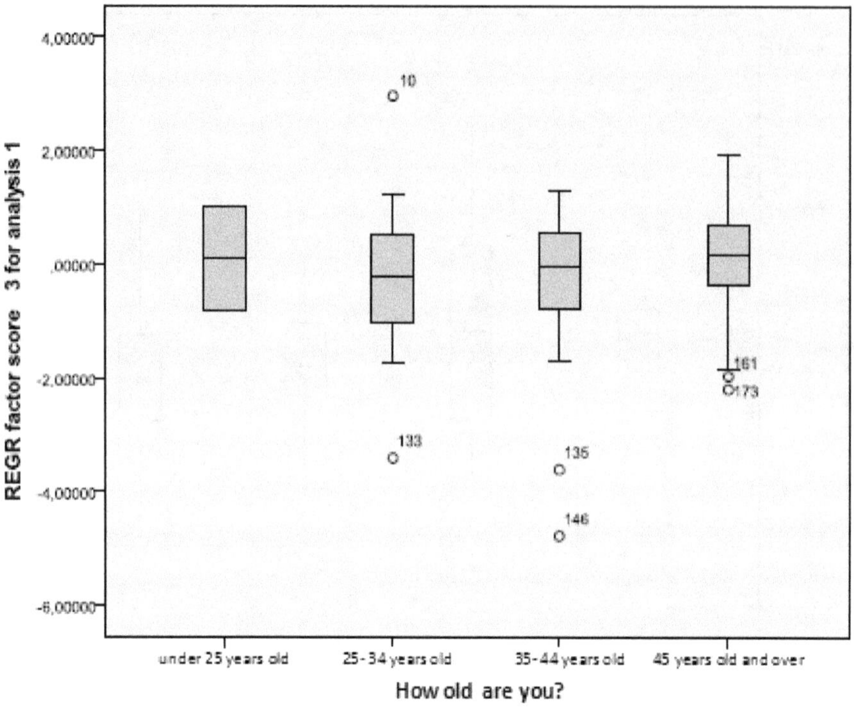

In terms of age (Figure 6-8), some differences are observed. Those under 25 years of age are all in the positives of the 1st and 2nd factorial axes. That is, they have more intention to adopt and consider the effectiveness of artificial intelligence to be positive. Of course, only 2 individuals in the sample are under 25 years of age. In the 3rd axis there is no difference in terms of age.

Figure 8. Characteristics of individuals by years of work experience in each axis

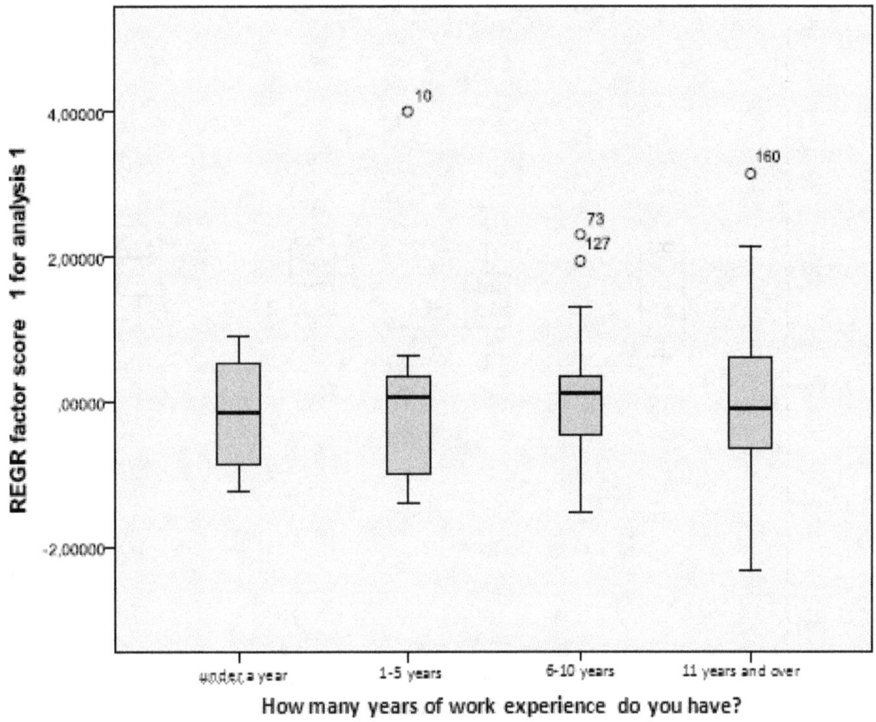

Figure 9. Characteristics of individuals by years of work experience in each axis

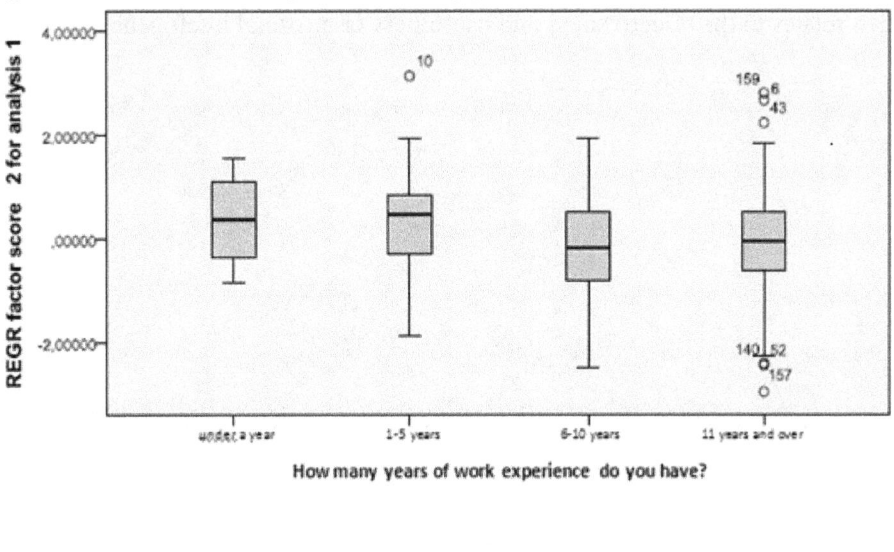

Figure 10. Characteristics of individuals by years of work experience in each axis

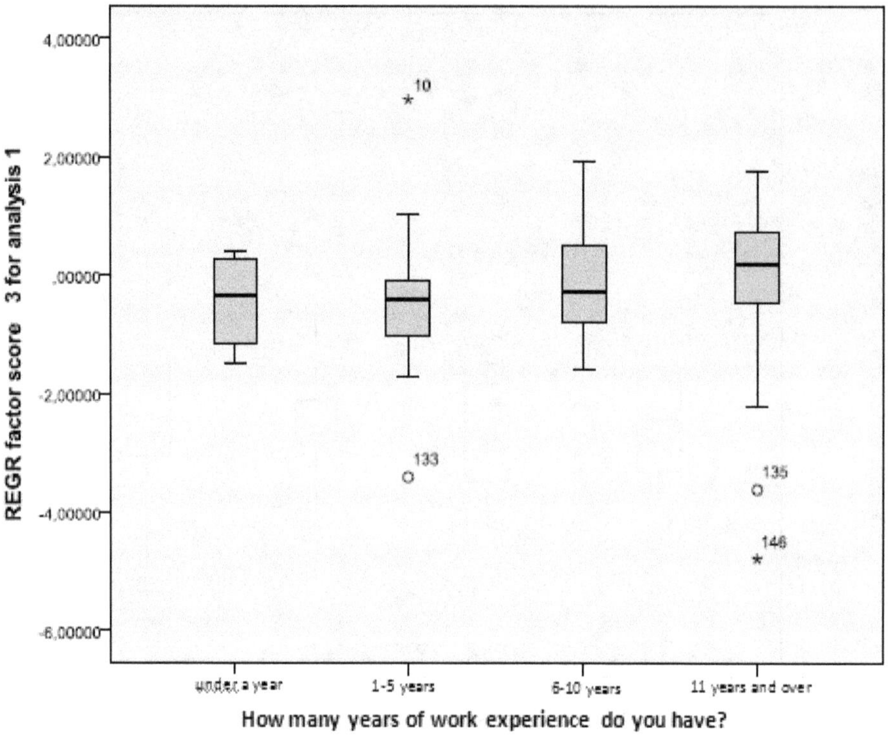

Experience (Figure 9-11) does not differ in the 1st and 2nd factorial axes. Those with work experience under 10 years are mainly in the negatives of the 3rd axis, which relates to the effectiveness and usefulness of artificial intelligence.

Figure 11. Characteristics of individuals by job title on each axis

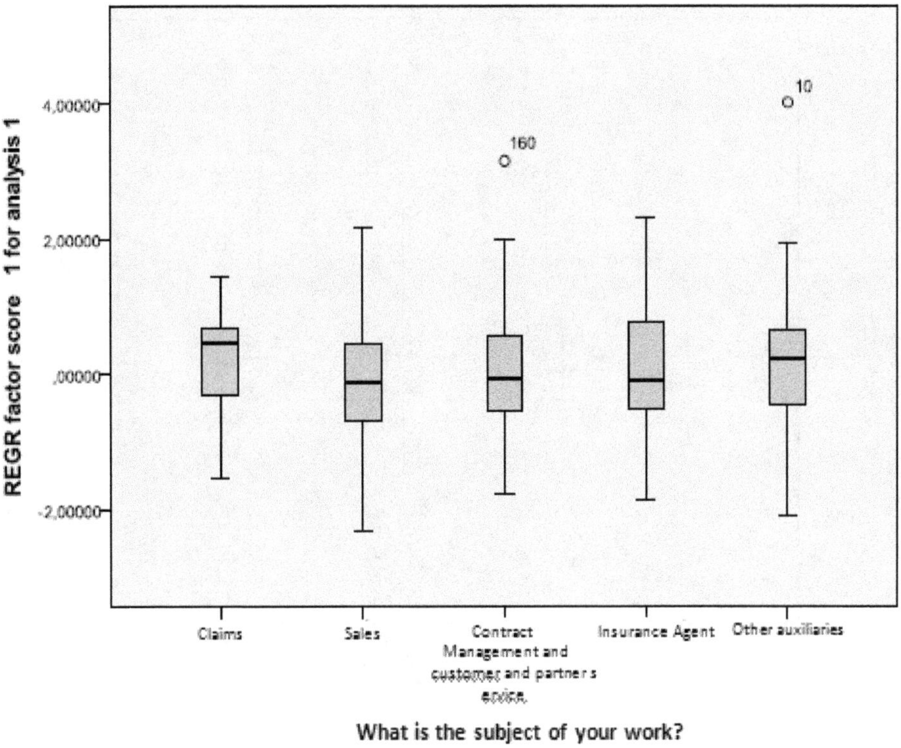

Figure 12. Characteristics of individuals by job title on each axis

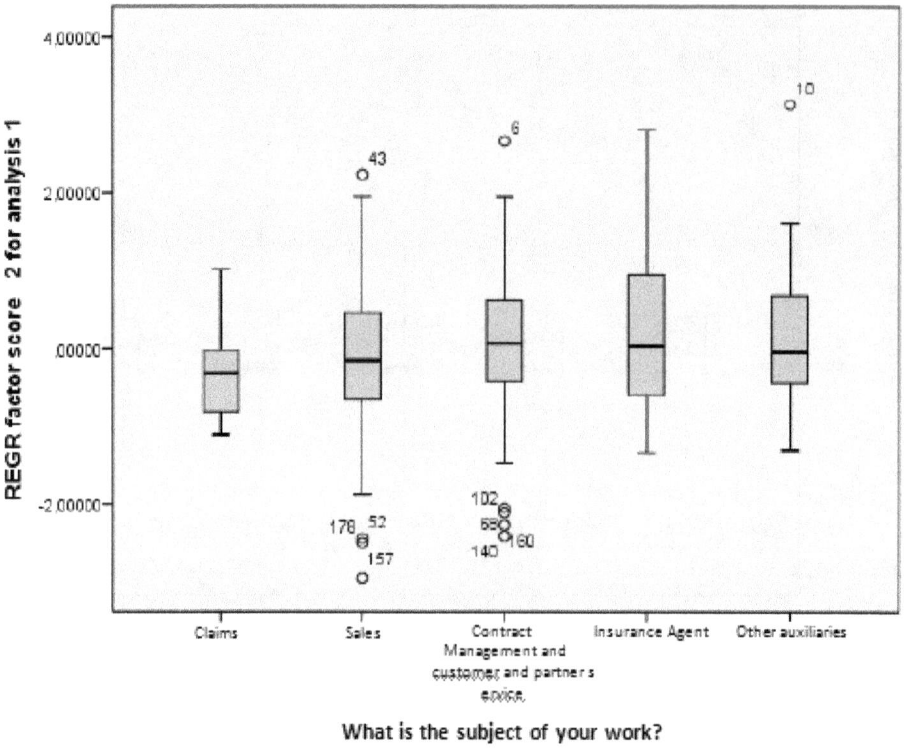

Figure 13. Characteristics of individuals by job title on each axis

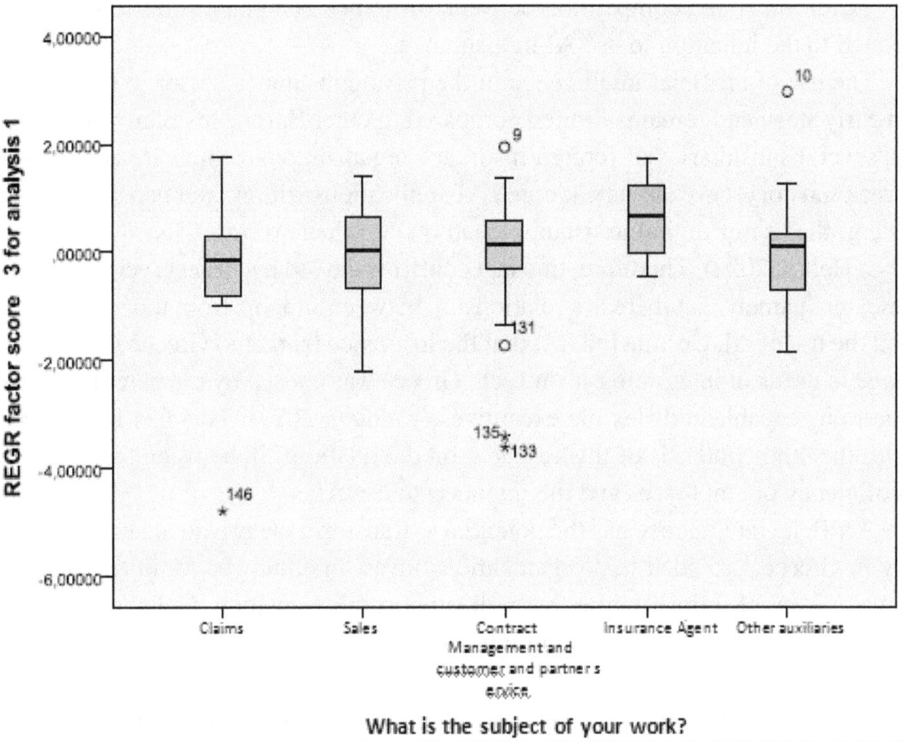

The job title is divided into five categories (four main ones and all the others as a 5th category). As can be seen in the diagram in Figure 12-14, the first axis is mainly related to the job title for damage compensation. Workers in compensation are on the negative side of the second factorial axis. The insurance agent category is on the positive side of the three-way axis.

DISCUSSION AND CONCLUSIONS

It is observed that there is a coexistence of the factors of support from top management and technological competence of the company and employees with the intention to adopt the use of AI in the insurance industry. That is, the 3rd and 4th hypotheses of the literature (Gupta, Ghardallou, Pandey, & Sahu, 2022; Twaissi, El-Khateeb, Al-Sharif, Almomany, & Abu Karaki, 2024; El-khateeb & AL-Omari, 2023) for the intention to adopt AI are verified. On the other hand, factors such as the expected benefit of insurance companies from the use of AI, the compatibility and ease of use of AI, the financial readiness of insurance organizations to acquire

AI technology, the effort to satisfy customer preferences, regulatory support from the government and competition between insurance companies do not seem to be related to the intention to use AI in insurance.

The use of artificial intelligence in the private insurance sector in Greece is at an early stage and remains limited compared to other European countries. However, several subsidiaries of foreign insurance organizations, which are active in the Greek territory, have already adopted AI applications within their capabilities such as e.g. the use of digital assistants (chatbots) on their websites (Next Dial, 2024, Ergo Hellas, 2023). Therefore, this fact confirms the 3rd hypothesis verified by this research, namely that there is a relationship between support from top management and the use of AI. Despite the fact that the insurance market in Greece is at an early stage in terms of integrating InsurTech, Greece was chosen by the parent company due to its capable and flexible executives (Kaloudi, 2023). This fact is consistent with the 4th hypothesis of this research on the relationship between technological proficiency of employees and the intention to use AI.

Artificial intelligence has the potential to transform the private insurance industry in Greece, provided that organizations invest in employee training and in the development of infrastructure that will support this transition. Collaboration with technology players and promoting innovation will be crucial for the success of AI in this field.

A key limitation of this research is the reduced use of artificial intelligence by insurance companies operating in Greece compared to companies abroad. This fact affects the responses of insurance industry employees, mainly regarding the benefits that the use of AI could offer in their work, as well as the complexity of using the new technology.

For further analysis of the data from this study, as well as for conducting a new study to examine the strength of similar research hypotheses, structural equation modeling (SEM) could be used. The analytical procedures provided by these systems allow researchers to evaluate the overall hypothesized structure of a model, simultaneously examining all the relationships between the dependent and independent variables. Structural equation modeling is commonly used as a method for validating various theoretical hypotheses, as it is not limited only to estimating the model parameters but also evaluates their fit to the data (Hoyle, 2012).

REFERENCES

Abed, S. S. (2020). Social commerce adoption using TOE framework: An empirical investigation of Saudi Arabian SMEs. *International Journal of Information Management, 53*, 102118. DOI: 10.1016/j.ijinfomgt.2020.102118

Aggarwal, A. (2022). Determinants of technology adaption within the framework of TOE: An insurance sector perspective. *ECS Transactions, 107*(1), 3417–3428. DOI: 10.1149/10701.3417ecst

Agrawal, A., Gans, J. S., & Goldfarb, A. (2019). Exploring the impact of artificial intelligence: Prediction versus judgment. *Information Economics and Policy, 47*, 1–6. DOI: 10.1016/j.infoecopol.2019.05.001

Ahmed, S., Alshater, M. M., Ammari, A., & Hammami, H. (2022). Artificial intelligence and machine learning in finance: A bibliometric review. *Research in International Business and Finance, 61*, 101646. DOI: 10.1016/j.ribaf.2022.101646

Ajzen, I. (1991). The theory of planned behavior. *Organizational Behavior and Human Decision Processes, 50*(2), 179–211. DOI: 10.1016/0749-5978(91)90020-T

Al-Dmour, H., Saad, N., Amin, E. B., Al-Dmour, R., & Al-Dmour, A. (2021). *The influence of the practices of big data analytics applications on bank performance: filed study*. VINE Journal of Information and Knowledge Management., DOI: 10.1108/VJIKMS-08-2020-0151

Al-Khatib, W. A. (2022). Big data analytics capabilities and green supply chain performance: Investigating the moderated mediation model for green innovation and technological intensity. *Business Process Management Journal, 28*(5/6), 1446–1461. DOI: 10.1108/BPMJ-07-2022-0332

Ali Abbasi, G., Abdul Rahim, N. F., Wu, H., Iranmanesh, M., & Keong, B. N. C. (2022). Determinants of SME's social media marketing adoption: Competitive industry as a moderator. *SAGE Open, 12*(1), 21582440211067220. DOI: 10.1177/21582440211067220

Aljumah, A. I., Nuseir, M. T., & Alam, M. M. (2021b). Traditional marketing analytics, big data analytics and big data systems quality and the success of new product development. *Business Process Management Journal, 27*(4), 1109–1121. DOI: 10.1108/BPMJ-11-2020-0527

Alkhater, N., Wills, G., & Walters, R. (2014). Factors influencing an organisation's intention to adopt cloud computing in Saudi Arabia. In 2014 IEEE 6th international conference on cloud computing technology and science (pp. 1040-1044). IEEE. DOI: 10.1109/CloudCom.2014.95

Ananda, S., Devesh, S., & Lawati, A. M. (2020). What factors drive the adoption of digital banking? An empirical study from the perspective of Omani retail banking. *Journal of Financial Services Marketing*, *25*(1-2), 14–24. DOI: 10.1057/s41264-020-00072-y

Bag, S., Luthra, S., Mangla, K. S., & Kazancoglou, Y. (2021). Leveraging big data analytics capabilities in making reverse logistics decisions and improving remanufacturing performance. *International Journal of Logistics Management*, *32*(3), 743758. DOI: 10.1108/IJLM-06-2020-0237

Baig, M. I., Yadegaridehkordi, E., & Nizam Bin Md Nasir, M. H. (2023). Influence of big data adoption on sustainable marketing and operation of SMEs: A hybrid approach of SEM-ANN. *Management Decision*, *61*(7), 2231–2253. DOI: 10.1108/MD-06-2022-0778

Baker, J. (2012). The technology–organization–environment framework. *Information Systems Theory: Explaining and Predicting Our Digital Society*, *1*, 231–245.

Barney, J. (1991). Firm resources and sustained competitive advantage. *Journal of Management*, *17*(1), 99–120. DOI: 10.1177/014920639101700108

Behl, A. (2020). Antecedents to firm performance and competitiveness using the lens of big data analytics: A cross cultural study. *Management Decision*, *6*(2), 369–387.

Camoit. How Information Technology (IT) Can Benefit Your Business. Retrieval date: 5 August 2024. https://camoitsolutions.ca/how-information-technology-it-can-benefit-your-business/

Cepeda, G., & Vera, D. (2007). Dynamic capabilities and operational capabilities: A knowledge management perspective. *Journal of Business Research*, *60*(5), 426–437. DOI: 10.1016/j.jbusres.2007.01.013

Ceylan, I.E. (2022). The effects of artificial intelligence on the insurance sector: emergence, applications, challenges, and opportunities. Account. Financ. Sustain. Gov. Fraud 225-241. .DOI: 10.1007/978-981-16-8997-0_13

Chatterjee, S., Nguyen, B., Ghosh, S. K., Bhattacharjee, K. K., & Chaudhuri, S. (2020). Adoption of artificial intelligence integrated CRM system: An empirical study of Indian organizations. *The Bottom Line (New York, N.Y.)*, *33*(4), 359–375. DOI: 10.1108/BL-08-2020-0057

Chen, G., Xie, P., Dong, J., & Wang, T. (2019). Understanding programmatic creative: The role of AI. *Journal of Advertising*, *48*(4), 347–355. DOI: 10.1080/00913367.2019.1654421

Collins, P. D., Hage, J., & Hull, F. M. (1988). Organizational and technological predictors of change in automaticity. *Academy of Management Journal*, *31*(3), 512–543. DOI: 10.2307/256458

Cosentino, A. (2024). The Role of Artificial Intelligence in the Insurance Business. Retrieval date: 4 June 2024. https://aqabaconf.com/images/uploads/Andrea_Aqaba.pdf

Davis, F. D., Bagozzi, R. P., & Warshaw, P. R. (1989). User acceptance of computer technology: A comparison of two theoretical models. *Management Science*, *35*(8), 982–1003. DOI: 10.1287/mnsc.35.8.982

DeBrusk, C. (2024). Technology Complexity And Its Impact On Innovation. Retrieval date: 8 August 2024. https://www.oliverwyman.com/our-expertise/insights/2022/jan/technology-complexity-and-its-impact-on-innovation.html

Dexe, J., Franke, U., & Rad, A. (2021). Transparency and insurance professionals: A study of Swedish insurance practice attitudes and future development. *The Geneva Papers on Risk and Insurance. Issues and Practice*, *46*(4), 547–572. DOI: 10.1057/s41288-021-00207-9 PMID: 33686323

Dorner, D. (1990). The logic of failure. *Philosophical Transactions of the Royal Society of London. Series B, Biological Sciences*, *327*(1241), 463–473. PMID: 1970892

Dutt, R. (2020). The impact of artificial intelligence on healthcare insurances. In *Artificial Intelligence in Healthcare* (pp. 271–293). Elsevier., DOI: 10.1016/B978-0-12-818438-7.00011-3

El-khateeb, A. I., & AL-Omari, O. H. (2023). Study the Impact of Artificial Intelligence Applications on Insurance Industry: A case of Jordan. *2023 WEI.*

El Khatib, M. M., Al-Nakeeb, A., & Ahmed, G. (2019). Integration of Cloud Computing with Artificial Intelligence and Its Impact on Telecom Sector—A Case Study. iBusiness, 11(01), 1.

Ergo Hellas. (2023). ERGO Insurance in the era of Artificial Intelligence with "Journey", the new Chatbot that changes the way it communicates with its customers. Retrieval date: 19 October 2024. https://www.ergohellas.gr/news/ergo-introduces-ai-chatbot-xara (In Greek).

Gupta, S., Ghardallou, W., Pandey, D. K., & Sahu, G. P. (2022). Artificial intelligence adoption in the insurance industry: Evidence using the technology–organization–environment framework. *Research in International Business and Finance*, *63*, 101757. DOI: 10.1016/j.ribaf.2022.101757

Hasani, T., & O'Reilly, N. (2021). Analyzing antecedents affecting the organizational performance of start-up businesses. *Journal of Entrepreneurship in Emerging Economies*, *13*(1), 107–130. DOI: 10.1108/JEEE-08-2019-0116

Hentzen, J. K., Hoffmann, A., Dolan, R., & Pala, E. (2021). Artificial intelligence in customer-facing financial services: A systematic literature review and agenda for future research. *International Journal of Bank Marketing*. Advance online publication. DOI: 10.1108/IJBM-09-2021-0417

Hossain, M. A., Quaddus, M., & Islam, N. (2016). Developing and validating a model explaining the assimilation process of RFID: An empirical study. *Information Systems Frontiers*, *18*(4), 645–663. DOI: 10.1007/s10796-014-9537-y

Hoyle, R. H. (Ed.). (2012). *Handbook of structural equation modeling*. Guilford press.

IBA. (2024). The Top 5 Challenges Facing the Insurance Industry Today. Retrieval date: 18 August 2024. https://ibapplications.com/content-library/blog/the-top-5-challenges-facing-the-insurance-industry-today/

Javaid, S. M. (2024). The Importance of New Technology Adoption for Success. Retrieval date: 6 August 2024. https://www.linkedin.com/pulse/importance-new-technology-adoption-success-shaikh-muzaffar-javaid

Jones, R. (2024). The Role of Leadership in Driving Technology Adoption. Retrieval date: 6 August 2024. https://www.trainingfolks.com/blog/the-role-of-leadership-in-driving-technology-adoption

Kaloudi (2023). DGTAL: Artificial intelligence in insurance market services. Retrieval date: 19 October 2024. https://www.powergame.gr/synenteyxeis/422850/dgtal-i-techniti-noimosyni-stis-ypiresies-tis-asfalistikis-agoras/ (In Greek).

Kankanamge, N., Yigitcanlar, T., & Goonetilleke, A. (2021). Public perceptions on artificial intelligence driven disaster management: Evidence from Sydney, Melbourne and Brisbane. *Telematics and Informatics*, *65*, 101729. DOI: 10.1016/j.tele.2021.101729

Khan, A., Talukder, S. M., Islam, T. Q., & Islam, N. A. (2022). *The impact of business analytics capabilities on innovation, information quality, agility and firm performance: the moderation role of industry dynamism.* VINE Journal of Information and Knowledge Management., DOI: 10.1108/VJIKMS-01-2022-0027

Kirvan. P. business resilience. (2024). Retrieval date: 12 August 2024. https://www.techtarget.com/searchcio/definition/business-resilience

Levio Consulting Inc. (2024). How is Your Company Reacting to New InsurTech Competition? Retrieval date: 13 August 2024. https://levioconsulting.com/insights/how-is-your-company-reacting-to-new-insurtech-competition/

Liu, X., Gao, L., Lu, J., & Lioliou, E. (2016). Environmental risks, localization and the overseas subsidiary performance of MNEs from an emerging economy. *Journal of World Business*, *51*(3), 356–368. DOI: 10.1016/j.jwb.2015.05.002

Lutfi, A., Alrawad, M., Alsyouf, A., Almaiah, M. A., Al-Khasawneh, A., Al-Khasawneh, A. L., Alshira'h, A. F., Alshirah, M. H., Saad, M., & Ibrahim, N. (2023). Drivers and impact of big data analytic adoption in the retail industry: A quantitative investigation applying structural equation modeling. *Journal of Retailing and Consumer Services*, *70*, 103129. DOI: 10.1016/j.jretconser.2022.103129

Lv, P., Xiong, H. (2022). Can FinTech improve corporate investment efficiency? Evidence from China. Res. Int. Bus. Financ. 60, 101571 https://doi.org/. ribaf.2021.101571.DOI: 10.1016/j

Marg, E. R. P. Ltd. (2024). Understanding the Principles of Insurance: Safeguarding Your Future. Retrieval date: 15 August 2024. https://margcompusoft.com/m/principles-of-insurance-your-future/

Maroufkhani, P., Ismail, W. K. W., & Ghobakhloo, M. (2020). Big data analytics adoption model for small and medium enterprises. *Journal of Science and Technology Policy Management*, *11*(4), 483–502. DOI: 10.1108/JSTPM-02-2020-0018

McEvily, S. K., Eisenhardt, K. M., & Prescott, J. E. (2004). The global acquisition, leverage, and protection of technological competencies. *Strategic Management Journal*, *25*(8-9), 713–722. DOI: 10.1002/smj.425

Moliterno, T. P., & Wiersema, M. F. (2007). Firm performance, rent appropriation, and the strategic resource divestment capability. *Strategic Management Journal*, *28*(11), 1065–1087. DOI: 10.1002/smj.630

Muir-Wood. The 10 Major Risks Shaping Insurance Today. (2024). Retrieval date: 18 August 2024. https://www.rms.com/blog/2024/05/07/the-major-risks-shaping-insurance-today

Mullins, M., Holland, C. P., & Cunneen, M. (2021). Creating ethics guidelines for artificial intelligence and big data analytics customers: The case of the consumer European insurance market. *Patterns (New York, N.Y.)*, *2*(10), 100362. DOI: 10.1016/j.patter.2021.100362 PMID: 34693379

Mushtaq, R., Gull, A. A., Shahab, Y., & Derouiche, I. (2022). Do financial performance indicators predict 10-K text sentiments? An application of artificial intelligence. *Research in International Business and Finance, 61*, 101679. DOI: 10.1016/j.ribaf.2022.101679

Na, S., Heo, S., Han, S., Shin, Y., & Roh, Y. (2022). Acceptance model of artificial intelligence (AI)-based technologies in construction firms: Applying the Technology Acceptance Model (TAM) in combination with the Technology–Organisation–Environment (TOE) framework. *Buildings (Basel, Switzerland), 12*(2), 90. DOI: 10.3390/buildings12020090

Next Dial. (2024). Christos Theodoridis: Allianz promotes leading. Retrieval date: 19 October 2024. https://www.nextdeal.gr/asfalistikes-eidiseis/idiotiki-asfalisi/139191/hristos-theodoridis-i-allianz-proothei-koryfaies (In Greek).

Nguyen, T. L., Nguyen, V. P., & Dang, T. V. D. (2022). Critical factors affecting the adoption of artificial intelligence: An empirical study in Vietnam. *The Journal of Asian Finance, Economics and Business, 9*(5), 225–237. DOI: 10.13106/jafeb.2020.vol7.no5.225

Njegomir, V., & Demko-Rihter, J. (2023). InsurTech: new competition to traditional insurers and impact on the economic growth. In *Digital transformation of the financial industry: approaches and applications* (pp. 133–150). Springer International Publishing. DOI: 10.1007/978-3-031-23269-5_8

Oliveira, T. & Martins, M. F. (2011). Literature review of information technology adoption models at firm level. Electronic journal of information systems evaluation, 14(1), pp110-121.

Owlift. Top Management Support in Innovation. (2024). Retrieval date: 8 August 2024. https://www.owlift.com/blog/submission/top-management-support-in-innovation/

Pearson. (2024). Major HR Challenge for Insurance Companies: Attracting Young Talent to Maintain Their Dynamism. Retrieval date: 18 August 2024. https://www.talentlens.com/Insights/blog/2024/05/hr-challenges-insurance-companies.html

Pinochet, L. H. C., Amorim, G. D. C. B., Junior, D. L., & De Souza, C. A. (2021). Consequential factors of Big Data Analytics Capability: How firms use data in the competitive scenario. *Journal of Enterprise Information Management, 34*(5), 1407–1417.

Qaffas, A. A., Ilmudeen, A., Almazmomi, N. K., Alharbi, I. M. (2022). The impact of big data analytics talent capability on business intelligent infrastructure to achieve firm performance, .DOI: 10.1108/FS-01-2021-0002

Rahman, M., Ming, T. H., Baigh, T. A., & Sarker, M. (2021). Adoption of artificial intelligence in banking services: An empirical analysis. *International Journal of Emerging Markets*. Advance online publication. DOI: 10.1108/IJOEM-06-2020-0724

Ramanathan, R., Ramanathan, U., & Bentley, Y. (2018). The debate on flexibility of environmental regulations, innovation capabilities and financial performance–A novel use of DEA. *Omega*, *75*, 131–138. DOI: 10.1016/j.omega.2017.02.006

Ramdani, B., & Kawalek, P. (2007). SME adoption of enterprise systems in the Northwest of England: An environmental, technological, and organizational perspective. In Organizational Dynamics of Technology-Based Innovation: Diversifying the Research Agenda: IFIP TC 8 WG 8.6 International Working Conference, June 14–16, Manchester, UK (pp. 409-429). Springer US.

Rawat, S., Rawat, A., Kumar, D., & Sabitha, A. S. (2021). Application of machine learning and data visualization techniques for decision support in the insurance sector. *International Journal of Information Management Data Insights*, *1*(2), 100012. DOI: 10.1016/j.jjimei.2021.100012

Rodrigues, A. R. D., Ferreira, F. A. F., Teixeira, F. J. C. S. N., & Zopounidis, C. (2022). Artificial intelligence, digital transformation and cybersecurity in the banking sector: A multi-stakeholder cognition-driven framework. *Research in International Business and Finance*, *60*, 101616. DOI: 10.1016/j.ribaf.2022.101616

Rogers, E. (1995). *Diffusion of innovations* (Paperback, F., Ed.).

Rogers, E. M., Singhal, A., & Quinlan, M. M. (2014). Diffusion of innovations. In *An integrated approach to communication theory and research* (pp. 432–448). Routledge.

Salonga, R. 4 External Factors that Affect Businesses. Retrieval date: 8 August 2024. https://sciencepark.com.ph/blog/factors-that-affect-businesses/

Sanwal, T., & Sareen, P. (2021). The relevance of social intelligence for effective optimization of retirement and successful ageing. *Ageing International*, •••, 1–16. PMID: 34744217

Shahbazi, H. (2024). Leveraging the TOE Framework to Shape Your Enterprise Technology Strategy. Retrieval date: 5 August 2024. https://www.linkedin.com/pulse/leveraging-toe-framework-shape-your-enterprise-hassan-shahbazi

Sharma, S., Singh, G., Islam, N., & Dhir, A. (2022). Why do SMEs adopt artificial intelligence-based chatbots? *IEEE Transactions on Engineering Management*, *71*, 1773–1786. DOI: 10.1109/TEM.2022.3203469

Singh, R., Sharma, P., Foropon, C., & Belal, H. M. (2022). The role of big data and predictive analytics in the employee retention: A resource-based view. *International Journal of Manpower*, *43*(2), 411–425. DOI: 10.1108/IJM-03-2021-0197

Srivastava, D. K., Kumar, V., Ekren, B. Y., Upadhyay, A., Tyagi, M., & Kumari, A. (2022). Adopting Industry 4.0 by leveraging organisational factors. *Technological Forecasting and Social Change*, *176*, 121439. DOI: 10.1016/j.techfore.2021.121439

Su, X., Zeng, W., Zheng, M., Jiang, X., Lin, W., & Xu, A. (2021). Big data analytics capabilities and organizational performance: The mediating effect of dual innovation. *European Journal of Innovation Management*, *25*(4), 1142–1157. DOI: 10.1108/EJIM-10-2020-0431

TheoryHub. Technology-Organization-Environment Framework. Retrieval date: 5 August 2024. https://open.ncl.ac.uk/academic-theories/23/technology-organization-environment-framework/

Tornatzky, L., & Fleischer, M. (1990). *The process of technology innovation.*

Twaissi, N. M., El-Khateeb, A., Al-Sharif, M., Almomany, G. A., & Abu Karaki, M. A. (2024). The rising role of Artificial Intelligence in Jordan's insurance industry. *Journal of Tianjin University Science and Technology*, *57*(4), 403–417.

Vanguard, X. Insurance Industry Challenges: Navigating the Landscape in 2024. Retrieval date: 12 August 2024. https://vanguard-x.com/software-development/insurance-industry-challenges-navigating-the-landscape-in-2024/

Venkatesh, V., Morris, M. G., Davis, G. B., & Davis, F. D. (2003). User acceptance of information technology: Toward a unified view. *Management Information Systems Quarterly*, *27*(3), 425–478. DOI: 10.2307/30036540

Von Treuer, K., Karantzas, G., McCabe, M., Mellor, D., Konis, A., Davison, T. E., & O'Connor, D. (2018). Organizational factors associated with readiness for change in residential aged care settings. *BMC Health Services Research*, *18*(1), 1–6. DOI: 10.1186/s12913-018-2832-4 PMID: 29390999

Vorecol (2024). Impact of artificial intelligence in driving digital transformation. Retrieved May 6, 2024, https://vorecol.com/blogs/blog-impact-of-artificial-intelligence-in-driving-digitaltransformation-8835

Wade, M., & Hulland, J. (2004). The resource-based view and information systems research: Review, extension, and suggestions for future research. *Management Information Systems Quarterly*, *28*(1), 107–142. DOI: 10.2307/25148626

Wamba, F. S., Akter, S., & De Bourmont, M. (2018). Quality dominant logic in big data analytics and find performance. *Business Process Management Journal, 25*(3), 512528.

Wang, Y., Lo, H. P., & Yang, Y. (2004). The constituents of core competencies and firm performance: Evidence from high-technology firms in China. *Journal of Engineering and Technology Management, 21*(4), 249–280. DOI: 10.1016/j.jengtecman.2004.09.001

Wang, Y., Xiuping, S., & Zhang, Q. (2021). Can fintech improve the efficiency of commercial banks?—An analysis based on big data. *Research in International Business and Finance, 55*, 101338. DOI: 10.1016/j.ribaf.2020.101338

Chapter 10
Legal Entropy in AI Governance

Spiros Kontis
Frederick University, Cyprus

Sofia Anastasiadou
https://orcid.org/0000-0001-6404-5003
University of Western Macedonia, Greece & Neapolis University Pafos, Cyprus

Lazaros Anastasiadis
University of Peloponnese, Greece

Lambrini Seremeti
https://orcid.org/0000-0002-0663-5408
Agricultural University of Athens, Greece

ABSTRACT

The integration of Artificial Intelligence (AI) into various sectors of society has introduced significant challenges to legal procedures, resulting in what can be called legal entropy. This concept refers to the increasing disorder, unpredictability and complexity within legal systems as they attempt to regulate rapidly evolving technologies. This chapter explores the manifestations of legal entropy in AI governance, including regulatory uncertainty, inconsistent legal interpretation, algorithmic opacity, and ethical and liability dilemmas. It examines the factors contributing to this phenomenon, including the rapid pace of technological advances, fragmented regulatory approaches, and the erosion of legal predictability. To manage and mitigate legal entropy, the chapter proposes several strategies, such as developing adaptive legal frameworks, enhancing transparency and accountability in AI systems, ensuring human oversight, promoting international cooperation, bridging the

DOI: 10.4018/979-8-3693-9576-9.ch010

expertise gap and encouraging innovation in legal technology.

INTRODUCTION

Generally, the term Artificial Intelligence (AI) refers to the simulation of human intelligence in machines, which have been programmed in such a manner that their way of thinking and learning resembles that of human beings. AI systems improve over time through exposure to data, identifying patterns, and making predictions or decisions with minimal human intervention. In many areas, like finance, healthcare and marketing, big data systems use AI algorithms to clean and prepare data by identifying anomalies, handling missing values, and transforming it into usable formats. This data is then used by big data applications that run over the cloud (Souravlas et al. 2022; Souravlas et al. 2022; Souravlas et al. 2023a Souravlas et al. 2023).

As Artificial Intelligence (AI) technologies become integral to sectors from healthcare to finance (Papademetriou et al., 2012; 2023; 2024) and law enforcement, they bring with them unprecedented regulatory challenges (Rashid and Kausik, 2024). The rapid evolution of AI has led to what can be described as legal entropy – an increase in disorder, unpredictability, and complexity within legal systems as they attempt to regulate technologies that continuously change in scope and capability (Mylrea and Robincon, 2023). The term of legal entropy, drawn from the concept of entropy originating from thermodynamics, refers to the degree of disorder or randomness within a system (Kostic, 2014). Legal entropy, applied to AI governance, similarly represents a state of disorder and unpredictability within the regulatory landscape (Sichelman, 2021; Chipiga, 2023), due to various factors that impact legal stability and continuity in the era of AI (Seremeti and Kougias, 2024).

More precisely, legal systems, which are often slow to adapt, find themselves struggling to keep up with the rapid development of AI technologies and the novel issues they introduce (Seremeti and Kougias, 2019). This has resulted in regulatory uncertainty, where laws and regulations struggle to define the boundaries of AI's legal and ethical implications. Inconsistent interpretations of AI-related laws have emerged, leading to a patchwork of legal responses that vary across jurisdictions, creating confusion and undermining the effectiveness of governance efforts (Chennupati, 2024). The opacity of many AI algorithms, often described as "black boxes," complicates efforts to assess accountability, liability, and fairness (Wischmeyer, 2020), further fueling legal entropy.

In light of these challenges, this chapter offers a comprehensive examination of how legal entropy manifests in the context of AI governance. It explores the various dimensions of this phenomenon, from regulatory uncertainty to the dilemmas of algorithmic accountability, and highlights the risks that an unpredictable legal environment poses for innovation and public trust in AI systems. However, the chapter also offers solutions to mitigate legal entropy and bring stability to AI governance. It proposes the development of adaptive legal frameworks that can more easily accommodate the fast-changing nature of AI, enhanced transparency and accountability mechanisms to address the opacity of algorithms, and the importance of ensuring human oversight in AI decision-making processes. Additionally, it emphasizes the need for international cooperation to harmonize regulations and bridge the expertise gap between technologists and legal professionals. By advocating for innovation in legal technology, the chapter suggests that new tools can help legal systems stay agile and responsive to the demands of the AI-driven future. Ultimately, the chapter aims to provide a roadmap for managing the complexities of AI governance and ensuring that legal systems remain both efficient and fair in the face of technological advancements.

FACTORS CONTRIBUTING TO LEGAL ENTROPY

One of the primary drivers of legal entropy in AI governance is the *unprecedented speed of technological innovation*. AI technologies evolve at an extraordinary rate, with new breakthroughs emerging suddenly across different fields. For example, advancements in machine learning algorithms, natural language processing, and computer vision are reshaping industries and societies in real time (Rawas, 2024). However, the legislative process is inherently slower, often relying on lengthy discussions, consultations, and reviews before new laws or regulations are enacted. This disparity in the speed of technological progress and legal adaptation results in legal systems that cannot keep pace with AI innovations (Zaidan and Ibrahim, 2024). When laws lag behind technological developments, they become outdated, leading to regulatory gaps and inconsistencies. This situation creates confusion for businesses, policymakers, and individuals, as they are left to navigate a regulatory landscape that fails to address emerging challenges. The inability of laws to quickly adapt to AI's rapid evolution is a central factor contributing to legal entropy in this domain.

Another significant factor contributing to legal entropy is the *erosion of legal predictability*, due to the inherent complexity and opacity of AI systems. AI technologies, especially those built on machine learning, are often "black boxes," meaning that their decision-making processes are not easily understood by humans (Fomin and Astromskis, 2023). Unlike traditional software systems, which operate based on predefined rules and logic, many AI models evolve through data patterns and experience. This makes it difficult for regulators, lawmakers, and even developers themselves to predict or explain the outcomes of AI-driven processes. The complexity of AI raises several regulatory challenges. For example, if an AI system makes a biased decision, it may be difficult to identify the root cause of the problem, let alone determine accountability. Similarly, AI systems may behave unpredictably in unfamiliar situations, creating potential risks that existing laws are ill-equipped to address. This lack of transparency and understanding (Cheong, 2024) exacerbates legal entropy, as the legal frameworks struggle to govern technologies that are too complicated to regulate effectively.

AI governance is further complicated by the *fragmentation of legal frameworks across different jurisdictions* (Robles and Mallinson, 2023). AI is a global technology, with its applications crossing national borders and affecting people worldwide. However, countries approach AI regulation in vastly different ways, often leading to a patchwork of laws, standards, and ethical guidelines (Miazi, 2023). The European Union has taken a more proactive stance with its proposed Artificial Intelligence Act, which seeks to regulate high-risk AI systems across member states. In contrast, the United States lacks a unified federal approach, with different States implementing their own AI regulations or relying on sector-specific guidelines. This lack of harmonization results in regulatory fragmentation, which can create confusion for AI developers and businesses operating across multiple jurisdictions. Companies must navigate a complex web of regulations, which may differ in their scope, enforcement mechanisms, and ethical requirements. This disjointed regulatory environment not only increases compliance costs but also leads to inconsistent standards, undermining the ability to manage AI technologies effectively on a global scale. Fragmentation of legal frameworks is a critical factor in the manifestation of legal entropy, as it prevents the establishment of coherent, universally accepted standards for AI governance.

MANIFESTATIONS OF LEGAL ENTROPY

One of the most apparent manifestations of legal entropy in AI governance is *regulatory uncertainty*, reflecting the chaotic and fragmented evolution of legal frameworks in response to rapidly advancing technologies. This uncertainty arises from the difficulty of reconciling traditional legal structures with the dynamic and transformative nature of AI (Scholes, 2025). Unlike traditional sectors where regulations evolve at a slower pace, AI is characterized by its fast-paced development and constant innovation. New AI techniques, such as deep learning and reinforcement learning, emerge excessively, each with unique challenges in terms of regulation, ethics, and accountability. In response, legal frameworks often become outdated or overly simplistic, unable to keep up with the intricacies of these technologies. This creates a situation where laws are either too broad, leaving significant gaps in regulation, or too specific, stifling future advancements. The European Union's proposed AI Act, for instance, has been criticized for being too rigid in defining high-risk AI systems, potentially excluding new AI applications that may pose risks in the future. As AI evolves (Wachter, 2024), regulators often find themselves playing catch-up, which further contributes to the entropy in legal systems. Moreover, the legal response to AI often comes in the form of amendments, revisions, and piecemeal updates, rather than coherent overhauls. This patchwork approach to updating laws can result in contradictory or overlapping regulations that fail to address the underlying issues comprehensively. As legal frameworks become increasingly disorganized and incoherent, their ability to provide clear guidance and enforceable standards becomes weakened, making the governance of AI even more complex.

Inconsistent legal interpretation is another prominent manifestation of legal entropy in AI governance, where ambiguity in applying existing laws to novel AI scenarios leads to conflicting decisions and unpredictability. This inconsistency arises from varying judicial, administrative, and legislative perspectives across jurisdictions, often influenced by differing cultural, economic, and political priorities. Indeed, the regulatory landscape for AI remains highly fragmented, with different countries enacting their own laws, policies, and ethical guidelines (Huang et al., 2024). For instance, the European Union has been proactive in introducing comprehensive AI regulations, such as the Artificial Intelligence Act, aimed at ensuring AI systems are developed and deployed safely and ethically. Conversely, other countries, like the United States, have a more fragmented approach, with federal-level guidelines largely absent and states like California taking the lead in AI regulation. This patchwork regulatory environment creates confusion and inefficiency for AI developers and users (Xi, 2025). Companies operating across multiple jurisdictions must navigate a maze of conflicting standards, which increases compliance costs, slows innovation, and risks undermining the global benefits of AI. Legal entropy here arises from the lack of uniformity and coherence in regulatory efforts, making it difficult to effectively govern AI technologies in a way that ensures both safety and innovation. For example, interpretations of privacy rights, intellectual property, and liability in AI applications can differ significantly, creating a fragmented legal landscape. Such discrepancies undermine the clarity essential for developers, businesses, and users to navigate compliance confidently. This inconsistency highlights the necessity for harmonized guidelines and adaptive frameworks that reduce entropy and provide a cohesive approach to AI governance.

Algorithmic opacity, or the difficulty in understanding and interpreting how AI systems make decisions, is a significant manifestation of legal entropy in AI governance. This opacity creates challenges for regulators and courts in assessing accountability, fairness, and compliance with existing legal standards (Frosio, 2024). The complexity of AI models, especially those leveraging deep learning, often renders their inner workings inaccessible to non-specialists, including legal professionals.

This lack of transparency fuels uncertainty, as laws designed for human decision-making processes struggle to address the inscrutability of algorithmic outcomes (Novelli et al., 2023). Consequently, algorithmic opacity exacerbates regulatory fragmentation and inconsistent enforcement, amplifying legal entropy. Addressing this issue requires developing standards for explainability and fostering collaboration between technologists and legal experts to demystify AI systems within the governance framework.

AI governance is not only a matter of technical regulation but also involves deep ethical considerations (Koridena et al., 2024). AI systems, particularly those involved in decision-making, raise critical questions about accountability, transparency, and fairness (Poli et al., 2025). For example, when AI is used in criminal justice, hiring practices, or healthcare, the decisions made by these systems can have profound effects on individuals and communities. However, the current legal landscape struggles to address these ethical concerns effectively. The issue of accountability is a prime example of legal entropy. AI systems can operate autonomously, making decisions without direct human involvement (Wong, 2020). When an AI system causes harm—whether through an unfair hiring decision, a biased loan approval, or even a fatal autonomous vehicle accident—the question of who is responsible becomes murky. Is it the developer of the algorithm, the company that deployed the system, or the end user who implemented it? In many cases, the existing legal frameworks are ill-equipped to assign liability and accountability in a clear and consistent manner. The lack of clear standards and the difficulty in pinpointing responsibility contribute to the *ethical and liability dilemmas* in AI governance, representing another manifestation of legal entropy.

STRATEGIES FOR MITIGATING LEGAL ENTROPY

The rapid advancement of artificial intelligence (AI) has brought immense benefits to society, ranging from automation in industries to breakthroughs in healthcare and scientific research (Vinothkumar and Karunamurthy, 2023). However, AI’s growth has also introduced challenges, particularly in the realm of legal governance. Legal entropy refers to the gradual deterioration of legal systems, often leading to fragmentation, incoherence, and inefficiency. In the context of AI, legal entropy manifests as a result of regulatory fragmentation, outdated standards, accountability issues, and the fast-evolving nature of AI technologies. To manage AI's societal impact and mitigate the consequences of legal entropy, several strategies can be employed. These strategies focus on creating a more coherent, inclusive, and adaptable legal framework for AI governance.

- *Developing Unified and Flexible Global Regulatory Frameworks.* One of the most significant challenges in AI governance is the fragmentation of regulations across different jurisdictions. AI operates on a global scale, and its impact transcends national borders. As countries enact their own laws and regulations, the result is a patchwork of rules that create confusion and inefficiencies for both developers and users of AI technologies. To mitigate legal entropy, a key strategy involves the development of unified and flexible global regulatory frameworks. Efforts toward global coordination, such as those promoted by organizations like the Organization for Economic Co-operation and Development (OECD) or the United Nations, can help create common standards for AI regulation. These frameworks can focus on key areas such as safety, accountability, transparency, and ethical standards while allowing countries to adapt them to local contexts. A flexible approach, rather than rigid or overly specific regulations, would enable legal systems to keep pace with the rapid evolution of AI technologies. For instance, the OECD AI Principles provide a non-binding set of guidelines for responsible AI, which can serve as a foundation for global cooperation and consistency in AI governance. By promoting the development of international standards and cooperation, policymakers can reduce legal fragmentation and increase the effectiveness of AI governance across borders.
- *Emphasizing Adaptive and Iterative Legislation.* The evolving nature of AI technology means that traditional legal frameworks often become outdated quickly. To counteract legal entropy caused by outdated regulations, adaptive and iterative legislation can be an essential strategy. Instead of enacting one-size-fits-all, long-term laws that may become obsolete as AI evolves, regulators can adopt more dynamic approaches to legislation. One approach is the implementation of sandbox models, which allow AI developers to test their innovations in controlled environments with limited legal liability, subject to specific rules. These sandboxes can enable legislators to observe how AI systems operate in practice and adjust regulations based on real-world data. For example, the UK's AI and Data Governance Sandbox allows companies to pilot AI solutions and receive regulatory feedback before deploying them at scale. This iterative approach to regulation allows legal systems to respond to technological changes more swiftly. Additionally, legislation can be framed with built-in mechanisms for periodic review and updates. For instance, sunset clauses—where regulations automatically expire after a set period unless renewed—can ensure that laws remain relevant and adaptable to future technological developments. These adaptive approaches help prevent legal frameworks from becoming rigid, fragmented, or incoherent as AI evolves.

- *Establishing Clear Accountability and Ethical Guidelines.* The complexity of AI systems often makes it difficult to pinpoint who is responsible when something goes wrong. Whether it's a self-driving car causing an accident or an algorithm making biased decisions in hiring, the question of accountability is a critical concern. Legal entropy manifests here through the lack of clear accountability, leaving legal systems disorganized and ill-equipped to assign liability. To mitigate this, clear accountability and ethical guidelines must be established at the outset. One approach involves defining clear legal responsibilities for AI developers, users, and organizations. For instance, AI systems could be classified based on risk levels, with higher-risk systems subject to more stringent regulations. The EU's Artificial Intelligence Act is one such attempt to classify AI applications by risk, with higher-risk applications like biometric identification or critical infrastructure subject to more rigorous oversight. In addition, ethical guidelines should be incorporated into the design and deployment of AI systems, ensuring that systems are aligned with human rights and values. Algorithmic transparency is an essential element of this strategy, as it enables individuals and organizations to understand how AI systems make decisions. Laws that require companies to disclose the underlying logic, data sources, and decision-making processes behind their AI models can foster trust and accountability. AI systems should be subject to audits, with independent oversight bodies ensuring compliance with ethical standards. By clarifying legal responsibilities and embedding ethical considerations in AI design and deployment, the risks of legal entropy—such as confusion over accountability or unethical use of AI—can be significantly reduced.
- *Promoting Public Engagement and Inclusive Legal Processes.* AI technologies have the potential to significantly impact society, yet many legal frameworks are designed by a small group of technocrats and policymakers without sufficient input from the broader public. This lack of inclusivity exacerbates legal entropy by creating regulatory frameworks that may not reflect the values or concerns of diverse groups. To combat this, public engagement and inclusive legal processes are critical strategies. Public consultations, citizen juries, and stakeholder dialogues can be used to gather input from various sectors of society, including marginalized groups that may be disproportionately affected by AI technologies. By involving the public in AI policy discussions, governments can ensure that legal frameworks reflect a wide range of societal concerns, leading to more balanced and robust regulations. In addition, engaging in cross-sectoral collaboration is vital. AI governance should involve not only legal experts but also ethicists, sociologists, industry professionals, and the general public. The diverse perspectives brought to the

table can help ensure that AI governance remains aligned with human rights, fairness, and justice.

- *Fostering Collaboration Between Industry and Regulators.* Another critical strategy for mitigating legal entropy is fostering collaboration between AI developers and regulators. The fast pace of AI development often leads to a disconnect between those creating the technology and those regulating it. A more collaborative approach can help bridge this gap and ensure that regulatory frameworks remain relevant and practical. Regulatory bodies should work closely with industry groups to understand the technical challenges associated with AI and develop regulations that are both enforceable and conducive to innovation. Joint working groups, task forces, and advisory boards, composed of experts from both the public and private sectors, can be established to provide guidance and recommendations on AI policy. These collaborations can help to identify emerging risks early and ensure that regulations can be adapted in real-time to keep pace with technological advancements. For instance, the Partnership on AI, which includes companies like Google, Amazon, and Microsoft, as well as nonprofits and academic institutions, is an example of a multi-stakeholder effort to ensure AI is developed in a responsible and ethical manner. By fostering ongoing dialogue between regulators and the private sector, AI governance can become more responsive, efficient, and aligned with technological progress.

Legal entropy in AI governance is a real and growing concern, but it is not insurmountable. By adopting strategies such as developing unified global regulatory frameworks, implementing adaptive legislation, establishing clear accountability guidelines, promoting public engagement, and fostering collaboration between industry and regulators, legal systems can better manage the challenges posed by AI. These strategies not only help mitigate legal entropy but also ensure that AI technologies are governed in a way that maximizes their potential benefits while minimizing risks and harms. Through these proactive measures, policymakers can create a legal landscape that is robust, flexible, and capable of evolving with the rapidly advancing field of artificial intelligence.

CONCLUSION

The rapid integration of AI into diverse sectors has created unprecedented challenges for legal systems, exemplified by the phenomenon of legal entropy. As AI technologies continue to advance at a pace far exceeding the adaptability of traditional legal frameworks, the disorder and unpredictability within governance structures are likely to intensify unless proactive measures are taken. This chapter has explored the multifaceted nature of legal entropy in AI governance, highlighting key manifestations such as regulatory uncertainty, inconsistent legal interpretation, algorithmic opacity, and ethical and liability dilemmas. These challenges underscore the urgent need for adaptive, transparent, and inclusive approaches to governance.

Addressing legal entropy requires a combination of strategies that balance innovation with accountability and fairness. Developing unified global regulatory frameworks can reduce fragmentation and promote harmonization, while adaptive legislation allows for responsive governance in the face of technological evolution. Clear accountability and ethical guidelines can enhance trust and transparency, while public engagement and cross-sector collaboration ensure that AI governance reflects diverse perspectives and societal values. By fostering cooperation between regulators and industry, policymakers can bridge the gap between technical advancements and legal oversight, creating a governance environment that is both robust and dynamic.

Ultimately, the goal of AI governance should be to create a legal ecosystem capable of accommodating the complexity and rapid evolution of AI while safeguarding public trust and protecting fundamental rights. Through deliberate and innovative approaches, the legal system can not only mitigate the risks associated with legal entropy but also harness AI's potential to drive progress across society. By navigating the challenges of legal entropy effectively, policymakers can lay the groundwork for an AI-driven future that is ethical, equitable, and sustainable.

REFERENCES

Chennupati, A. (2024). The evolution of AI: What does the future hold in the next two years. *World Journal of Advanced Engineering Technology and Sciences*, 12(1), 022-028. https://doi.org/DOI: 10.30574/wjaets.2024.12.1.0176

Cheong, B. C. (2024). Transparency and accountability in AI systems: Safeguarding wellbeing in the age of algorithmic decision-making. *Frontiers in Human Dynamics*, *6*, 1421273. Advance online publication. DOI: 10.3389/fhumd.2024.1421273

Chipiga, I. V. (2023). Legal entropy in International Law. *Russian Journal of Legal Studies*, *10*(2), 113–120. DOI: 10.17816/RJLS322823

Fomin, V. V., & Astromskis, P. (2023). The black box problem. In: Gordon, J.S. (ed) *Philosophy and Human Rights*. Brill, 393, 112-125. https://doi.org/DOI: 10.1163/9789004682900_012

Frosio, G. (2024). Algorithmic enforcement tools: Governing opacity with due process. In Francese, S., & King, R. (Eds.), *Driving Forensic Innovation in the 21st Century* (pp. 195–218). Springer., DOI: 10.1007/978-3-031-56556-4_9

Huang, K., Joshi, A., Dun, S., & Hamilton, N. (2024). AI regulations. In: Huang, K., Wang, Y., Goertzel, B., Li, Y., Wright, S. Ponnapalli, J. (eds) *Generative AI Security. Future of Business and Finance*. Springer, Cham, 61-98. https://doi.org/DOI: 10.1007/978-3-031-54252-7_3

Koridena, B. K., Malaiyappan, J. N. A., & Tadimarri, A. (2024). Ethical considerations in the development and deployment of AI systems. *European Journal of Technology*, *8*(2), 41–53. DOI: 10.47672/ejt.1890

Kostic, M. M. (2014). The elusive nature of entropy and its physical meaning. *Entropy (Basel, Switzerland)*, *16*(2), 953–967. DOI: 10.3390/e16020953

Miazi, M.A.N. (2023). Interplay of legal frameworks and artificial intelligence (AI): A global perspective. *Law and Policy Review*, 2(2), 01-25. https://doi.org/DOI: 10.32350/lrp.22.01

Mylrea, M., & Robinson, N. (2023). Artificial Intelligence (AI) trust framework and maturity model: Applying an entropy lens to improve security, privacy, and ethical AI. *Entropy (Basel, Switzerland)*, *25*(10), 1429. DOI: 10.3390/e25101429 PMID: 37895550

Nove, I. C., Taddeo, M., & Floridi, L. (2023). Accountability in artificial intelligence: What it is and how it works. *AI & Society*, *39*(4), 1871–1882. DOI: 10.1007/s00146-023-01635-y

Papademetriou, , C. (2012). To what extent is the Turing Test Still Important? *Pliroforiki*, *1*(22), 28–32.

Papademetriou, C., Ragazou, K., & Garefalakis, A. (2023). Adapting Artificial Intelligence in Cypriot Hotel Industry: The Views of Hotel Managers. *Proceedings of Eurasia Business and Economics Society Conference*. Springer Nature Switzerland (Eds), 143-155.

Papademetriou, C., Ragazou, K., Garefalakis, A., & Anastasiadou, S. (2024). The Role of Artificial Intelligence in Employee Wellness and Mental Health. In Global, I. G. I. (Ed.), *Human Resource Strategies in the Era of Artificial Intelligence* (pp. 29–54). DOI: 10.4018/979-8-3693-6412-3.ch002

Poli, P. K. R., Pamidi, S., & Poli, S. K. R. (2025). Unraveling the ethical conundrum of artificial intelligence: A synthesis of literature and case studies. *Augmented Human Research*, *10*(1), 2. DOI: 10.1007/s41133-024-00077-5

Rashid, A. B., & Kausik, M. A. (2024). AI revolutionizing industries worldwide: A comprehensive overview its diverse applications. *Hybrid Advances*, *7*, 100277. DOI: 10.1016/j.hybadv.2024.100277

Rawas, S. (2024). AI: The future of humanity. *Discover Artificial Intelligence*, *4*(25), 25. Advance online publication. DOI: 10.1007/s44163-024-00118-3

Robles, P., & Mallinson, D. J. (2023). Catching up with AI: Pushing toward a cohesive governance framework. *Politics & Policy*, *51*(3), 355–372. DOI: 10.1111/polp.12529

Scholes, M. S. (2025). Artificial intelligence and uncertainty. *Risk Sciences*, *1*, 100004. DOI: 10.1016/j.risk.2024.100004

Seremeti, L., & Kougias, I. (2019). Legal issues within ambient intelligence environments. *Proceedings of the 10th International Conference on Information, Intelligence, Systems and Applications (IISA)*, Patras, Greece, 1-2. https://doi.org/DOI: 10.1109/IISA.2019.8900748

Seremeti, L., & Kougias, I. (2024). The AI spectrum under the doctrine of necessity: Towards the flexibility of the future legal praxis. *Computers and Artificial Intelligence*, *2*(1), 1258. DOI: 10.59400/cai.v2i1.1258

Sichelman, T. (2021). Quantifying legal entropy. *Frontiers in Physics (Lausanne)*, *9*, 665054. DOI: 10.3389/fphy.2021.665054

Souravlas, S., & Anastasiadou, S. (2022). On Implementing Social Community Clouds Based on Markov Models. *IEEE Transactions on Computational Social Systems*. Advance online publication. DOI: 10.1109/TCSS.2022.3213273

Souravlas, S., Anastasiadou, S., Economides, Th., & Katsavounis, S. (2023). Probabilistic Community Detection in Social Networks. *IEEE Access : Practical Innovations, Open Solutions, 11*, 25629–25641. DOI: 10.1109/ACCESS.2023.3257021

Souravlas, S., Anastasiadou, S., & Kostoglou, I. (2022). A Novel Method for General Hierarchical System Modeling Via Colored Petri Nets Based on Transition Extractions from Real Data Sets. *Applied Sciences (Basel, Switzerland)*, *13*(1), 339. DOI: 10.3390/app13010339

Souravlas, S., Anastasiadou, S. D., Tantalaki, N., & Katsavounis, S. (2022). A Fair, Dynamic Load Balanced Task Distribution Strategy for Heterogeneous Cloud Platforms Based on Markov Process Modeling. *IEEE Access : Practical Innovations, Open Solutions, 10*, 26149–26162. DOI: 10.1109/ACCESS.2022.3157435

Vinothkumar, J. and Karunamurthy, A. (2023). Recent advancements in artificial intelligence technology: Trends and implications. *International Journal of Multidisciplinary Scientific Research and Development*, 2(1), 01-11. https://doi.org/DOI: 10.54368/qijmsrd.2.1.0003

Wachter, S. (2024). Limitations and loopholes in the EU AI Act and AI liability directives: What this means for the European Union, the United States, and beyond. *SSRN*, *26*(3), 671–718. DOI: 10.2139/ssrn.4924553

Wischmeyer, T. (2020). Artificial intelligence and transparency: Opening the black box, *Regulating Artificial Intelligence*, 75-101. https://doi.org/DOI: 10.1007/978-3-030-32361-5_4

Wong, A. (2020). The laws and regulation of AI and autonomous systems. In Strous, L., Johnson, R., Grier, D. A., & Swade, D. (Eds.), *Unimagined Futures – ICT Opportunities and Challenges* (Vol. 555, pp. 38–54). Springer., DOI: 10.1007/978-3-030-64246-4_4

Xi, R. (2025). On emerging technologies: The old regime, and the proactivity. *Cardozo International & Comparative Law Review*, 8(1).

Zaidan, E., & Ibrahim, I. A. (2024). AI governance in a complex and rapidly changing regulatory landscape: A global perspective. *Humanities & Social Sciences Communications, 11*(1), 1121. DOI: 10.1057/s41599-024-03560-x

Chapter 11
Shifting Grounds in Exploring Diverse Approaches to AI Regulation:
Comparative Analysis of Google, EU, and IFLA Perspectives on AI Policy

Shalini Pandey
https://orcid.org/0009-0002-7960-0166
SBS' Balaji Law College, Pune, India

Aditya Agrawal
O.P. Jindal Global University, India

Shailesh Kumar Pandey
Hidayatullah National Law University, India

Md Mudassir Imam
Faculty of Law, Aligarh Muslim University, India

ABSTRACT

This chapter investigates the regulatory stance of Google and the International Federation of Library Associations and Institutions alongside the European Union through a post-Fordist French regulation school perspective. The analysis of various documents and ideological assessment demonstrates that Google upholds technology development and economic achievement while promoting solutionism and optimism

DOI: 10.4018/979-8-3693-9576-9.ch011

under a philosophical framework that views intelligence and societal formations from an essentialist liberal perspective. The EU supports adaptable regulations that confirm liberal economic principles but keeps its regulatory oversight mechanisms weak. IFLA maintains an inconsistent stance by criticizing AI innovation and capitalism from a human-centric liberal frame and embracing AI development as an inevitable force. All actors follow post-Fordist ideologies, but ethical and human rights considerations against capitalist positions stand out as fundamental critiques of AI control systems, demonstrating contradictions in the discussion regarding AI regulations and societal effects

INTRODUCTION

Artificial Intelligence (AI) has progressed at a breakneck pace in recent years and has already been applied in various ways. However, the regulation of AI has not seen the same explosive growth. This became particularly evident in 2023 when the Screen Actors Guild-American Federation of Television and Radio Artists (SAG-AFTRA) and the Writers Guild of America (WGA) went on a months-long strike against working conditions in the American film industry. Among their concerns was using AI in screenwriting and acting to cut costs and reduce the number of employees (Anguiano, 2023; Contreras, 2023). Similarly, AI has raised issues in the literary world, such as when it was revealed that ProseCraft, a now-defunct website aimed at analyzing and evaluating prose, used data from 25,000 published book manuscripts without the author's knowledge or consent (Geraets, 2023). The rapid advancement of AI has once again sparked debates about the right to creative expression, the exploitation of digital and manual labor, source criticism, copyright, and technical regulation. These are pressing questions for legislative actors, AI-developing companies, and cultural and informational institutions like archives, museums, and libraries (Robles Carrillo 2020 conclusion; Cath, Wachter, Mittelstadt, Taddeo & Floridi 2018 p. 505f). About the United Nations' Agenda 2030 goals—such as decent work and economic growth, sustainable industry and consumption, and reduced inequality (Globalamålen.se)—AI development presents ethical challenges. These challenges must be addressed as technology is integrated into current regulatory frameworks and new AI regulations are created.

As a field of research, Artificial Intelligence has existed since the 1950s, first defined during the Dartmouth Research Project as a machine programmed to behave in a way that would be considered intelligent if performed by a human (McCarthy, Minsky, Rochester & Shannon 1955 in Kaplan & Haenlein 2019 p. 17). At the time of writing, a search for the term "artificial intelligence" yields approximately 214,000 articles in the Web of Science database and 184,000 articles in Scopus, most of which have been published in the 2020s. These studies are primarily tied to computer science, engineering, mathematics, and medicine disciplines. Much of this research focuses on AI's technical development and practical application, such as healthcare. However, some studies adopt more critical perspectives on AI development, examining AI regulation and ethical frameworks. For instance, they explore what constitutes a "good AI society" (Palladino 2023 abstract; Cath, Wachter, Mittelstadt, Taddeo & Floridi 2018 p. 507; Robles Carrillo 2020 conclusion; Wirtz, Weyerer, & Sturm 2020 p. 822). Nevertheless, research comparing the ethical and ideological approaches of different actors and highlighting how these actors themselves define a "good AI society" is lacking. In the field of library and information science, current research is mainly exploratory. Studies address topics such as specific conceptual understandings of AI, librarians' attitudes toward AI, and the relationship between AI development and core library values (Vogus, 2023, p. 309; Subaveerapandiyan, Sunanthini & Amees, 2023 p. 503; Barsha & Munshi 2024 p. 7; Bridges, Elroy & Welhouse 2024 p. 66). Research on libraries and capitalism, which examines how libraries as institutions can be understood through different capitalist theories, is also available (Stevenson, 2011; Stevenson, 2016). However, there is a lack of studies investigating the relationship between libraries, other societal actors, AI, and regulation and how such regulation might be developed and negotiated internationally.

BACKGROUND

AI research is broad and multifaceted, but the research needs identified in the introduction are explored in depth in this subchapter, which presents and explores three aspects of AI research: AI and capitalism, AI and ethics, and AI and libraries. These aspects will then be used to discuss the topic's relevance further and justify the choice of the French regulation school as the chapter's theoretical framework. AI and capitalism are often critically discussed in the broader context of digital capitalism, which refers to a form of capitalism leveraging digital technology development to accumulate capital (Harvey, 1989, p. 191; Bhattacharyya, 2024, p. 121). Digital capitalism provides a critical perspective on AI development and regulation and is a natural bridge from earlier critiques of capitalism to contemporary AI research. However, much of this research operates at a high level of abstraction, often obscuring AI's concrete societal effects and the specific roles of actors involved. The design and implementation of AI regulation are also rarely examined in detail. AI regulation receives slightly more attention within the realm of AI ethics, which examines the ethical policies, laws, principles, and guidelines that shape AI development (Siau & Wang, 2023, p. 74). As noted earlier, several studies have explored

AI regulation and ethical frameworks, reflecting on what constitutes a "good AI society," which values are central to "good" societal development, and how these values are impacted by AI (Robles Carrillo 2020 conclusion; Chen, Ahn & Wang 2023; Wirtz, Weyerer, & Sturm 2020 p. 822; Cath, Wachter, Mittelstadt, Taddeo & Floridi 2018 p. 507). AI ethics thus offers insights into the normative, social, and legal frameworks of AI regulation while highlighting the ethical conflicts shaping AI development. However, ethics is a broad and interpretive concept, making it a somewhat porous foundation for theoretical development. Furthermore, the connection between AI development and capitalism is often absent.

A more practice-oriented perspective is provided by research on AI and libraries, focusing on how AI is understood conceptually, how it impacts libraries, and how attitudes toward AI are expressed in library operations and among librarians themselves (Vogus, 2023, p. 309; Lund, Khan & Yuvaraj 2024 p. 4; Subaveerapandiyan, 2023, p. 14; Subaveerapandiyan, Sunanthini & Amees 2023, p. 503; Barsha & Munshi, 2024, p. 7; Bridges, Elroy & Welhouse 2024 p. 66). This segment of AI research primarily highlights the tangible effects and questions AI development raises for libraries at a local level. In contrast to research on digital capitalism and AI ethics, this perspective lacks a broader view of AI's global consequences and more profound reflections on libraries' relationships with other actors in the context of AI development. There is, however, library and information science research that bridges the chapter of capitalism and libraries. In two studies, Siobhan Stevenson examines changes in the relationship between librarians and library users and how library work can be understood through the French regulation school's concept of post-Fordism (Stevenson, 2016; Stevenson, 2011). Although Stevenson's studies are relatively small in scale and focused primarily on the library as an institution, they illuminate a theoretical framework that has not been widely applied in library and information science research. As described in the introductory chapter, there is a lack of research investigating the relationship between AI, regulation, and actors with commercial, political, and cultural interests. Based on existing research, there is also a need to examine how AI regulation is designed and implemented, the specific roles of actors in AI regulation, and more profound reflections on libraries' relationships with other actors in AI development. This is important to investigate because the design and implementation of AI regulation and the actors involved will shape how AI is applied and perceived in society. This could significantly affect everything from employment opportunities to ethical and legal rights. As part of the public sector and an institution concerned with culture, information, and human practices, this issue is significant for libraries and library and information science. Unlike digital capitalism and AI ethics, the French regulation school and its concept of post-Fordism provide a more concrete and well-defined theoretical framework for examining the relationship between AI regulation and the systems of capital accumulation built around AI. The French regulation school thus offers an opportunity to explore the relationship between AI, regulation, and involved actors at a deeper level, uniting library and information science research with critical research on capitalism and ethics. This theory can, therefore, contribute new insights into the ideological similarities and differences in how various societal actors approach AI regulation.

This chapter aims to compare the approaches to AI regulation adopted by the AI-focused company Google, the International Federation of Library Associations and Institutions (IFLA), and the European Union (EU), focusing on the ideological themes revealed in the tensions between these approaches. Subsequently, these approaches will be analyzed through the lens of the French regulation school's perspective on post-Fordist regulation.

The research questions for the chapter are:

1. How do Google's, the EU's, and IFLA's approaches to AI regulation compare?
2. What ideological themes are revealed in the different approaches?
3. How can these approaches be understood from the perspective of the French regulation school's theory of post-Fordist regulation?

MAIN FOCUS OF THE CHAPTER

This chapter is conducted as a document chapter. Data collection involves close reading of the EU's Proposal for European AI Act (2021/0106), IFLA's A Library Strategic Approach to AI (2023), and Google's Perspectives on Issues in AI Governance (n.d.). These documents will be analyzed through an ideology analysis to identify and thematize the central themes and values regarding AI and AI regulation. The analysis will then compare Google's, the EU's, and IFLA's approaches using the French regulation school's perspective on post-Fordist regulation, broken down into its characteristic features. A strength of document studies is that documents constitute "non-reactive" chapter material (Bryman, 2018, p. 657), meaning they are not influenced by the researcher's values or perceptions, unlike interviews (ibid.). However, documents are often written with specific audiences and aim to convey a favorable impression of the authors or organizations, shaping their formulation and content (Bryman, 2018, p. 674). This ideological slant can be an asset since this chapter aims to uncover the ideologies embedded in the organizations' approaches to AI regulation.

Ideology analysis was chosen as the analysis method to explore the organizations' approaches. This method helps reveal the values and interests that informally and implicitly characterize organizations and how these values are used to legitimize specific societal conditions or goals (Alvesson & Deetz 2022, pp. 120f; Boréus & Bergström 2018, pp. 136ff; Eagleton 2007, pp. 28f, cited in Lund 2015, p. 184). However, ideology analysis and critique risk premature judgment, as they are often based on critical, sometimes harmful, assumptions (Alvesson & Deetz, 2022, p. 128). To address this, this chapter incorporates elements of positive ideology analysis, where the concrete aspects of ideology are first identified and then linked to the interests of social groups and actors (Liedman 1989 in Lund 2015, p. 182).

LITERATURE REVIEW

AI And Digital Capitalism

Research on AI and capitalism is closely intertwined with the broader critical discourse on digital capitalism, which refers to capitalism that utilizes digital technology to accumulate capital (Harvey, 1989, p. 191; Bhattacharyya, 2024, p. 121). Studies on digital capitalism focus on revealing processes unique to this form of capitalism, such as the increasingly blurred boundary between capitalist organizations and social infrastructure, the normalization and invisibility of digital technologies in society, and the concealment of labor to promote the vision of an automated society (Bhattacharyya, 2024, p. 123; Pasquinelli 2023, p. 8; Harvey, 1989, p. 152; Cath, Wachter, Mittelstadt, Taddeo & Floridi 2018, p. 507). Grounded in Marxism, a societal ideology that examines capitalism's impact on labor and economic development, this research explores fundamental capitalist processes, such as "accumulation by dispossession" (Harvey 2003, cited in Bhattacharyya 2024, p. 12). This refers to the tendency of accumulation systems to enhance some individuals' capital by exploiting, marginalizing, and excluding specific, often racialized, societal groups (Harvey, 1989, p. 180; Bhattacharyya 2024, pp. 6, 12, 15 & 124; Morozov 2013, p. xii). Digital capitalism is used by researchers to explain AI technology as a reformulation of capitalist strategies while recycling old capitalist logic, challenging the notion of AI development as inherently good and inevitable (Ericson, Dobbe & Lindgren 2024, p. 323; Pasquinelli, 2023, p. 246). Researchers also argue that automation of tasks creates social hierarchies by redefining labor systems based on the quantification and ranking of intelligence, seeking to make AI capital independent of labor (Pasquinelli, 2023, pp. 21f; Karppi & Granata, 2019, p. 874; Dyer-Witheford, Kjøsen & Steinhoff 2019, p. 32; Khereiche, 2020, p. 75). The oligopoly of the AI industry uses this to influence social behaviors, steering labor and society toward capitalist interests (Bhattacharyya 2024, pp. 126 & 129f; Harvey 1989, pp. 158f; Dyer-Witheford, Kjøsen & Steinhoff 2019, pp. 32-42, cited in Khereiche 2020, p. 75). To counter digital capitalism, proposals such as digital socialism, which aims to unify workers from the ground up through mobilization based on workers' realities and needs, and digital Marxist-humanist communication theory, advocating for publicly owned and managed internet and society, have been suggested (Englert, Woodcock & Cant 2020, p. 142; Fuchs 2020, p. 335). Several studies imply that AI development and regulation cannot occur without first addressing capitalism and its principles.

AI, Regulation, and Ethics

AI ethics is a distinct field within AI research, emerging from the 21st century's discussions on machine ethics (Siau & Wang, 2020, p. 74). A key theoretical distinction within the field separates AI ethics, encompassing policies, laws, principles, and guidelines for AI development, from ethical AI, which refers to AI exhibiting ethical behavior (ibid.). AI ethics primarily examines the legal, normative, and social frameworks that regulate AI development. A critique raised within AI ethics is how the emphasis on technological innovation obscures structural ethical inequalities. The field also critiques how ethical frameworks are operationalized and simplified into mathematical representations aligned with measurable ideals of technological research and associated corporations, contributing to technological solutionism (Heilinger 2022, pp. 9f; Palladino 2023, Chapter 2). Studies on AI regulation and ethical frameworks in the public sector reflect on what constitutes a "good AI society," the values central to "good" societal development, and how these values are impacted by AI development. These studies differentiate ethical and legal frameworks, arguing that ethical principles such as transparency, accountability, and positive outcomes are necessary to encourage beneficial AI use, while legal frameworks are needed to deter harmful applications (Robles Carrillo 2020 conclusion; Chen, Ahn & Wang 2023; Wirtz, Weyerer & Sturm 2020, p. 822; Cath, Wachter, Mittelstadt, Taddeo & Floridi 2018, p. 507). In the absence of previous AI legislation, it is predicted that legal frameworks will rely on human norms, rights, and values (Wirtz, Weyerer & Sturm 2020, p. 822). However, pervasive capitalist ideals—such as technological solutionism, flexibility, and innovation as inherently good—risk aligning human values with capitalist interests (Harvey 1989, pp. 158f & 180; Morozov 2013, p. xii). This highlights a complex dilemma, as private and commercial actors primarily drive AI development, while ethical frameworks are expected to be based on human rights and existing transnational normative structures (Palladino 2023, abstract; Wirtz, Weyerer & Sturm 2020, p. 822).

AI and Libraries

A practice-oriented library perspective is most prominent in library and information science research on AI and AI regulation. This research focuses on understanding specific conceptualizations of AI, librarians' attitudes toward AI, and how AI development aligns with core library values. Some studies adopt an overall positive view, describing AI as enhancing the efficiency, accessibility, and user-friendliness of library services while potentially reducing digital divides in society. Challenges identified in these studies are often practical implementation barriers, such as insufficient knowledge and attitudes among librarians, inadequate funding, or the need for more substantial digital infrastructure (Vogus 2023, p. 309; Lund, Khan & Yuvaraj 2024, p. 4; Subaveerapandiyan 2023, p. 14; Subaveerapandiyan, Sunanthini & Amees 2023, p. 503; Barsha & Munshi 2024, p. 7; Chhetri 2023, p. 1; Pence, 2022, p. 141). Other studies take a more critical stance, highlighting concerns such as AI's potential to complicate the information environment, fears of job displacement for librarians, and the potential conflict between AI development and library core values, such as equality, diversity, inclusion, intellectual freedom, open access, and privacy (Cox & Mazumdar, 2022, p. 330; Subaveerapandiyan 2023, p. 14; Bridges, Elroy & Welhouse 2024, p. 66; Subaveerapandiyan, Sunanthini & Amees 2023, p. 503; Chhetri 2023, p. 1).

THEORETICAL FRAMEWORK

The French regulation school, originating from Michel Aglietta's theory of capitalist regulation (Aglietta, 1987), focuses on how systems of capital accumulation are regulated, stabilized, and defended over time through historically grounded social and infrastructural systems (Leckie & Given, 2010, p. 6; Stevenson 2011, pp. 774f; Aglietta 1987, pp. 380ff). Unlike Marx's theory that class tensions in capitalism would ultimately lead to its collapse, the French regulation school argues that social changes occur within the capitalist system by adapting regimes of accumulation and modes of regulation (Leckie & Given, 2010, p. 2; Stevenson 2011, pp. 774f).

Regimes of Accumulation and Modes of Regulation

Modes of regulation encompass the laws, norms, practices, and policies that form the foundation for operating regimes of accumulation, the structures designed for capital accumulation (ibid.). These regimes and modes rely on each other in a symbiotic relationship. Through state intervention, the relationship between regimes of accumulation and modes of regulation reconciles labor and capital with technological developments. This reconciliation is shaped by the sociohistorical context in which it occurs, meaning it changes over time (Marx, 1857; Leckie & Given 2010, p. 4; Dyer-Witheford 1999, pp. 55f, cited in Lund, pp. 105f; Stevenson 2011, pp. 774 & 777; Hollingsworth & Boyer 1997, pp. 36ff).

By reproducing ideologies such as individualism, social mobility, and equal opportunity, a stable and relatively permanent social and economic hierarchy is established based on the balance between the state, capital, and labor (Leckie & Given, 2010, p. 6; Aglietta 1987, pp. 383ff). When conflicts arise between the state, capital, and labor—and thus between regimes of accumulation and modes of regulation—a crisis can occur, necessitating the renegotiation of new conditions (Leckie & Given 2010, pp. 4f; Stevenson, 2011, p. 775). The regulation school sees such crises as inevitable due to capitalism's tendency toward overaccumulation of profits and debt, which regulation seeks to counterbalance. The state must, therefore, balance regulation between national interests and market dynamics (Harvey 1989, pp. 171 & 185). Using the state as a "lender of the last resort" (Harvey, 1989, p. 168) can stabilize the system in the short term. However, over time, this creates such an imbalance between regimes and modes that the system collapses and requires renegotiation (ibid.).

Fordism and Post-Fordism

Aglietta and the French regulation school argue that a significant shift occurred during the 1960s and 1970s (Aglietta 1987, pp. 383f). They describe the specific relationships between regimes of accumulation and modes of regulation before and after this shift using the concepts of Fordism and Post-Fordism. The fall of Fordism and the subsequent rise of post-Fordism brought changes in how social costs of labor were distributed. Fordism's top-down organizational structure, authoritarian leadership, large workforces, and factory-based mass production of goods eventually created debts and social disparities so extensive that state intervention was no longer effective (Lipietz 1992, p. 16, cited in Stevenson 2011, p. 776; Harvey 1989, pp. 168ff). The shift to post-Fordism emphasized flexible accumulation (Aglietta 2000, p. 385, cited in Lund 2015, p. 104f; Harvey 1989, pp. 152 & 191). Characterized by flexibility, post-Fordism is marked by information-intensive and network-based economies reliant on just-in-time production, the internationalization of labor, and corresponding legislation to regulate it (Stevenson, 2011, p. 776; Harvey, 1989, p. 195). With information as the primary commodity, success depended on privileged and rapid access to information and quickly turning it into marketable goods. This compression of time and space in the labor market and the need for control over information flows fostered mergers, acquisitions, and the globalization of local markets into a unified capitalist system with shared or overlapping modes of regulation (Harvey 1989, pp. 152, 155f & 158ff).

Ideology and Regulation in Post-Fordism

The language of regulatory policy documents is not neutral but "bears the imprint of the ideological struggles of which it is a product" (Stevenson, 2016, p. 196). The ideologies promoted through such documents can either include or exclude actors (Harvey, 1989, p. 138). Harvey highlights values like corporate and national pride and loyalty as central to capitalism, which function as tools of social control through competitive individualism—tying an individual's sense of success to their status in the company—and legitimizing prevailing relations between the state, capital, and labor (Harvey 1989, pp. 123 & 171). Given the centrality of control over information for capital growth and the system's instability requiring continuous innovation, post-Fordist ideology emphasizes development as inevitable and inherently beneficial (Harvey, 1989, p. 180). These promoted ideologies are even more critical for the relatively young field of AI development, as the state cannot rely on existing legislation. Instead, it may turn to normative regulation theory, which emphasizes ideals, human values, rights, and ethics (Wirtz, Weyerer & Sturm 2020, p. 822). Thus, the construction of regulatory frameworks for AI development will likely be heavily influenced by post-Fordist ideology and its associated ideals.

In this chapter, the French regulation school's theory of regulation is interpreted as a framework where regimes of accumulation and modes of regulation exist symbiotically and are shaped by their specific sociohistorical context. Modes of regulation are understood as the laws, norms, practices, and policies that underpin the functioning of regimes of accumulation. In the context of AI, modes of regulation are the laws, norms, practices, and policies designed to enable AI development to accumulate capital.

Five key features characterize the post-Fordist mode of regulation:

1. Information-intensive and network-based economies.
2. Just-in-time production.
3. Internationalization of labor and legislation.
4. The need for control over information flows for market success.
5. Competitive individualism, combined with a focus on normative regulation and human rights about AI.

These five features will be the framework for comparing Google's, the EU's, and IFLA's approaches to AI regulation, shedding light on alignments and tensions within post-Fordist ideology.

METHODOLOGY

Qualitative data collection methods such as in-depth interviews, field observations, and small-scale document studies are often employed for research questions that are exploratory and reflective, emphasizing the subjective perspective of the interviewee or research context (Bryman, 2018, p. 561). Document studies, the chosen method for this chapter, involve analyzing materials not explicitly created for research purposes but which nonetheless hold scientific interest, such as diaries, articles, reports, or legal texts (Bryman 2018, pp. 656f). A key advantage of document studies is that documents are "non-reactive" research materials (Bryman, 2018, p. 657), meaning they are not influenced by the researcher's values or opinions, unlike interviews. Furthermore, documents generated by organizations, authorities, and companies can be seen as representations of their social and organizational realities, offering more profound insights into their ethical, social, and ideological approaches than interviews with a few individuals could provide (Bryman, 2018, p. 674).

However, documents are often written with specific audiences in mind and aim to convey a favorable impression of the authors or organizations, influencing their content and formulation (Bryman, 2018, p. 674). This characteristic is advantageous for this chapter, as the aim is to uncover the ideologies present in the organizations' approaches to AI regulation.

In qualitative research, purposive sampling is often used to strategically select research participants or objects based on the research questions and how representative the sample is of reality (Bryman, 2018, p. 496). This can include techniques like a snowball, theoretical, and generic purposive sampling. In this chapter, generic purposive sampling was used to select documents representing various organizational types—corporations, transnational unions, and non-governmental organizations—providing a range of perspectives on AI regulation. Publicly and digitally accessible documents were identified for each organizational type, and the final selection was based on how well the documents addressed the research questions.

The chapter is based on a close reading of three documents:

1. **Google's Perspectives on Issues in AI Governance**: This white chapter outlining Google's views on AI regulation offers a corporate perspective, including insights into internal AI regulation and government and international framework proposals. Of the 30 pages, 27 were closely analyzed, with three pages read in the overview due to their limited relevance to the research questions.
2. **EU's Proposal for European AI Act (2021/0106)**: A legislative proposal addressing AI risks, protecting fundamental rights, and positioning the EU as a leader in AI regulation and innovation. Only the first 16 pages, comprising

the introduction and justification, were closely read to align with the scope of the other documents. The remaining sections were used as reference material.

3. **IFLA's A Library Strategic Approach to AI (2023)**: This document outlines IFLA's reflections on how libraries should approach AI and support local decision-making on AI-related issues. All 20 pages were closely analyzed.

The documents were analyzed through an ideology analysis, which examined explicit ideologies, assumptions, naturalizations, universalizations, and silences in the documents. In this context, ideology is "the patterns and regularities in people's mental constructions" (Boréus & Bergström, 2018, p. 136), shaping organizations and social institutions informally and implicitly.

This chapter employs **positive ideology analysis**, first identifying concrete aspects of ideology and then linking them to the interests of social groups and actors (Liedman 1989, cited in Lund 2015, p. 182). The analysis proceeds in two steps:

1. Identify themes and make interpretative comments on each actor's approach to AI regulation.
2. Summarizing and analyzing these themes concerning the actors' interests.

Elements of critical ideology analysis are also included, assuming underlying capitalist interests in Google's ideologies and similar tendencies in the EU's stance, enabling a stronger connection to the French regulation school's critique of capitalism.

The second part of the analysis compares the ideological approaches identified by Google, the EU, and IFLA to the post-Fordist features outlined in the theoretical chapter. These features include:

1. Just-in-time production and time-space compression.
2. Internationalization of labor and legislation.
3. Control over information flows.
4. Competitive individualism.
5. Normative regulation and human rights.

The presence or absence of these characteristics in the documents highlights alignments with and deviations from the post-Fordist ideology.

RESULTS

The following results chapter presents Google's, EU's, and IFLA's approaches to AI regulation, divided into three overarching ideological themes for each text. At the end of each theme, the respective actor's approach and the naturalizations, silences, and assumptions that have been identified will be summarised, followed by a more comprehensive summary at the end of each subchapter.

Google

Google asserts that AI development has accelerated to the point where it has become *"[a] part of the fabric of modern life"* (p. 2). AI is thus presented as a natural and increasingly invisible part of everyday life. This serves as the foundation for the document's purpose: to urge the state, authorities, and non-governmental organizations to make significant contributions to discussions on AI regulation (ibid.). Therefore, AI regulation is portrayed as a process subject to discussion and negotiation. This call for dialogue leads to three main themes.

Regulation with Restraint and Technological Solutionism

Google states that the power over how society should use AI lies in the hands of the state, whose primary role is to oversee collaboration between the industry and other stakeholders to "*ensure good outcomes*" (pp. 6, 31). This effectively absolves Google of responsibility for how AI should be used and coordinated in society. The document does not provide specific examples of what "*good outcomes*" entail. However, it emphasizes the need to regulate the misuse of AI—both intentional and unintentional—and to balance law enforcement with privacy and human rights (pp. 18, 29, 31). This implies that AI is inherently good but can be misused by malicious actors. The state's role, therefore, primarily ensures compliance with laws and prevents these bad actors from infringing on the rights of AI users. At the same time, Google argues that regulation must be done "*within reason*" (p. 18). Throughout the document, it warns that overly restrictive regulation could have "*considerable downsides*" (p. 29), such as hindering socially beneficial innovation, reducing competition, misplacing responsibility, stifling free speech on ideas, and increasing legal uncertainty (pp. 29–30). AI innovation is thus portrayed as positive, and hindering its development is equated to violating companies' (such as Google's) freedom of expression. By using terms like *"discussion," "collaboration," "guidance," "consultation," and "conversation,"* Google frames AI regulation as something to be negotiated and co-constructed, where collaborative, multi-stakeholder cooperation with the state in a supportive and advisory role is the best way to achieve timely solutions to AI challenges "*without impeding its promise*" (p. 6). Google repeatedly claims that current non-AI-specific legislation is sufficient to meet the regulatory needs of the AI market (pp. 4, 6, 29, 30, 31). Implicitly, Google favors weak regulation or continued deregulation of AI development. Instead, it suggests updating legislation based on the specific sectors where AI is intended to be used, such as medicine or law enforcement, and doing so thoughtfully and cautiously: "*Google recommends a cautious approach for governments concerning liability in AI systems since the wrong frameworks might place unfair blame, stifle innovation, or even reduce safety. Any changes to the general liability framework should come only after thorough research establishing the failure of the existing contract, tort, and other laws.*" (p. 30) Google thus argues that changes to the legal framework should only occur after the current framework is proven insufficient. However, the same cautious approach does not apply to AI development and innovation.

Instead, Google prioritizes regulation that strengthens users' confidence and trust in AI systems (pp. 10, 12). This is justified by describing how algorithms can make decisions more consistently and with fewer errors than humans, dismissing the belief that human oversight of AI improves safety as a "*fallacy*" (p. 26). The narrative painted is that humans are more irrational and prone to error than AI; therefore, our reliance on human supervisors and decision-makers is misguided. These arguments lean heavily on technological solutionism and optimism, the idea that societal problems have solutions, which lie in innovation and technological progress—with AI being more likely to provide these solutions than humans due to its superior intelligence. While Google emphasizes that companies are ultimately responsible for ensuring AI technology does not fall into the hands of "*bad actors*" (p. 21), it also argues that the state should work on clarifying the ethical expectations and demands placed on the market through mechanisms such as safety certifications and definitions of "*best practices*" (pp. 23, 25, 28). This work, however, should be collaborative, with the optimal regulatory framework being "*flexible and able to keep pace with developments*" (p. 31) by delegating regulation to self- and co-regulatory practices (ibid.). What remains unsaid is that this places a significant portion of regulatory power in the hands of companies, which can choose whether to adhere to or ignore certifications and best-practice recommendations. Thus, weaker regulations provide companies like Google considerable leeway to develop AI based on their interests.

Pragmatism and Uniformity

As previously mentioned, Google encourages governments to clarify expectations and requirements for AI usage through collaboration with society, companies, and AI users. This includes explanation standards, safety precautions lists, human oversight requirements in AI systems, and general accountability frameworks (p. 4).

Ideally, these measures should be rooted in human rights and values such as privacy and equality (p. 6). However, this pragmatic perspective assumes that human rights can be translated into concrete, operationalized, or quantified standards, reflecting an underlying belief that such rights can be measured. Google suggests practical measures such as introducing safety certifications that AI systems must meet to be sold on the market or creating "*best practice*" recommendations in collaboration with AI developers and other policy stakeholders (pp. 9, 13, 18, 25). Additionally, Google proposes developing universally agreed-upon definitions of key concepts, such as fairness, to facilitate their application in AI algorithms (p. 15). This regulation is technology-focused mainly, aiming to address algorithmic bias through standards and operationalization of core values. However, this approach obscures biases inherent in AI programmers and training data and the process by which established standards become naturalized and taken for granted over time. Since certifications place most of the regulatory authority in the hands of companies (as discussed in 5.1.1), businesses hold significant influence over the standards that are eventually normalized. Google also emphasizes the importance of international uniformity in standards and regulations to "*relieve pressure on individual countries and regions to advance a controversial use of technology just because others might be doing so, preventing a race to the bottom*" (p. 6). Interestingly, businesses are not mentioned in this "*race to the bottom,*" even though capitalism and corporate competition are primary drivers of accelerating AI development. According to Google, common standards would level the playing field for AI developers, encourage more responsible use of AI, and increase trust in AI tools in society (pp. 6, 18). This framing portrays safe and unsafe AI as being created by users rather than Google while reinforcing that AI regulation must be negotiated among businesses, governments, and other stakeholders.

Flexibility and Innovation as Essential Goods

In addition to its emphasis on non-restrictiveness, pragmatism, and uniformity, Google argues that AI regulation must also be flexible, as reflected in its description of the optimal regulatory framework: "*Google believes the optimal governance regime is flexible and able to keep pace with developments while respecting cultural differences. We believe that self and co-regulatory approaches will remain the most effective practical way to address and prevent AI-related problems in most instances, within the boundaries already set by sector-specific regulation.*" (p. 31) Sector-specific regulation is a recurring suggestion from Google to avoid stifling innovation while enabling precise adjustments that align with the company's economic and social priorities (pp. 5, 30). Flexibility and "*just-in-time*" production and regulation emerge as a dominant ideal throughout the document. Sector-specific regulation is also presented as a way to accommodate cultural differences. However, this is contradicted by Google's position as a global company that advocates for common standards and frameworks, even within specific sectors. As the quote above highlights, flexibility also implies that regulation must keep pace with technological advancements and shifts in social values (p. 30). Thus, regulation is expected to follow innovation rather than being constrained by regulation, positioning businesses as the driving and guiding force in development. Global development—specifically its acceleration—is portrayed as inherently good and desirable. This perspective is further evident in Google's description of AI as "*a powerful, multi-purpose technology with the potential to transform industrial and societal processes alike*" (p. 6). AI is consistently described in broadly favorable terms, with transformative potential comparable to technologies like genetic modification (GMO), IVF treatments, nuclear energy, research into harmful PCBs, and space exploration (pp. 6–7). In several places, Google also claims that AI is less prone to social bias than humans and can make more consistent, creative, and fair decisions (pp. 15, 17, 19). This assumes that AI can radically transform social processes without social bias, framing social processes as rational and separate from human emotions, thoughts, and biases. This perspective aligns with a liberal and essentialist view of society instead of a constructivist one. Google emphasizes that the opportunities provided by AI development and its positive qualities outweigh the potential adverse effects caused by the "*[misuse of a small fraction of bad actors]*" (p. 22). Regulating AI development is thus portrayed as restricting a positive societal force. At the same time, responsibility is described as "*an intrinsically human property*" (p. 28), meaning that the function and consequences of AI ultimately fall under human accountability. This effectively shifts responsibility for adverse outcomes away from AI systems and, consequently, away from the companies developing them.

EU

According to the EU, the upcoming AI legislation aims to establish "*harmonized rules for artificial intelligence*" (p. 1) to unite AI regulation under a single legal framework. This is emphasized as particularly important due to the rapid development of AI, which can provide the European economy with competitive advantages but also pose risks to fundamental EU rights (ibid.). Through three overarching themes, the EU positions itself as the primary decision-making authority on AI regulation and the standard to which member states and their markets should adhere.

The Single Market and Innovation

AI regulation is presented as a key component of the EU's "*digital single market strategy*" (p. 6), which primarily seeks to ensure the uniform and harmonious functioning of the internal market (pp. 1, 6). The concept of the single market is mentioned multiple times (pp. 3, 6, 7, 9, 10), including once in capital letters: "*the Single Market*" (p. 6). This assumes that EU member states are or should be viewed as a market and a unified economy, thus naturalizing and reinforcing the EU's position as the ultimate authority over AI development. The concept of unified regulation stemming from the EU is also promoted through the idea of the single market. The EU argues that regulation at the national level would fragment the market and create legal uncertainty, which would "*slow market uptake of AI*" (p. 6). A swift development and adoption of AI and the EU's sole control over this progress are essential. The single market is also portrayed as an innovation utopia—an ecosystem that enhances digital autonomy (p. 10). Using the term "*ecosystem*" naturalizes AI as an integral part of the socioeconomic cycle. At the same time, the emphasis on digital autonomy reflects an assumption that harmony within this cycle is rooted in liberal values and ideals of freedom. The regulatory framework is intended to be "*robust and flexible*" (p. 3). The "*robust*" aspect refers to uniformity in member states' legislation, ensuring that AI systems are safe, reliable, and aligned with fundamental rights and Union values (pp. 1, 3, 5, 6). Simultaneously, the framework is robust in its flexibility, designed to be sustainable over time, and relevant to new AI developments and societal changes (pp. 3, 15). In practice, this means a normatively binding framework with the EU as the leading authority, though it is general enough to apply over time, which renders it relatively vague. Society's role is also somewhat obscured by the focus on the economy and market stimulation.

The "*flexible*" aspect of the legal framework is implemented through a "*sector-by-sector and case-by-case approach*" to regulating and assessing risks (p. 8). This reduces business compliance costs, avoiding a slowdown in AI development (pp. 3, 10, 13, 14). Three ideological threads emerge from this reasoning: Speed of development is framed as a strong reason for less restrictive regulation, emphasizing development as inherently positive. Regulation is individualized on a case-by-case basis, aligning with liberal ideals. Reducing businesses' compliance costs is prioritized, reflecting capitalist values and obscuring that the EU benefits from this setup by reducing its administrative burden. The legislation mainly focuses on regulating "*high-risk*" AI systems, including those used in healthcare, traffic and energy systems, education, candidate evaluations, border surveillance, and other systems that raise "*justified cause for concern*" (pp. 3, 24). For non- "*high-risk*" AI systems, only voluntary codes of conduct and "minimal transparency obligations" are applied (p. 7). Implicitly, "*high-risk*" AI systems are assumed to threaten fundamental rights and societal systems, requiring regulation. In contrast, other AI systems are considered reliable and should not face restrictions, leaving control mainly in the hands of companies. Non- "*high-risk*" systems are also exempt from transparency requirements if such transparency infringes on freedom of expression (pp. 5, 15). In this context, freedom of expression is reinterpreted as the right to innovate and develop new AI systems. Limiting companies' ability to develop AI freely is equated to restricting an individual's freedom of expression, promoting self-regulation as a right.

Control and Conformity

Beyond regulating to safeguard the single market's innovation and interests, the EU also advocates for "*regulatory intervention*" (p. 1) to ensure that AI development aligns with the Union's values and that AI is safe, ethical, and reliable (ibid.). Two undertones emerge here: first, the rapid pace of development is acknowledged as positive and problematic; second, there is an assumption that EU intervention is necessary to guide development in a positive and ethical direction. The EU justifies legal regulation based on "*the need for a uniform application of the new rules*" (p. 7), with these new rules referring to the EU AI Act. Terms such as "*uniformity,*" "*harmony,*" "*consistency,*" "*coherence,*" and especially "*conformity*" are frequently used in the text, underscoring that uniformity is seen as desirable. Combined with an interest in maintaining "the Union's digital sovereignty" (p. 6) and shaping global AI norms and standards (pp. 1, 5, 6), the EU positions itself as one of, if not the ultimate authority on AI development. However, it also becomes evident that the EU's authority is rooted in the unity of its member states. Justifying the EU's control over AI development in its member states relies on promoting uniformity as a positive goal. High-risk AI systems are to be regulated through reporting to an EU-controlled database and monitored before, during, and after production to counteract opacity, complexity, bias, unpredictability, and, to some extent, autonomous behavior (pp. 2, 7, 10, 15). Unlike the generally positive view of AI the EU has previously portrayed, high-risk AI is opaque, complex, biased, and unpredictable. However, the EU proposes no "*regulatory burdens*" (p. 7) for non-high-risk AI systems, presenting regulation as negative and restrictive.

The flexibility of AI regulation also ensures that legislation can adapt to the pace of AI development and the emergence of "*new concerning situations*" (p. 3). These concerning situations seem to be tied explicitly to high-risk AI systems, as the EU establishes mandatory codes of conduct for these systems and imposes substantial fines of up to 30 million Euros or 6% of a company's annual revenue for violations (pp. 4, 9, 11, 82). This creates strong economic incentives to comply with regulations and avoid having AI projects classified as high-risk. This reflects the assumption that capitalism drives societal development. At the same time, the EU notes that its stakeholders and partners—such as academia, businesses, local authorities, non-commercial organizations, and individual citizens (pp. 7–8)—have warned against legal duplication, contradictory legislation, and overregulation (p. 8). This is used to justify shifting responsibility for reporting high-risk AI systems to the EU database entirely onto AI providers. This obscures the EU's interest in maintaining a free market while allowing the EU to partially absolve itself of responsibility for the consequences of weaker regulation.

Trust, Ethical Values, and Fundamental Rights

A key aim of the EU's AI regulation is to promote the adoption of AI in the market and society by building "*an ecosystem of trust*" (p. 1), giving users confidence to embrace AI-based solutions (ibid.). This contributes to the naturalization and eventual normalization of AI in society, aligning with the ideology of technological solutionism—AI is seen as inherently trustworthy, sound, and a positive force for societal transformation. The so-called ecosystem's shortcomings are attributed to AI users rather than to AI or its development. The EU frames AI as a positive societal force with "*the ultimate aim of increasing human well-being*" (p. 1). This broadens the focus from innovation, market interests, and control to humans and society. However, implicit in this vision is that improving human well-being occurs through trust in and acceptance of AI technology, driven by market forces. The EU also states that it is in the Union's interest to "*ensure that Europeans can benefit from new technologies*" (p. 1), presenting access to these technologies as inherently advantageous. Notably, the EU explicitly mentions Europeans, implying that it is not in the EU's interest to ensure the same benefits reach non-Europeans. From the perspective of the EU's vision of the single market, non-Europeans appear more as competitors than as individuals with the same fundamental rights.

Beyond revisiting existing legislation, the EU ensures that Europeans' rights are fully respected (p. 2). These rights include privacy, protection against discrimination, freedom of expression, freedom of organization, fair investigation and trial rights, the presumption of innocence, and the right to defense (p. 11). The EU claims its proposed law will enhance these rights, suggesting that AI development risks infringing on privacy, enabling discrimination, or violating principles of criminal justice without legal regulation. Furthermore, the EU emphasizes that the legislation should ensure individuals are appropriately informed about AI systems and have the free choice not to use or be profiled by such systems (pp. 13–14). This reflects a liberalist notion of individuals as free and rational agents. The EU also states that the law will positively impact specific groups' rights, such as workers' rights to fair conditions, consumer protection, children's rights, the inclusion of persons with disabilities, and the right to environmental protection (p. 11). However, the EU notes these considerations are "*applicable in certain domains*" (ibid.). This could be interpreted as these rights not applying to all EU citizens or AI developers not needing to consider them universally. The latter interpretation likely applies, as sustainable development, accessibility for persons with disabilities, and workforce diversity are described as "*voluntary commitments*" (p. 16). This creates an image where more liberal rights, such as freedom of expression and privacy, are prioritized over social-liberal rights like protection and support for vulnerable groups.

The justification for the proposed law also highlights concerns over high-risk AI systems' potential to manipulate individuals, exploit the vulnerabilities of groups like children and persons with disabilities, and cause physical or psychological harm (pp. 12–13). As a result, the EU argues that the legislation will impose certain restrictions on corporate rights, such as freedom of enterprise, artistic and scientific freedom, and intellectual property rights (p. 11). Similar to earlier discussions on freedom of expression, human rights like artistic and scientific freedom are ascribed to corporations, creating a narrative where AI development is framed as a corporate right. By limiting the potential adverse effects of AI to high-risk systems, malicious actors, and exceptional cases, the EU preserves the image of AI as a positive societal force.

IFLA

The purpose of IFLA's document is to highlight considerations and dilemmas libraries may face when implementing AI (p. 2). The document expresses hope that it can "*support local decision-making about AI*" (ibid.), suggesting that IFLA aspires to influence how AI is regulated locally.

Access (Openness) and Ethical Concerns

IFLA emphasizes that libraries can influence AI implementation in libraries and other institutions by promoting openness, privacy, and accessibility (pp. 10–11). This suggests that IFLA views AI as inherently closed, privacy-invasive, and inaccessible. Ethical regulation by external actors is deemed particularly important because AI development is dominated by "*Big Tech companies*" (ibid.), which are seen as the primary cause of AI's current ethical deficiencies. Nonetheless, AI technology is also acknowledged as having the potential to enhance access to information and knowledge (pp. 3, 5). Despite IFLA's reservations about the commercial nature of AI development, access to AI is framed as inherently positive, somewhat obscuring the ethical tensions inherent in AI systems. IFLA raises concerns about libraries' "*capacity and readiness to develop [and implement] AI systems*" (p. 13). Therefore, the central issue is whether libraries should implement AI or not. This positions

AI implementation as inevitable and naturalized. To remain relevant, IFLA recommends adopting an uncritical stance in the hope of gaining "*a seat at the table*" (p. 19), allowing it to highlight accessibility and ethical issues. This reflects a sense of powerlessness in the face of technological development, where control is placed in the hands of AI developers and corporations rather than IFLA or the library sector. Social and normative efforts, such as educating and informing users to encourage AI literacy, are also described as the library's "*natural role*" in AI development (p. 5). This implies that users interact with AI uncritically and that AI interaction requires critical literacy skills. Thus, interacting with AI is portrayed as an increasingly normalized aspect of the digital information landscape—something to be accepted and prepared for rather than challenged.

Change and Staying "Up-to-Date"

In IFLA's SWOT analysis, one identified threat is that "*[t]he speed of change, particularly initiated by ChatGPT, makes it difficult for institutions to respond in a timely way*" (p. 11). In this context of rapid development and the need to stay "*up-to-date*" with new information, IFLA emphasizes the importance of responding flexibly to change, primarily as these shifts "*are driven by actors beyond influence or control*" (p. 11). While these actors are not explicitly identified, the surrounding text discusses the impact of ChatGPT's success (pp. 11–12), implying that these actors are likely companies and other industry-related stakeholders. This suggests that corporations are perceived as forces outside libraries' influence and control, effectively positioning capitalism as a force similarly beyond influence and control. Consequently, IFLA's primary focus is to remain relevant and current rather than to question prevailing systems and developments. This includes proactive efforts to continuously train library staff as "*a proactive strategy for keeping the workforce adaptable and competitive in a rapidly changing landscape*" (p. 15). Therefore, flexibility and informational competitiveness are crucial for libraries to thrive in the capitalist paradigm. At the same time, IFLA distances itself from current policies' "*productivity agenda*" (p. 12), highlighting potential adverse effects such as job cuts, increased pressure on staff, and heightened surveillance (ibid.). This critique reflects a negative view of increased technological presence and the expectation that staff remain flexible and perpetually productive. However, as noted earlier, these expectations of adaptability and competitiveness are deemed essential, making IFLA's critique appear more symbolic than substantive. This is further underscored by the suggestion that AI could assist librarians by drafting policies, documents, and other administrative content to "*create more space for higher value, skilled work*" (p. 11). This implies that drafting policies is less important than preparing for, adapting to, and being flexible toward AI developments.

ANALYSIS

In this chapter, the approaches analyzed in the results section regarding Google's, the EU's, and IFLA's stances on AI regulation are further explored through the lens of the French Regulation School's understanding of post-Fordism. Specifically, five defining categories of post-Fordism are operationalized: just-in-time production and compression of time and space, internationalization of labor and legislation, control over information flows, competitive individualism, and normative regulation and human rights. The final section summarises the analysis.

Just-in-Time Production and Compression of Time and Space

The emphasis on flexible accumulation in post-Fordism redefined the relationship between regimes of accumulation and modes of regulation, manifesting in just-in-time production and compression of time and space. This refers to shorter production windows and minimized physical or digital space for products (Harvey, 1989). AI, being inherently digital, sees minimal discussion on spatial compression, but temporal compression is a recurring theme in all three texts. Both Google and the EU portray AI innovation as inherently positive, building arguments for accelerating development and production. Faster innovation is equated with societal improvement, subtly legitimizing a quicker capital turnover. Weak regulation is justified through this optimistic framing of innovation, obscuring the time costs associated with regulation. Flexible, sector-specific, and "*just-in-time*" regulation facilitates faster AI production and innovation. However, the EU's establishment of legal frameworks for "*high-risk*" AI systems, which somewhat slow development, indicates partial resistance to post-Fordist temporal compression. Google, too, acknowledges the risks of accelerated AI development, warning of a societal "race to the bottom" (p. 6). IFLA, in particular, critiques ideals like flexibility, productivity, and competition—key pillars of just-in-time production—advocating for stronger regulation grounded in social-liberal values. Despite these critiques, IFLA's perception of AI development as uncontrollable and inevitable undermines its rejection of post-Fordist temporal compression. Similarly, Google obscures the role of corporate competition in its critique of a "*race to the bottom*," the EU's pursuit of a "*robust yet flexible*" framework results in regulation so broad it lacks meaningful restrictions. All three actors' distancing from post-Fordist temporal compression appears more symbolic than substantive.

Control Over Information Flows

Post-Fordism emphasizes control over information flows as critical to capital growth, alongside the necessity for continuous innovation to stabilize the capitalist system. This control manifests through market mergers, acquisitions, and the ideology that progress is inevitable and inherently good (Harvey, 1989). All three texts reflect the ideology of inevitable innovation, albeit with varied implications. IFLA conveys a sense of powerlessness against AI development's uncontrollable and naturalized pace, criticizing its commercial drivers. This frames AI as unavoidable but not inherently beneficial. The EU and Google similarly view slowing AI development as equivalent to stifling a positive societal force. However, the EU considers "*high-risk*" AI systems problematic, requiring regulatory intervention. This dual perspective—viewing innovation as inevitable yet sometimes destructive—may reveal a crack in post-Fordist ideology or underscore the EU's efforts to legitimize its control over "*high-risk*" systems and their associated information flows. An apparent competition for regulatory control also emerges. Google frames AI and innovation as beneficial in justifying weak regulations, such as voluntary certifications and codes of conduct, leaving significant power in corporate hands. While the EU also advocates for weak regulation, it does so within the context of the single EU market, geographically centralizing AI governance under its authority. In contrast, IFLA's rhetoric focuses on creating conditions for future influence, suggesting that control may be achieved by embracing capitalist ideals and aligning with dominant market narratives. Post-Fordism links regulatory power to the ability to steer AI development and control information exchanges, aligning governance with institutional economic and social interests. However, alongside this competition for control, all three actors exhibit a diffusion of responsibility. Google assigns ethical oversight to states, while the EU shifts responsibility onto companies and users by presenting adherence to human rights as voluntary. Lacking direct control over AI development, IFLA focuses on equipping users and institutions with critical literacy and social-liberal values, attempting to mitigate the harm caused by capitalist-driven AI advancements. However, in doing so, IFLA downplays its critique of the capitalist system, rendering its opposition less effective. In many ways, the three organizations' perspectives on control and innovation seem to coincide with the post-Fordist ideology, as control over information flows is seen as the key to success, and innovation is presented as inevitable. However, in the EU, particularly IFLA, questioning AI and AI development is good. This part of the post-Fordist ideology thus seems to be intact in its practice, but tensions exist in its theoretical basis.

Internationalization of Labor and Legislation

As described in section 6.2, one consequence of information as a commodity and flexible accumulation is the acquisition of competitors and the internationalization of local markets into a connected economic system. This process leads to regulatory frameworks becoming unified or overlapping (Aglietta, 2000, p. 385; Lund 2015, p. 104f; Harvey 1989, pp. 152, 155f, 158ff & 191). This section examines Google's, the EU's, and IFLA's approaches to labor and AI legislation internationalization trends. All three texts exhibit tendencies toward internationalization, but the EU most explicitly advocates for internationalized legislation. This is evident in its descriptions of the single market and its frequent use of terms like uniformity, harmonization, and conformity. The EU's primary argument is that a single market reduces legal uncertainty, obscuring the EU's economic gains from a free market and reducing administrative burdens. Similarly, Google uses the reduction of legal uncertainty to argue for collectively constructed "best-practice" recommendations and certifications, meaning Google only needs to adhere to one set of guidelines, making it easier to choose whether to comply. Weak regulation is also framed as a way to respect cultural differences, which contradicts the idea that Google is a global company advocating for universally negotiated global standards and frameworks. IFLA, on the other hand, argues for internationalization to counteract the adverse effects of AI development. This includes societal mobilization by external actors and the establishment of commons for AI training data and other resources. Internationalization is thus framed as a method for socially regulating AI development and a way for collective efforts to create an equivalent counterforce to capitalism.

The acquisition of competitors and the internationalization of labor are not explicitly addressed in any of the texts, likely due to Google's and the EU's recurring tendency to obscure societal and human aspects in favor of an economic and technological focus. While society is more visible in IFLA's text, discussions of labor primarily center on AI and capitalism's expansive spread and its potential threats to the librarian profession. Thus, the documents focus on the internationalization of AI as labor, reflected in trends such as training data acquisition. The analysis suggests that this aspect of post-Fordist ideology largely remains intact. Notably, all the organizations studied are international: IFLA is an international library organization, the EU is an economic union of European countries, and Google is, in IFLA's words, a global Big Tech company. Since the existence of these organizations relies on a perceived need for international bodies, their calls for international AI regulation may not necessarily reflect their stance on AI regulation specifically but rather a foundational requirement for their operations. However, this requirement may be rooted in post-Fordist ideology, though no definitive conclusions can be drawn from the material studied.

Competitive Individualism

Harvey posits that competitive individualism can serve as a form of social control by tying individuals' sense of success to their status within a company. Fostering individual loyalty and pride toward a company or nation is identified as central to capitalism (Harvey 1989, pp. 123 & 171). Trust, competition, and a liberal view of humans as free and rational can thus be interpreted as core aspects of competitive individualism, which this section explores. The texts contain calls to trust AI systems, indirectly urging trust in the capitalist market's ability to bring about positive societal changes through AI development. Google promotes this through a liberal and essentialist view of intelligence, portraying AI as more intelligent, consistent, less prone to social bias, and more reliable than humans. The EU, in turn, assumes that improving human well-being occurs through trust in AI technology and market-driven development. Embracing AI development is equated with caring for the future and acting rationally, linking an individual's sense of success and responsibility to trust in AI and, by extension, the companies behind its development. In contrast to Google and the EU, IFLA advocates for trust in social-liberal and humanistic values and collaborative knowledge-sharing around AI, aiming to create trustworthy AI. At the same time, companies and capitalism are seen as beyond IFLA's influence and control, leaving the organization with no choice but to adopt an uncritical stance toward capitalist norms and ideals to remain relevant. From the context of competitive individualism, IFLA's position suggests there is no alternative but to trust AI development, companies, and capitalism.

Competitive individualism typically pits individuals against one another. However, Google positions AI in competition with humans instead, portraying AI as superior in more complimentary, rational, and "*intelligent*" decision-making. This can be seen as humanizing and elevating AI, obscuring the underlying biases of AI programmers or training data. Interestingly, this view, which ties individual merit to success, combines a non-rational view of humans, departing from the liberal notion of humans as rational beings often associated with competitive individualism. The EU, by contrast, embraces a more "*traditional*" form of competitive individualism, where humans are seen as free, rational, and capable of choosing whether or not to use AI systems, placing ethical responsibility and demands on the individual. However, the EU's responsibility to protect fundamental human rights does not extend to all people—non-Europeans are portrayed as competition. Competitive individualism is thus expressed in the EU's encouragement of competition between individual markets, with Europe interpreted as a unified market stimulated by EU AI-regulating legislation. Although IFLA criticizes the "productivity agenda" (p. 12), it also expresses a similar view to the EU, where competitiveness and participation in the capitalist system are essential for organizations like libraries to succeed. The EU and IFLA regard competition as a prerequisite for innovation and maintaining their respective organizations' relevance. Overall, post-Fordist competitive individualism is upheld in all the texts, though Google's reasoning hints at a potential renegotiation of its criteria. IFLA's critical stance also highlights ideological tensions within the theory.

Normative Regulation and Human Rights

Given the nascent nature of AI development and the lack of historical precedent for AI regulation, post-Fordist AI regulation is predicted to incorporate elements of normative regulation theory, heavily relying on human ideals and rights (Wirtz, Weyerer & Sturm 2020, p. 822). This section examines how Google's, the EU's, and IFLA's approaches align with human rights principles. In all three texts, the potential of AI to strengthen human rights is emphasized, though with varying perspectives. Both Google and the EU portray AI and AI innovation as positive societal forces that can solve societal issues and improve society. The EU additionally assumes that trust in AI technology enhances human well-being. Consequently, overly restrictive AI regulation appears to limit progress in achieving equality and well-being for all. In contrast, IFLA adopts a more cautious stance, advocating for AI access as a universal right but emphasizing that external actors should regulate AI development using social-liberal and humanistic values to ensure positive progress. While Google's and the EU's technologically solutionist and optimistic positions imply that human rights can and should adapt to AI development within a capitalist framework, IFLA advocates for the reverse: AI development should adapt to human rights.

Human rights are used not only to present AI development positively but also to criticize AI development and its current regulatory approaches. IFLA strongly opposes commercially driven AI development, suggesting that companies perpetuate biases, fail to protect individual privacy, and restrict access to AI systems. These shortcomings in respecting human rights are used to argue for stricter, humanistically oriented AI regulation. Similarly, the EU employs the argument of safeguarding human rights to justify stricter regulation of "high-risk" AI systems, as these systems are seen as capable of exposing vulnerable individuals to psychological and physical risks. Thus, human rights serve as an ethical benchmark to navigate the risks of AI systems and determine regulatory measures. However, there are indications that this "*ethical benchmark*" is adapted to the organizations' other interests, including economic ones. In the EU's document, liberal rights like freedom of expression are portrayed as more important than social-liberal rights, such as protecting vulnerable groups, by limiting the latter to specific circumstances, meaning not all AI developers need to apply them. Conversely, Google suggests that human rights should be operationalized into voluntary "*best-practice*" guidelines and certifications. This contributes to a technology-focused approach, which, at its core, implies that only those rights that can be quantified in a way deemed acceptable by the company will be respected. Such an approach frames human rights as conditional and flexible, meaning that specific conditions must be met for these rights to be recognized and for individuals to "deserve" their rights.

Another adjustment seen in the EU and Google's approaches is the transfer of human rights from individuals to corporations. Restrictions on AI innovation and self-regulation are equated with limitations on corporate freedom of expression, artistic freedom, and scientific freedom. By framing AI innovation and self-regulation as corporate rights, the definition of human rights is renegotiated to support innovation and, by extension, capitalist interests. Human rights are thus utilised both to legitimise and criticise capitalism. Legitimation occurs by highlighting AI innovation and development as positive forces, framing them as corporate rights, and depicting human rights as conditional and flexible. On the other hand, criticism uses human rights as an ethical yardstick to argue for stricter regulation and distance AI development from capitalist motives. This dual use of human rights reflects an ongoing negotiation and conflict within post-Fordist ideology, particularly evident in IFLA's approach.

DISCUSSION

Previous research has highlighted how digital capitalism reconfigures capitalist logic to leverage AI technology for capital accumulation (Harvey, 1989, p. 191; Bhattacharyya, 2024, p. 121; Pasquinelli, 2023, p. 246). This is reflected in the chapter's findings, as post-Fordist traits such as the internationalization of legislation and just-in-time production are used to advocate for weak AI regulation and market-driven AI development. Google's portrayal of AI as a legitimate competitor to human labor mirrors the drive for AI capital independent of human labor identified in previous studies (Bhattacharyya 2024, p. ix; Harvey 1989, pp. 158f; Dyer-Witheford, Kjøsen & Steinhoff 2019, p. 32; Khereiche 2020, p. 75). However, this is done through an approach that diverges from the traditionally liberal image of capitalism by adopting a more irrational view of humanity. Another similarity lies in the normalization of AI in society, which obscures the labor required to monitor, control, repair, and supply data to AI systems (Cath, Wachter, Mittelstadt, Taddeo & Floridi 2018, p. 507; Pasquinelli 2023, p. 8). All three analyzed organizations view AI development and integration into society as inevitable and natural, emphasizing AI as a form of labor while obscuring the human labor involved. Unlike prior studies, this chapter highlights a user perspective by examining how users are socially regulated and assigned ethical responsibility for AI development by Google and the EU. This contributes to a more nuanced understanding of how capitalist approaches impact society. The chapter also identifies skepticism from the EU and, notably, IFLA regarding the ideology that AI and innovation are inherently good. Previous research often portrays such skepticism as critical research tasks (Ericson, Dobbe & Lindgren 2024, p. 323; Pasquinelli, 2023, p. 246), suggesting that this skepticism rarely reflects among real-world actors. This chapter, however, indicates that digital capitalism is less uniform and universally accepted than prior research suggests. Research also positions digital socialism and Marxist-humanist communication theory as counterpoints to digital capitalism (Englert, Woodcock & Cant 2020, p. 142; Fuchs 2020, p. 335). While IFLA's rejection of the "productivity agenda" and advocacy for social mobilization and public AI training data resemble these ideologies, IFLA also appears resigned to the impossibility of overcoming capitalism. The analyzed organizations seem to consider a future AI development without capitalism unattainable.

AI, Regulation, and Ethics

Similarities to the chapter's findings are also evident in AI, regulation, and ethics. The EU proposes stringent regulation for "high-risk" AI systems and weaker certification-based regulation for other AI systems. This aligns with Robles Carrillo's argument that discouraging harmful AI use requires legal frameworks while encouraging positive use only requires normative frameworks (Robles Carrillo 2020, conclusion). However, unlike prior research, the organizations do not profoundly reflect on what constitutes a "good" AI society (Robles Carrillo 2020, conclusion; Cath, Wachter, Mittelstadt, Taddeo & Floridi 2018, p. 507). Instead, their focus is on creating positive AI development. For Google, this entails a free market and lightly regulated AI development, while IFLA emphasizes human rights-driven AI development. The EU adopts a more fragmented approach, combining elements of Google's and IFLA's perspectives. A critique highlighted by AI ethics is that the focus on technological innovation fosters technological solutionism, reducing ethical frameworks to simplified mathematical representations (Heilinger 2022, pp. 9f; Palladino 2023, chapter 2). This tendency is also evident in the chapter's findings, where both Google's and the EU's proposals for codes of conduct and certifications rest on the assumption that human rights can be operationalized and quantified. The findings further confirm Wirtz, Weyerers, and Sturm's prediction that AI regulation will rely on normative regulation theory (2020, p. 822), as human rights are invoked to legitimize and critique capitalism. This aligns with the argument that capitalist norms may reshape human values (Harvey 1989, pp. 158f & 180; Morozov 2013, p. xii), as seen in the ways the EU and Google frame human rights as conditional, flexible, and variably significant depending on their alignment with capitalist ideals. Moreover, this chapter highlights a unique dimension absent in prior research:

the redefinition of who is granted human rights. The EU and Google, for instance, attribute freedom of expression to corporations to justify the notion that innovation is a corporate right.

AI and Libraries

Finally, the findings, particularly IFLA's stance, can be discussed about AI and library research. Like previous studies, IFLA's position is generally practice-oriented, aiming to prepare libraries and related organizations for stringent regulation of "high-risk" AI systems and the weaker certification-based regulation proposed for other AI systems. However, IFLA displays a more pessimistic view of AI development than, for instance, Pence (2022), expressing a sense of helplessness regarding libraries' dependence on capitalist organizations. Concerns are also raised about the current AI development's conflict with library values such as accessibility, privacy, and openness, mirroring criticisms from earlier researchers (Cox & Mazumdar, 2022, p. 330; Subaveerapandiyan 2023, p. 14; Bridges, Elroy & Welhouse 2024, p. 66; Stevenson 2011, pp. 777 & 787; Subaveerapandiyan, Sunanthini & Amees 2023, p. 503; Chhetri 2023, p. 1). Overall, this chapter adopts a broader and more theoretical perspective than previous research by also analyzing AI development from the perspectives of corporations and legislators. It provides a more nuanced and critical view of how AI development might impact libraries and society.

CONCLUSION

Google, the EU, and IFLA's approaches to AI and AI regulation share similarities and differences. A consistent theme in Google's reasoning is that AI development should be regulated through codes of conduct and certifications, placing ethical, coordinating, and societal responsibility on the state while leaving power in companies' hands. Google justifies this by portraying AI development with weak regulation in the best possible light, with AI innovation framed as a corporate right and AI itself as more intelligent, consistent, and less prone to social biases than humans. A technological and economic focus, technological solutionism, optimism, and a liberal and essentialist view of intelligence and society thus mark Google's perspective on AI regulation. Despite the EU's emphasis on a singular market and regulation, its view on AI and AI regulation appears fragmented. Similar to Google, AI innovation is described as a positive societal force, which is used to justify why it should be as fast as possible and largely unrestricted by regulation. The EU also approaches technological solutionism by promoting weaker regulation based on liberal and capitalist ideals, emphasizing flexibility, technological development, and autonomy. However, there are many exceptions within this innovation utopia, with "high-risk" AI systems' rapid development viewed as problematic. Meanwhile, the human rights that the EU claims AI protects are presented as conditional and flexible. The robust and flexible framework the EU strives for thus, in practice, becomes a regulatory framework based on flexible, liberal, and capitalist ideals, where only specific exceptions are regulated robustly.

IFLA's approach to AI and AI regulation is highly contradictory compared to Google and the EU. On the one hand, IFLA firmly distances itself from commercially driven AI development, in contrast to Google's and the EU's primary positions. Instead, IFLA emphasizes the regulation by external actors through social mobilization, the spread of social-liberal and humanist values, and the sharing of resources and information in common to guide AI development in a positive direction. On the other hand, AI development, AI implementation, and the surrounding capitalist system are portrayed as inevitable, uncontrolled, naturalized, and all-encompassing, leaving IFLA powerless, with the only option being to adopt a non-problematic stance and adapt to capitalist norms. This results in IFLA's social-liberal and human-centered criticism of AI development and capitalism appearing more formal than real. Therefore, Google, the EU, and IFLA's positions on AI and AI regulation align with several aspects of the French regulatory school's view on post-Fordism but also differ in certain respects. Internationalization of legislation is a characteristic trait that all three organizations highlight as desirable. However, tensions emerge concerning post-Fordism's just-in-time production and compression of time and space, the need for control over information flows for success, and competitive individualism. The EU, particularly IFLA, questions the notion of AI and AI development being inherently good, and at Google, an ongoing redefinition of the human perspective within competitive individualism is apparent. However, these doubts about the inevitability of AI development appear more formal than real. The enormous cracks in the post-Fordist ideology become visible in the context of human rights, as these are used both to legitimize and critique capitalism.

Overall, all three organizations' positions on AI and AI regulation are strongly influenced by capitalism and the post-Fordist ideologies of the French regulatory school. However, cracks emerge, especially in the EU's and IFLA's uncertainties regarding AI development's ethical and human consequences. This makes human rights a central focus and the most substantial criticism of the capitalist approach to AI and its regulation. Several aspects of the study's methodology and execution are open to criticism. First, the interpretation of Google's, the EU's, and IFLA's documents was based solely on the author's reading and prior understanding, which could mean that specific nuances in the organizations' positions may not have been identified or the identified themes may have been subconsciously influenced by the author's subjectivity, especially given the ideological-critical assumptions made during the ideological analysis of Google's and, to some extent, the EU's capitalist interests. This may have influenced the results or led to premature analysis. To strengthen the results, further readings could have been conducted to identify overlooked perspectives and nuances, or the thematization could have been done in discussion with one or more colleagues to reduce the risk of subjective interpretations. A stronger connection to positive ideological analysis could also have been made by consistently conducting the analysis in two steps and avoiding including ideological criticism.

Given that AI development is rapidly changing and evolving, there is also a risk that the documents studied in the study will become less representative of the organizations' views on AI regulation over time, negatively affecting the study's sustainability and relevance. The study could have been conducted using more documents or over an extended period to address this. Finally, since all the organizations studied are international, internationalization as an ideal may not necessarily reflect the organizations' views on AI regulation or a post-Fordist approach to AI regulation. Had one of the study objects been a national or local organization, the study could have more clearly examined internationalization due to post-Fordism. It is evident, however, that the French regulatory school and its understanding of post-Fordism provide new perspectives on the informational, technological, and social impact AI has and may have on society, thereby adding a critical capitalist perspective to library and information science. Future research could examine other organizations or documents using the French regulatory school to build on this. Given that labor was largely overlooked in the perspectives identified in this study, further research could explore labor's perspectives on AI compared to the organizations they work for through interviews or observational studies. The qualitative approach of this study could also be enriched with various forms of quantitative studies, which can highlight a broader range of actors and general changes over time.

REFERENCES

Aglietta, M. (1987). *A theory of capitalist regulation*. Verso.

Aglietta, M. (2000). *A theory of capitalist regulation*. Verso.

Alvesson, M., & Deetz, S. (2022). *Kritisk samhällsvetenskaplig metod*. Studentlitteratur.

Andrews, T. (2012). What is social constructionism? *The Grounded Theory Review*, *11*(1).

Anguiano, D. (2023, December 6). Sag-Aftra union ratifies strike-ending contract with Hollywood studios. *The Guardian*. https://www.theguardian.com/culture/2023/dec/05/sag-aftra-union-ratifies-contract-hollywood-studios (accessed January 31, 2024).

Barsha, S., & Munshi, S. A. (2024). Implementing artificial intelligence in library services: A review of current prospects and challenges of developing countries. *Library Hi Tech News*, *41*(1), 7–10. DOI: 10.1108/LHTN-07-2023-0126

Bhattacharyya, G. (2024). *The futures of racial capitalism*. Polity Press.

Boréus, K., & Bergström, G. (Eds.). (2018). *Textens mening och makt: Metodbok i samhällsvetenskaplig text- och diskursanalys*. Studentlitteratur.

Bridges, L. M., McElroy, K., & Welhouse, Z. (2024). Generative artificial intelligence: 8 critical questions for libraries. *Journal of Library Administration*, *64*(1), 66–79. DOI: 10.1080/01930826.2024.2292484

Bryman, A. (2018). *Samhällsvetenskapliga metoder*. Studentlitteratur.

Cath, C., Wachter, S., Mittelstadt, B., Taddeo, M., & Floridi, L. (2018). Artificial intelligence and the 'good society': The US, EU, and UK approach. *Science and Engineering Ethics*, *24*(2), 505–528. PMID: 28353045

Chen, Y.-C., Ahn, M. J., & Wang, Y.-F. (2023). Artificial intelligence and public values: Value impacts and governance in the public sector. *Sustainability (Basel)*, *15*(6), 4796. DOI: 10.3390/su15064796

Chhetri, P. (2023). Analyzing the strengths, weaknesses, opportunities, and threats of AI in libraries. *Library Philosophy and Practice*, *2023*(07), 1–14.

Contreras, B. (2023, September 28). Screenwriters secured a new deal for AI. For actors, the fight could be even harder. *Los Angeles Times*. https://www.latimes.com/entertainment-arts/business/story/2023-09-28/screenwriters-secured-a-new-deal-for-ai-for-actors-the-fight-could-be-even-harder (accessed January 31, 2024).

Cox, A. M., & Mazumdar, S. (2022). Defining artificial intelligence for librarians. *Journal of Librarianship and Information Science*, •••, 330–340.

Domingues, J. M. (2017). From citizenship to social liberalism or beyond? Some theoretical and historical landmarks. *Citizenship Studies*, *21*(2), 167–181. DOI: 10.1080/13621025.2017.1279798

Dyer-Witheford, N., Kjøsen, A. M., & Steinhoff, J. (2019). *Inhuman power: Artificial intelligence and the future of capitalism*. Pluto Press. DOI: 10.2307/j.ctvj4sxc6

Englert, S., Woodcock, J., & Cant, C. (2020). Digital workerism: Technology, platforms, and the circulation of workers' struggles. *TripleC*, *18*(1), 132–145. DOI: 10.31269/triplec.v18i1.1133

Ericson, P., Dobbe, R., & Lindgren, S. (2024). Tracing class and capitalism in AI research. *TripleC*, *22*(1), 307–328. DOI: 10.31269/triplec.v22i1.1464

European Union. (2024). AI Act. https://digital-strategy.ec.europa.eu/en/policies/regulatory-framework-ai (accessed April 18, 2024).

Fuchs, C. (2020). Towards a critical theory of communication as renewal and update of Marxist humanism in the age of digital capitalism. *Journal for the Theory of Social Behaviour*, *50*(3), 335–356. DOI: 10.1111/jtsb.12247

Geraets, N. (2023, August 9). Authors furious as 'wildly unethical' AI website hoovers up books. *The Sydney Morning Herald*. https://www.smh.com.au/culture/books/it-filled-me-with-rage-authors-furious-as-ai-website-hoovers-up-books-20230809-p5dv0j.html (accessed January 31, 2024).

Harvey, D. (1989). *The condition of postmodernity*. Blackwell.

Heilinger, J.-C. (2022). The ethics of AI ethics: A constructive critique. *Philosophy & Technology*, *35*(3), 61. DOI: 10.1007/s13347-022-00557-9

Hollingsworth, J. R., & Boyer, R. (Eds.). (1997). *Contemporary capitalism: The embeddedness of institutions*. Cambridge University Press. DOI: 10.1017/CBO9781139174701

Kaplan, A., & Haenlein, M. (2019). Siri, Siri, in my hand: Who's the fairest in the land? On the interpretations, illustrations, and implications of artificial intelligence. *Business Horizons*, *62*(1), 15–25. DOI: 10.1016/j.bushor.2018.08.004

Karppi, T., & Granata, Y. (2019). Non-artificial non-intelligence: Amazon's Alexa and the frictions of AI. *AI & Society*, *34*(4), 867–876. DOI: 10.1007/s00146-019-00896-w

Khereiche, M. (2020). Book review: Inhuman power: Artificial intelligence and the future of capitalism. *Journal of Digital Social Research, 2*(2), 73–77. DOI: 10.33621/jdsr.v2i2.21

Leckie, G. J., Given, L. M., & Buschman, J. E. (Eds.). (2010). *Critical theory for library and information science: Exploring the social from across the disciplines*. Libraries Unlimited. DOI: 10.5040/9798400634420

Lund, B. D., Khan, D., & Yuvaraj, M. (2024). ChatGPT in medical libraries, possibilities and future directions: An integrative review. *Health Information and Libraries Journal, 41*(1), 4–15. DOI: 10.1111/hir.12518 PMID: 38200693

Marx, K. (1857). Introduction to a contribution to the critique of political economy. https://www.marxists.org/archive/marx/works/1859/critique-pol-economy/appx1.htm (accessed April 18, 2024).

Morozov, E. (2013). *To save everything, click here: The folly of technological solutionism*. PublicAffairs.

Newman, G. E., & Knobe, J. (2019). The essence of essentialism. *Mind & Language, 34*(5), 585–605. DOI: 10.1111/mila.12226

Palladino, N. (2023). A 'biased' emerging governance regime for artificial intelligence? How AI ethics get skewed moving from principles to practices. *Telecommunications Policy, 47*(5), 102479. DOI: 10.1016/j.telpol.2022.102479

Pasquinelli, M. (2023). *The eye of the master: A social history of artificial intelligence*. Verso.

Pence, H. E. (2022). Future of artificial intelligence in libraries. *The Reference Librarian, 63*(4), 133–143. DOI: 10.1080/02763877.2022.2140741

Robles Carrillo, M. (2020). Artificial intelligence: From ethics to law. *Telecommunications Policy, 44*(6), 101937. DOI: 10.1016/j.telpol.2020.101937

Siau, K., & Wang, W. (2020). Artificial intelligence (AI) ethics: Ethics of AI and ethical AI. *Journal of Database Management, 31*(2), 74–87. DOI: 10.4018/JDM.2020040105

Stevenson, S. (2011). New labour in libraries: The post-Fordist public library. *The Journal of Documentation, 67*(5), 773–790. DOI: 10.1108/00220411111164664

Stevenson, S. (2016). Immaterial labour, public librarians, and third-generation public libraries. *New Library World, 117*(3/4), 186–200. DOI: 10.1108/NLW-11-2015-0083

Subaveerapandiyan, A. (2023). Application of artificial intelligence (AI) in libraries and its impact on library operations review. *Library Philosophy and Practice*, 1-19.

Subaveerapandiyan, A., Sunanthini, C., & Amees, M. (2023). A study on the knowledge and perception of artificial intelligence. *IFLA Journal*, *49*(3), 503–513. DOI: 10.1177/03400352231180230

Titlestad, P. J. H. (2010). Liberalism. *English Academy Review*, *27*(2), 94–100. DOI: 10.1080/10131752.2010.514989

Vallentin, S., & Murillo, D. (2022). Ideologies of corporate responsibility: From neoliberalism to 'varieties of liberalism'. *Business Ethics Quarterly*, *32*(4), 635–670. DOI: 10.1017/beq.2021.43

Vogus, B. (2023). Generative AI and ChatGPT: Friend or foe for academic libraries? *Public Services Quarterly*, *19*(4), 309–312. DOI: 10.1080/15228959.2023.2266358

Wirtz, B. W., Weyerer, J. C., & Sturm, B. J. (2020). The dark sides of artificial intelligence: An integrated AI governance framework for public administration. *International Journal of Public Administration*, *43*(9), 818–829. DOI: 10.1080/01900692.2020.1749851

ADDITIONAL READING

Binns, R. (2018). Fairness in machine learning: Lessons from political philosophy. *Proceedings of the 2018 CHI Conference on Human Factors in Computing Systems*, 1-14. DOI: 10.1145/3173574.3174057

Binns, R., & Fagerberg, J. (2021). The impact of artificial intelligence on work and employment. *Research Policy*, *50*(1), 103830. DOI: 10.1016/j.respol.2020.103830

Crawford, K. (2021). *Atlas of AI: Power, politics, and the planetary costs of artificial intelligence*. Yale University Press.

Friedman, B., Kahn, P. H., & Borning, A. (2006). Value sensitive design and information systems. In *The handbook of information and computer ethics* (pp. 69–101). Wiley.

Gillespie, T. (2014). The relevance of algorithms. In *Media technologies: Essays on communication and the future of media* (pp. 167–194). MIT Press. DOI: 10.7551/mitpress/9042.003.0013

Gunkel, D. J. (2018). *Robot rights*. MIT Press. DOI: 10.7551/mitpress/11444.001.0001

Zuboff, S. (2019). *The age of surveillance capitalism: The fight for a human future at the new frontier of power*. PublicAffairs.

KEY TERMS AND DEFINITIONS

Artificial Intelligence (AI): Computer scientists create artificial human intelligence systems that learn to think and problem-solve like human beings. AI encompasses machine learning, neural networks, and natural language processing as its core member technologies.

Regulation: Rules and laws exist to regulate specific industrial operations and activities so they operate according to public policy requirements and safety regulations while meeting ethical expectations.

Technological Solutionism: The assumption that technical innovations solve every societal challenge taint deep social problems even when they simplify complex matters by addressing them through technology alone.

Post-Fordism: For industrial capitalism, post-Fordism represents a new phase that incorporates flexible novel methods coupled with global markets and technological breakthroughs alongside unique employee assignments compared to traditional automated manufacturing processes.

Capitalism: Within capitalism, industries and asset management that yield profit propel innovation to drive market competitiveness while economic growth accelerates from private sector operation and distribution of goods.

Ethics of AI: The vision explores how moral principles affect artificial intelligence system production, deployment and regulatory standards while addressing worries about fairness, understanding, responsibility and societal shifts.

Chapter 12
The Impact of AI on Legality and Regularity:
Navigating Societal Transformations

Lambrini Seremeti
https://orcid.org/0000-0002-0663-5408
University of Western Macedonia, Greece

ABSTRACT

This chapter explores the intertwined concepts of legality and regularity in the context of artificial intelligence (AI) and their role in managing societal transformations driven by AI integration. As AI increasingly permeates various aspects of human life, from healthcare to fundamental rights like freedom of assembly, it raises important legal and ethical questions. While legality refers to the normative nature of law, regularity focuses on how these norms are empirically observed in society. This chapter examines the challenges AI poses to both concepts, analyzing its potential to disrupt legal norms, challenge societal regularity, and spur rapid, often unpredictable, transformations. It also discusses the growing importance of transparency, accountability, fairness, trustworthiness, safety, and reliability as quality requirements for legal and ethical AI development. This chapter seeks to provide insights into the urgent need for regulating AI, ensuring its integration into society in a way that maximizes benefits while mitigating risks.

DOI: 10.4018/979-8-3693-9576-9.ch012

INTRODUCTION

The principal "raison d'être" of governments, whether democratic or authoritarian, is to protect their citizens from any form of invasion or transformative power in social cohesion. Their basic tool is regulation. Regulation is the set of laws, decrees, rules, practices or government formalities which govern the political economic and social domain (Baldwin et al, 2011). Reasons behind regulatory intervention are market failures, violation of human rights, disrespect for social values, ineffective innovation (Joskow and Noll, 1981). The ultimate purpose of legislation is to safeguard public order and to shape the common good. Thus, its efficiency and efficacy are of crucial importance. An efficient and effective regulation is based on certain criteria, such as necessity (i.e., there must be a reason for the State to intervene, as the promotion of human rights or the correction of a market failure), legitimacy (i.e., the regulators should be legally and socially legitimate to conduct the process, and the regulation should have a legal basis), targeting (i.e., regulation should focus on the issue at stake and avoid hitting other targets), proportionality (i.e., the regulation must have rules and allocate resources in a way that is proportional to the end it wants to achieve), stability (i.e., the regulation must be certain, the rules consistent, and the legal obligations predictable, to promote legal certainty), flexibility (i.e., it should be flexible to adapt to factual changes and remain relevant and effective face to the ever-changing circumstances), transparency and accountability (i.e., all the process of regulation must be accompanied by a justification of the decisions made, and be available to the public), and effectiveness (i.e., the regulation should constantly be evaluated to ensure it is beneficial and is achieving its goal) (Karpen, 2016). Obtaining a 'good regulation' is a challenging and complicated task. Establishing a well-functioning legal system is a key factor in successful efforts to achieve sustainable economic growth and promote life. The cornerstone for a good regulatory framework is its compliance with social principles, human rights, democracy, and the rule of law - as a rule to which the entire society, including the government, is bound (Tommasoli, 2013).

Undoubtedly, Artificial Intelligence (AI) has a catalytic effect on the formation of modern society, playing an active role in various aspects of everyday life (Crawford, 2021). The impact of AI systems should be considered not only from an individual perspective, but also from the perspective of society as a whole. Indeed, AI has become one of the main driving forces of modern industrial development as well as of the digital economy and now has a profound influence on the formation of social evolution, human communication, economic transactions, personal development and, thus, of most dimensions of human life (Pannu, 2015), (Nayak and Dutta, 2017), (Kamble and Shah, 2018), (Khyani et al., 2022). In this vein, the factors of appropriate design in order to achieve the balance between the evolution of AI and the legal order must be examined.

The following sections highlight the debate on the current AI impact on sudden and violent societal transformations, by focusing on legality and regularity. The interplay of these concepts reflects the broader concerns about AI's power and influence. It touches on the urgent need for adaptable, ethical frameworks that can anticipate AI's long-term impact on society, while recognizing the importance of fostering innovation in a safe and transparent manner. The growing importance of transparency, accountability, fairness, trustworthiness, safety, and reliability as quality requirements for legal and ethical AI development is also discussed.

THE IMPACT OF AI ON LEGALITY AND REGULARITY

Legality and regularity are interrelated concepts – there is no unanimous understanding of their semantic distinction. In a broad sense, legality refers to the normative nature of law, while regularity to the empirical one (Hildebrand, 2013). They are frequently invoked and in connection with various disputes regard the legitimization of specific actions. The purpose of examining the legality of actions taken by an entity is to determine whether it has acted lawfully, that is, under the Law, while the purpose of examining the regularity of actions taken is to clarify how the appropriate norms are being societally observed. Although, they are not clear-cut concepts, they have a substantial impact on the functioning of the societal reality, which aims at ensuring the stability and continuity of the legal order. Their in-depth investigation falls outside the scope of this study. Instead, this chapter focuses on the debate on the current AI impact on sudden and violent societal transformations.

It is generally accepted that societal transformations are triggered by the invasion of AI into daily activities. Indeed, AI has the potential to revolutionize sectors such as healthcare, transportation, finance, education, exercise of fundamental rights by individuals, altering the way of thinking and acting. In this vein, AI affects human life in both positive and negative ways. For example, the AI-empowered Internet and social media have changed the way groups or individuals exercise their right to freedom of assembly and association, enumerated in Art. 20 of the Universal Declaration of Human Rights. It states that "Everyone has the right to freedom of peaceful assembly and association". However, the digital potentials have posed a challenge to the extent of this right through its online expression. The online exercise of this right is beneficial for some social contexts where assembly and association may endanger lives or be banned and for vulnerable individuals who cannot afford to travel to protests. The alternative online manifestation of this right is compliant with legality, since it can be understood as the individuals' right coming together or forming groups peacefully in a public or private virtual space for some purpose. But it is not in confront with regularity, since this online right may be restricted due to unpredictable content blocking, state-sponsored cyberattacks, internet shutdowns or disruptions and surveillance (Ashraf, 2020).

By analyzing the key hurdles and dilemmas faced by AI research, this chapter aims to provide insights into the complexities of AI embedding into society through the lenses of legality and regularity, that is, to identify current legal and ethical challenges that lead to the answer of the main question "why to regulate AI?" As this is a pressing global concern, the following section seek to inform policy makers about the quality requirements of legal and regular AI.

QUALITY REQUIREMENTS OF LEGAL AND REGULAR AI

Transparency, accountability, fairness, trustworthiness, safety and reliability are frequently used as quality requirements in AI related debates aiming at maximizing the positive impacts of AI innovations on society and minimize potential harms (Balasubramanian et al., 2023). Indeed, transparent, accountable, fair, trustworthy, safe and reliable AI development and deployment is of paramount importance in order to prevent unintended consequences and mitigate potential risks during societal transformations (Thiebes et al., 2021). These quality features of AI depict legal and ethical principles and values (Akinrinola et al., 2024).

Transparency, trustworthiness, accountability, fairness, safety, and reliability are intertwined terms that are often defined too imprecisely; their conceptual lines get blurred. This is due to their multifaceted nature, which is context-dependent, and their manifold manifestations. Within the AI field, they have a connotation of societal (understanding how AI affects the individual's life and social reality), legal (ensuring that AI follows the Law), and ethical (making sure that AI behaves fairly and responsibly) implications. Although the number of publications in the field of AI combined with ethics, governance, and society have grown remarkably over the last four years, to understand the AI implications for the integrity of the society, it is important to analyze the above-mentioned terms from another perspective, by giving their key requirements, the goals they serve, as well as their interrelations.

When focusing on AI **transparency**, the literature often refers to explainability (the ability of an AI entity to provide understandable explanations for its decisions and actions), interpretability (human understanding about an AI entity's operation and behavior), and accountability (ensuring AI entities are held for their actions or decisions) (Larsson and Heintz, 2020).

AI **accountability** denotes the expectation that AI stakeholders comply with ethical and legal standards to ensure the proper functioning of AI entities. Accountability is narrowly defined in terms of answerability and through its goals of compliance with Law. It is conceived as the AI entities' quality linked to liability and regulation consequences (Novelli et al., 2023).

When focusing on AI **fairness**, many publications refer to statistical/probabilistic measures ensuring that decision support systems prevent disparate harm or benefit to different groups. It includes a quantification of unwanted bias especially in training data that leads to discrimination according to sensitive attributes such as gender, race, religion, as well as other ostensibly non-sensitive attributes such as salary, family structure, ZIP code (Feuerriegel et al., 2020).

AI **reliability** refers to an AI system performance without failure under given conditions. This quality requirement is an objective for the overall correctness of AI systems operation under the conditions of their expected use and over a given period of time (Silva et al., 2022).

AI **safety** refers to the severity of potential risks caused by AI systems related with harms in human life, health, property, or environment. Employing safety consideration in the AI development and deployment can prevent failures or conditions that can render AI systems dangerous (Schneider et al. 2022).

When focusing on AI **trustworthiness**, the literature refers to an umbrella term that is synthesized by the special characteristics of fairness, accountability, reliability, safety, and transparency aiming at reducing the negative socio-economic consequences of AI use. Addressing AI trustworthiness does not mean considering every characteristic on its own. Simultaneously, rarely do all characteristics apply in every setting, since some of the characteristics may be more or less important in any given situation. Thus, trustworthiness characteristics influence each other (Kaur et al., 2022).

All these terms play a very important role in the overall strive to societal transition, and they include addressing technical challenges in AI development, such as algorithmic bias, data privacy breaches and security vulnerabilities. Algorithmic bias refers to the inherent tendency of AI systems to reproduce existing biases in the training data or underlying assumptions made during algorithms development. This can lead to unfair or discriminatory outcomes, particularly in crucial domains like healthcare, hiring, and criminal justice (Islam, 2024), (Kumar et al., 2024). Data privacy breaches refer to failure to adequately protect sensitive information stored and transmitted across various digital platforms, which may result in financial losses, reputation damage, and legal consequences for organizations, individuals, and governments alike (Farayola et al., 2024). Regarding security, due to their pervasive nature, AI-based systems like robots are prone to diverse attacks by actors that aim to exploit vulnerabilities in the underlying technologies to threat the functionality, safety and reliability of systems. Security breaches can lead to accidents and property damage (Neupane et al., 2024).

In summary, transparency involves making AI processes and decision-making mechanisms understandable to users and stakeholders, ensuring that AI operations are open to scrutiny. Accountability requires that entities involved in the development and deployment of AI systems are responsible for their actions and the outcomes of their AI applications. Fairness demands that AI systems operate without bias, providing equitable outcomes for all individuals, regardless of background or identity. Trustworthiness is established when AI systems are reliable and can be depended upon to function as intended, without causing harm. Safety encompasses the need for AI systems to operate securely, preventing unintended or malicious actions that could cause damage. Reliability ensures that AI systems perform consistently and accurately over time, maintaining their effectiveness under various conditions.

The above-mentioned quality requirements and technical characteristics of AI systems represent the consensus views of academia, industry and governments about the AI challenges. Several studies have been published that discuss these challenges, by focusing either on more technical details or on specific sector (Sonko et al., 2024), (Jan et al., 2023). However, a distinguishing aspect of this Section is that it has been written for an audience who may not possess expert knowledge in AI technologies.

AI AFFECTS LEGAL PROCESSES AND ETHICAL VALUES

The advent of AI has recently complicated the relationship between legality and regularity. In this chapter, legality is used to refer to the laws and regulations ensuring social order, while regularity is used to denote actions, legal or not, which may not necessary be ethical. Resolving inconsistencies in legal process and adherence to fundamental ethical values are complementary issues for maintaining social order and effectively managing social change during punctual challenges such as the AI sudden integration into society. Uncertainties in development of AI, unpredictability and unforeseen uses of AI systems can make it difficult to identify the AI impact in both the short – and long – term. There are a number of challenges related to AI that are discussed on a philosophical, technical, societal, and regulatory level. Ensuring transparency, fairness, safety, reliability, and accountability, protecting privacy, preventing bias and discrimination, mitigating the risks of AI systems, preventing violations of fundamental human rights, and promoting innovation, are some of these challenges that also reflect the reasons to urgently regulate the AI development and deployment. This section presents a panoramic, non-exhaustive overview of these challenges by using the notions of legal processes and ethical values in order to emphasize to the dual nature of the same issue. In the AI field, legal processes and ethical values are occasionally used as they are interchangeable notions but a deeper insight may perceive they are indeed different (Nweke and Nweke, 2024).

Accepting that legal processes and ethical values exert rather different impulses on societal reality, their fundamental distinctions, from a philosophical aspect, may limited to the following: (a) Legal processes refer to the guidelines for conduct dictated by the current laws. Ethical values provide the principles and ideals upon which judgement is made of what is spatiotemporally more important. (b) Legal processes are based on a system of fundamental principles. Ethical values stimulate thinking. (c) Legal processes compel an entity to act in a predefined manner. Ethical values affect an entity's motivation. (d) Legal processes are consistent, affecting all equally. Ethical values may differ between human entities. In summary, legal processes refer to constraints dictated by the laws, while ethical values motivate actors to define priorities in life. Both notions reflect the concern of the AI integration into social cohesion. Legal processes are concerned with the extrospective judgement of decisions (Is the decision in alignment with the practice policies, procedures and guidelines? Is the decision acceptable under the applicable laws and regulations?), while ethical values are concerned with the introspective judgement of decisions (Does the decision conform to universal principles? Does the decision satisfy fairness?)

Extensive literature focuses on legal issues of AI, potential solutions, gaps and challenges, as well as affected human rights principles (Rodriguez, 2020). Indeed, legal issues related to AI risks and challenges has been discussed, from a legal perspective, in policy documents, academic literature, and media. Policy documents analyze how AI affects human rights (van Dijk et al., 2021), (Khan and Mer, 2023), (Yilma, 2023), (Breczko et al., 2021), (Huang et al., 2024). Academic literature mainly analyzes AI risks and challenges focusing on contexts with a high impact on social dynamics such as healthcare (Chikhaoui et al., 2022), defense (Molloy, 2021), transport (Taeihagh and Lim, 2021). Apart from the AI risks and challenges on specific domains, studies include issues related to intellectual property (Zakir et al., 2023), labor protection (De Stefano, 2020), algorithmic bias (Kordzadeh and Ghasemaghaei, 2021), discrimination (Heinrichs, 2022), unfairness (Pfeiffer et al., 2023), legal personality (Ziemianin, 2021), cybersecurity (Watney, 2020), accountability (Novelli et al., 2023), trustworthiness (Salloum, 2024), liability for harms (Yas et al., 2023), access to justice (Nowotko, 2021), transparency (Wulf and Seizov, 2020), surveillance (Saheb, 2023), democracy (Kan, 2024). The media coverage of AI legal issues investigates everyday incidents which reveal the urgent need of AI regulation in areas such as self-driving cars (Jelinski et al., 2021), autonomous weapon systems (Solovyeva and Hynek, 2018), algorithms creating art (Rani et al., 2023), etc.

According to the international literature, the issue of adherence to ethical values in ambient intelligence environments is examined in the light of three interrelated levels; institutional, social and individual (Khan et al., 2022), (Ayinla et al., 2024). At the institutional level, the dominant issue is whether AI entities should be given legal personality. At the societal level, issues of safeguarding individual rights and security are addressed, given their essential characteristic of autonomy. At the individual level, issues of responsibility, accountability and trust in AI systems are analyzed. Given that ethical values are culture-specific, various conceptual considerations have been developed for the impact of AI on social transformation. Indeed, the European Union (EU), the United States (US), and China, recognizing the ethical challenges posed by the integration of AI applications in all areas of human activity, have begun to take steps to address them (Hine and Floridi, 2022), (Dixon, 2022), (Saheb, 2024). The difference among the approaches is that they focus on the same ethical challenges, but from a different aspect, due to their different socio-cultures. The Western world places greater emphasis on the protection of individual integrity, privacy and the responsible use of AI over the rule of law and respect for fundamental rights. In the East, the use of AI is more oriented towards the benefit to the state and the country as a whole, even if this implies sacrifices from the perspective of individuals. Of course, this difference lies in the fact that in the West there is a tradition of individualism and humanism that places greater value on personal autonomy and dignity, whereas in the East the priority is social harmony and collective responsibility. A further difference lies in the extent and depth of the government's role. In the West it is limited to supervision and control, whereas in the East the authorities play a more direct and active interventionist role with regard to AI. These variations in approaches to aligning the use of AI with ethical values are mainly due to the fact that there is no commonly accepted understanding of what the core ethical values are (What is ethical or not is always the result of a function of many individualized ideas about the value or worthlessness of a given instance).

In conclusion, the legal and ethical dilemmas regarding AI which are extensively studied in the literature demonstrate that what remains constant is the anthropocentric approach based on the need to preserve the universal principles that should govern any societal transition. The primary objectives are to improve human life, to ensure that AI does not lead to humans' harm, to preserve human choices' autonomy, to safeguard that the development, use, and regulation of AI is based on the principles of Law.

CONCLUSION

The sudden and violent advent of AI has complicated the interplay between legality (legal norms) and regularity (ethical norms) that are the building Law-factors to prevent increasing divergences in societies from undermining their long-term stability.

Theoretically, this chapter contributes to an enriched understanding of the pressing need for a flexible legal framework that can keep pace with AI transformative impact. Practically, it offers insights for all stakeholders to identify the quality requirements of legal and regular AI. The fulfilment of these requirements is essential for safeguarding ethical values while embracing AI progress, and ensuring AI development and deployment is both legally sound and ethically responsible.

REFERENCES

Akinrinola, O., Okoye, C. C., Ofodile, O. C., & Ugochukwu, C. E. (2024). Navigating and reviewing ethical dilemmas in AI development: Strategies for transparency, fairness, and accountability. *GSC Advanced Research and Reviews, 18*(3), 50–58. DOI: 10.30574/gscarr.2024.18.3.0088

Ashraf, C. (2020). Artificial intelligence and the rights to assembly and association. *Journal of Cyber Policy, 5*(2), 163–179. DOI: 10.1080/23738871.2020.1778760

Ayinla, B. S., Amoo, O. O., Atadoga, A., Abrahams, T. O., Osasona, F., & Farayola, O. A. (2024). Ethical AI in practice: Balancing technological advancements with human values. *International Journal of Science and Research Archive, 11*(01), 1311–1326. DOI: 10.30574/ijsra.2024.11.1.0218

Balasubramaniam, N., Kouppinen, M., Rannisto, A., Hiekkanen, K., & Kujala, S. (2023). Transparency and explainability of AI systems: From ethical guidelines to requirements. *Information and Software Technology, 159*, 107197. https://doi.org/10.j.infsof.2023.107197/. DOI: 10.1016/j.infsof.2023.107197

Baldwin, R., Cave, M., & Lodge, M. (2011). What is 'good' regulation? *Understanding Regulation: Theory, Strategy, and Practice*, 2nd Edition, Oxford. DOI: 10.1093/acprof:osobl/9780199576081.003.0003

Breczko, A., Filipkowski, W., & Krasnicka, I. (2021). Ethics and the development of artificial intelligence: Challenges and dilemmas in the context of the 2030 United Nations agenda for sustainable development. In Kury, H., & Redo, S. (Eds.), *Crime Prevention and Justice in 2030, 355-380*. Springer., DOI: 10.1007/978-3-030-56227-4_17

Chikhaoui, E., Alajmi, A., & Sainte, S. L. M. (2022). Artificial intelligence applications in healthcare sector: Ethical and legal challenges. *Emerging Science Journal*, 6(4), 717-738. http://dx.doi.org/DOI: 10.28991/ESJ-2022-06-04-05

Crawford, K. (2021). *Atlas of AI*. Yale University Press., DOI: 10.12987/97800252392

De Stefano, V. (2020). Algorithmic bosses and what to do about them: Automation, artificial intelligence and labour protection. In Marino, D., & Monaca, M. (Eds.), *Economic and Policy Implications of Artificial Intelligence. Studies in Systems, Decision and Control* (Vol. 288, pp. 65–86). Springer., DOI: 10.1007/978-3-030-45340-4_7

Dixon, R. B. L. (2022). A principled governance for emerging AI regimes: Lessons from China, the European Union, and the United States. *AI and Ethics*, *3*(3), 793–810. DOI: 10.1007/s43681-022-00205-0

Farayola, O. A., Olorunfemi, O. L., & Shoetan, P. O. (2024). Data privacy and security in IT: A review of techniques and challenges. *Computer Science & IT Research Journal*, *5*(3), 606–615. DOI: 10.51594/csitrj.v5i3.909

Feuerriegel, S., Dolata, M., & Schwade, G. (2020). Fair AI: Challenges and opportunities. *Business & Information Systems Engineering*, *62*(4), 379–384. DOI: 10.1007/s12599-020-00650-3

Heinrichs, B. (2022). Discrimination in the age of artificial intelligence. *AI & Society*, *37*(1), 143–154. DOI: 10.1007/s00146-021-01192-2

Hildebrand, T. (2013). Tooley's account of the necessary connection between law and regularity. *Philosophical Studies*, *166*(1), 33–43. DOI: 10.1007/s11098-012-0023-4

Hine, E., & Floridi, L. (2022). Artificial intelligence with American values and Chinese characteristics: A comparative analysis of American and Chinese governmental AI policies. *AI & Society*, *39*(1), 257–278. DOI: 10.1007/s00146-022-01499-8

Huang, K., Joshi, A., Dun, S., & Hamilton, N. (2024). AI regulations. In Huang, K., Wang, Y., Goertzel, B., Li, Y., Wright, S., & Ponnapalli, J. (Eds.), *Generative AI Security. Future of Business and Finance* (pp. 61–98). Springer., DOI: 10.1007/978-3-031-54252-7_3

Islam, M. (2024). Exploring ethical dimensions in AI: Navigating bias and fairness in the field. *Journal of Artificial Intelligence General Science*, *1*(1), 13–17. DOI: 10.60087/jaigs.v1i1.p18

Jan, Z., Ahamed, F., Mayer, W., Patel, N., Grossmann, G., Stumptner, M., & Kuusk, A. (2023). Artificial intelligence for industry 4.0: Systematic review of applications, challenges, and opportunities. *Expert Systems with Applications*, *216*, 119456. DOI: 10.1016/j.eswa.2022.119456

Jelinski, L., Etzrodt, K., & Emgesser, S. (2021). Undifferentiated optimism and scandalized accidents: The media coverage of autonomous driving in Germany. *JCOM, Journal of Science Communication*, *20*(4), A02. DOI: 10.22323/2.20040202

Joskow, P.L. & Noll, R.G. (1981). Regulation in theory and practice: An overview. *Studies in Public Regulation*, 1-78.

Kamble, R. & Shah, D. (2018). Applications of artificial intelligence in human life. International *Journal of Research – Granthaalayah*, 6(6), 178-188. https://doi.org// DOI: 10.29121/granthaalayah.v6.i6.2018.1363

Kan, C. H. (2024). Artificial intelligence (AI) in the age of democracy and human rights: Normative challenges and regulatory perspectives. *International Journal of Eurasian Education and Culture*, 9(25), 145–166. DOI: 10.35826/ijoecc.1825

Karpen, U. (2016). Efficacy, Effectiveness, Efficiency: From Judicial to Managerial Rationality. In: Meßerschmidt, K., Oliver-Lalana, A. (eds) *Rational Lawmaking under Review*. Legisprudence Library, 3. Springer, Cham. https://doi.org/DOI: 10.1007/978-3-319-33217-8_12

Kaur, D., Uslu, S., Rittichier, K.J. & Durresi, A. (2022). Trustworthy artificial intelligence: A review. *ACM Computing Surveys*, 55(2), 39, 1-38. https://doi.org// DOI: 10.1145/3491209

Khan, A. A., Badshah, S., Liang, P., Waseem, M., Khan, B., Ahmad, A., Fahmideh, M., Niazi, M., & Akber, M. A. (2022). Ethics of AI: A systematic literature review of principles and challenges. *Proceedings of the 26th International Conference on Evaluation and Assessment in Software Engineering*, 383-392. https://doi.org//DOI: 10.1145/3530019.3531329

Khan, F., & Mer, A. (2023). Embracing artificial intelligence technology: Legal implications with special reference to European Union initiatives of data protection. In: Sood, K., Balusamy, B., Grima, S. (eds) *Digital Transformation, Strategic Resilience, Cyber Security and Risk Management*, 111, 119-141. https://doi.org/DOI: 10.1108/S1569-375920230001110007

Khyani, L., Rizvi, S. M., & Srivastava, A. (2022). Artificial intelligence and its applications in finance. *International Research Journal of Modernization in Engineering Technology and Science, 4*, 1208–1210.

Kordzadeh, N., & Ghasemaghaei, M. (2021). Algorithmic bias: Review, synthesis, and future research directions. *European Journal of Information Systems, 31*(3), 388–409. DOI: 10.1080/0960085X.2021.1927212

Kumar, R., Joshi, A., Sharan, H. O., Peng, S., & Dudhagara, C. R. (2024). *The Ethical Frontier on AI and Data Analysis*. IGI Global Publishing., DOI: 10.4018/979-8-3693-2964-1

Larsson, S., & Heintz, F. (2020). Transparency in artificial intelligence. *Internet Policy Review*, 9(2). Advance online publication. DOI: 10.14763/2020.2.1469

Molloy, B. T. (2021). Project governance for defense applications of artificial intelligence: An ethics-based approach. *Prism*, *9*(3), 106–121. https://www.jstor.org/stable/48640749/

Nayak, A., & Dutta, K. (2017). Impacts on machine learning and artificial intelligence on mankind. *International Conference on Intelligent Computing and Control*, 1-3. https://doi.org//DOI: 10.1109/I2C2.2017.8321908

Neupane, S., Mitra, S., Fernandez, I. A., Saha, S., Mittal, S., Chen, J., Pillai, N., & Rahimi, S. (2024). Security considerations in AI-robotics: A survey of current methods, challenges, and opportunities. *IEEE Access : Practical Innovations, Open Solutions*, *12*, 22072–22097. DOI: 10.1109/ACCESS.2024.3363657

Novelli, C., Taddeo, M., & Floridi, L. (2023). Accountability in artificial intelligence: What it is and how it works. *AI & Society*. Advance online publication. DOI: 10.1007/s00146-023-01635-y

Nowotko, P. M. (2021). AI in judicial application of law and the right to a court. *Procedia Computer Science*, *192*, 2220–2228. DOI: 10.1016/j.procs.2021.08.235

Nweke, O. C., & Nweke, G. J. (2024). Legal and ethical conundrums in the AI era: A multidisciplinary analysis. *International Law Research*, 13(1). https://orcid.org/0009-0009-6956-5345/

Pannu, A. (2015). Artificial intelligence and its application in different areas. *International Journal of Engineering and Innovative Technology*, 4(10), 79-84, ISSN: 2277-3754.

Pfeiffer, J., Gutschow, J., Haas, C., Moslein, F., Maspfuhl, O., Borgers, F., & Alpsancar, S. (2023). Algorithmic fairness in AI. *Business & Information Systems Engineering*, *65*(2), 209–222. DOI: 10.1007/s12599-023-00787-x

Rani, S., Jining, D., Shah, D., Xaba, S., & Singh, P. R. (2023). The role of artificial intelligence in art: A comprehensive review of a generative adversarial network portrait painting. In Vasant, P. (Eds.), *Intelligent Computing and Optimization. Lecture Notes in Networks and Systems, 852, 126-135*. Springer., DOI: 10.1007/978-3-031-50330-6_13

Rodriguez, R. (2020). Legal and human rights issues of AI: Gaps, challenges and vulnerabilities. *Journal of Responsible Technology*, *4*, 100005. DOI: 10.1016/j.jrt.2020.100005

Saheb, T. (2023). Ethically contentions aspects of artificial intelligence surveillance: A social science perspective. *AI and Ethics*, *3*(2), 369–379. DOI: 10.1007/s43681-022-00196-y PMID: 35874304

Saheb, T., & Saheb, T. (2024). Mapping ethical artificial intelligence policy landscape: A mixed method analysis. *Science and Engineering Ethics*, *30*(9), 9. Advance online publication. DOI: 10.1007/s11948-024-00472-6 PMID: 38451328

Salloum, S. A. (2024). Trustworthiness of the AI. In: Al-Marzouqi, A., Sallum, S.A., Al-Saidat, M., Aburayya, A. Gupta, B. (eds) *Artificial Intelligence in Education: The Power and Dangers of ChatGPT in the Classroom. Studies in Big Data*, 1441, 643-650. Springer, Cham. https://doi.org//DOI: 10.1007/978-3-031-52280-2_41

Schneider, J., Abraham, R., Meske, C., & Brocke, J. V. (2022). Artificial intelligence governance for businesses. *Information Systems Management*, *40*(3), 229–249. DOI: 10.1080/10580530.2022.2085825

Silva, A., Schrum, M., Hedlund-Botti, E., Gopalan, N., & Gombolay, M. (2022). Explainable artificial intelligence: Evaluating the objective and subjective impacts of xAI on human-agent interaction. *International Journal of Human-Computer Interaction*, *39*(7), 1390–1404. DOI: 10.1080/10447318.2022.2101698

Solovyeva, A., & Hynek, N. (2018). Going beyond the "killer robots" debate: Six dilemmas autonomous weapon systems raise. *Central European Journal of International and Security Studies*, *12*(3), 166–208.

Sonko, S., Adewusi, A. O., Obi, O. C., Onwusinkwue, S., & Atadoga, A. (2024). A critical review towards artificial intelligence: Challenges, ethical considerations, and the path forward. *World Journal of Advanced Research and Reviews*, *21*(03), 1262–1268. DOI: 10.30574/wjarr.2024.21.3.0817

Taeihagn, A., & Lim, H. S. M. (2021). Towards autonomous vehicles in smart cities: Risks and risk governance. In Hamid, U. Z. A., & Al-Turjman, F. (Eds.), *Towards Connected and Autonomous Vehicle Highways* (pp. 169–190). Springer., DOI: 10.1007/978-3-030-66042-0_7

Thiebes, S., Lins, S., & Sunyaev, A. (2021). Trustworthy artificial intelligence. *Electronic Markets*, *31*(2), 447–464. DOI: 10.1007/s12525-020-00441-4

Tommasoli, M. (2013). Rule of law and democracy: Addressing the gap between policies and practices. *UN Chronicle*, *49*(4), 29–31. DOI: 10.18356/e2c335d7-en

van Dijk, N., Casiraghi, S., & Gutwirth, S.Artificial Intelligence and Data Protection in the European Union. (2021). The "ethification" of ICT governance. Artificial intelligence and data protection in the European Union. *Computer Law & Security Review*, *43*, 105597. DOI: 10.1016/j.clsr.2021.105597

Watney, M. M. (2020). Artificial intelligence and its' legal risk to cybersecurity. *Proceedings of the ECCWS2020 19th European Conference on Cyber Warfare and Security*, 398-405.

Wulf, A. J., & Seizov, O. (2020). Artificial intelligence and transparency: A blueprint for improving the regulation of AI applications in the EU. *European Business Law Review*, *31*(4), 611–640. DOI: 10.54648/EULR2020024

Yas, N., Qaruty, R. A., Hadi, S. A., & AlAdeedi, A. (2023). Civil liability and damage arising from artificial intelligence. *Migration Letters : An International Journal of Migration Studies*, *20*(5), 430–446. DOI: 10.59670/ml.v20i5.3554

Yilma, K. (2023). Emerging technologies and human rights at the United Nations. *IEEE Technology and Society Magazine*, *42*(1), 54–64. DOI: 10.1109/MTS.2023.3241297

Zakir, M.H., Kham, S.H., Saeed, Z. & Sajida (2023). The impact of artificial intelligence on intellectual property rights. *International Journal of Human and Society*, 3(4), 312-319. https://ijhs.com.pk/index.php/IJHS/article/view/330/

Ziemianin, K. (2021). Civil legal personality of artificial intelligence. Future or utopia? *Internet Policy Review*, *10*(2), 1–22. DOI: 10.14763/2021.2.1544

Chapter 13
The Status Quo of AI Governance:
Global Approaches and Challenges

Lambrini Seremeti
https://orcid.org/0000-0002-0663-5408
University of Western Macedonia, Greece

ABSTRACT

AI governance is a multifaceted challenge due to the lack of a universally accepted definition of AI, its various manifestations, and the rapidly evolving nature of AI technologies. This chapter examines the current state of AI governance across continents, highlighting the socio-political contexts, legal frameworks, and regulatory efforts in Europe, Asia, the Americas, Africa, and beyond. With governance, legislation, and regulation forming the core of responsible AI development, each region adopts different approaches based on its priorities and capacities. The chapter explores Europe's pioneering AI Act, the U.S.'s innovation-driven, Asia's regulatory diversity, the nascent stage of governance in Africa, and Australia's emerging strategies. Furthermore, it addresses the role of corporations in developing self-regulatory frameworks in the absence of comprehensive global AI regulations. This chapter provides a comprehensive overview of how nations and corporations are navigating the governance of AI, setting the stage for future regulatory developments and international cooperation.

DOI: 10.4018/979-8-3693-9576-9.ch013

INTRODUCTION

Defining AI governance is challenging due to the lack of consensus on the AI definition, its constituent elements, as well as, its manifold manifestations. In general, AI governance refers to the development and implementation of policies, regulations, and standards to ensure responsible and ethical use of AI technologies (Madan and Ashok, 2023). A growing body of the literature covers three guiding forces in AI governance (law, ethics and technology) that are complementary (Cath, 2018). Indeed, issues related to laws to govern the impact of AI, AI ethical frameworks, and technical approaches like algorithmic impact assessments and building trustworthiness through system validation have been extensively investigated, across the globe (Camilleri, 2024), (Walter, 2024), (Roberts et al., 2024), (Erman and Furendal, 2024).

The following sections highlight how different continents so far have dealt with AI governance. Each continent's approach reflects its unique socio-political context and technological priorities, ranging from strict regulatory frameworks in Europe to more flexible, innovation-driven approaches in the U.S., and early-stage policy development in Africa and parts of Asia. While all initiatives aim to govern the ethical use of artificial intelligence, they differ in scope, applicability, and regulatory focus (Tallberg et al., 2023), (Birkstedt et al., 2023). Furthermore, in the absence of comprehensive global AI regulation, corporate initiatives (Olatoye et al., 2024) that lead in creating their own ethical guidelines and self-regulatory frameworks for AI development are discussed.

AI GOVERNANCE ACROSS THE GLOBE

AI governance across the globe encompasses a diverse range of approaches, as countries struggle to balance innovation with ethical considerations. Due to the lack of a unified international standard about developing and employing safe AI systems, different regions have developed their own policies, guidelines, and regulatory frameworks for AI integration into everyday life. These frameworks address issues such as transparency, accountability, and privacy, while also attempt to mitigate risks related to social impact of AI technology, reflecting the diverse socio-political, economic, and technological landscapes of each region.

In **Europe**, there have been initiatives to regulate AI on the level of the European Union, but also on the level of its individual members states—although the EU regulations would eventually apply to all of its member states. The *EU's Artificial Intelligence Act*, which came into force in August 2024, categorizes AI systems by risk level and imposes strict requirements on high-risk systems, including conformity assessments and human oversight. The Act also bans certain AI applications deemed unacceptable, such as social scoring by governments. This legislation represents a pioneering effort to ensure AI development aligns with European values, emphasizing transparency, accountability, and the protection of fundamental rights (Cancela-Outeda, 2024). At the same time, non-EU countries, such as Switzerland, the UK, Russia have also been discussing how to best set up AI governance structures. Indeed, the national AI strategy of Switzerland emphasizes the responsible development and use of AI, by including measures to promote research and innovation in AI, while also addressing ethical and societal concerns. The UK has also taken steps to regulate AI, by publishing a *White Paper on AI*, in 2021, which set out a vision for a "responsible, trustworthy, and innovative" AI ecosystem. Russia has also adopted a number of AI-related regulations that are focused primarily on promoting the development and use of AI in the country, and they do not address the ethical and societal concerns raised by AI. In addition to the AI Act, Europe has also taken a leadership role on the global stage. The Council of Europe adopted the first legally binding *International Treaty on AI Governance* in May 2024. This treaty, while primarily shaped by EU and US influence, represents a significant step in global AI governance by creating a legal framework for the entire AI lifecycle and addressing private sector responsibilities. Overall, Europe is leading the way in AI governance with the most comprehensive and advanced regulatory framework globally.

The status quo of AI governance in **Asia** varies significantly across different countries, reflecting the region's diversity in regulatory approaches and technological development (Xu et al., 2024). China is at the forefront of AI governance in Asia, with a strong emphasis on regulation and development. The Chinese government has implemented several targeted regulations focusing on specific AI applications, such as generative AI and algorithmic recommendations. These include the 2023 *Generative AI Measures* and the 2021 *Algorithm Recommendation Provisions*. China's AI governance approach is heavily influenced by its broader data governance framework, which prioritizes national security and public order. India is also advancing in AI governance, although it is still in the process of developing comprehensive AI regulations. Existing AI applications in India fall under the broader *Information Technology Act* 2000. India has drafted several AI guidelines and frameworks, including the *National AI Strategy* and ethical guidelines, but formal legislation specific to AI is yet to be enacted. The Indian government's approach has been to promote innovation while addressing ethical and data privacy concerns. In Southeast Asia, AI governance is generally less developed. Countries like Cambodia are in the early stages of considering AI regulation, primarily focusing on broader digital governance issues like data protection and cybersecurity. Singapore, however, stands out with its proactive stance on AI governance, having developed the *Model AI Governance*

Framework and other guidelines to promote responsible AI deployment. The region also has collective initiatives, such as the *ASEAN Guide on AI Governance and Ethics*, which provides recommendations for the responsible use of AI across member states. A significant challenge for AI governance in Asia is the diversity of regulatory environments and technological landscapes across the region. This makes it difficult to implement uniform AI regulations, unlike the more cohesive approach seen in the EU. Additionally, the influence of global regulations like the EU AI Act is pushing Asian countries to consider stricter AI governance frameworks, which could impact innovation and competitiveness. Overall, AI governance in Asia is evolving rapidly, with leading nations like China and India driving significant regulatory efforts, while other countries are still developing their frameworks in response to both domestic needs and international pressures.

AI governance in **the Americas**, particularly in the United States, Canada, and Brazil, has seen significant developments recently. The Biden administration has taken a proactive stance on AI governance, emphasizing the need to balance innovation with risk mitigation. Key initiatives include the *Blueprint for an AI Bill of Rights*, published in October 2022, which, while not legally binding, outlines core principles for the development of safe and ethical AI systems (Hine and Floridi, 2023). In October 2023, an executive order was issued, mandating safety testing and risk assessments for advanced AI systems, particularly those developed by leading tech companies. This order also introduced "know-your-customer" requirements for cloud service providers and set standards for federal agencies regarding AI safety and privacy. The U.S. has also been active in international AI governance efforts, collaborating with the EU and other G7 countries to establish safety and transparency standards. Canada's approach is guided by the *Artificial Intelligence and Data Act (AIDA)*, which is part of the broader Digital Charter Implementation Act. AIDA aims to regulate AI systems by requiring companies to assess the potential risks of their AI technologies and implement measures to mitigate these risks. The Act also seeks to protect the public from potential harms related to AI, ensuring that AI systems operate transparently and are subject to accountability . Brazil is emerging as a leader in AI governance in Latin America. The country has been working on a comprehensive AI law, *Bill 2338/2023*, which emphasizes transparency, accountability, and bias mitigation. The proposed legislation requires organizations to conduct regular public impact assessments of high-risk AI systems and imposes significant fines for non-compliance. This bill reflects Brazil's commitment to creating a robust regulatory framework that ensures the responsible use of AI. Overall, AI governance in the Americas is evolving rapidly, with each country taking unique approaches to balance innovation, safety, and ethical considerations in AI development and deployment.

AI governance in **Africa** is still in its formative stages, characterized by a patchwork of policies, frameworks, and initiatives at both the continental and national levels (Ayana et al., 2024). The African Union (AU) has taken significant steps by introducing the *Continental Artificial Intelligence Strategy for Africa*, which aims to harness AI for development while ensuring ethical considerations are embedded in its deployment. However, the strategy is more of a guiding framework, and its implementation across member states varies widely. At the national level, only a few countries have made strides in AI governance. For example, Mauritius has partial legislation that touches on AI, particularly in sectors like investment management. Other countries, such as Tunisia, have developed draft policies or white papers on AI, while a handful of nations like Kenya and South Africa have established expert commissions or task forces to explore AI-related issues. Despite these efforts, the majority of African countries lack comprehensive AI-specific legislation. Most regulations related to AI are embedded within broader data protection laws, with around 30 countries addressing AI indirectly through automated decision-making provisions in their data protection frameworks. Additionally, only four countries have articulated a national AI strategy, reflecting a slow but growing awareness of the need for targeted governance in this rapidly evolving field. The challenges in AI governance in Africa are significant, including infrastructural deficits, limited technical expertise, and the need for policies that reflect the continent's unique socio-economic context. However, the AU's strategic initiatives and the increasing number of national efforts indicate a growing commitment to leveraging AI responsibly for Africa's development.

Australia's approach to AI governance is still developing. It is characterized by a mix of existing laws, voluntary guidelines, and ongoing consultations aimed at creating a more comprehensive regulatory framework (Kao, 2024). For example, AI that uses personal data is subject to the *Privacy Act 1988*, while AI used in medical devices falls under the *Therapeutic Goods Act 1989*. This approach allows existing laws to be adapted as AI technologies evolve, but it has also highlighted the need for more targeted regulations to address AI's unique challenges. The Australian government has been actively seeking public and industry input on AI governance. In June 2023, the Department of Industry, Science, and Resources released a discussion paper on *Safe and Responsible AI in Australia*. This paper outlined potential risks associated with AI and proposed measures to enhance public trust and confidence in AI systems. The feedback from this consultation will inform the development of future regulations and policies. The *Australian AI Ethics Framework*, introduced in 2019, serves as a set of voluntary principles guiding the responsible design, development, and implementation of AI. These principles align with international standards, such as the OECD's AI guidelines, and are intended to complement more formal regulatory measures. Both public and private organizations in Australia have begun implementing their own AI governance frameworks. These efforts include ethical guidelines for AI usage, risk management strategies, and transparency measures. The federal government has also issued guidance for the public sector, including the *Digital Transformation Agency's advice on AI adoption*. While these efforts are a step in the right direction, challenges remain. Public trust in AI in Australia is currently low, which affects the rate of AI adoption. The government's strategy moving forward will need to balance innovation with effective risk management to build this trust.

Antarctica is governed by the *Antarctic Treaty System (ATS)*, an international agreement that regulates human activities on the continent, with a focus on scientific research and environmental protection (Lord, 2020). As of now, there is no specific AI governance framework tailored to Antarctica. Any use of AI in Antarctica, such as for research purposes or environmental monitoring, including climate modeling, wildlife monitoring, and logistical support in extreme conditions, would fall under the general principles of the Treaty, which emphasize peaceful use, scientific collaboration, and environmental protection. AI is increasingly being used in Antarctica for scientific research. However, the governance of these AI applications is typically managed by the institutions and countries conducting the research, in line with the rules of the ATS. Any AI deployment in Antarctica would need to consider the ethical and environmental guidelines set out by the ATS. This includes ensuring that AI technologies do not disrupt the fragile ecosystems or interfere with the continent's status as a natural reserve. Given that the governance of Antarctica is based on international cooperation, any future developments in AI governance would likely involve collaboration between the signatories of the ATS. This could include agreements on the ethical use of AI, data sharing, and ensuring that AI advancements support the treaty's goals. Overall, while Antarctica does not have a formal AI governance framework, the principles of the ATS provide a foundational structure for any AI-related activities on the continent. The focus remains on ensuring that AI technologies are used in a way that aligns with the treaty's objectives of peaceful use, scientific research, and environmental preservation.

In summary, each continent's approach reflects its unique socio-political context and technological priorities, ranging from strict regulatory frameworks in Europe to more flexible, innovation-driven approaches in the U.S., and early-stage policy development in Africa and parts of Asia.

AI GOVERNANCE THROUGH CORPORATE INITIATIVES

In the absence of comprehensive national and international regulations for artificial intelligence (AI), many corporations are taking the lead in creating their own guidelines and frameworks for responsible AI development and deployment (Cloete, 2024). This initiative is driven by various factors, including the potential risks associated with AI, the need to foster public trust, and the aim to ensure that AI practices align with corporate values and societal norms. The lack of clear regulations presents several challenges for businesses, such as uncertainty about what constitutes acceptable behavior in AI, which can make companies hesitant to advance AI technologies due to concerns over legal and reputational risks. Additionally, without standardized regulations, companies face difficulties in comparing and benchmarking their AI practices against those of their peers, potentially hindering the establishment of best practices and leading to inconsistencies across different industries.

In response to these challenges, many companies have begun developing their own ethical guidelines and principles for AI. These frameworks typically address important issues such as data privacy, fairness, accountability, and transparency (Fritz and Giardini, 2024), (Akhtar et al., 2024). Some organizations have even set up AI ethics boards or committees to oversee their AI practices and provide guidance. A notable example is OpenAI, which has established guidelines for developing safe and beneficial artificial general intelligence (AGI) with a focus on value alignment, safety, and robustness. Similarly, major tech companies like Microsoft, IBM, and Meta have proposed their own AI regulations and ethical principles, advocating for global agreements and declarations to promote responsible AI development. Additionally, collaborative networks such as the Partnership on AI (PAI) and the Global AI Council (GAC) are working to develop shared guidelines and principles, emphasizing fairness, accountability, transparency, and safety. These efforts highlight the current reliance on corporate self-regulation to fill the gap left by the absence of comprehensive AI governance frameworks.

CONCLUSION

Globally, industry representatives, governments, academics, and civil society are engaged in discussions about the necessity and timing of legal-regulatory frameworks for emerging technologies, and whether ethical or technical approaches alone might be sufficient. Even if these questions are addressed, there remains the critical issue of determining whether our current ethical and regulatory frameworks adequately encompass the full impact of these technologies. Indeed, while various regions are developing their own AI regulations, these efforts often disjointed lead to regulatory fragmentation.

Our thought toward AI governance is to differentiate between ethical guidelines and rule-of-law, drawing upon the principles of legal positivism. By employing legal positivism, which emphasizes that the legitimacy of laws comes from their formal creation and adherence to established procedures rather than moral considerations, we adhere to clarify the distinct roles of ethical guidelines and legal rules (Siliquini-Cinelli, 2024). Ethical guidelines often focus on moral values and best practices, while rule-of-law principles ensure that regulations are systematically established, clearly defined, and consistently applied. This distinction helps to create a more structured and predictable framework for AI governance, ensuring that ethical considerations are integrated into the regulatory process while maintaining the clarity and enforceability of legal standards.

REFERENCES

Akhtar, M. A. K., Kumar, M., & Nayyar, A. (2024). Towards Ethical and Socially Responsible Explainable AI: Challenges and Opportunities. In: Kacprzyk, J. (ed.) *Studies in Systems, Decision and Control*, 551.

Ayana, G., Dese, K., Nemomssa, H. D., Habtamu, B., Mellado, B., Badu, K., Yamba, E., Faye, S. L., Ondua, M., Vsagha, D., Nkweteyim, D., & Kong, J. D. (2024). Decolonizing global AI governance: Assessment of the state of decolonized AI governance in sub-saharan Africa. *Royal Society Open Science*, *11*(8), 231994. Advance online publication. DOI: 10.1098/rsos.231994 PMID: 39113766

Birkstedt, T., Minkkinen, M., Tandon, A., & Mantymaki, M. (2023). AI governance: Themes, knowledge gaps and future agendas. *Internet Research*, *33*(7), 133–167. DOI: 10.1108/INTR-01-2022-0042

Camilleri, M. A. (2024). Artificial intelligence governance: Ethical considerations and implications for social responsibility. *Expert Systems: International Journal of Knowledge Engineering and Neural Networks*, *41*(7), e13406. DOI: 10.1111/exsy.13406

Cancela-Outeda, C. (2024). The EU's AI act: A framework for collaborative governance. *Internet of Things : Engineering Cyber Physical Human Systems*, *27*, 101291. DOI: 10.1016/j.iot.2024.101291

Cath, C. (2018). Governing artificial intelligence: Ethical, legal and technical opportunities and challenges. *Philosophical Transactions. Series A, Mathematical, Physical, and Engineering Sciences*, *376*(2133), 2133. DOI: 10.1098/rsta.2018.0080 PMID: 30322996

Cloete, F. (2024). Governing artificial intelligence (AI) and other technologies in the digital era. *Administratio Publica*, *32*(1), 1–30.

Erman, E., & Furendal, M. (2024). Artificial Intelligence and the political legitimacy of global governance. *Political Studies*, *72*(2), 421–441. DOI: 10.1177/00323217221126665

Fritz, J., & Giardini, T. (2024). Emerging contours of AI governance and the three layers of regulatory heterogeneity. *Digital Policy Alert Working Paper* 24-001.

Hine, E., & Floridi, L. (2023). The blueprint for an AI bill of rights: In search of enaction, at risk of inaction. *Minds and Machines*, *33*(2), 285–292. Advance online publication. DOI: 10.1007/s11023-023-09625-1

Kao, K. T. (2024). From robodebt to responsible AI: Sociotechnical imaginaries of AI in Australia. *Communication Research and Practice, 10*(3), 387–397. DOI: 10.1080/22041451.2024.2346420

Lord, T. (2020). The Antarctic Treaty System and the peaceful governance of Antarctica: The role of the ATS in promoting peace at the margins of the world. *The Polar Journal, 10*(1), 3–21. DOI: 10.1080/2154896X.2020.1757821

Madan, R., & Ashok, M. (2023). AI adoption and diffusion in public administration: A systematic literature review and future research agenda. *Government Information Quarterly*, *40*(1), 101774. DOI: 10.1016/j.giq.2022.101774

Olatoye, F. O., Awonuga, K. F., Mhlongo, N. Z., Ibeh, C. V., Elufloye, O. A., & Ndubuisi, N. L. (2024). AI and ethics in business: A comprehensive review of responsible AI practices and corporate responsibility. *International Journal of Science and Research Archive*, *11*(01), 1433–1443. DOI: 10.30574/ijsra.2024.11.1.0235

Roberts, H., Hine, E., Taddeo, M., & Floridi, L. (2024). Global AI goverance: Barriers and pathways forward. *International Affairs*, *100*(3), 1275–1286. DOI: 10.1093/ia/iiae073

Sinquini-Cinelli, L. (2024). Methodological legal positivism. In *Scientia Iuris. Ius Gentium: Comparative Perspectives on Law and Justice* (Vol. 11, pp. 311–356). Springer., DOI: 10.1007/978-3-031-51936-9_5

Tallberg, J., Erman, E., Furendal, M., Geith, J., Klamberg, K. & Lundgren, M. (2023). The global governance of artificial intelligence: Next steps for empirical and normative research. *International Studies Review*, 25(3), viad40.

Walter, Y. (2024). Managing the race to the moon: Global policy and governance in artificial intelligence regulation – A contemporary overview and an analysis of socioeconomic consequences. *Discover Artificial Intelligence*, *4*(14), 14. Advance online publication. DOI: 10.1007/s44163-024-00109-4

Xu, J., Lee, T., & Goggin, G. (2024). AI governance in Asia: Policies, praxis and approaches. *Communication Research and Practice*, *10*(3), 275–287. Advance online publication. DOI: 10.1080/22041451.2024.2391204

Compilation of References

Abbott, R. (2022). Artificial Intelligence and Intellectual Property: An Introduction. SSRN Electronic Journal. DOI: 10.2139/ssrn.4065150

Abed, S. S. (2020). Social commerce adoption using TOE framework: An empirical investigation of Saudi Arabian SMEs. *International Journal of Information Management, 53*, 102118. DOI: 10.1016/j.ijinfomgt.2020.102118

Aggarwal, A. (2022). Determinants of technology adaption within the framework of TOE: An insurance sector perspective. *ECS Transactions*, *107*(1), 3417–3428. DOI: 10.1149/10701.3417ecst

Aglietta, M. (1987). *A theory of capitalist regulation*. Verso.

Agrawal, A., Gans, J. S., & Goldfarb, A. (2019). Exploring the impact of artificial intelligence: Prediction versus judgment. *Information Economics and Policy*, *47*, 1–6. DOI: 10.1016/j.infoecopol.2019.05.001

Ahmed, S., Alshater, M. M., Ammari, A., & Hammami, H. (2022). Artificial intelligence and machine learning in finance: A bibliometric review. *Research in International Business and Finance*, *61*, 101646. DOI: 10.1016/j.ribaf.2022.101646

Ajzen, I. (1991). The theory of planned behavior. *Organizational Behavior and Human Decision Processes*, *50*(2), 179–211. DOI: 10.1016/0749-5978(91)90020-T

Akhtar, M. A. K., Kumar, M., & Nayyar, A. (2024). Towards Ethical and Socially Responsible Explainable AI: Challenges and Opportunities. In: Kacprzyk, J. (ed.) *Studies in Systems, Decision and Control*, 551.

Akinrinola, O., Okoye, C.C., Ofodile, O.C. and Ugochukwn, C.E. (2024). Navigating and reviewing ethical dilemmas in AI development: Strategies for transparency, fairness, and accountability. *GSC Advanced Research and Reviews*, 18(03), 050-058. https://doi.org/DOI: 10.30574/gscarr.2024.183.0088

Akinrinola, O., Okoye, C. C., Ofodile, O. C., & Ugochukwu, C. E. (2024). Navigating and reviewing ethical dilemmas in AI development: Strategies for transparency, fairness, and accountability. *GSC Advanced Research and Reviews*, *18*(3), 50–58. DOI: 10.30574/gscarr.2024.18.3.0088

Alarie, B., Niblett, A., & Yoon, A. (2016). Regulation by Machine. SSRN Electronic Journal. DOI: 10.2139/ssrn.2878950

Al-Dmour, H., Saad, N., Amin, E. B., Al-Dmour, R., & Al-Dmour, A. (2021). *The influence of the practices of big data analytics applications on bank performance: filed study*. VINE Journal of Information and Knowledge Management., DOI: 10.1108/VJIKMS-08-2020-0151

Alessa, H. (2022). The role of Artificial Intelligence in Online Dispute Resolution: A brief and critical overview. *Information & Communications Technology Law*, *31*(3), 319–342. DOI: 10.1080/13600834.2022.2088060

Ali Abbasi, G., Abdul Rahim, N. F., Wu, H., Iranmanesh, M., & Keong, B. N. C. (2022). Determinants of SME's social media marketing adoption: Competitive industry as a moderator. *SAGE Open*, *12*(1), 21582440211067220. DOI: 10.1177/21582440211067220

Ali, O., Abdelbaki, W., Shrestha, A., Elbasi, E., Alryalat, M. A. A., & Dwivedi, Y. (2023). A systematic literature review of artificial intelligence in the healthcare sector: Benefits, challenges, methodologies, and functionalities. *Journal of Innovation & Knowledge*, *8*(1), 100333. DOI: 10.1016/j.jik.2023.100333

Aljumah, A. I., Nuseir, M. T., & Alam, M. M. (2021b). Traditional marketing analytics, big data analytics and big data systems quality and the success of new product development. *Business Process Management Journal*, *27*(4), 1109–1121. DOI: 10.1108/BPMJ-11-2020-0527

Alkhater, N., Wills, G., & Walters, R. (2014). Factors influencing an organisation's intention to adopt cloud computing in Saudi Arabia. In 2014 IEEE 6th international conference on cloud computing technology and science (pp. 1040-1044). IEEE. DOI: 10.1109/CloudCom.2014.95

Al-Khatib, W. A. (2022). Big data analytics capabilities and green supply chain performance: Investigating the moderated mediation model for green innovation and technological intensity. *Business Process Management Journal*, *28*(5/6), 1446–1461. DOI: 10.1108/BPMJ-07-2022-0332

Almada, M. (2023). Governing the Black Box of Artificial Intelligence. SSRN Electronic Journal. DOI: 10.2139/ssrn.4587609

Alvesson, M., & Deetz, S. (2022). *Kritisk samhällsvetenskaplig metod.* Studentlitteratur.

Amanathan, U. (2019). Aadhaar: Surveillance, control, and dispossession. In Jayasankar, K. P. (Eds.), *Digital States of Surveillance* (pp. 36–55). Oxford University Press.

Ananda, S., Devesh, S., & Lawati, A. M. (2020). What factors drive the adoption of digital banking? An empirical study from the perspective of Omani retail banking. *Journal of Financial Services Marketing*, *25*(1-2), 14–24. DOI: 10.1057/s41264-020-00072-y

Andrews, T. (2012). What is social constructionism? *The Grounded Theory Review*, *11*(1).

Anguiano, D. (2023, December 6). Sag-Aftra union ratifies strike-ending contract with Hollywood studios. *The Guardian*. https://www.theguardian.com/culture/2023/dec/05/sag-aftra-union-ratifies-contract-hollywood-studios (accessed January 31, 2024).

Angwin, J., Larson, J., Mattu, S., & Kirchner, L. (2016). Machine bias: There's software used across the country to predict future criminals. And it's biased against blacks. *ProPublica*. https://www.propublica.org/article/machine-bias-risk-assessments-in-criminal-sentencing

Anjaria, K., & Mishra, A. (2017). Relation between cybernetics and information security: From Norbert Wiener's perspectives. *Kybernetes*, *46*(10), 1654–1673. DOI: 10.1108/K-04-2017-0129

Anjum, N., & Dutta, P. (2022). Identifying Counterfeit Products using Blockchain Technology in Supply Chain System. 2023 17th International Conference on Ubiquitous Information Management and Communication (IMCOM), 1. DOI: 10.1109/IMCOM53663.2022.9721789

Arora, A., Barrett, M., Lee, E., Oborn, E., & Prince, K. (2023). Risk and the future of AI: Algorithmic bias, data colonialism, and marginalization. *Information and Organization*, *33*(3), 100478. DOI: 10.1016/j.infoandorg.2023.100478

Artificial Intelligence Collides with Patent Law. (2023). https://www.weforum.org/whitepapers/artificial-intelligence-collides-with-patent-law

Artificial Intelligence in Intellectual Property Administration. (2023). https://www.wipo.int/about-ip/en/artificial_intelligence/ip_administration.html

Asaro, P. M. (2016). The liability problem for autonomous artificial agents. In Calo, R., Froomkin, A. M., & Kerr, I. (Eds.), *Robot law* (pp. 303–318). Edward Elgar Publishing.

Ashraf, C. (2020). Artificial intelligence and the rights to assembly and association. *Journal of Cyber Policy*, *5*(2), 163–179. DOI: 10.1080/23738871.2020.1778760

Atata, B. (2024). Artificial intelligence and the right to be forgotten. *International Journal of Research Publication and Reviews*, *5*(8), 4300–4310. DOI: 10.55248/gengpi.5.0824.2310

Atrey, I. (2023). Revolutionising the legal industry: The intersection of artificial intelligence and law. Available at *SSRN*: https://ssrn.com/abstract=4632440 or http://dx.doi.org/DOI: 10.2139/ssrn.4632440

Awoyomi, T. (2024). *Legal issues associated with artificial intelligence (AI). SSRN.* https://doi.org/DOI: 10.2139/ssrn.4750140

Ayana, G., Dese, K., Nemomssa, H. D., Habtamu, B., Mellado, B., Badu, K., Yamba, E., Faye, S. L., Ondua, M., Vsagha, D., Nkweteyim, D., & Kong, J. D. (2024). Decolonizing global AI governance: Assessment of the state of decolonized AI governance in sub-saharan Africa. *Royal Society Open Science*, *11*(8), 231994. Advance online publication. DOI: 10.1098/rsos.231994 PMID: 39113766

Ayinla, B. S., Amoo, O. O., Atadoga, A., Abrahams, T. O., Osasona, F., & Farayola, O. A. (2024). Ethical AI in practice: Balancing technological advancements with human values. *International Journal of Science and Research Archive*, *11*(01), 1311–1326. DOI: 10.30574/ijsra.2024.11.1.0218

Bag, A., Chaturvedi, A., Sneha, , & Tiwari, R. (2024). Navigating the Legal Landscape of AI-Induced Property Damage. *Advances in Computational Intelligence and Robotics*, *185*, 185–210. Advance online publication. DOI: 10.4018/979-8-3693-1565-1.ch011

Bag, S., Luthra, S., Mangla, K. S., & Kazancoglou, Y. (2021). Leveraging big data analytics capabilities in making reverse logistics decisions and improving remanufacturing performance. *International Journal of Logistics Management*, *32*(3), 743758. DOI: 10.1108/IJLM-06-2020-0237

Baig, M. I., Yadegaridehkordi, E., & Nizam Bin Md Nasir, M. H. (2023). Influence of big data adoption on sustainable marketing and operation of SMEs: A hybrid approach of SEM-ANN. *Management Decision*, *61*(7), 2231–2253. DOI: 10.1108/MD-06-2022-0778

Bailenson, J. N. (2018). *Experience on demand: What virtual reality is, how it works, and what it can do*. W. W. Norton & Company.

Baird, A., & Schuller, B. (2020). Considerations for a more ethical approach to data in AI: On data representation and infrastructure. *Frontiers in Big Data*, *3*, 25. DOI: 10.3389/fdata.2020.00025 PMID: 33693398

Baker, J. (2012). The technology–organization–environment framework. *Information Systems Theory: Explaining and Predicting Our Digital Society*, *1*, 231–245.

Bala, J., Kellar, M., & Ramberg, F. (2017). Predictive analytics for litigation case management. *Proceedings of the IEEE international Conference on Big Data*, Boston, MA, USA, 3826-3830. https://doi.org/DOI: 10.1109/BigData.2017.8258384

Balasubramaniam, N., Kauppinen, M., Rannisto, A., Hiekkanen, K., & Kujala, S. (2023). Transparency and explainability of AI systems: From ethical guidelines to requirements. *Information and Software Technology*, *159*, 107197. DOI: 10.1016/j.infsof.2023.107197

Baldwin, R., Cave, M., & Lodge, M. (2011). What is 'good' regulation? *Understanding Regulation: Theory, Strategy, and Practice*, 2nd Edition, Oxford. DOI: 10.1093/acprof:osobl/9780199576081.003.0003

Banisar, D. (2011). The right to information and privacy: Balancing rights and managing conflicts. *World Bank Institute Governance Working Paper*. Available at *SSRN*: https://ssrn.com/abstract=1786473 or http://dx.doi.org/DOI: 10.2139/ssrn.1786473

Barnett, J., & Treleaven, P. (2023). Algorithmic Dispute Resolution. DOI: 10.1093/comjnl/bxx103

Barney, J. (1991). Firm resources and sustained competitive advantage. *Journal of Management*, *17*(1), 99–120. DOI: 10.1177/014920639101700108

Barsha, S., & Munshi, S. A. (2024). Implementing artificial intelligence in library services: A review of current prospects and challenges of developing countries. *Library Hi Tech News*, *41*(1), 7–10. DOI: 10.1108/LHTN-07-2023-0126

Batool, A., Zowghi, D., & Bano, M. (2024). AI governance: A systematic literature review. *Research Square*. https://doi.org/DOI: 10.21203/rs.3.rs-4784792/v1

Behl, A. (2020). Antecedents to firm performance and competitiveness using the lens of big data analytics: A cross cultural study. *Management Decision*, *6*(2), 369–387.

Belenguer, L. (2022). AI bias: Exploring discriminatory algorithmic decision-making models and the application of possible machine-centric solutions adapted from the pharmaceutical industry. *AI and Ethics*, *2*(4), 771–787. DOI: 10.1007/s43681-022-00138-8 PMID: 35194591

Benefo, E. O., Tingler, A., White, M., Cover, J., Torres, L., Broussard, C., Shirmohammadi, A., Pradham, A. K., & Patra, D. (2022). Ethical, legal, social, and economic (ELSE) implications of artificial intelligence at a global level: A scientometrics approach. *AI and Ethics*, *2*(4), 667–682. DOI: 10.1007/s43681-021-00124-6

Berger, K. M. (2023). Using AI To Track AI Patents At The USPTO. https://www.mondaq.com/unitedstates/patent/1008772/using-ai-to-track-ai-patents-at-the-uspto

Bex, F. J. (2024). AI, law and beyond: A transdisciplinary ecosystem for the future of AI & law. *Artificial Intelligence and Law*. Advance online publication. DOI: 10.1007/s10506-024-09404-y

Bhalla, N., Brooks, L., & Leach, T. (2023). Ensuring a 'responsible' AI future in India: RRI as an approach for identifying the ethical challenges from an Indian perspective. *AI and Ethics*. Advance online publication. DOI: 10.1007/s43681-023-00370-w

Bharati, R. K. (2024). Ethical implications of AI in criminal justice: Balancing efficiency and due process. *RESEARCH REVIEW International Journal of Multidisciplinary*, *9*(7), 93–105. DOI: 10.31305/rrijm.2024.v09.n07.014

Bhattacharyya, G. (2024). *The futures of racial capitalism*. Polity Press.

Bianchini, F. (2023). Autopoiesis of artificial: From systems to cognition. *Bio Systems*, *230*, 104936. DOI: 10.1016/j.biosystems.2023.104936 PMID: 37279825

Biega, A. J., Potash, P., Daumé, H., Diaz, F., & Finck, M. (2020). Operationalizing the legal principle of data minimization for personalization. In *Proceedings of the 43rd International ACM SIGIR Conference on Research and Development in Information Retrieval (SIGIR '20)* (pp. 399–408). Association for Computing Machinery. https://doi.org/DOI: 10.1145/3397271.3401034

Biju, P. R., & Gayathri, O. (2024). The Indian approach to Artificial Intelligence: An analysis of policy discussions, constitutional values, and regulation. *AI & Society*, *39*(5), 2321–2335. DOI: 10.1007/s00146-023-01685-2

Birkstedt, T., Minkkinen, M., Tandon, A., & Manrymaki, M. (2023). AI governance: Themes, knowledge gaps and future agendas. *Internet Research*, *33*(7), 133–167. https://di.org/10.1108/INTR-01-2022-0042. DOI: 10.1108/INTR-01-2022-0042

Boréus, K., & Bergström, G. (Eds.). (2018). *Textens mening och makt: Metodbok i samhällsvetenskaplig text- och diskursanalys*. Studentlitteratur.

Bostrom, N. (2014). *Superintelligence: Paths, dangers, strategies*. Oxford University Press.

Braga, J., Stiubieuer, I., Henriques, P., & Cananea, H. (2024). How multistakeholder governance can shape responsible AI. *OSFPreprints*. https://doi.org//DOI: 10.31219/osf.io/kdw52

Breczko, A., Filipkowski, W., & Krasnicka, I. (2021). Ethics and the development of artificial intelligence: Challenges and dilemmas in the context of the 2030 United Nations agenda for sustainable development. In Kury, H., & Redo, S. (Eds.), *Crime Prevention and Justice in 2030, 355-380*. Springer., DOI: 10.1007/978-3-030-56227-4_17

Bridges, L. M., McElroy, K., & Welhouse, Z. (2024). Generative artificial intelligence: 8 critical questions for libraries. *Journal of Library Administration*, *64*(1), 66–79. DOI: 10.1080/01930826.2024.2292484

Bruyne, J. D., Gool, E. V., & Gils, T. (2021). Tort law and damage caused by AI systems. In De Bruyne, J., & Vanleenhove, C. (Eds.), *Artificial intelligence and the law* (pp. 359–404). Centrum voor Verbintenissen-en Goederenrecht. Intersentia. DOI: 10.1017/9781839701047.015

Bryman, A. (2018). *Samhällsvetenskapliga metoder*. Studentlitteratur.

Buckland, R. (2023). *AI, judges and judgement: Setting the scene*. M-RCBG Associate Working Paper Series 2023.220, Harvard University, Cambridge, MA.

Buiten, M. C. (2024). Product liability for defective AI. *European Journal of Law and Economics*, *57*(1-2), 239–273. DOI: 10.1007/s10657-024-09794-z

Buiten, M., de Streel, A., & Peitz, M. (2023). The law and economics of AI liability. *Computer Law & Security Review*, *48*, 105794. DOI: 10.1016/j.clsr.2023.105794

Cai, D., Tan, M., & Cai, J. (2011). The VAT tax burden warning model and modification based on CTAIS system data. *2011 2nd International Conference on Artificial Intelligence, Management Science and Electronic Commerce, AIMSEC 2011 - Proceedings*, 2653 – 2656. DOI: 10.1109/AIMSEC.2011.6011092

Cai, D., Zhang, A., & Cai, J. (2011). The improvement on China's regional standard value added tax revenue estimate method - The construction, application and verification of standard rate model. *2011 2nd International Conference on Artificial Intelligence, Management Science and Electronic Commerce, AIMSEC 2011 - Proceedings*, 783 – 786. DOI: 10.1109/AIMSEC.2011.6010234

Calo, R. (2017). Artificial intelligence policy: A primer and roadmap. *U.C. Davis Law Review, 51*(2), 399–414.

Camilleri, M. A. (2024). Artificial intelligence governance: Ethical considerations and implications for social responsibility. *Expert Systems: International Journal of Knowledge Engineering and Neural Networks, 41*(7), e13406. DOI: 10.1111/exsy.13406

Camoit. How Information Technology (IT) Can Benefit Your Business. Retrieval date: 5 August 2024. https://camoitsolutions.ca/how-information-technology-it-can-benefit-your-business/

Cancela-Outeda, C. (2024). The EU's AI act: A framework for collaborative governance. *Internet of Things : Engineering Cyber Physical Human Systems, 27*, 101291. DOI: 10.1016/j.iot.2024.101291

Cath, C. (2018). Governing artificial intelligence: Ethical, legal and technical opportunities and challenges. *Philosophical Transactions. Series A, Mathematical, Physical, and Engineering Sciences, 376*(2133), 2133. DOI: 10.1098/rsta.2018.0080 PMID: 30322996

Cath, C., Wachter, S., Mittelstadt, B., Taddeo, M., & Floridi, L. (2018). Artificial intelligence and the 'good society': The US, EU, and UK approach. *Science and Engineering Ethics, 24*, 505–528. DOI: 10.1007/s11948-017-9901-7 PMID: 28353045

Cepeda, G., & Vera, D. (2007). Dynamic capabilities and operational capabilities: A knowledge management perspective. *Journal of Business Research, 60*(5), 426–437. DOI: 10.1016/j.jbusres.2007.01.013

Ceylan, I.E. (2022). The effects of artificial intelligence on the insurance sector: emergence, applications, challenges, and opportunities. Account. Financ. Sustain. Gov. Fraud 225-241. .DOI: 10.1007/978-981-16-8997-0_13

Cha, S. (2024). Towards an international regulatory framework for AI safety: Lessons from the IAEA's nuclear safety regulations. *Humanities & Social Sciences Communications, 11*(1), 506. DOI: 10.1057/s41599-024-03017-1

Chatterjee, S., Nguyen, B., Ghosh, S. K., Bhattacharjee, K. K., & Chaudhuri, S. (2020). Adoption of artificial intelligence integrated CRM system: An empirical study of Indian organizations. *The Bottom Line (New York, N.Y.)*, *33*(4), 359–375. DOI: 10.1108/BL-08-2020-0057

Chaudhry, P. E. (2023). Changing levels of intellectual property rights protection for global firms: A synopsis of recent U.S. and EU trade enforcement strategies. DOI: 10.1016/j.bushor.2006.03.002

Chen, G., Xie, P., Dong, J., & Wang, T. (2019). Understanding programmatic creative: The role of AI. *Journal of Advertising*, *48*(4), 347–355. DOI: 10.1080/00913367.2019.1654421

Cheng, J., & Zeng, J. (2022). Shaping AI's future? China in global AI governance. *Journal of Contemporary China*, *32*(143), 794–810. DOI: 10.1080/10670564.2022.2107391

Chennupati, A. (2024). The evolution of AI: What does the future hold in the next two years. *World Journal of Advanced Engineering Technology and Sciences*, 12(1), 022-028. https://doi.org/DOI: 10.30574/wjaets.2024.12.1.0176

Chen, Y.-C., Ahn, M. J., & Wang, Y.-F. (2023). Artificial intelligence and public values: Value impacts and governance in the public sector. *Sustainability (Basel)*, *15*(6), 4796. DOI: 10.3390/su15064796

Cheong, B. C. (2024). Transparency and accountability in AI systems: Safeguarding wellbeing in the age of algorithmic decision-making. *Frontiers in Human Dynamics*, *6*, 1421273. Advance online publication. DOI: 10.3389/fhumd.2024.1421273

Chesterman, S. (2020). Artificial intelligence and the limits of legal personality. *The International and Comparative Law Quarterly*, *69*(4), 819–844. DOI: 10.1017/S0020589320000366

Chhetri, P. (2023). Analyzing the strengths, weaknesses, opportunities, and threats of AI in libraries. *Library Philosophy and Practice*, *2023*(07), 1–14.

Chien, C. V., Kim, M., Raj, A., & Rathish, R. (2024). How generative AI can help address the access to justice gap through the courts. *Loyola of Los Angeles Law Review*, Forthcoming. Available at *SSRN*: https://ssrn.com/abstract=4683309

Chikhaoui, E., Alajmi, A., & Sainte, S. L. M. (2022). Artificial intelligence applications in healthcare sector: Ethical and legal challenges. *Emerging Science Journal*, 6(4), 717-738. http://dx.doi.org/DOI: 10.28991/ESJ-2022-06-04-05

Chimuka, G. (2019). Impact of artificial intelligence on patent law. Towards a new analytical framework – [the Multi-Level Model]. *World Patent Information*, *59*, 101926. DOI: 10.1016/j.wpi.2019.101926

Chipiga, I. V. (2023). Legal entropy in International Law. *Russian Journal of Legal Studies*, *10*(2), 113–120. DOI: 10.17816/RJLS322823

Choi, J. H., & Schwarcz, D. (2023). AI assistance in legal analysis: An empirical study. *Journal of Legal Education, 73*(forthcoming, 2024). Available at *SSRN*: https://ssrn.com/abstract=4539836

Choung, H., David, P., & Ling, T.-W. (2024). Acceptance of AI-powered facial recognition technology in surveillance scenarios: Role of trust, security, and privacy perceptions. *Technology in Society*, *79*, 102721. DOI: 10.1016/j.techsoc.2024.102721

Cloete, F. (2024). Governing artificial intelligence (AI) and other technologies in the digital era. *Administratio Publica*, *32*(1), 1–30.

Collenette, J., Atkinson, K., & Bench-Capon, T. (2023). Explainable AI tools for legal reasoning about cases: A study on the European Court of Human Rights. *Artificial Intelligence*, *317*, 103861. DOI: 10.1016/j.artint.2023.103861

Collins, P. D., Hage, J., & Hull, F. M. (1988). Organizational and technological predictors of change in automaticity. *Academy of Management Journal*, *31*(3), 512–543. DOI: 10.2307/256458

Contreras, B. (2023, September 28). Screenwriters secured a new deal for AI. For actors, the fight could be even harder. *Los Angeles Times*. https://www.latimes.com/entertainment-arts/business/story/2023-09-28/screenwriters-secured-a-new-deal-for-ai-for-actors-the-fight-could-be-even-harder (accessed January 31, 2024).

Cordeschi, R. (2004). The Blackwell Guide to the Philosophy of Computing and Information. *Cybernetics*, *186*, 186–196. Advance online publication. DOI: 10.1002/9780470757017.ch14

Corrêa, N. K., Galvão, C., Santos, J. W., Pino, C. D., Pinto, E. P., Barbosa, C., Massmann, D., Mambrini, R., Galvão, L., Terem, E., & Oliveira, N. D. (2022). Worldwide AI Ethics: a review of 200 guidelines and recommendations for AI governance [Review of Worldwide AI Ethics: a review of 200 guidelines and recommendations for AI governance]. arXiv (Cornell University). Cornell University. https://doi.org/DOI: 10.48550/arXiv.2206

Cosentino, A. (2024). The Role of Artificial Intelligence in the Insurance Business. Retrieval date: 4 June 2024. https://aqabaconf.com/images/uploads/Andrea_Aqaba.pdf

Cox, A. M., & Mazumdar, S. (2022). Defining artificial intelligence for librarians. *Journal of Librarianship and Information Science*, **•••**, 330–340.

Crawford, K. (2021). *Atlas of AI*. Yale University Press., DOI: 10.12987/97800252392

Crawford, K., & Joler, V. (2018). Anatomy of an AI System: The Amazon Echo as an Anatomical Map of Human Labor, Data, and Planetary Resources. *Open Journal of Social Sciences*, *12*(2).

Cummings, M. L. (2018). Artificial intelligence and the future of education. *AI Magazine*, *39*(3), 25–36. DOI: 10.1609/aimag.v39i3.2807

D.B. S. (Ed.). (2019). International Scientific Conference, FarEastCon 2018. *Smart Innovation, Systems and Technologies, 139.*

da Silva, L. (2020). Concepts in Policy and Governance: A Framework for Analysis. *Public Administration Journal*, *28*(1), 77–88.

Dastin, J. (2018, October 10). Amazon scrapped 'sexist AI' recruiting tool. *Reuters*. https://www.reuters.com/article/us-amazon-com-jobs-automation-insight-idUSKCN1MK08G

Davis, F. D., Bagozzi, R. P., & Warshaw, P. R. (1989). User acceptance of computer technology: A comparison of two theoretical models. *Management Science*, *35*(8), 982–1003. DOI: 10.1287/mnsc.35.8.982

de Almeida, P. G. R., dos Santos, C. D., & Farias, J. S. (2021). Artificial intelligence regulation: A framework for governance. *Ethics and Information Technology*, *23*(4), 505–525. DOI: 10.1007/s10676-021-09593-z

de Oliveira, L. F., da Silva Gomes, A., Enes, Y., Branco, T. V. C., Pires, R. P., Bolzon, A., & Demo, G. (2022). Path and future of artificial intelligence in the field of justice: A systematic literature review and a research agenda. *SN Social Sciences*, *2*(9), 180. DOI: 10.1007/s43545-022-00482-w

De Stefano, V. (2020). Algorithmic bosses and what to do about them: Automation, artificial intelligence and labour protection. In Marino, D., & Monaca, M. (Eds.), *Economic and Policy Implications of Artificial Intelligence. Studies in Systems, Decision and Control* (Vol. 288, pp. 65–86). Springer., DOI: 10.1007/978-3-030-45340-4_7

De'Shazer, M. (2024). Advancing Legal Reasoning: The Integration of AI to Navigate Complexities and Biases in Global Jurisprudence with Semi-Automated Arbitration Processes (SAAPs). arXiv (Cornell University). https://doi.org/DOI: 10.48550/arXiv.2402

DeBrusk, C. (2024). Technology Complexity And Its Impact On Innovation. Retrieval date: 8 August 2024. https://www.oliverwyman.com/our-expertise/insights/2022/jan/technology-complexity-and-its-impact-on-innovation.html

Devineni, S. K. (2024). AI in data privacy and security. *International Journal of Artificial Intelligence and Machine Learning*, *3*, 35–49.

Dexe, J., Franke, U., & Rad, A. (2021). Transparency and insurance professionals: A study of Swedish insurance practice attitudes and future development. *The Geneva Papers on Risk and Insurance. Issues and Practice*, *46*(4), 547–572. DOI: 10.1057/s41288-021-00207-9 PMID: 33686323

Dhanol, J. (2023). Whether Artificial Intelligence Is a Person or Machine: An Analysis under Patent Law. *International Journal of Law and Social Sciences*, *1*, 1–8. Advance online publication. DOI: 10.60143/ijls.v7.i1.2021.22

Dignum, V. (2019). *Responsible Artificial Intelligence: How to develop and use AI in a responsible way*. Springer. DOI: 10.1007/978-3-030-30371-6

Ding, J., Huang, Y., Ni, K., Wang, X., Wang, Y., & Wang, Y. (2022). Intellectual Property Evaluation Utilizing Machine Learning. arXiv (Cornell University). https://doi.org//arxiv.2208.08611DOI: 10.48550

Distinto, I., Guarino, N., & Masolo, C. (2013). A well-founded ontological framework for modeling personal income tax. *Proceedings of the International Conference on Artificial Intelligence and Law*, 33 – 42. DOI: 10.1145/2514601.2514606

Dixon, R. B. L. (2022). A principled governance for emerging AI regimes: Lessons from China, the European Union, and the United States. *AI and Ethics*, *3*(3), 793–810. DOI: 10.1007/s43681-022-00205-0

Domingues, J. M. (2017). From citizenship to social liberalism or beyond? Some theoretical and historical landmarks. *Citizenship Studies*, *21*(2), 167–181. DOI: 10.1080/13621025.2017.1279798

Donnelly, M., & Young, A. (1999). TAXTUTOR: An intelligent tutoring system for Canadian tax. *New Review of Applied Expert Systems and Emerging Technologies*, *5*, 99–112.

Dorner, D. (1990). The logic of failure. *Philosophical Transactions of the Royal Society of London. Series B, Biological Sciences*, *327*(1241), 463–473. PMID: 1970892

Dubljevic, V. (2024). Colleges and universities are important stakeholders for regulating large language models and other emerging AI. *Technology in Society*, *76*, 102480. DOI: 10.1016/j.techsoc.2024.102480

Dutt, R. (2020). The impact of artificial intelligence on healthcare insurances. In *Artificial Intelligence in Healthcare* (pp. 271–293). Elsevier., DOI: 10.1016/B978-0-12-818438-7.00011-3

Dwivedi, D. (2024). Algorithmic bias: A challenge for ethical artificial intelligence (AI). In Heggde, G. S., Patra, S. K., & Panda, R. (Eds.), *Immersive technology and experiences* (pp. 57–75). Palgrave Macmillan., DOI: 10.1007/978-981-99-8834-1_5

Dyer-Witheford, N., Kjøsen, A. M., & Steinhoff, J. (2019). *Inhuman power: Artificial intelligence and the future of capitalism*. Pluto Press. DOI: 10.2307/j.ctvj4sxc6

Ejjami, R. (2024). AI-driven justice: Evaluating the impact of artificial intelligence on legal systems. *International Journal of Finance and Management Research*, *6*(3), 23969. Advance online publication. DOI: 10.36948/ijfmr.2024.v06i03.23969

El Khatib, M. M., Al-Nakeeb, A., & Ahmed, G. (2019). Integration of Cloud Computing with Artificial Intelligence and Its Impact on Telecom Sector—A Case Study. iBusiness, 11(01), 1.

El-khateeb, A. I., & AL-Omari, O. H. (2023). Study the Impact of Artificial Intelligence Applications on Insurance Industry: A case of Jordan. *2023 WEI.*

Elliott, K., Price, R., Shaw, P., Spiliotopoulos, T., Ng, M., Coopamootoo, K., & van Moorsel, A. (2021). Towards an Equitable Digital Society: Artificial Intelligence (AI) and Corporate Digital Responsibility (CDR). *Society*, *58*(3), 179–188. DOI: 10.1007/s12115-021-00594-8 PMID: 34149122

Eneh, C. (2023). Enhancing regulatory compliance monitoring with AI. *Journal of AI-assisted Scientific Discovery*, *3*(2), 534–548.

Engel, C., Linhardt, L., & Schubert, M. (2024). Code is law: How COMPAS affects the way the judiciary handles the risk of recidivism. *Artificial Intelligence and Law*. Advance online publication. DOI: 10.1007/s10506-024-09389-8

Englert, S., Woodcock, J., & Cant, C. (2020). Digital workerism: Technology, platforms, and the circulation of workers' struggles. *TripleC*, *18*(1), 132–145. DOI: 10.31269/triplec.v18i1.1133

Ergo Hellas. (2023). ERGO Insurance in the era of Artificial Intelligence with "Journey", the new Chatbot that changes the way it communicates with its customers. Retrieval date: 19 October 2024. https://www.ergohellas.gr/news/ergo-introduces-ai-chatbot-xara (In Greek).

Ericson, P., Dobbe, R., & Lindgren, S. (2024). Tracing class and capitalism in AI research. *TripleC*, *22*(1), 307–328. DOI: 10.31269/triplec.v22i1.1464

Erman, E., & Furendal, M. (2024). Artificial Intelligence and the political legitimacy of global governance. *Political Studies*, *72*(2), 421–441. DOI: 10.1177/00323217221126665

Eshraghian, J. K. (2020). Human ownership of artificial creativity. *Nature Machine Intelligence*, *2*(3), 157–160. DOI: 10.1038/s42256-020-0161-x

European Commission. (2021). Proposal for a regulation laying down harmonised rules on artificial intelligence (Artificial Intelligence Act). https://eur-lex.europa.eu/legal-content/EN/TXT/?uri=CELEX:52021PC0206

European Union. (2016). Regulation (EU) 2016/679 of the European Parliament and of the Council (General Data Protection Regulation). https://eur-lex.europa.eu/eli/reg/2016/679/oj

European Union. (2024). AI Act. https://digital-strategy.ec.europa.eu/en/policies/regulatory-framework-ai (accessed April 18, 2024).

Exploring the Impact of Generative AI on Intellectual Property Law and the Future of Artistic Expression. (2023). https://issuu.com/ethicalintelligence-equation/docs/equation_issue_v/s/24638929

Farayola, M. M., Tal, I., Connolly, R., Saber, T., & Bendechache, M. (2023). Ethics and trustworthiness of AI for predicting the risk of recidivism: A systematic literature review. *Information (Basel)*, *14*(8), 426. DOI: 10.3390/info14080426

Farayola, O. A., Olorunfemi, O. L., & Shoetan, P. O. (2024). Data privacy and security in IT: A review of techniques and challenges. *Computer Science & IT Research Journal*, *5*(3), 606–615. DOI: 10.51594/csitrj.v5i3.909

Fazel, S., Burghart, M., Fanshawe, T., Gil, S. D., Monahan, J., & Yu, R. (2022). The predictive performance of criminal risk assessment tools used at sentencing: Systematic review of validation studies. *Journal of Criminal Justice*, *81*, 101902. DOI: 10.1016/j.jcrimjus.2022.101902 PMID: 36530210

Fenglin, Y., Zhao, Y., & Turdi, M. (2020). Challenges of the Intellectual Property System in the Age of Artificial Intelligence. *American Journal of Applied Scientific Research*, *6*(1), 24. DOI: 10.11648/j.ajasr.20200601.13

Ferguson, A. G. (2017). *The rise of big data policing: Surveillance, race, and the future of law enforcement*. New York University Press. DOI: 10.18574/nyu/9781479854608.001.0001

Ferrara, E. (2023). Fairness And Bias in Artificial Intelligence: A Brief Survey of Sources, Impacts, And Mitigation Strategies. arXiv (Cornell University). https://doi.org/DOI: 10.48550/arXiv.2304

Feuerriegel, S., Dolata, M., & Schwade, G. (2020). Fair AI: Challenges and opportunities. *Business & Information Systems Engineering*, *62*(4), 379–384. DOI: 10.1007/s12599-020-00650-3

Financial Conduct Authority. (2023). Regulatory sandbox. https://www.fca.org.uk/firms/innovation/regulatory-sandbox

Floridi, L., & Cowls, J. (2019). A unified framework of five principles for AI in society. *Harvard Data Science Review*, *1*(1). Advance online publication. DOI: 10.1162/99608f92.8cd550d1

Fomin, V. V., & Astromskis, P. (2023). The black box problem. In: Gordon, J.S. (ed) *Philosophy and Human Rights*. Brill, 393, 112-125. https://doi.org/DOI: 10.1163/9789004682900_012

Fontes, C., Hohma, E., Corrigan, C. C., & Lütge, C. (2022). AI-powered public surveillance systems: Why we (might) need them and how we want them. *Technology in Society*, *71*, 102137. DOI: 10.1016/j.techsoc.2022.102137

Fosch-Villaronga, E., Kieseberg, P., & Li, T. (2017). Humans forget, machines remember: Artificial intelligence and the right to be forgotten. *Computer Security & Law Review (Forthcoming)*. Available at *SSRN*: https://ssrn.com/abstract=3018186

Friederich, S. (2024). Symbiosis, not alignment, as the goal for liberal democracies in the transition to artificial general intelligence. *AI and Ethics*, *4*(2), 315–324. DOI: 10.1007/s43681-023-00268-7

Fritz, J., & Giardini, T. (2024). Emerging contours of AI governance and the three layers of regulatory heterogeneity. *Digital Policy Alert Working Paper* 24-001.

Frolova, E. E., & Ermakova, E. P. (2021). Utilizing artificial intelligence in legal practice. In Inshakova, A. O., & Frolova, E. E. (Eds.), *Smart Technologies for the Digitisation of Industry: Entrepreneurial Environment. Smart Innovation, Systems and Technologies* (Vol. 254, pp. 17–27). Springer., DOI: 10.1007/978-981-16-4621-8_2

Frosio, G. (2024). Algorithmic enforcement tools: Governing opacity with due process. In Francese, S., & King, R. (Eds.), *Driving Forensic Innovation in the 21st Century* (pp. 195–218). Springer., DOI: 10.1007/978-3-031-56556-4_9

Fuchs, C. (2020). Towards a critical theory of communication as renewal and update of Marxist humanism in the age of digital capitalism. *Journal for the Theory of Social Behaviour*, *50*(3), 335–356. DOI: 10.1111/jtsb.12247

Fukuyama, F. (2016). Governance: What do we know, and how do we know it? *Annual Review of Political Science*, *19*(1), 89–105. DOI: 10.1146/annurev-polisci-042214-044240

Galindo, L., Perset, K., & Sheeka, F. (2021). *An overview of national AI strategies and policies. OECD Going Digital Toolkit Notes, 14*. OECD Publishing., DOI: 10.1787/c05140d9-

Garcia-Macia, D., & Goyal, R. (2020). Technological and Economic Decoupling in the Cyber Era. SSRN Electronic Journal. DOI: 10.5089/9781513561677.001

Geraets, N. (2023, August 9). Authors furious as 'wildly unethical' AI website hoovers up books. *The Sydney Morning Herald*. https://www.smh.com.au/culture/books/it-filled-me-with-rage-authors-furious-as-ai-website-hoovers-up-books-20230809-p5dv0j.html (accessed January 31, 2024).

Geroulanos, S., & Weatherby, L. (2020). Cybernetics and the human sciences. *History of the Human Sciences*, *33*(1), 3–11. DOI: 10.1177/0952695119887098

Gilbert, S. (2024). The EU passes the AI Act and its implications for digital medicine are unclear. *npj. Digital Medicine*, *7*(1), 135. DOI: 10.1038/s41746-024-01116-6 PMID: 38778162

Goddard, M. (2017). The EU General Data Protection Regulation (GDPR): European regulation that has a global impact. *International Journal of Market Research*, *59*(6), 703–705. DOI: 10.2501/IJMR-2017-050

Golbin, I., Rao, A. S., Hadjarian, A., & Krittman, D. (2020). Responsible AI: A Primer for the Legal Community. 2021 IEEE International Conference on Big Data (Big Data). DOI: 10.1109/BigData50022.2020.9377738

Goldsteen, A., Ezov, G., Shmelkin, R., Moffie, M., & Farkash, A. (2022). Data minimization for GDPR compliance in machine learning models. *AI and Ethics*, *2*(2), 477–491. DOI: 10.1007/s43681-021-00095-8

González, I., & Mateos, A. (2019). Multilayer Identification: Combining N-Grams, TF-IDF and Monge-Elkan in Massive Real Time Processing. *Lecture Notes in Computer Science (Including Subseries Lecture Notes in Artificial Intelligence and Lecture Notes in Bioinformatics), 11676 LNAI*, 213 – 223. DOI: 10.1007/978-3-030-26773-5_19

Gordon, J. S. (2021). AI and law: Ethical, legal, and socio-political implications. *AI & Society, 36*(2), 403–404. DOI: 10.1007/s00146-021-01194-0

Gray, J., & Suzor, N. (2020). Playing with machines: Using machine learning to understand automated copyright enforcement at scale. *Big Data & Society, 7*(1), 205395172091996. DOI: 10.1177/2053951720919963

Greene, T., Shmueli, G., Fell, J., Lin, C.-F., Shope, M., & Liu, H. (2020). The Hidden Inconsistencies Introduced by Predictive Algorithms in Judicial Decision Making.

Grossi, V., Giannotti, F., Pedreschi, D., Manghi, P., Pagano, P., & Assante, M. (2021). Data science: A game changer for science and innovation. *International Journal of Data Science and Analytics, 11*(2), 263–278. DOI: 10.1007/s41060-020-00240-2

Guadamuz, A. (2024). A Scanner Darkly: Copyright Liability and Exceptions in Artificial Intelligence Inputs and Outputs. *GRUR International, 73*(2), 111–127. DOI: 10.1093/grurint/ikad140

Gupta, S., Ghardallou, W., Pandey, D. K., & Sahu, G. P. (2022). Artificial intelligence adoption in the insurance industry: Evidence using the technology–organization–environment framework. *Research in International Business and Finance, 63*, 101757. DOI: 10.1016/j.ribaf.2022.101757

Hacker, P., Krestel, R., Grundmann, S., & Naumann, F. (2020). Explainable AI under contract and tort law: Legal incentives and technical challenges. *Artificial Intelligence and Law, 28*(4), 415–439. DOI: 10.1007/s10506-020-09260-6

Hagendorff, T. (2020). The ethics of AI ethics: An evaluation of guidelines. *Minds and Machines, 30*(1), 99–120. DOI: 10.1007/s11023-020-09517-8

Harvey, D. (1989). *The condition of postmodernity*. Blackwell.

Hasani, T., & O'Reilly, N. (2021). Analyzing antecedents affecting the organizational performance of start-up businesses. *Journal of Entrepreneurship in Emerging Economies, 13*(1), 107–130. DOI: 10.1108/JEEE-08-2019-0116

He, W. (2011). Tax incentive and technology innovation: The empirical research based on the listed companies. *2011 2nd International Conference on Artificial Intelligence, Management Science and Electronic Commerce, AIMSEC 2011 - Proceedings*, 7284 – 7291. DOI: 10.1109/AIMSEC.2011.6010554

Heilinger, J.-C. (2022). The ethics of AI ethics: A constructive critique. *Philosophy & Technology, 35*(3), 61. DOI: 10.1007/s13347-022-00557-9

Heinrichs, B. (2022). Discrimination in the age of artificial intelligence. *AI & Society, 37*(1), 143–154. DOI: 10.1007/s00146-021-01192-2

Hentzen, J. K., Hoffmann, A., Dolan, R., & Pala, E. (2021). Artificial intelligence in customer-facing financial services: A systematic literature review and agenda for future research. *International Journal of Bank Marketing*. Advance online publication. DOI: 10.1108/IJBM-09-2021-0417

Henz, P. (2021). Ethical and legal responsibility for artificial intelligence. *Discover Artificial Intelligence*, *1*(2), 2. Advance online publication. DOI: 10.1007/s44163-021-00002-4

Hijmans, H., & Raab, C. (2022). Ethical dimensions of the GDPR, AI regulation, and beyond. *Direito Público*, *18*(100). Advance online publication. DOI: 10.11117/rdp.v18i100.6197

Hildebrand, T. (2013). Tooley's account of the necessary connection between law and regularity. *Philosophical Studies*, *166*(1), 33–43. DOI: 10.1007/s11098-012-0023-4

Hildebrandt, M. (2016). *Smart Technologies and the End(s) of Law: Novel Entanglements of Law and Technology*. Edward Elgar Publishing.

Hilty, R. M., Hoffmann, J., & Scheuerer, S. (2021). Intellectual Property Justification for Artificial Intelligence. In *Oxford University Press eBooks* (p. 50). Oxford University Press., DOI: 10.1093/oso/9780198870944.003.0004

Hine, E., & Floridi, L. (2022). Artificial intelligence with American values and Chinese characteristics: A comparative analysis of American and Chinese governmental AI policies. *AI & Society*, *39*(1), 257–278. DOI: 10.1007/s00146-022-01499-8

Hine, E., & Floridi, L. (2023). The blueprint for an AI bill of rights: In search of enaction, at risk of inaction. *Minds and Machines*, *33*(2), 285–292. Advance online publication. DOI: 10.1007/s11023-023-09625-1

Hinterleitner, M., Knill, C., & Steinebach, Y. (2023). The growth of policies, rules, and regulations: A review of the literature and research agenda. *Regulation & Governance*, *18*(2), 637–654. DOI: 10.1111/rego.12511

Hollingsworth, J. R., & Boyer, R. (Eds.). (1997). *Contemporary capitalism: The embeddedness of institutions*. Cambridge University Press. DOI: 10.1017/CBO9781139174701

Hossain, M. A., Quaddus, M., & Islam, N. (2016). Developing and validating a model explaining the assimilation process of RFID: An empirical study. *Information Systems Frontiers*, *18*(4), 645–663. DOI: 10.1007/s10796-014-9537-y

How Google Fights Piracy. (2023). https://www.blog.google/documents/25/GO806_Google_FightsPiracy_eReader_final.pdf

Hoyle, R. H. (Ed.). (2012). *Handbook of structural equation modeling*. Guilford press.

Huang, K., Joshi, A., Dun, S., & Hamilton, N. (2024). AI regulations. In Huang, K., Wang, Y., Goertzel, B., Li, Y., Wright, S., & Ponnapalli, J. (Eds.), *Generative AI Security. Future of Business and Finance* (pp. 61–98). Springer., DOI: 10.1007/978-3-031-54252-7_3

Hung, T. W., & Yen, C. P. (2023). Predictive policing and algorithmic fairness. *Synthese*, *201*(6), 206. DOI: 10.1007/s11229-023-04189-0

IBA. (2024). The Top 5 Challenges Facing the Insurance Industry Today. Retrieval date: 18 August 2024. https://ibapplications.com/content-library/blog/the-top-5-challenges-facing-the-insurance-industry-today/

Imogen, P. V., Sreenidhi, J., & Nivedha, V. (2024). AI-powered legal documentation assistant. *Journal of Artificial Intelligence and Capsule Networks*, *6*(2), 210–226. DOI: 10.36548/jaicn.2024.2.007

Intelligence, G. A. the impact on intellectual property crimes. (2023). https://www.eurojust.europa.eu/sites/default/files/assets/generative-ai-impact-to-ip-crimes.pdf

Islam, M. (2024). Exploring ethical dimensions in AI: Navigating bias and fairness in the field. *Journal of Artificial Intelligence General Science*, *1*(1), 13–17. DOI: 10.60087/jaigs.v1i1.p18

Jan, Z., Ahamed, F., Mayer, W., Patel, N., Grossmann, G., Stumptner, M., & Kuusk, A. (2023). Artificial intelligence for industry 4.0: Systematic review of applications, challenges, and opportunities. *Expert Systems with Applications*, *216*, 119456. DOI: 10.1016/j.eswa.2022.119456

Javaid, S. M. (2024). The Importance of New Technology Adoption for Success. Retrieval date: 6 August 2024. https://www.linkedin.com/pulse/importance-new-technology-adoption-success-shaikh-muzaffar-javaid

Jelinski, L., Etzrodt, K., & Emgesser, S. (2021). Undifferentiated optimism and scandalized accidents: The media coverage of autonomous driving in Germany. *JCOM, Journal of Science Communication*, *20*(4), A02. DOI: 10.22323/2.20040202

Jerker, D., & Svantesson, B. (2023). The characteristics making Internet communication challenge traditional models of regulation. DOI: 10.1093/ijlit/eai002

Jiang, H. H., Brown, L. T., Cheng, J. Y.-Y., Khan, M., Gupta, A., Workman, D., Hanna, A., Flowers, J., & Gebru, T. (2023). AI Art and its Impact on Artists. 363. DOI: 10.1145/3600211.3604681

Jobin, A., Ienca, M., & Vayena, E. (2019). The global landscape of AI ethics guidelines. *Nature Machine Intelligence*, *1*(9), 389–399. DOI: 10.1038/s42256-019-0088-2

Jones, R. (2024). The Role of Leadership in Driving Technology Adoption. Retrieval date: 6 August 2024. https://www.trainingfolks.com/blog/the-role-of-leadership-in-driving-technology-adoption

Joseph, J. (2024). Predicting crime or perpetuating bias? The AI dilemma. *AI & Society*. Advance online publication. DOI: 10.1007/s00146-024-02032-9

Joshi, D. (2024). AI governance in India – law, policy and political economy. *Communication Research and Practice*, *10*(3), 328–339. DOI: 10.1080/22041451.2024.2346428

Joskow, P.L. & Noll, R.G. (1981). Regulation in theory and practice: An overview. *Studies in Public Regulation*, 1-78.

Kabir, M. S., & Alam, M. N. (2023). The role of AI technology for legal research and decision making. *International Journal of Advanced Research*, *10*(1), 2395–0056.

Kaloudi (2023). DGTAL: Artificial intelligence in insurance market services. Retrieval date: 19 October 2024. https://www.powergame.gr/synenteyxeis/422850/dgtal-i-techniti-noimosyni-stis-ypiresies-tis-asfalistikis-agoras/ (In Greek).

Kamble, R. & Shah, D. (2018). Applications of artificial intelligence in human life. International *Journal of Research – Granthaalayah*, 6(6), 178-188. https://doi.org// DOI: 10.29121/granthaalayah.v6.i6.2018.1363

Kaminski, M. E. (2020). Understanding Transparency in Algorithmic Accountability. In *Cambridge University Press eBooks* (p. 121). Cambridge University Press., DOI: 10.1017/9781108680844.006

Kan, C. H. (2024). Artificial intelligence (AI) in the age of democracy and human rights: Normative challenges and regulatory perspectives. *International Journal of Eurasian Education and Culture*, *9*(25), 145–166. DOI: 10.35826/ijoecc.1825

Kankanamge, N., Yigitcanlar, T., & Goonetilleke, A. (2021). Public perceptions on artificial intelligence driven disaster management: Evidence from Sydney, Melbourne and Brisbane. *Telematics and Informatics*, *65*, 101729. DOI: 10.1016/j.tele.2021.101729

Kao, K. T. (2024). From robodebt to responsible AI: Sociotechnical imaginaries of AI in Australia. *Communication Research and Practice*, *10*(3), 387–397. DOI: 10.1080/22041451.2024.2346420

Kaplan, A., & Haenlein, M. (2019). Siri, Siri, in my hand: Who's the fairest in the land? On the interpretations, illustrations, and implications of artificial intelligence. *Business Horizons*, *62*(1), 15–25. DOI: 10.1016/j.bushor.2018.08.004

Karpen, U. (2016). Efficacy, Effectiveness, Efficiency: From Judicial to Managerial Rationality. In: Meßerschmidt, K., Oliver-Lalana, A. (eds) *Rational Lawmaking under Review*. Legisprudence Library, 3. Springer, Cham. https://doi.org/DOI: 10.1007/978-3-319-33217-8_12

Karppi, T., & Granata, Y. (2019). Non-artificial non-intelligence: Amazon's Alexa and the frictions of AI. *AI & Society*, *34*(4), 867–876. DOI: 10.1007/s00146-019-00896-w

Kauffman, M. E., & Soares, M. N. (2020). AI in legal services: New trends in AI-enabled legal services. *Service Oriented Computing and Applications*, *14*(4), 223–226. DOI: 10.1007/s11761-020-00305-x

Kaur, D., Uslu, S., Rittichier, K.J. & Durresi, A. (2022). Trustworthy artificial intelligence: A review. *ACM Computing Surveys*, 55(2), 39, 1-38. https://doi.org// DOI: 10.1145/3491209

Kaur, N., & Kaur, M. (2024). Role of artificial intelligence in the Indian courts. *International Journal of Law, Policy and Social Review*, *6*(1), 17-20. https://www .lawjournals.net/assets/archives/2024/vol6issue1/5124.pdf

Kendal, E. (2022). Ethical, legal and social implications of emerging technology (ELSIET) symposium. *Journal of Bioethical Inquiry*, *19*(3), 363–370. DOI: 10.1007/ s11673-022-10197-5 PMID: 35749026

Khan, F., & Mer, A. (2023). Embracing artificial intelligence technology: Legal implications with special reference to European Union initiatives of data protection. In: Sood, K., Balusamy, B., Grima, S. (eds) *Digital Transformation, Strategic Resilience, Cyber Security and Risk Management*, 111, 119-141. https://doi.org/DOI: 10.1108/S1569-375920230000111C007

Khan, A. A., Badshah, S., Liang, P., Waseem, M., Khan, B., Ahmad, A., Fahmideh, M., Niazi, M., & Akber, M. A. (2022). Ethics of AI: A systematic literature review of principles and challenges. *Proceedings of the 26th International Conference on Evaluation and Assessment in Software Engineering*, 383-392. https://doi.org//DOI: 10.1145/3530019.3531329

Khan, A., Talukder, S. M., Islam, T. Q., & Islam, N. A. (2022). *The impact of business analytics capabilities on innovation, information quality, agility and firm performance: the moderation role of industry dynamism.* VINE Journal of Information and Knowledge Management., DOI: 10.1108/VJIKMS-01-2022-0027

Kharchenko, V., Fesenko, H., & Illiashenko, O. (2022). Quality Models for Artificial Intelligence Systems: Characteristic-Based Approach, Development and Application. *Sensors (Basel)*, *22*(13), 4865. DOI: 10.3390/s22134865 PMID: 35808361

Khereiche, M. (2020). Book review: Inhuman power: Artificial intelligence and the future of capitalism. *Journal of Digital Social Research*, *2*(2), 73–77. DOI: 10.33621/jdsr.v2i2.21

Khyani, L., Rizvi, S. M., & Srivastava, A. (2022). Artificial intelligence and its applications in finance. *International Research Journal of Modernization in Engineering Technology and Science*, *4*, 1208–1210.

Kirvan. P. business resilience. (2024). Retrieval date: 12 August 2024. https://www.techtarget.com/searchcio/definition/business-resilience

Koene, A., Dowthwaite, L., Seth, S., & Webb, H. (2021). Algorithmic bias: Impact on children's mental health. *The Lancet. Child & Adolescent Health*, *5*(3), 174–176. DOI: 10.1016/S2352-4642(21)00013-5

Koivula, K., Shamsuzzoha, A., & Shamsuzzaman, M. (2024). Application of artificial intelligence as a knowledge creation instrument in tax procedures. *Engineering Applications of Artificial Intelligence*, *133*, 108417. Advance online publication. DOI: 10.1016/j.engappai.2024.108417

Korba, A. A., Sebaa, S., Mabrouki, M., Ghamri-Doudane, Y., & Benatchba, K. (2024). A Life-long Learning Intrusion Detection System for 6G-Enabled IoV. 2022 International Wireless Communications and Mobile Computing (IWCMC), 1773. DOI: 10.1109/IWCMC61514.2024.10592500

Kordzadeh, N., & Ghasemaghaei, M. (2021). Algorithmic bias: Review, synthesis, and future research directions. *European Journal of Information Systems*, *31*(3), 388–409. DOI: 10.1080/0960085X.2021.1927212

Koridena, B. K., Malaiyappan, J. N. A., & Tadimarri, A. (2024). Ethical considerations in the development and deployment of AI systems. *European Journal of Technology*, *8*(2), 41–53. DOI: 10.47672/ejt.1890

Kostic, M. M. (2014). The elusive nature of entropy and its physical meaning. *Entropy (Basel, Switzerland)*, *16*(2), 953–967. DOI: 10.3390/e16020953

Kostka, G., Steinacker, L., & Meckel, M. (2021). Between security and convenience: Facial recognition technology in the eyes of citizens in China, Germany, the United Kingdom, and the United States. *Public Understanding of Science (Bristol, England), 30*(6), 671–690. DOI: 10.1177/09636625211001555 PMID: 33769157

Kougias, I., Seremeti, L., & Kalogeras, D. (2016). Promoting inclusion in higher education by adopting the theoretical framework of autopoiesis. *Proceedings of the 11th MIBES Conference*, Heraklion, Crete.

Krafft, P. M., Young, M., Katell, M., Huang, K., & Bugingo, G. (2020). Defining AI in policy versus practice. *Proceedings of the AAAI/ACM Conference on AI, Ethics, and Society*, 72-78. https://doi.org/DOI: 10.1145/3375627.3375835

Kumar, R., Joshi, A., Sharan, H. O., Peng, S., & Dudhagara, C. R. (2024). *The Ethical Frontier on AI and Data Analysis*. IGI Global Publishing., DOI: 10.4018/979-8-3693-2964-1

Kusumaputra, A., Sudarsono, S., Fadli, M., & Sukarmi, . (2023). CYBERSTATE: AN ALTERNATIVE TO BUILDING LEGAL UNIFICATION BRINGING ABOUT LEGAL ORDER IN CYBERSOCIETY. *Russian Journal of Agricultural and Socio-Economic Sciences, 139*(7), 3–8. DOI: 10.18551/rjoas.2023-07.01

Lagioia, F., Rovatti, R., & Sartor, G. (2023). Algorithmic fairness through group parities? The case of COMPAS-SAPMOC. *AI & Society, 38*(2), 459–478. DOI: 10.1007/s00146-022-01441-y

Larsson, S., & Heintz, F. (2020). Transparency in artificial intelligence. *Internet Policy Review, 9*(2). Advance online publication. DOI: 10.14763/2020.2.1469

Lawrence, C., Cui, I., & Ho, D. (2023). The bureaucratic challenge to AI governance: An empirical assessment of implementation at U.S. Federal Agencies. *Proceedings of the 2023 AAAI/ACM Conference on AI, Ethics, and Society*, 606-652. https://doi.org/DOI: 10.1145/3600211.3604701

Laycock, A. (2023). European Patent Office Gives Guidance On Artificial Intelligence And Machine Learning. https://www.mondaq.com/uk/patent/750954/european-patent-office-gives-guidance-on-artificial-intelligence-and-machine-learning

Leckie, G. J., Given, L. M., & Buschman, J. E. (Eds.). (2010). *Critical theory for library and information science: Exploring the social from across the disciplines.* Libraries Unlimited. DOI: 10.5040/9798400634420

Lee, Y., Bradford, B., & Posch, K. (2024). The effectiveness of big data-driven predictive policing: Systematic review. *Justice Evaluation Journal*. https://doi.org/DOI: 10.1080/24751979.2024.2371781

Levio Consulting Inc. (2024). How is Your Company Reacting to New InsurTech Competition? Retrieval date: 13 August 2024. https://levioconsulting.com/insights/how-is-your-company-reacting-to-new-insurtech-competition/

Lewis, D., Filip, D., & Pandit, H. (2020). An ontology for standardizing trustworthy AI. In Hessami, A., & Shaw, P. (Eds.), *Factoring Ethics in Technology* (pp. 65–86). Policy Making, Regulation and AI., DOI: 10.5772/intechopen.97478

Liang, W., Tadesse, G. A., Ho, D., Fei-Fei, L., Zaharia, M., Zhang, C., & Zou, J. (2022). Advances, challenges and opportunities in creating data for trustworthy AI. *Nature Machine Intelligence*, *4*(8), 669–677. DOI: 10.1038/s42256-022-00516-1

Lin, Y. (2023). E-commerce and Online Dispute Resolution in Hong Kong. *Amicus Curiae*, *4*(3), 542–551. DOI: 10.14296/ac.v4i3.5615

Liu, H., Xia, Q., & Xu, J. (2011). Notice of Retraction: Taxpayer compliance in China: A prospect theory analysis. *2011 2nd International Conference on Artificial Intelligence, Management Science and Electronic Commerce, AIMSEC 2011 - Proceedings*, 7292 – 7297. DOI: 10.1109/AIMSEC.2011.6009750

Liu, J., & Zhou, G. (2011). Analysis on China's individual income tax self-declaration system - Problems, guidance and strategies. *2011 2nd International Conference on Artificial Intelligence, Management Science and Electronic Commerce, AIMSEC 2011 - Proceedings*, 1930 – 1933. DOI: 10.1109/AIMSEC.2011.6011083

Liu, H. Y., Maas, M., Danaher, J., Scarcella, L., Lexer, M., & Van Rompaey, L. (2020). Artificial intelligence and legal disruption: A new model for analysis. *Law, Innovation and Technology*, *12*(2), 205–258. DOI: 10.1080/17579961.2020.1815402

Liu, X., Gao, L., Lu, J., & Lioliou, E. (2016). Environmental risks, localization and the overseas subsidiary performance of MNEs from an emerging economy. *Journal of World Business*, *51*(3), 356–368. DOI: 10.1016/j.jwb.2015.05.002

Liu, Y., Zhang, J., Wu, S., & Pathan, M. S. (2021). Research on digital copyright protection based on the hyperledger fabric blockchain network technology. *PeerJ. Computer Science*, *7*, e709. Advance online publication. DOI: 10.7717/peerj-cs.709 PMID: 34616889

Li, W. (2024). A study on factors influencing designers' behavioral intention in using AI-generated content for assisted design: Perceived anxiety, perceived risk, and UTAUT. *International Journal of Human-Computer Interaction*, •••, 1–14. DOI: 10.1080/10447318.2024.2310354

Lord, T. (2020). The Antarctic Treaty System and the peaceful governance of Antarctica: The role of the ATS in promoting peace at the margins of the world. *The Polar Journal, 10*(1), 3–21. DOI: 10.1080/2154896X.2020.1757821

Lu, Z., & Nam, I. (2021). Research on the Influence of New Media Technology on Internet Short Video Content Production under Artificial Intelligence Background. Complexity, 2021(1). DOI: 10.1155/2021/8875700

Luger, G.F. (2025). AI ethical issues: From a social perspective. *Artificial Intelligence: Principles and Practice*, 573-599. https://doi.org/DOI: 10.1007/978-3-031-57437-5_26

Lund, B. D., Khan, D., & Yuvaraj, M. (2024). ChatGPT in medical libraries, possibilities and future directions: An integrative review. *Health Information and Libraries Journal, 41*(1), 4–15. DOI: 10.1111/hir.12518 PMID: 38200693

Lu, O., Zhu, L., Xu, X., Whittle, J., Zowghi, D., & Jacquet, A. (2024). Responsible AI pattern catalogue: A collection of best practices for AI governance and engineering. *ACM Computing Surveys, 56*(7), 1–35. DOI: 10.1145/3626234

Lutfi, A., Alrawad, M., Alsyouf, A., Almaiah, M. A., Al-Khasawneh, A., Al-Khasawneh, A. L., Alshira'h, A. F., Alshirah, M. H., Saad, M., & Ibrahim, N. (2023). Drivers and impact of big data analytic adoption in the retail industry: A quantitative investigation applying structural equation modeling. *Journal of Retailing and Consumer Services, 70*, 103129. DOI: 10.1016/j.jretconser.2022.103129

Lv, P., Xiong, H. (2022). Can FinTech improve corporate investment efficiency? Evidence from China. Res. Int. Bus. Financ. 60, 101571 https://doi.org/. ribaf.2021.101571.DOI: 10.1016/j

Lynskey, O. (2023). Complete and effective data protection. *Current Legal Problems, 76*(1), 297–344. DOI: 10.1093/clp/cuad009

Maas, M. M. (2024). *Concepts in advanced AI governance: A literature review of key terms and definitions*. AI Foundations Report, Institute for Law & AI.

Madan, R., & Ashok, M. (2023). AI adoption and diffusion in public administration: A systematic literature review and future research agenda. *Government Information Quarterly, 40*(1), 101774. DOI: 10.1016/j.giq.2022.101774

Madaoui, N. (2024). The impact of artificial intelligence on legal systems: Challenges and opportunities. *Problems of Legality, 1*(164), 285–303. DOI: 10.21564/2414-990X.164.289266

Mansoor, S. I., & Wani, S. A. (2025). Harnessing ethical AI: Measures of redressing hate speech in the social media context. In Chakraborty, S. (Ed.), *Ethical AI solutions for addressing social media influence and hate speech* (pp. 37–62). IGI Global Scientific Publishing., DOI: 10.4018/979-8-3693-9904-0.ch003

Marda, V. (2018). Artificial intelligence policy in India: A framework for engaging the limits of data-driven decision-making. *Philosophical Transactions. Series A, Mathematical, Physical, and Engineering Sciences, 376*(2133), 20180087. DOI: 10.1098/rsta.2018.0087 PMID: 30323001

Marg, E. R. P. Ltd. (2024). Understanding the Principles of Insurance: Safeguarding Your Future. Retrieval date: 15 August 2024. https://margcompusoft.com/m/principles-of-insurance-your-future/

Maroufkhani, P., Ismail, W. K. W., & Ghobakhloo, M. (2020). Big data analytics adoption model for small and medium enterprises. *Journal of Science and Technology Policy Management, 11*(4), 483–502. DOI: 10.1108/JSTPM-02-2020-0018

Marx, K. (1857). Introduction to a contribution to the critique of political economy. https://www.marxists.org/archive/marx/works/1859/critique-pol-economy/appx1 .htm (accessed April 18, 2024).

Maturana, H. R., & Varela, F. J. (1980). *Autopoiesis and Cognition: The realization of the living*. Springer. DOI: 10.1007/978-94-009-8947-4

McDonald, L. (2023). AI systems and liability: An assessment of the applicability of strict liability & a case for limited legal personhood for AI. *The St Andrews Law Journal, 3*(1), 5–21. Advance online publication. DOI: 10.15664/stalj.v3i1.2645

McEvily, S. K., Eisenhardt, K. M., & Prescott, J. E. (2004). The global acquisition, leverage, and protection of technological competencies. *Strategic Management Journal, 25*(8-9), 713–722. DOI: 10.1002/smj.425

McGrath, S. K., & Whitty, S. J. (2018). Accountability and responsibility defined. *International Journal of Managing Projects in Business, 11*(3), 687–707. DOI: 10.1108/IJMPB-06-2017-0058

Miazi, M.A.N. (2023). Interplay of legal frameworks and artificial intelligence (AI): A global perspective. *Law and Policy Review*, 2(2), 01-25. https://doi.org/ DOI: 10.32350/lrp.22.01

Mittelstadt, B. (2019). Principles alone cannot guarantee ethical AI. *Nature Machine Intelligence, 1*(11), 501–507. DOI: 10.1038/s42256-019-0114-4

Mittelstadt, B. D., Allo, P., Taddeo, M., Wachter, S., & Floridi, L. (2016). The ethics of algorithms: Mapping the debate. *Big Data & Society*, *3*(2), 2053951716679679. Advance online publication. DOI: 10.1177/2053951716679679

Mohamed, E., Quteishat, A., Qtaishat, A., & Mohammad, A. (2024). Exploring the role of AI in modern legal practice: Opportunities, challenges, and ethical implications. *Journal of Electrical Systems*.

Moliterno, T. P., & Wiersema, M. F. (2007). Firm performance, rent appropriation, and the strategic resource divestment capability. *Strategic Management Journal*, *28*(11), 1065–1087. DOI: 10.1002/smj.630

Molloy, B. T. (2021). Project governance for defense applications of artificial intelligence: An ethics-based approach. *Prism*, *9*(3), 106–121. https://www.jstor.org/stable/48640749/

Mondschein, C. F., & Monda, C. (2019). The EU's General Data Protection Regulation (GDPR) in a research context. In Kubben, P., Dumontier, M., & Dekker, A. (Eds.), *Fundamentals of clinical data science* (pp. 65–82). Springer., DOI: 10.1007/978-3-319-99713-1_5

Morozov, E. (2013). *To save everything, click here: The folly of technological solutionism*. PublicAffairs.

Mühlhoff, R., & Ruschemeier, H. (2024). Updating purpose limitation for AI: A normative approach from law and philosophy. *SSRN*. https://doi.org/DOI: 10.2139/ssrn.4711621

Muir-Wood. The 10 Major Risks Shaping Insurance Today. (2024). Retrieval date: 18 August 2024. https://www.rms.com/blog/2024/05/07/the-major-risks-shaping-insurance-today

Mulgan, T. (2016). Superintelligence: Paths, dangers, strategies.

Mullins, M., Holland, C. P., & Cunneen, M. (2021). Creating ethics guidelines for artificial intelligence and big data analytics customers: The case of the consumer European insurance market. *Patterns (New York, N.Y.)*, *2*(10), 100362. DOI: 10.1016/j.patter.2021.100362 PMID: 34693379

Munshi, M. F., & Barai, S. (2022). IP Rights to AI-Generated Works: Barriers Presented by Existing Law and Reformations Needed. *Canadian Journal of Business and Information Studies*, *37*, 37–46. Advance online publication. DOI: 10.34104/cjbis.022.037046

Mushtaq, R., Gull, A. A., Shahab, Y., & Derouiche, I. (2022). Do financial performance indicators predict 10-K text sentiments? An application of artificial intelligence. *Research in International Business and Finance*, *61*, 101679. DOI: 10.1016/j.ribaf.2022.101679

Mylrea, M., & Robinson, N. (2023). Artificial Intelligence (AI) trust framework and maturity model: Applying an entropy lens to improve security, privacy, and ethical AI. *Entropy (Basel, Switzerland)*, *25*(10), 1429. DOI: 10.3390/e25101429 PMID: 37895550

Na, S., Heo, S., Han, S., Shin, Y., & Roh, Y. (2022). Acceptance model of artificial intelligence (AI)-based technologies in construction firms: Applying the Technology Acceptance Model (TAM) in combination with the Technology–Organisation–Environment (TOE) framework. *Buildings (Basel, Switzerland)*, *12*(2), 90. DOI: 10.3390/buildings12020090

Nayak, A., & Dutta, K. (2017). Impacts on machine learning and artificial intelligence on mankind. *International Conference on Intelligent Computing and Control*, 1-3. https://doi.org//DOI: 10.1109/I2C2.2017.8321908

Neupane, S., Mitra, S., Fernandez, I. A., Saha, S., Mittal, S., Chen, J., Pillai, N., & Rahimi, S. (2024). Security considerations in AI-robotics: A survey of current methods, challenges, and opportunities. *IEEE Access : Practical Innovations, Open Solutions*, *12*, 22072–22097. DOI: 10.1109/ACCESS.2024.3363657

New York City Council. (2021). Int. No. 1894-A: A local law to amend the administrative code of the city of New York, in relation to automated employment decision tools. https://www.nyc.gov/assets/dca/downloads/pdf/about/Local-Law-144-Automated-Employment-Decision-Tools.pdf

Newman, G. E., & Knobe, J. (2019). The essence of essentialism. *Mind & Language*, *34*(5), 585–605. DOI: 10.1111/mila.12226

Next Dial. (2024). Christos Theodoridis: Allianz promotes leading. Retrieval date: 19 October 2024. https://www.nextdeal.gr/asfalistikes-eidiseis/idiotiki-asfalisi/139191/hristos-theodoridis-i-allianz-proothei-koryfaies (In Greek).

Nguyen, T. L., Nguyen, V. P., & Dang, T. V. D. (2022). Critical factors affecting the adoption of artificial intelligence: An empirical study in Vietnam. *The Journal of Asian Finance, Economics and Business*, *9*(5), 225–237. DOI: 10.13106/jafeb.2020.vol7.no5.225

Nisbet, R., Miner, G., & Yale, K. (2018). IBM Watson. Elsevier eBooks, 773. DOI: 10.1016/B978-0-12-416632-5.00022-0

Njegomir, V., & Demko-Rihter, J. (2023). InsurTech: new competition to traditional insurers and impact on the economic growth. In *Digital transformation of the financial industry: approaches and applications* (pp. 133–150). Springer International Publishing. DOI: 10.1007/978-3-031-23269-5_8

Novelli, C., Taddeo, M., & Floridi, L. (2024). Accountability in artificial intelligence: What it is and how it works. *AI & Society*, *39*(4), 1871–1882. DOI: 10.1007/s00146-023-01635-y

Nowotko, P. M. (2021). AI in judicial application of law and the right to a court. *Procedia Computer Science*, *192*, 2220–2228. DOI: 10.1016/j.procs.2021.08.235

Ntoutsi, E., Fafalios, P., Gadiraju, U., Iosifidis, V., Nejdl, W., Vidal, M.-E., Ruggieri, S., Turini, F., Papadopoulos, S., Krasanakis, E., Kompatsiaris, I., Kinder-Kurlanda, K., Wagner, C., Karimi, F., Fernandez, M., Alani, H., Berendt, B., Kruegel, T., Heinze, C., & Staab, S. (2020). Bias in data-driven artificial intelligence systems—An introductory survey. *Wiley Interdisciplinary Reviews. Data Mining and Knowledge Discovery*, *10*(3), e1356. DOI: 10.1002/widm.1356

Nweke, O. C., & Nweke, G. J. (2024). Legal and ethical conundrums in the AI era: A multidisciplinary analysis. *International Law Research*, 13(1). https://orcid.org/0009-0009-6956-5345/

O'Neil, C. (2017). *Weapons of math destruction: How big data increases inequality and threatens democracy*. Crown Publishing Group.

ÓhÉigeartaigh, S. S., Whittlestone, J., Liu, Y., Zeng, Y., & Liu, Z.ÓhÉigeartaigh. (2020). Overcoming barriers to cross-cultural cooperation in AI ethics and governance. *Philosophy & Technology*, *33*(4), 571–593. DOI: 10.1007/s13347-020-00402-x

Olatoye, F. O., Awonuga, K. F., Mhlongo, N. Z., Ibeh, C. V., Elufloye, O. A., & Ndubuisi, N. L. (2024). AI and ethics in business: A comprehensive review of responsible AI practices and corporate responsibility. *International Journal of Science and Research Archive*, *11*(01), 1433–1443. DOI: 10.30574/ijsra.2024.11.1.0235

Oliveira, T. & Martins, M. F. (2011). Literature review of information technology adoption models at firm level. Electronic journal of information systems evaluation, 14(1), pp110-121.

Online Dispute Resolution Standards of Practice. (2023). https://www.icann.org/resources/pages/odr-standards-of-practice-2012-02-25-en

Orwat, C., Bareis, J., Folberth, A., Jahnel, J., & Wabephul, C. (2024). Normative challenges of risk regulation of artificial intelligence. *NanoEthics*, *18*(2), 11. DOI: 10.1007/s11569-024-00454-9

Owlift. Top Management Support in Innovation. (2024). Retrieval date: 8 August 2024. https://www.owlift.com/blog/submission/top-management-support-in-innovation/

Pack, H. (2022). Regulation of artificial intelligence in the United States. In M. A. Grau Ruiz (Ed.), *Interactive robotics: Legal, ethical, social and economic aspects* (Vol. 30, pp. 367–380). Biosystems & Biorobotics. Springer. https://doi.org/DOI: 10.1007/978-3-031-04305-5_38

Pagallo, U. (2013). *The laws of robots: Crimes, contracts, and torts* (Vol. 10). Springer Science & Business Media., DOI: 10.1007/978-94-007-6564-1

Pagan, N., Baumann, J., Elokda, E., Pasquale, G. D., Bolognani, S., & Hannák, A. (2023). A Classification of Feedback Loops and Their Relation to Biases in Automated Decision-Making Systems. arXiv (Cornell University). /arxiv.2305.06055DOI: 10.1145/3617694.3623227

Palladino, N. (2023). A 'biased' emerging governance regime for artificial intelligence? How AI ethics get skewed moving from principles to practices. *Telecommunications Policy*, *47*(5), 102479. DOI: 10.1016/j.telpol.2022.102479

Pannu, A. (2015). Artificial intelligence and its application in different areas. *International Journal of Engineering and Innovative Technology*, 4(10), 79-84, ISSN: 2277-3754.

Papademetriou, C., Ragazou, K., & Garefalakis, A. (2023). Adapting Artificial Intelligence in Cypriot Hotel Industry: The Views of Hotel Managers. *Proceedings of Eurasia Business and Economics Society Conference*. Springer Nature Switzerland (Eds), 143-155.

Papademetriou, C. (2012). To what extent is the Turing Test Still Important? *Pliroforiki*, *1*(22), 28–32.

Papademetriou, C., Ragazou, K., Garefalakis, A., & Anastasiadou, S. (2024). The Role of Artificial Intelligence in Employee Wellness and Mental Health. In Global, I. G. I. (Ed.), *Human Resource Strategies in the Era of Artificial Intelligence* (pp. 29–54). DOI: 10.4018/979-8-3693-6412-3.ch002

Pasquinelli, M. (2023). *The eye of the master: A social history of artificial intelligence*. Verso.

Patil, U. (2023). South Africa Grants A Patent With An Artificial Intelligence (AI) System As The Inventor – World's First!! https://www.mondaq.com/india/patent/1122790/south-africa-grants-a-patent-with-an-artificial-intelligence-ai-system-as-the-inventor-world39s-first

Paul, R. (2024). The politics of regulating AI technologies: Towards AI competition states. In: Paul, R., Carmel, E. & Cobbe, J. (eds) *Handbook on Public Policy and Artificial Intelligence*, 261-279. https://doi.org/DOI: 10.4337/9781803922171.00028

Pearson. (2024). Major HR Challenge for Insurance Companies: Attracting Young Talent to Maintain Their Dynamism. Retrieval date: 18 August 2024. https://www.talentlens.com/Insights/blog/2024/05/hr-challenges-insurance-companies.html

Pence, H. E. (2022). Future of artificial intelligence in libraries. *The Reference Librarian*, *63*(4), 133–143. DOI: 10.1080/02763877.2022.2140741

Perez-Des Rosiers, D. (2021). AI application in surveillance for public safety: Adverse risks for contemporary societies. In Keskin, T., & Kiggins, R. D. (Eds.), *Towards an international political economy of artificial intelligence* (pp. 95–114). Palgrave Macmillan., DOI: 10.1007/978-3-030-74420-5_6

Pfeiffer, J., Gutschow, J., Haas, C., Moslein, F., Maspfuhl, O., Borgers, F., & Alpsancar, S. (2023). Algorithmic fairness in AI. *Business & Information Systems Engineering*, *65*(2), 209–222. DOI: 10.1007/s12599-023-00787-x

Picht, P. G., & Thouvenin, F. (2023). AI and IP: Theory to Policy and Back Again – Policy and Research Recommendations at the Intersection of Artificial Intelligence and Intellectual Property. *IIC; International Review of Industrial Property and Copyright Law*, *54*(6), 916–940. DOI: 10.1007/s40319-023-01344-5

Pinochet, L. H. C., Amorim, G. D. C. B., Junior, D. L., & De Souza, C. A. (2021). Consequential factors of Big Data Analytics Capability: How firms use data in the competitive scenario. *Journal of Enterprise Information Management*, *34*(5), 1407–1417.

Poli, P. K. R., Pamidi, S., & Poli, S. K. R. (2025). Unraveling the ethical conundrum of artificial intelligence: A synthesis of literature and case studies. *Augmented Human Research*, *10*(1), 2. DOI: 10.1007/s41133-024-00077-5

Porvazník, J., & Ljudvigová, I. (2016). General Theory of Systems, Cybernetics and Evaluation of Human Competence by Solving Present Crisis Problems of Civilisation. *Procedia: Social and Behavioral Sciences*, *230*, 112–120. DOI: 10.1016/j.sbspro.2016.09.014

Power, D. J., Heavin, C., & O'Connor, Y. (2021). Balancing privacy rights and surveillance analytics: A decision process guide. *Journal of Business Analytics*, *4*(2), 155–170. DOI: 10.1080/2573234X.2021.1920856

Qaffas, A. A., Ilmudeen, A., Almazmomi, N. K., Alharbi, I. M. (2022). The impact of big data analytics talent capability on business intelligent infrastructure to achieve firm performance, .DOI: 10.1108/FS-01-2021-0002

Quteishat, E.M.A., Qtaishat, A. and Qutcishat, A.M.A. (2024). Exploring the role of AI in modern legal practice: Opportunities, challenges, and ethical implications. *Journal of Electrical Systems*, 20-6s, 3040-3050.

Quteishat, E. M. A., Qtaishat, A., & Quteishat, A. M. A. (2024). Exploring the role of AI in modern legal practice: Opportunities, challenges, and ethical implications. *Journal of Educational Studies*, *20*(6s), 3040–3050. Advance online publication. DOI: 10.52783/jes.3320

Radanliev, P., Roure, D. D., Kleek, M. V., Santos, O., & Ani, U. (2020). Artificial intelligence in cyber physical systems. *AI & Society*, *36*(3), 783–796. DOI: 10.1007/s00146-020-01049-0 PMID: 32874020

Radi, P. R., & Noninska, I. S. (2020). Challenges of the digital age for privacy and personal data protection. *Mathematical Biosciences and Engineering*, *17*(5), 5288–5303. DOI: 10.3934/mbe.2020286 PMID: 33120553

Rahman, M., Ming, T. H., Baigh, T. A., & Sarker, M. (2021). Adoption of artificial intelligence in banking services: An empirical analysis. *International Journal of Emerging Markets*. Advance online publication. DOI: 10.1108/IJOEM-06-2020-0724

Rahmatian, A. (2015). Cyberspace and intellectual property rights. In *Edward Elgar Publishing eBooks*. Edward Elgar Publishing., DOI: 10.4337/9781782547396.00013

Ramanathan, R., Ramanathan, U., & Bentley, Y. (2018). The debate on flexibility of environmental regulations, innovation capabilities and financial performance–A novel use of DEA. *Omega*, *75*, 131–138. DOI: 10.1016/j.omega.2017.02.006

Ramdani, B., & Kawalek, P. (2007). SME adoption of enterprise systems in the Northwest of England: An environmental, technological, and organizational perspective. In Organizational Dynamics of Technology-Based Innovation: Diversifying the Research Agenda: IFIP TC 8 WG 8.6 International Working Conference, June 14–16, Manchester, UK (pp. 409-429). Springer US.

Rani, S., Jining, D., Shah, D., Xaba, S., & Singh, P. R. (2023). The role of artificial intelligence in art: A comprehensive review of a generative adversarial network portrait painting. In Vasant, P. (Eds.), *Intelligent Computing and Optimization. Lecture Notes in Networks and Systems, 852, 126-135*. Springer., DOI: 10.1007/978-3-031-50330-6_13

Rashid, A. B., & Kausik, M. A. (2024). AI revolutionizing industries worldwide: A comprehensive overview its diverse applications. *Hybrid Advances*, *7*, 100277. DOI: 10.1016/j.hybadv.2024.100277

Rawas, S. (2024). AI: The future of humanity. *Discover Artificial Intelligence*, *4*(1), 25. DOI: 10.1007/s44163-024-00118-3

Rawat, S., Rawat, A., Kumar, D., & Sabitha, A. S. (2021). Application of machine learning and data visualization techniques for decision support in the insurance sector. *International Journal of Information Management Data Insights*, *1*(2), 100012. DOI: 10.1016/j.jjimei.2021.100012

Rayhan, S. (2023). *AI superintelligence and human existence: A comprehensive analysis of ethical, societal, and security implications*. https://doi.org/DOI: 10.13140/RG.2.2.12922.26561

Reidenberg, J., Robinson, D. G., & YUt, H. (2023). Accountable Algorithms. https://www.semanticscholar.org/paper/Accountable-Algorithms-Reidenberg-Reidenberg/da812fbacd6edddbbe3a53625804f32edf7ed0ea

Riccio, G. (2013). Old Economy v. New Economy: Intellectual Property, Global Wrongs and Private Remedies. SSRN Electronic Journal. DOI: 10.2139/ssrn.2543852

Riedl, M. O. (2020). Human-centered artificial intelligence and narrative intelligence. *Communications of the ACM*, *63*(12), 62–71. DOI: 10.1145/3381831

Risser, H. M., & Bottoms, B. L. (2020). Emotion recognition, AI, and children's rights. *Journal of Children and Media*, *14*(3), 325–341. DOI: 10.1080/17482798.2020.1778487

Roberts, H., Cowls, J., Hine, E., Morley, J., Wang, V., Taddeo, M., & Floridi, L. (2022). Governing artificial intelligence in China and the European Union: Comparing aims and promoting ethical outcomes. *The Information Society*, *39*(2), 79–97. DOI: 10.1080/01972243.2022.2124565

Roberts, H., Cowls, J., Morley, J., Taddeo, M., Wang, V., & Floridi, L. (2021). The Chinese approach to artificial intelligence: An analysis of policy, ethics, and regulation. *AI & Society*, *36*(1), 59–77. DOI: 10.1007/s00146-020-00992-2

Roberts, H., Hine, E., Taddeo, M., & Floridi, L. (2024). Global AI goverance: Barriers and pathways forward. *International Affairs*, *100*(3), 1275–1286. DOI: 10.1093/ia/iiae073

Robles Carrillo, M. (2020). Artificial intelligence: From ethics to law. *Telecommunications Policy*, *44*(6), 101937. DOI: 10.1016/j.telpol.2020.101937

Robles, P., & Mallinson, D. J. (2023). Catching up with AI: Pushing toward a cohesive governance framework. *Politics & Policy*, *51*(3), 355–372. DOI: 10.1111/polp.12529

Rodrigues, A. R. D., Ferreira, F. A. F., Teixeira, F. J. C. S. N., & Zopounidis, C. (2022). Artificial intelligence, digital transformation and cybersecurity in the banking sector: A multi-stakeholder cognition-driven framework. *Research in International Business and Finance*, *60*, 101616. DOI: 10.1016/j.ribaf.2022.101616

Rodriguez, R. (2020). Legal and human rights issues of AI: Gaps, challenges and vulnerabilities. *Journal of Responsible Technology*, *4*, 100005. DOI: 10.1016/j.jrt.2020.100005

Rogers, E. (1995). *Diffusion of innovations* (Paperback, F., Ed.).

Rogers, E. M., Singhal, A., & Quinlan, M. M. (2014). Diffusion of innovations. In *An integrated approach to communication theory and research* (pp. 432–448). Routledge.

Rosa, A. D., Bartolini, F., & Piva, A. (2003). Application of Intelligent Agents in a Notice and Takedown Process, Proceedings of SPIE, the International Society for Optical Engineering. *Proceedings of SPIE - the International Society for Optical Engineering*, *5018*, 275–283. DOI: 10.1117/12.473371

Russell, S. J., & Norvig, P. (2016). *Artificial intelligence: A modern approach* (3rd ed.). Pearson Education.

Saheb, T. (2023). Ethically contentions aspects of artificial intelligence surveillance: A social science perspective. *AI and Ethics*, *3*(2), 369–379. DOI: 10.1007/s43681-022-00196-y PMID: 35874304

Saheb, T., & Saheb, T. (2024). Mapping ethical artificial intelligence policy landscape: A mixed method analysis. *Science and Engineering Ethics*, *30*(9), 9. Advance online publication. DOI: 10.1007/s11948-024-00472-6 PMID: 38451328

Salloum, S. A. (2024). Trustworthiness of the AI. In: Al-Marzouqi, A., Sallum, S.A., Al-Saidat, M., Aburayya, A. Gupta, B. (eds) *Artificial Intelligence in Education: The Power and Dangers of ChatGPT in the Classroom. Studies in Big Data*, 1441, 643-650. Springer, Cham. https://doi.org//DOI: 10.1007/978-3-031-52280-2_41

Salonga, R. 4 External Factors that Affect Businesses. Retrieval date: 8 August 2024. https://sciencepark.com.ph/blog/factors-that-affect-businesses/

Sano, K., Hagiwara, S., & Tojo, S. (2012). An intuitionistic investigation of prerequisite-effect structure. *Lecture Notes in Computer Science (Including Subseries Lecture Notes in Artificial Intelligence and Lecture Notes in Bioinformatics), 7258 LNAI*, 170 – 183. DOI: 10.1007/978-3-642-32090-3_15

Santoni de Sio, F., & Mecacci, G. (2021). Four responsibility gaps with artificial intelligence: Why they matter and how to address them. *Philosophy & Technology*, *34*(4), 1057–1084. DOI: 10.1007/s13347-021-00450-x

Sanwal, T., & Sareen, P. (2021). The relevance of social intelligence for effective optimization of retirement and successful ageing. *Ageing International*, •••, 1–16. PMID: 34744217

Saranya, A., & Subhashini, R. (2023). A systematic review of explainable artificial intelligence models and applications: Recent developments and future trends. *Decision Analytics Journal*, *7*, 100230. DOI: 10.1016/j.dajour.2023.100230

Sarirete, A., Balfagih, Z., Brahimi, T., Lytras, M. D., & Visvizi, A. (2022). Artificial intelligence and machine learning research: Towards digital transformation at a global scale. *Journal of Ambient Intelligence and Humanized Computing*, *13*(7), 3319–3321. DOI: 10.1007/s12652-021-03168-y

Sarkar, A. (2023).. . *Exploring Perspectives on the Impact of Artificial Intelligence on the Creativity of Knowledge Work: Beyond Mechanised Plagiarism and Stochastic Parrots.*, *1*, 1–17. Advance online publication. DOI: 10.1145/3596671.3597650

Sayyed, H. (2024). Artificial intelligence and criminal liability in India: Exploring legal implications and challenges. *Cogent Social Sciences*, *10*(1), 2343195. Advance online publication. DOI: 10.1080/23311886.2024.2343195

Scherer, M. U. (2016). Regulating Artificial Intelligence Systems: Risks, Challenges, Competencies, and Strategies. *Harvard Journal of Law & Technology*, *29*(2), 353–400.

Schneider, J., Abraham, R., Meske, C., & Brocke, J. V. (2022). Artificial intelligence governance for businesses. *Information Systems Management*, *40*(3), 229–249. DOI: 10.1080/10580530.2022.2085825

Scholes, M. S. (2025). Artificial intelligence and uncertainty. *Risk Sciences*, *1*, 100004. DOI: 10.1016/j.risk.2024.100004

Schulze, K. K., & Mock, R. P. (2021). THE ROBOTIC REVOLUTION: A TAX POLICY COLLISION COURSE. *Temple Law Review*, *93*(2), 301–341.

Seremeti, L., & Kougias, I. (2019). Legal issues within ambient intelligence environments. *Proceedings of the 10th International Conference on Information, Intelligence, Systems and Applications (IISA)*, Patras, Greece, 1-2. https://doi.org/DOI: 10.1109/IISA.2019.8900748

Seremeti, L., & Kougias, I. (2021a). The legalhood of artificial intelligence: AI applications as energy services. *Journal of Artificial Intelligence and Systems*, *3*, 83–92.

Seremeti, L., & Kougias, I. (2021b). Category theory as interpretation law model in artificial intelligence era. *Journal of Artificial Intelligence and Systems*, *3*, 35–47.

Seremeti, L., & Kougias, I. (2024). The AI spectrum under the doctrine of necessity: Towards the flexibility of the future legal praxis. *Computers and Artificial Intelligence*, *2*(1), 1258.

Shackelford, S. J., & Raymond, A. (2014). Building the Virtual Courthouse: Ethical Considerations for Design, Implementation, and Regulation in the World of ODR. SSRN Electronic Journal. DOI: 10.2139/ssrn.2387912

Shahbazi, H. (2024). Leveraging the TOE Framework to Shape Your Enterprise Technology Strategy. Retrieval date: 5 August 2024. https://www.linkedin.com/pulse/leveraging-toe-framework-shape-your-enterprise-hassan-shahbazi

Shah, M., & Sureja, N. (2024). A comprehensive review of bias in deep learning models: Methods, impacts, and future directions. *Archives of Computational Methods in Engineering*. Advance online publication. DOI: 10.1007/s11831-024-10134-2

Shahriar, S., Allana, S., Hazratifard, S. M., & Dara, R. (2023). A survey of privacy risks and mitigation strategies in the artificial intelligence life cycle. *IEEE Access : Practical Innovations, Open Solutions*, *11*, 61829–61854. DOI: 10.1109/ACCESS.2023.3287195

Shao, C., Nah, S., Makady, H., & McNealy, J. (2024). Understanding user attitudes towards AI-enabled technologies: An integrated model of self-efficacy, TAM, and AI ethics. *International Journal of Human-Computer Interaction*, •••, 1–13. DOI: 10.1080/10447318.2024.2331858

Sharkey, N. (2019). Autonomous weapons systems, killer robots and human dignity. *Law, Innovation and Technology*, *11*(1), 107–128.

Sharma, S. (2024). Benefits or concerns of AI: A multistakeholder responsibility. *Futures*, *157*, 103328. DOI: 10.1016/j.futures.2024.103328

Sharma, S., Singh, G., Islam, N., & Dhir, A. (2022). Why do SMEs adopt artificial intelligence-based chatbots? *IEEE Transactions on Engineering Management*, *71*, 1773–1786. DOI: 10.1109/TEM.2022.3203469

Sheehan, M. (2023). China's AI regulations and how they get made. *Horizons: Journal of International Relations and Sustainable Development*, 24, 108–125. https://www.jstor.org/stable/48761167

Shekhar, R. (2020). Artificial Creations: Ascription, Ownership, Time-Specific Monopolies. arXiv (Cornell University). https://doi.org/DOI: 10.48550/arXiv.2010

Shen, A. (2024). AI ethics and governance at international standards. *International IT Journal of Research*, *2*(1), 8–14.

Shi, A., & Wu, W. (2011). Analysis on consolidated taxation in the context of head-quarters economy under independent corporation accounting. *2011 2nd International Conference on Artificial Intelligence, Management Science and Electronic Commerce, AIMSEC 2011 - Proceedings*, 160 – 163. DOI: 10.1109/AIMSEC.2011.6010251

Shin, D., Hameleers, M., Park, Y. J., Kim, J. N., Trielli, D., Diakopoulos, N., Helberger, N., Lewis, S. C., Westlund, O., & Baumann, S. (2022). Countering algorithmic bias and disinformation and effectively harnessing the power of AI in media. *Journalism & Mass Communication Quarterly*, *99*(4), 887–907. DOI: 10.1177/10776990221129245

Siau, K., & Wang, W. (2020). Artificial intelligence (AI) ethics: Ethics of AI and ethical AI. *Journal of Database Management*, *31*(2), 74–87. DOI: 10.4018/JDM.2020040105

Sichelman, T. (2021). Quantifying legal entropy. *Frontiers in Physics (Lausanne)*, *9*, 665054. DOI: 10.3389/fphy.2021.665054

Silva, A., Schrum, M., Hedlund-Botti, E., Gopalan, N., & Gombolay, M. (2022). Explainable artificial intelligence: Evaluating the objective and subjective impacts of xAI on human-agent interaction. *International Journal of Human-Computer Interaction*, *39*(7), 1390–1404. DOI: 10.1080/10447318.2022.2101698

Singapore IP Strategy 2030. (2024). https://www.ipos.gov.sg/manage-ip/singapore-ip-strategy-2030

Singhal, A., Neveditsin, N., Tanveer, H., & Mago, V. (2024). Toward fairness, accountability, transparency, and ethics in AI for social media and health care: Scoping review. *JMIR Medical Informatics*, *12*, e50048. DOI: 10.2196/50048 PMID: 38568737

Singh, M. (2024). Review on role of artificial intelligence in the life of legal profession. *International Journal of Legal Science and Innovation*, *6*(3), 1087–1096. DOI: 10.10000/IJSI.1996

Singh, R., Sharma, P., Foropon, C., & Belal, H. M. (2022). The role of big data and predictive analytics in the employee retention: A resource-based view. *International Journal of Manpower*, *43*(2), 411–425. DOI: 10.1108/IJM-03-2021-0197

Sinquini-Cinelli, L. (2024). Methodological legal positivism. In *Scientia Iuris. Ius Gentium: Comparative Perspectives on Law and Justice* (Vol. 11, pp. 311–356). Springer., DOI: 10.1007/978-3-031-51936-9_5

Slade, S., Prinsloo, P., & Khalil, M. (2019). Learning analytics at the intersection of ethics and education. *British Journal of Educational Technology*, *50*(6), 3031–3043. DOI: 10.1111/bjet.12861

Sneha, A., Agrawal, A., Singh, A. K., & Ranjan, R. (2024). Can AI Propel Sustainable Finance Towards Achieving SDGs? *Advances in Finance, Accounting, and Economics*, *281*, 281–310. Advance online publication. DOI: 10.4018/979-8-3693-7580-8.ch013

Solovyeva, A., & Hynek, N. (2018). Going beyond the "killer robots" debate: Six dilemmas autonomous weapon systems raise. *Central European Journal of International and Security Studies*, *12*(3), 166–208.

Sonko, S., Adewusi, A. O., Obi, O. C., Onwusinkwue, S., & Atadoga, A. (2024). A critical review towards artificial intelligence: Challenges, ethical considerations, and the path forward. *World Journal of Advanced Research and Reviews*, *21*(03), 1262–1268. DOI: 10.30574/wjarr.2024.21.3.0817

Souravlas, S., & Anastasiadou, S. (2020). Pipelined Dynamic Scheduling of Big Data Streams. *Applied Sciences (Basel, Switzerland)*, *10*(14), 4796. DOI: 10.3390/app10144796

Souravlas, S., & Anastasiadou, S. (2022). On Implementing Social Community Clouds Based on Markov Models. *IEEE Transactions on Computational Social Systems*. Advance online publication. DOI: 10.1109/TCSS.2022.3213273

Souravlas, S., Anastasiadou, S. D., Tantalaki, N., & Katsavounis, S. (2022). A Fair, Dynamic Load Balanced Task Distribution Strategy for Heterogeneous Cloud Platforms Based on Markov Process Modeling. *IEEE Access : Practical Innovations, Open Solutions*, *10*, 26149–26162. DOI: 10.1109/ACCESS.2022.3157435

Souravlas, S., Anastasiadou, S., Economides, Th., & Katsavounis, S. (2023). Probabilistic Community Detection in Social Networks. *IEEE Access : Practical Innovations, Open Solutions*, *11*, 25629–25641. DOI: 10.1109/ACCESS.2023.3257021

Souravlas, S., Anastasiadou, S., & Katsavounis, S. (2021). A survey on the recent advances of deep community detection. *Applied Sciences (Basel, Switzerland)*, *11*(16), 7179. DOI: 10.3390/app11167179

Souravlas, S., Anastasiadou, S., & Katsavounis, S. (2021b). More on Pipelined Dynamic Scheduling of Big Data Streams. *Applied Sciences (Basel, Switzerland)*, *11*(1), 61. DOI: 10.3390/app11010061

Souravlas, S., Anastasiadou, S., & Kostoglou, I. (2022). A Novel Method For General Hierarchical System Modeling Via Colored Petri Nets Based on Transition Extractions From Real Data Sets. *Applied Sciences (Basel, Switzerland)*, *13*(1), 339. DOI: 10.3390/app13010339

Souravlas, S., Anastasiadou, S., Tantalaki, N., & Katsavounis, S. (2021). A dynamic load balanced task distribution strategy for heterogeneous cloud platforms based on Markov process modeling. *IEEE Access : Practical Innovations, Open Solutions*, *10*, 2169–3536. https://ieeexplore.ieee.org/document/9729723

Souravlas, S., Katsavounis, S., & Anastasiadou, S. (2020). On Modeling and Simulation of Resource Allocation Policies in Cloud Computing Using Colored Petri Nets. *Applied Sciences (Basel, Switzerland)*, *10*(16), 5644. DOI: 10.3390/app10165644

Srivastava, D. K., Kumar, V., Ekren, B. Y., Upadhyay, A., Tyagi, M., & Kumari, A. (2022). Adopting Industry 4.0 by leveraging organisational factors. *Technological Forecasting and Social Change*, *176*, 121439. DOI: 10.1016/j.techfore.2021.121439

Stahl, B. C. (2023). Embedding responsibility in intelligent systems: From AI ethics to responsible AI ecosystems. *Scientific Reports*, *13*(1), 7586. DOI: 10.1038/s41598-023-34622-w PMID: 37202436

Stevenson, S. (2011). New labour in libraries: The post-Fordist public library. *The Journal of Documentation*, *67*(5), 773–790. DOI: 10.1108/00220411111164664

Stevenson, S. (2016). Immaterial labour, public librarians, and third-generation public libraries. *New Library World*, *117*(3/4), 186–200. DOI: 10.1108/NLW-11-2015-0083

Stix, C., & Maas, M. M. (2021). Bridging the gap: The case for an "incompletely theorized agreement" on AI policy. *AI and Ethics*, *1*(3), 261–271. DOI: 10.1007/s43681-020-00037-w

Straub, V. J., Morgan, D., Bright, J., & Margetts, H. (2023). Artificial intelligence in government: Concepts, standards, and a unified framework. *Government Information Quarterly*, *40*(4), 101881. DOI: 10.1016/j.giq.2023.101881

Stroppa, M. (2023). Legal and ethical implications of autonomous cyber capabilities: A call for retaining human control in cyberspace. *Ethics and Information Technology*, *25*(1), 7. Advance online publication. DOI: 10.1007/s10676-023-09679-w

Subaveerapandiyan, A. (2023). Application of artificial intelligence (AI) in libraries and its impact on library operations review. *Library Philosophy and Practice*, 1-19.

Subaveerapandiyan, A., Sunanthini, C., & Amees, M. (2023). A study on the knowledge and perception of artificial intelligence. *IFLA Journal*, *49*(3), 503–513. DOI: 10.1177/03400352231180230

Subramaniyan, M., Skoogh, A., Bokrantz, J., Sheikh, M. A., Thürer, M., & Chang, Q. (2021). Artificial intelligence for throughput bottleneck analysis – State-of-the-art and future directions. *Journal of Manufacturing Systems*, *60*, 734–751. DOI: 10.1016/j.jmsy.2021.07.021

Su, X., Zeng, W., Zheng, M., Jiang, X., Lin, W., & Xu, A. (2021). Big data analytics capabilities and organizational performance: The mediating effect of dual innovation. *European Journal of Innovation Management*, *25*(4), 1142–1157. DOI: 10.1108/EJIM-10-2020-0431

Taeihagn, A., & Lim, H. S. M. (2021). Towards autonomous vehicles in smart cities: Risks and risk governance. In Hamid, U. Z. A., & Al-Turjman, F. (Eds.), *Towards Connected and Autonomous Vehicle Highways* (pp. 169–190). Springer., DOI: 10.1007/978-3-030-66042-0_7

Tallberg, J., Erman, E., Furendal, M., Geith, J., Klamberg, K. & Lundgren, M. (2023). The global governance of artificial intelligence: Next steps for empirical and normative research. *International Studies Review*, 25(3), viad40.

Tallberg, J., Lundgren, M., & Geith, J. (2024). AI regulation in the European Union: Examining non-state actor preferences. *Business and Politics*, *26*(2), 218–239. DOI: 10.1017/bap.2023.36

Talukder, Md. A., Hasan, K. F., Islam, Md. M., Uddin, Md. A., Akhter, A., Yousuf, M. A., Alharbi, F., & Moni, M. A. (2022). A Dependable Hybrid Machine Learning Model for Network Intrusion Detection. arXiv (Cornell University). https://doi.org/ DOI: 10.48550/arXiv.2212

Taylor, I. (2023). Justice by algorithm: The limits of AI in criminal sentencing. *Criminal Justice Ethics*, *42*(3), 193–213. DOI: 10.1080/0731129X.2023.2275967

Technology Trends, W. I. P. O. 2019. (2021). https://www.wipo.int/publications/en/details.jsp?id=4386

Teubner, G. (1988). *Autopoietic Law: A new approach to Law and Society*. Walter de Gruyter.

Thelisson, E., & Verma, H. (2024). Conformity assessment under the EU AI Act general approach. *AI and Ethics*, *4*(1), 113–121. DOI: 10.1007/s43681-023-00402-5

TheoryHub. Technology-Organization-Environment Framework. Retrieval date: 5 August 2024. https://open.ncl.ac.uk/academic-theories/23/technology-organization-environment-framework/

Thiebes, S., Lins, S., & Sunyaev, A. (2021). Trustworthy artificial intelligence. *Electronic Markets*, *31*(2), 447–464. DOI: 10.1007/s12525-020-00441-4

Thirumagal, P. G., Raj, M. A., Naser, S. J., Hussien, N. A., & Abbas, J. K. and vinayagam, S. (2024). Efficient contract analysis and management through AI-powered tool: Time savings and error reduction in legal document review. *Proceedings of the 19th International Conference on Science Technology Engineering and Mathematics*, Chennai, India, 1-6. https://doi.org/DOI: 10.1109/ICONSTEM60960.2024.10568823

Titlestad, P. J. H. (2010). Liberalism. *English Academy Review*, *27*(2), 94–100. DOI: 10.1080/10131752.2010.514989

Tommasoli, M. (2013). Rule of law and democracy: Addressing the gap between policies and practices. *UN Chronicle*, *49*(4), 29–31. DOI: 10.18356/e2c335d7-en

Tornatzky, L., & Fleischer, M. (1990). *The process of technology innovation*.

Tsamados, A., Aggarwal, N., Cowls, J., Morley, J., Roberts, H., Taddeo, M., & Floridi, L. (2022). The ethics of algorithms: Key problems and solutions. *AI & Society*, *37*(1), 215–230. DOI: 10.1007/s00146-021-01154-8

Twaissi, N. M., El-Khateeb, A., Al-Sharif, M., Almomany, G. A., & Abu Karaki, M. A. (2024). The rising role of Artificial Intelligence in Jordan's insurance industry. *Journal of Tianjin University Science and Technology*, *57*(4), 403–417.

UNESCO. (2021). Recommendation on the ethics of artificial intelligence. https://unesdoc.unesco.org/ark:/48223/pf0000381137

Unicane, I., Knight, W., Leach, T., Stahl, B. C., & Wanjiku, W. G. (2020). Framing governance for a contested emerging technology: Insights from AI policy. *Policy and Society*, *40*(2), 158–177. DOI: 10.1080/14494035.2020.1855800

USPTO issues inventorship guidance and examples for AI-assisted inventions. (2024). https://www.uspto.gov/subscription-center/2024/uspto-issues-inventorship-guidance-and-examples-ai-assisted-inventions

Vallentin, S., & Murillo, D. (2022). Ideologies of corporate responsibility: From neoliberalism to 'varieties of liberalism'. *Business Ethics Quarterly*, *32*(4), 635–670. DOI: 10.1017/beq.2021.43

Vallor, S. (2016). *Technology and the virtues: A philosophical guide to a future worth wanting*. Oxford University Press. DOI: 10.1093/acprof:oso/9780190498511.001.0001

van Dijk, N., Casiraghi, S., & Gutwirth, S.Artificial Intelligence and Data Protection in the European Union. (2021). The "ethification" of ICT governance. Artificial intelligence and data protection in the European Union. *Computer Law & Security Review*, *43*, 105597. DOI: 10.1016/j.clsr.2021.105597

Vanguard, X. Insurance Industry Challenges: Navigating the Landscape in 2024. Retrieval date: 12 August 2024. https://vanguard-x.com/software-development/insurance-industry-challenges-navigating-the-landscape-in-2024/

Varona, D., & Suarez, J. L. (2022). Discrimination bias, fairness, and trustworthy AI. *Applied Sciences (Basel, Switzerland)*, *12*(12), 5826. DOI: 10.3390/app12125826

Vehar, F., & Gils, T. (2020). I'm sorry AI, I'm afraid you can't be an author (for now). *Journal of Intellectual Property Law & Practice*, *15*(9), 718–726. DOI: 10.1093/jiplp/jpaa106

Venkatesh, V., Morris, M. G., Davis, G. B., & Davis, F. D. (2003). User acceptance of information technology: Toward a unified view. *Management Information Systems Quarterly*, *27*(3), 425–478. DOI: 10.2307/30036540

Verschuuren, J. (2009). *The Impact of Legislation. A Critical Analysis of Ex Ante Evaluation*. ISSN. DOI: 10.1163/ej.9789004170209.i-280

Vinothkumar, J. and Karunamurthy, A. (2023). Recent advancements in artificial intelligence technology: Trends and implications. *International Journal of Multidisciplinary Scientific Research and Development*, 2(1), 01-11. https://doi.org/DOI: 10.54368/qijmsrd.2.1.0003

Vinuesa, R., Azizpour, H., Leite, I., Balaam, M., Dignum, V., Domisch, S., Felländer, A., Langhans, S. D., Tegmark, M., & Fuso Nerini, F. (2020). The role of artificial intelligence in achieving the Sustainable Development Goals. *Nature Communications*, *11*(1), 233. DOI: 10.1038/s41467-019-14108-y PMID: 31932590

Vogus, B. (2023). Generative AI and ChatGPT: Friend or foe for academic libraries? *Public Services Quarterly, 19*(4), 309–312. DOI: 10.1080/15228959.2023.2266358

Von Treuer, K., Karantzas, G., McCabe, M., Mellor, D., Konis, A., Davison, T. E., & O'Connor, D. (2018). Organizational factors associated with readiness for change in residential aged care settings. *BMC Health Services Research, 18*(1), 1–6. DOI: 10.1186/s12913-018-2832-4 PMID: 29390999

Vorecol (2024). Impact of artificial intelligence in driving digital transformation. Retrieved May 6, 2024, https://vorecol.com/blogs/blog-impact-of-artificial-intelligence-in-driving-digitaltransformation-8835

Wachter, S. (2024). Limitations and loopholes in the EU AI Act and AI liability directives: What this means for the European Union, the United States, and beyond. *SSRN, 26*(3), 671–718. DOI: 10.2139/ssrn.4924553

Wachter, S., Mittelstadt, B., & Floridi, L. (2017). Why a right to explanation of automated decision-making does not exist in the general data protection regulation. *International Data Privacy Law, 7*(2), 76–99. DOI: 10.1093/idpl/ipx005

Wade, M., & Hulland, J. (2004). The resource-based view and information systems research: Review, extension, and suggestions for future research. *Management Information Systems Quarterly, 28*(1), 107–142. DOI: 10.2307/25148626

Walter, Y. (2024). Managing the race to the moon: Global policy and governance in artificial intelligence regulation—A contemporary overview and an analysis of socioeconomic consequences. *Discover Artificial Intelligence, 4*(14), 14. Advance online publication. DOI: 10.1007/s44163-024-00109-4

Wamba, F. S., Akter, S., & De Bourmont, M. (2018). Quality dominant logic in big data analytics and find performance. *Business Process Management Journal, 25*(3), 512528.

Wang, Y., Lo, H. P., & Yang, Y. (2004). The constituents of core competencies and firm performance: Evidence from high-technology firms in China. *Journal of Engineering and Technology Management, 21*(4), 249–280. DOI: 10.1016/j.jengtecman.2004.09.001

Wang, Y., & Wang, P. (2020). New Personal Tax Collection Management System Based on Artificial Intelligence and Its Application in the Middle Class. *Journal of Physics: Conference Series, 1574*(1), 012105. Advance online publication. DOI: 10.1088/1742-6596/1574/1/012105

Wang, Y., Xiuping, S., & Zhang, Q. (2021). Can fintech improve the efficiency of commercial banks?—An analysis based on big data. *Research in International Business and Finance*, *55*, 101338. DOI: 10.1016/j.ribaf.2020.101338

Wani, S. A., & Mansoor, S. I. (2025). Criminal justice system in the age of artificial intelligence: Exploring rights, risks, and responsibilities in the digital era. In Kaunert, C., Raghav, A., Ravesangar, K., Singh, B., & Riswandi, B. (Eds.), *Artificial intelligence in peace, justice, and strong institutions* (pp. 67–92). IGI Global Scientific Publishing., DOI: 10.4018/979-8-3693-9395-6.ch004

Watney, M. M. (2020). Artificial intelligence and its' legal risk to cybersecurity. *Proceedings of the ECCWS2020 19th European Conference on Cyber Warfare and Security*, 398-405.

Weber, P., Carl, K. V., & Hinz, O. (2024). Applications of explainable artificial intelligence in finance – a systematic review of finance, information systems, and computer science literature. *Management Review Quarterly*, *74*(2), 867–907. DOI: 10.1007/s11301-023-00320-0

When, A. I. S. P. I. An Alternative Model for Patent Law at the 3A Era. (2024). https://cardozolawreview.com/artificial-intelligence-systems-produce-inventions/

Whittlestone, J., Nyrup, R., Alexandrova, A., & Cave, S. (2019). The role and limits of principles in AI ethics: Towards a focus on tensions. Proceedings of the AAAI/ACM Conference on AI, Ethics, and Society, 195–200. DOI: 10.1145/3306618.3314289

Wirtz, B. W., Weyerer, J. C., & Sturm, B. J. (2020). The dark sides of artificial intelligence: An integrated AI governance framework for public administration. *International Journal of Public Administration*, *43*(9), 818–829. DOI: 10.1080/01900692.2020.1749851

Wischmeyer, T. (2020). Artificial intelligence and transparency: Opening the black box, *Regulating Artificial Intelligence*, 75-101. https://doi.org/DOI: 10.1007/978-3-030-32361-5_4

Wong, A. (2020). The laws and regulation of AI and autonomous systems. In Strous, L., Johnson, R., Grier, D. A., & Swade, D. (Eds.), *Unimagined Futures – ICT Opportunities and Challenges. IFIP Advances in Information and Communication Technology* (Vol. 555, pp. 38–54). Springer., DOI: 10.1007/978-3-030-64246-4_4

Wulf, A. J., & Seizov, O. (2020). Artificial intelligence and transparency: A blueprint for improving the regulation of AI applications in the EU. *European Business Law Review*, *31*(4), 611–640. DOI: 10.54648/EULR2020024

Xi, R. (2025). On emerging technologies: The old regime, and the proactivity. *Cardozo International & Comparative Law Review*, 8(1).

Xiao, Y. (2022). Decoding Authorship: Is There Really no Place for an Algorithmic Author Under Copyright Law? *IIC; International Review of Industrial Property and Copyright Law, 54*(1), 5–25. DOI: 10.1007/s40319-022-01269-5

Xue, M., Zhang, Y., Wang, J., & Liu, W. (2021). Intellectual Property Protection for Deep Learning Models: Taxonomy, Methods, Attacks, and Evaluations. *IEEE Transactions on Artificial Intelligence, 3*(6), 908–923. DOI: 10.1109/TAI.2021.3133824

Xu, J., Lee, T., & Goggin, G. (2024). AI governance in Asia: Policies, praxis and approaches. *Communication Research and Practice, 10*(3), 275–287. Advance online publication. DOI: 10.1080/22041451.2024.2391204

Yas, N., Qaruty, R. A., Hadi, S. A., & AlAdeedi, A. (2023). Civil liability and damage arising from artificial intelligence. *Migration Letters : An International Journal of Migration Studies, 20*(5), 430–446. DOI: 10.59670/ml.v20i5.3554

Yilma, K. (2023). Emerging technologies and human rights at the United Nations. *IEEE Technology and Society Magazine, 42*(1), 54–64. DOI: 10.1109/MTS.2023.3241297

Yurkevich, E. V., & Kryukova, L. N. (2021). Model design as a new socio-cyber-physical systems creating mechanism. *Journal of Physics: Conference Series, 1864*(1), 12089. DOI: 10.1088/1742-6596/1864/1/012089

Zadeh, S. A., Iwendi, C., Uhumuavbi, I., & Boulouard, Z. (2023). A New AI-Based Approach for Rental Tax Evasion Management in Iran (Ethical Consideration). *Lecture Notes in Networks and Systems, 735 LNNS*, 451 – 468. DOI: 10.1007/978-3-031-37164-6_34

Zafar, A. (2024). Balancing the scale: Navigating ethical and practical challenges of artificial intelligence (AI) integration in legal practices. *Discover Artificial Intelligence, 4*(1), 27. DOI: 10.1007/s44163-024-00121-8

Zaidan, E., & Ibrahim, I. A. (2024). AI governance in a complex and rapidly changing regulatory landscape: A global perspective. *Humanities & Social Sciences Communications, 11*(1), 1121. DOI: 10.1057/s41599-024-03560-x

Zakir, M.H., Kham, S.H., Saeed, Z. & Sajida (2023). The impact of artificial intelligence on intellectual property rights. *International Journal of Human and Society*, 3(4), 312-319. https://ijhs.com.pk/index.php/IJHS/article/view/330/

Zekos, G. I. (2021). AI and legal issues. In *Economics and Law of Artificial Intelligence* (pp. 401–460). Springer., DOI: 10.1007/978-3-030-64254-9_10

Zhang, D., Badilla, J., Tong, H., & Wang, D. (2018). An End-to-End Scalable Copyright Detection System for Online Video Sharing Platforms. *2016 IEEE/ACM International Conference on Advances in Social Networks Analysis and Mining (ASONAM)*, 626. DOI: 10.1109/ASONAM.2018.8508288

Zhang, D., Finckenberg-Broman, P., & Hoang, T.. (2024). Right to be forgotten in the era of large language models: Implications, challenges, and solutions. *AI and Ethics*. Advance online publication. DOI: 10.1007/s43681-024-00573-9

Zhang, Y. (2023). Analysis of the status of artificial intelligence as the subject of law from the perspective of autopoiesis. *Beijing Law Review*, *14*(3), 1–12.

Zhang, Y., Hao, S., & Li, S. (2023). Development And Application of Electronic Tax Declaration Robot for Individual Income Tax Based on Uipath. *ACM International Conference Proceeding Series*, 620 – 624. DOI: 10.1145/3656766.3656870

Zhuk, A. (2023). Navigating the legal landscape of AI copyright: A comparative analysis of EU, US, and Chinese approaches. *AI and Ethics*, *4*(4), 1299–1306. DOI: 10.1007/s43681-023-00299-0

Ziemianin, K. (2021). Civil legal personality of artificial intelligence. Future or utopia? *Internet Policy Review*, *10*(2), 1–22. DOI: 10.14763/2021.2.1544

Zuboff, S. (2019). *The age of surveillance capitalism*. PublicAffairs.

Zuboff, S. (2019). *The age of surveillance capitalism: The fight for a human future at the new frontier of power*. PublicAffairs.

Zulić, H. (2019). How AI can Change/Improve/Influence Music Composition, Performance and Education: Three Case Studies. *INSAM Journal of Contemporary Music Art and Technology*, 2(2), 100–114. DOI: 10.51191/issn.2637-1898.2019.2.2.100

. (2018). A Study on matters necessary for promoting the mediation industry in Korea in the Fourth stage of the Industrial Revolution: Focus on JAMS and AAA in the U.S. , 59(3), 201. DOI: 10.35275/pnulaw.2018.59.3.007

About The Contributors

Sofia Anastasiadou is a Professor of Statistics and Research Methodology, Biostatistics Biomedical Research Methodology and at the School Health Sciences of the University of Western Macedonia (UOWM). She is the Deam of the Health Sciences of UOWM, Senate Member, and Member of post graduate studies committee. She is also a Member of the Senate and a MODIP Member of the same University. Her teaching focuses in the field of cognitive Research Methodology (Quantitative and Qualitative), Educational Research and Statistical Data Analysis, Big Data. She has written three books on Statistics and Research Methodology and has published over 300 articles in International and Greek Journals as well as in International and Greek Conferences. She has participated in scientific dialogues/ round tables in more than 200 lectures at International and Greek Conferences. She has organized and co-organized Greek and International Scientific Conferences. She is also a Member of a number of Scientific Committees of International Conferences and is an Associate Editor in a number of International Journals. Since the spring semester 2021 she works as a Collaborative Academic Staff teaching in the Distance Learning Program of Special Education at the School of Education and Social Sciences at Frederick University.

Lamprini Seremeti is a Collaborative Academic Staff at Frederick University since 2017. She is also a Lecturer in Programming in the Department of Agricultural Economics & Rural Development at the School of Applied Economics and Social Science of the Agricultural University of Athens. Her teaching experience in Higher Education Institutions, since 2005, involves cognitive subjects such as expert systems, artificial intelligence, semantic web, business management, programming languages, calculus, algebra, statistics, differential equations, research methodology, informatics applied in pedagogy. She has also served as a teacher of Informatics, Mathematics and Special Education in Primary and Secondary Schools, since 2001.Dr Seremeti holds a PhD in Computer Science with a focus on propagating knowledge in networks of aligned ontologies from Hellenic Open University; a Master in Special Education from University of Rome; a Master in Pure Mathematics from University of Patras; a Bachelor in Mathematics from University of Patras; a Bachelor in Informatics from University of Western Greece; and a Bachelor in Law from University of Nicosia. She has also participated as a researcher in EU-funded projects, in which, her tasks involved mathematical modeling, data processing, knowledge representation and management, and conceptualization of heterogeneous environments (socio-economic, educational, biomedical, ambient intelligent). Dr Seremeti has published her research work in peer-reviewed international journals (14 articles) and book chapters (5 articles), and has presented her work in international peer-reviewed conferences (30 articles). Her research interests focus on theories applied in inclusive education, interpretation of Law in ambient intelligent environments, knowledge representation and management through ontologies, mathematical modeling.

Andreas Masouras is an Associate Professor of Communication and Marketing in the Department of Economics & Business at Neapolis University. He holds a PhD with distinction from the Department of Political Science and International Relations at the University of the Peloponnese. The title of his doctoral dissertation is "Entrepreneurship and Competitiveness through the Lens of Institutional Analysis: The Case of Cyprus," which is available in the National Archive of Doctoral Dissertations. He coordinates the following programs: the conventional MBA, the distance MBA (English-speaking), and the MBA in Tourism (distance learning). He is actively writing scientific articles and participates in international conferences. His book, "Entrepreneurship in Small and Medium-Sized Enterprises", published by the American publishing house Nova, has been indexed in the Scopus book list.

Lazaros Anastasiadis is a political Scientist. He holds a master Degree in Informatics, AUTH and cuttently has followed a PhD Degree from the University of Patras, Greece. He has published over many articles in International and Greek Journals as well as in International and Greek Conferences. He has participated in scientific dialogues/round tables at International and Greek Conferences.

***

Charilaos Amarantidis works at Physics/Natural Sciences Department, Democritus University of Thrace / Kavala Campus, Greece.

Nikita Biswal is a dedicated legal scholar who completed her B.A.LL.B (Hons.) from the prestigious University Law College, Utkal University. With a passion for intellectual property law and its evolving landscape, she is currently pursuing an LL.M. in Intellectual Property at CHRIST (Deemed to be University), Delhi NCR. Her academic journey reflects a commitment to excellence and a keen interest in understanding the intersection of law, innovation, and creativity.

Giannoula Florou is a proferssor at Accounting and Finance/Management Science and Accounting Deoartment, Democritus University of Thrace / Kavala Campus.

Angelos Iliopoulos, a postgraduate student pursuing an MBA in Business Administration at Neapolis University Pafos. I am also a graduate of the Hellenic Military Academy. I have a strong interest in organizational management and the ethical use of Artificial Intelligence in recruitment. My professional experience as a Second Lieutenant in the Special Forces has provided me with practical knowledge of human resource practices and personnel evaluation. My current research focuses on exploring the opportunities and ethical challenges of AI in recruitment processes.

Akankshya Kanungo is a dedicated legal scholar who completed her B.A.LL.B (Hons.) from the prestigious University Law College, Utkal University. With a passion for intellectual property law and its evolving landscape, she is currently pursuing an LL.M. in Intellectual Property & Trade Law at CHRIST (Deemed to be University), Delhi NCR. Her academic journey reflects a commitment to excellence and a keen interest in understanding the intersection of law, innovation, and creativity.

Hina Kausar is a distinguished legal scholar specializing in Family Law. She holds a Ph.D. in Family Law from Aligarh Muslim University (AMU), Aligarh, where she also completed her BA.LLB. (Hons.) and LLM in Commercial Law. A dedicated academician, she qualified the UGC NET exam in 2013, demonstrating her expertise in the field of law. Currently, Dr. Kausar serves as an Assistant Professor (Selection Grade) at the School of Law, UPES Dehradun, where she contributes to legal education and research. Her academic journey reflects a strong commitment to legal scholarship, with a focus on both family law and commercial law.

Mohammed Salim Baitullah Khan With over 25 years of academic and professional experience, Dr. Mohammed Salim Baitullah Khan holds multiple advanced degrees, including a Ph.D. in Law, a Ph.D. (HC) from the USA, an M.Phil. (Gold Medalist), MBA in Operations Management, M.A. in Rural Development, LL.M., and B.A. His areas of specialization include Sports Law, Intellectual Property Rights, and Business Law. His research interests span Arbitration, Mediation, Constitutional Law, Sports Law, Animal Law, and IPR.

Spyros Kontis is an Electronics Engineer with over 17 years of experience in computer science, robotics education, and information security. He holds a Master's degree in Information Security and Electronic Terrorism from Seattle University (USA), a Master's in Special Education, and has completed postgraduate studies in Child Psychology. He is currently a PhD candidate focusing on AI-based emotional state analysis and the ethical implications of AI in education and mental health. He is the founder and director of Corfu Robotiki, an educational center specializing in programming and robotics, and has published the book "Informatics for Greek High School Students", which serves as a comprehensive resource for students preparing for national exams. He also collaborates as an external examiner for postgraduate dissertations at the Norwegian University of Science and Technology (NTNU).

Sheikh Inam Ul Mansoor (BA.LLB Hon's, LLM, CCPT WIPO, Ph.D. International Trade Law) is a highly accomplished academician presently working as an Assistant Professor Law at the School of Law, Dayananda Sagar University in Bangalore, India. With a strong background in law and a passion for academia, Dr. Sheikh has made significant contributions to the field through his extensive research and publications. Pursued his BA. LLB (Hon's) from University of Kashmir, LLM from JNU Jaipur and Ph.D. International Trade Law from LPU Punjab. Prior to his academic career, Dr. Sheikh served as an Advocate and Solicitor at the Jammu and Kashmir High Court and other subordinate courts in Jammu and Kashmir. This experience as a legal practitioner has provided him with valuable insights into the practical application of law and enhanced his understanding of legal dynamics. As an Assistant Professor Law at Dayananda Sagar University, Dr. Sheikh Inam Ul Mansoor continues to make significant contributions to the legal field through his research, teaching, and involvement in various professional activities.

Abhinash Mohanta pursued a three-year LLB program at Ganjam Law College, Berhampur, under Berhampur University. He further advanced his academic journey by enrolling in the Master of Laws (LLM) program in Business Law at the P.G. Department of Law, Berhampur University, graduating in 2017. Currently, he is pursuing a Ph.D. in Law at KIIT Deemed to be University, with a research focus on critical areas such as refugee and human rights. In addition to his academic endeavors, Abhinash has authored several Scopus-indexed papers covering diverse topics, including AI, environment, migration, crime, intellectual property, and refugee studies.

Stavros Valsamidis is prof at the Accounting and Finance/Management Department Science and Accounting, Democritus University of Thrace / Kavala Campus,

Govind Yadav is an Assistant Professor of Law at the School of Law, Manipal University, Jaipur. He holds a doctorate in law and brings a rich blend of academic rigor and practical insight to his teaching. His areas of expertise include constitutional law, administrative law, and legal theory. Dr. Yadav is committed to nurturing analytical and research skills among students and has contributed to various academic publications and conferences. His approach to legal education emphasizes clarity, critical analysis, and a strong foundation in both theory and practice.

Index

A

B

C

D

E

M

P

R

S

T

www.ingramcontent.com/pod-product-compliance
Lightning Source LLC
LaVergne TN
LVHW081338300926
849161LV00008B/2011
9798369395769